1994

A Green Dinosaur Day

A Guide for Developing Thematic Units in Literature-Based Instruction, K–6

PATRICIA L. ROBERTS

California State University, Sacramento

Graphics by Anson Jew

ALLYN AND BACON

Boston   London   Toronto   Sydney   Tokyo   Singapore

Copyright © 1993 by Allyn and Bacon
A Division of Simon & Schuster, Inc.
160 Gould Street
Needham Heights, Massachusetts 02194

Library of Congress Cataloging-in-Publication Data
Roberts, Patricia
   A green dinosaur day : a guide for developing thematic units in
   literature-based instruction, K-6 / Patricia L. Roberts ; graphics
   by Anson Jew.
      p.   cm.
   Includes bibliographical references.
   ISBN 0-205-14007-6
   1. Education, Elementary—Curricula.   2. Literature—Study and
teaching (Elementary)   3. Interdisciplinary approach in education.
I. Title.
LB1570.R55   1992
372.19—dc20   92-26441
                                                           CIP

Printed in the United States of America
10 9 8 7 6 5 4 3 2 1   96 95 94 93 92

To these fine teachers who are interested in thematic units:

Elizabeth Aldridge, Laura Bardini, Stefani Brown, Jann Carlson, Lizabeth Coleman, Valerie Collins, Kristie Darras, Jacque Farrell, Penny Hocking, Marilyn Hylton, Louise Ito, Debbie Krieger, Patricia Lao, Shirleen MacKenzie, Karen Mercante, Phillip Newport, Pamela Reed, Sheila Simmons, and Janice Wirth

Contents

Chapter 6
How May I Integrate Mathematics and Science?   117

Chapter 7
What Resources Are Available to Me? 151

Chapter 8
How Can I Meet the Needs of Diverse Students? 167

Preface

A Green Dinosaur Day: A Guide for Developing Thematic Units in Literature-Based Instruction, K–6 is a resource for preservice and inservice teachers new to literature-based instruction. In this guidebook, you will find an organizational plan for developing a thematic unit for literature-based instruction for grades K–6. A dinosaur unit is used as an example throughout the chapters as well as selected instructional resources—including 26 reproducible pages—to support the unit. You will see ways that a content topic can be used as a theme and infused with a literacy curriculum and you will also get ideas for integrating social studies (social sciences), natural sciences, and other curriculum areas. You will find approaches for assessing and evaluating the progress of students as they study a thematic unit and you will learn how to review the related research findings that support literature-based instruction. Further, you will be able to link the suggestions in this book to other topics and use the ideas to develop themed units of your choice.

Chapter 1 discusses ways to begin a thematic unit and Chapter 2 focuses on how a literacy curriculum mixes with content and how literature-based instruction occurs through an example of a fourth-grade class and their activities during A Green Dinosaur Day. A literature base and different book-related inquiries for a study about dinosaurs are presented in Chapter 3. Teaching techniques and classroom organizational plans are reviewed in Chapter 4. In Chapter 5, there are ideas for infusing social sciences and expressive arts, and in Chapter 6, suggestions for integrating math, natural science, and computer software are given. Chapter 7 has additional resources for literature-based units and materials for a specific unit on dinosaurs and Chapter 8 discusses the needs of diverse students. In Chapter 9, approaches for assessing and evaluating the students' progress are reviewed and research findings that support literature-based instruction are presented in Chapter 10. The book concludes with 26 reproducibles to assist you in your teaching.

To support your focus, specific examples about dinosaurs are given in this book. The topic of dinosaurs is the theme because students' interest in dinosaurs often is as great as the words they use in describing the dinosaurs themselves—giant, colossal, huge—and then may turn from dinosaurs to studies of the environment, energy, or other related areas. The topic of dinosaurs in this text includes:

- Content from natural science/paleontology.
- An opportunity for students to work in a manner of a scientist.
- Lines of student inquiry about (1) *How* did we find out about dinosaurs? (2) *What* did we find out about dinosaurs? (3) *How* can we share what we learned with others? (4) *What* is it we still don't know about dinosaurs? and (5) *What* can we investigate?
- Ways scientists make deductions from primary evidence as students study ways scientists gather information.
- Prehistoric mysteries that exist currently and allow students to make predictions in their studies.
- Ways people work together in a scientific community.
- Ways for students to become effective democratic citizens as they keep informed on current issues affecting society. For instance, students interact with present-day issues such as ways to preserve an endangered species or

protect forests both in and outside the United States. Specifically, they may show their concern about preserving Mexico's rain forest, the Lacandona jungle in Chiapas, realizing 60 percent of Lacandona has been lost since 1970. They can report to others what they discover about the jungle's minimum ecosystem and the effects of clearing and burning the jungle and planting crops.

- Related studies that interest students, for example: (1) the earth as an ecosystem, (2) species endangerment and extinction, (3) geology, (4) earth history, and (5) other topics based on the students' inquiries.

Organization of the Book

The Core of Structure is a graphic organizer for this text and its components show the relationships in literature-based instruction when instruction centers around a theme. Ironically, the idea of the integration of a literature-based unit is best shown by the separation of a unit's components—its building blocks—in the Core of Structure. The Core of Structure, seen as a blank oval, is a visual metaphor. As you read the chapters, you will see the relationships in literature-based instruction that relate to the concept of a thematic unit. The blank oval represents a teacher's determination to develop a literature-based unit of instruction.

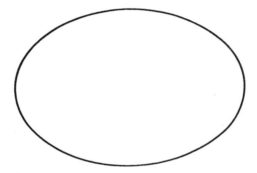

Blank Core of Structure to Implement Thematic Unit for Literature-Based Instruction

Now an empty oval, the Core will show the building of relationships in a unit by adding a wedge-shaped component representing information vital to a unit as each chapter is read. Each component and its related chapter has information for you to consider when developing a thematic unit. All of the components come together as a complete whole in the last chapter, where you will see the finished visual metaphor that looks like this:

Core of Structure to Implement Thematic Unit for Literature-Based Instruction

To show ways each segment contributes to the building of a unit, each one of the ten components in the Core of Structure is considered separately in a related chapter:

Component 1: Begin to Plan
Component 2: Infuse Literacy Curriculum
Component 3: Select Literature Base
Component 4: Select Teaching Techniques
Component 5: Integrate Social Studies and Expressive Arts
Component 6: Integrate Mathematics and Science
Component 7: Locate Resources
Component 8: Meet Needs of Diverse Students
Component 9: Assess and Evaluate
Component 10: Use Research to Support Practice

In the final figure of the Core of Structure in the last chapter, each component touches all of the others in the center of the Core to show its relationship to the other components. The visual metaphor points out the importance of each component to the thematic unit: Each is an integral part needed in total planning, each has a place in the concept of a unit, and each plays a valuable part in building an effective plan for literature-based instruction in the elementary classroom.

Considering the components separately as the different chapters are read will help focus your thinking on the importance of each component in literature-based instruction, guide you as you generate ideas related to each area, and serve as a unit outline as you concentrate on ways to expand your planning. Considering each component will help identify lines of inquiry and projects related to the theme and enable you to visualize additional depth in planning in curriculum areas—perhaps beginning with simple concrete projects and then moving to more complex abstract ones.

In the Core of Structure, the components of information will also assist you in planning and implementing a unit. The Core and its components guide you as you read and serve as tools to help you review the information in this book. For instance, the Core can be a useful study guide in learning and researching the component topics and can be a personal note-taking device as you review the topics presented in the chapters. To facilitate note taking, each chapter begins with Teacher Reflections—phrases to stimulate your thoughts about thematic units and literature-based instruction. To support your teaching, findings from research related to instruction in an elementary classroom are in Classroom Updates throughout the book. To further assist you, black line masters (reproducibles) are identified within various chapters. These reproducibles are found at the end of the book. Extensions (activities), endnotes, and suggested readings for teachers are listed at the end of each chapter. In the bibliographies of children's books, those currently in print are identified with an asterisk. The other books are available in juvenile collections at large universities, elementary school library collections, private collections of teachers and librarians, and children's book departments at public libraries.

Of course, you can begin reading any chapter related to a component that interests you the most. For instance, you may want to turn first to Chapter 7, Resources, to find book selection aids to help you locate children's books you need, or you may want to turn to Chapter 9, Meeting the Needs of Diverse Students, and consider the needs of students before you select a unit topic. After you have read all of the chapters, turn to the last one again and review the final figure of the Core of Structure that visually shows the integration needed in the development of a thematic unit in literature-based instruction.

Acknowledgments

A Green Dinosaur Day: A Guidebook for Developing Thematic Units in Literature-Based Instruction, K–6 was supported by field testing in a selected classroom in Elk Grove, California, by teachers and librarians who contributed resources, and by support from mentor teachers and university professors. Consulting with teachers in school districts allowed me to work with educators as they developed and improved their own literature-based curricula. My sincere appreciation goes to the following contributors: John Dickinson, elementary school student; Barbara Striplen, student teacher supervisor; Janet D. M. Tucker, professional substitute teacher who contributed guidelines for being a substitute teacher; Kristie Darras, primary-grade teacher, the contributor of a dinosaur unit for first grade found in some of the vignettes in the chapters; Sheila Simmons, upper-elementary grade teacher who suggested a "panel of experts" idea; and the other elementary teachers who offered ideas for this text.

Colleagues at California State University, Sacramento, gave needed criticism and impetus for refinement and changes. Consulting with Dr. Victoria Jew, coordinator of Title VII Curriculum Improvement Project and contributing author to Chapter 5 and the "Sheltered English" portion of Chapter 8, allowed me to present a Core of Structure as a visual graphic organizer. Additionally, Dr. Janie Low, associate chair of the Department of Teacher Education (1991–92), was a contributing author to the section, "Preparing Your Students for Learning" in Chapter 4, and Dr. Chris Hasegawa, a valued colleague, performed an important service as science consultant.

Librarians from California State University, Sacramento, provided needed assistance for which I am most grateful: Roz Van Auker, curriculum librarian, and Kathryn King, librarian in the InterLibrary Loan Department, deserve special thanks for their contributions, support, and hard work. Also, the dedicated educators who reviewed this manuscript offered many valuable suggestions that were appreciated and are offered my thanks: Sandra Baker, elementary school teacher, Munster, Indiana, and Marcia Modlo, educational administrator, Vestal, New York.

My sincere appreciation goes to Anson Jew, illustrator, for his artistic talent and computer skills. His graphics add the needed visuals and enhance the text of this book.

Finally, I would like to acknowledge the special people at Allyn and Bacon who helped make this book a reality: Mylan Jaixen, editor-in-chief, who supported the project; Sean Wakely, senior editor/education, who first saw this as a helpful resource for teachers; and Susan Hutchinson, editorial assistant, who took a special interest in this book.

Patricia L. Roberts

Chapter 1 _____

How May I Plan a Thematic Unit?

Teacher Reflections for Chapter 1

Chapter 1 relates to a professional overview about ways to:

- Initiate a thematic unit
- Integrate a unit with curricular areas
- Use different approaches to start a thematic unit
- Refer to the Core of Structure to plan an approach to a unit

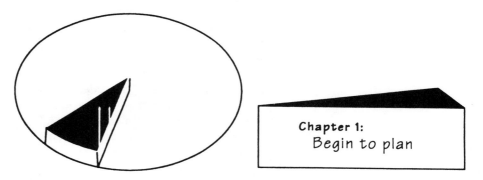

Component in Core of Structure to Implement a Thematic Unit for Literature-Based Instruction: Begin to Plan

Introduce "A Green Dinosaur Day" and Go Beyond

"Tyrannosaurus raised his head and rolled his evil eye . . ."[1] and looked your way. In jest, you sense tyrannosaurus knows you want a thematic unit about dinosaurs. Tyrannosaurus keeps an eye on you as you plan "A Green Dinosaur Day," the first day of planned literature-based language instruction about dinosaurs in an elementary classroom. Literature-based instruction goes beyond a first day when a teacher infuses a literacy curriculum with a content curriculum in a unit format. The unit includes text materials of all kinds, uses large blocks of time, explores a theme, and, on purpose, integrates knowledge from several disciplines. A theme (topic) includes literature, natural science, social sciences, and ways to express information about our natural and social environment; it includes the arts of language (listening, speaking, reading, writing), mathematics, and other expressive arts (painting, dramatizing, and interacting with music). A question looms: *When a teacher starts a literature-based thematic unit on a topic such as dinosaurs, how may a teacher begin?*

If you are like other teachers interested in whole-language learning and its principles (real people using real language for real purposes [Goodman, 1986]), you will be quite excited as you use these principles to begin a literature-based unit! When using language for real purposes, a literature-based unit can support the whole-language philosophy. However, it is also possible that a literature-based unit will not support the whole-language philosophy if language is not used for authentic purposes. After your first excitement about all this wears off and you think more about implementing this instruction, a mild anxiousness may begin in your mind. This anxiety generates other questions to consider:

- How should I prepare a thematic unit? How can I infuse a literacy curriculum with a content curriculum?
- In the unit, how will I lead students toward social interaction in the community so they interact with people and "give something back"?
- What multicultural contributions can be included? What teaching ensures concepts about plurality (recognizing different cultures), empowerment (ownership, sense of belonging, internal motivation for learning), and status-equivalency procedures (each student has status) in the classroom?
- How can I meet the needs of diverse students?
- What supportive resources are available?
- What research backs up my teaching plans?
- How can I encourage the participation of other teachers in a support group for literature-based instruction?

Implementing a thematic unit in an elementary classroom can be quite troublesome (and a trouble). Few writers can say all the words needed for every teacher about developing thematic units for literature-based instruction in the beginning paragraphs of a book on this subject. However, you will recognize the importance in beginning to plan and in starting with ways to initiate a thematic unit. Thus, this book begins with that topic—initiating a unit.

Topic A: Initiating a Thematic Unit

To begin a unit, you should decide which of the many approaches is most appropriate for your class, considering the interests, skills, and abilities of your particular students. A unit can begin in various ways. For example, an introduction to a unit's content can start with an artifact, a book, or a computer simulation. You can initiate a unit with a field trip, an item from a trip related to the topic, or with visits to exhibits or museums. You can begin with a problem to solve, a learning center, or a current event or supplementary books for reading about a theme and the content. You can start with the students' questions, with students' roleplaying, or with a visiting resource person from your community. Indeed, any of these beginnings will interest students in a unit of study.

Artifacts

Artifacts, a special kind of topic introduction for a unit, enhance learning for girls and boys interested in real-life examples. Children cannot depend on verbal explanations only. If, for example, during a unit about dinosaurs, the youngsters discuss fossils and what information fossils tell us, they need hands-on experience with fossils to develop further concepts about fossils. The children experience materials, such as those in a fossil kit with a 70-million-year-old dinosaur bone (Childcraft) or the fossil kits of a apatosaurus/brontosaurus or tryannosaurus (Casual Living). Working with a triceratops kit (Smithsonian Institution) allows students to unearth fragments of a fossil, reassemble its pieces, discuss the experience, and write about what was learned. This approach provides opportunities for girls and boys to cluster in groups and involve themselves in an authentic language activity. Handling an artifact can introduce a dinosaur unit and arouse the students' curiosity—they'll ask many questions about it and can record their questions on the board to begin their study.

As another example of beginning a unit with an artifact, a primary-grade teacher gathered the girls and boys on a rug near her and showed a clear plastic container filled with sand. Buried in the sand, an aptosaurus bone fossil (Childcraft) waited to be uncovered. After locating the fossil, students passed it around their semi-circle, looked at it, and the teacher asked them to tell their observations about it. On small bone-shaped paper, students then wrote a few lines telling their thoughts about the bone. The students' thoughts about the bone fossil were read aloud, told to others, rewritten in larger manuscript, and then displayed on class charts that were read by the whole group.

After excavating the fossil, the students asked more questions about it—a springboard for further activities. To infuse the literacy curriculum with content about the fossil and to demonstrate reading aloud, the teacher told the students that portions of a book, *100 Dinosaurs From A to Z* (Grosset & Dunlap, 1986) by Ron Wilson, would be read to them to tell some of the scientists' observations about the dinosaur and the parts of the United States where the fossil was found. In this learning situation, the teacher became a facilitator and helped students discover dinosaurs—the intellectual giants of their time—as a topic of interest for their lines of inquiry.

With an artifact as a positive force in concept building, this teacher led the students on subsequent days to study the work of a particular type of scientist—the paleontologist—and to another time period—the prehistoric time of dinosaurs. The teacher focused on contributions of paleontologists from many cultures and countries and on paleontology as an aspect of science studied across cultures throughout the world. To do this, the teacher linked happenings in the present back to what happened in the past and compared the extinction of animal species now with the extinction of dinosaurs. The teacher compared animal species endangered now with some of the species surviving during the dinosaurs' extinction and compared the habitats of animals endangered now with the changed habitat leading to the dinosaurs' demise. This link from the present to the past about endangered species and their habitats led to social interactions in the classroom as well as to social activities outside the classroom as the children met with park rangers, museum workers, and local scientists in the community. Social action for the teacher began, too, when the teacher invited other teachers to join her to form a small support/empowerment group on literature-based instruction. The teachers in the support group met regularly to discuss teaching, learning, classroom research, and social activities in the community related to the curriculum (see Chapter 5).

Audiovisual Presentations

The new and often very exciting audiovisual material for instruction seems to reject a traditional text-oriented approach. For instance, while seeing *Evolution* (Texture Films), a wordless video presentation, sixth-grade students listened for ways music helped tell the story and looked for three important observations they learned while observing the video. After seeing the video, the students talked about ways they thought music helped tell the story and discussed the information they gained from their observations. To record their observations, the students developed a word association (word relationships) map on the board and wrote what they knew about the process of evolution (Pehrsson & Denner, 1989). Also in the study, the students kept a record in learning logs (a daily record of learning in notebooks) of what they discovered as they followed their selected lines of inquiry about the work of paleontologists and the types of dinosaurs. Visually emphasizing more dinosaur discoveries, *Evolution* (Crowell, 1987) by Joanna Cole was read aloud and the pictures discussed. It reported ways scientists put together pieces of the puzzle about the chain of life from fossils. Then the students returned to their original word association map to add the information they gained from listening to the book. Along with other audiovisual materials and trade books, the students used a science text as one of the many resource books in their classroom.

Books

A children's trade book, particularly one related to the theme, helps girls and boys learn about content. Showing how a trade (library) book starts a unit, a second-grade teacher selected Jeannie Baker's *Where the Forest Meets the Sea* (Greenwillow, 1988) to generate children's interest and questions. Baker's illustrations show a boy and his father spending a day along the sandy beaches of a creek flowing through a tangled primordial forest. This remote place is reached by boat and an observant student notices the boat's name, *Time Machine*. Baker places the shapes of the past on the pages—aboriginal children, ancient trees, husky dinosaurs, and other extinct animals. Different perspectives are seen, too: from inside the hollow of an enormous old tree, from outside the tree, and from the past. Without borders, each illustration goes across two pages so children see Baker's interpretation of the vastness of nature. Creating textures, Baker uses clay, paints, and natural materials in the pictures. With these present-day materials, Baker gives girls and boys a look into the future with her pictures about the past and shows how the past developed in the forest and then how it disappeared or was destroyed. Sad to see the day end in the story, the father assures the boy they will return to the forest, a contrast with the last question: *But will the forest still be here when we come back?* Baker's book offers opportunities for the students to imagine what life was like in past times, discuss what happened in the illustrations, and explore the content related to the unit further.

Later in the day, some students reviewed Baker's story again about the young boy who steps into the past and discovers the old growth Australian rain forest with a video (Films, Inc./Film Australia). After seeing the video, the girls and boys in their literature response groups (groups where something is said or done as an answer to questions generated from the material) related information from this video to their own lives. They talked about current threats to America's forests and what they know related to the condition of today's trees and forests.

In a fourth-grade class, another teacher read aloud Virginia Lee Burton's *Life Story* (Houghton Mifflin, 1963) to show Burton's use of the "life is a stage" metaphor. Both print and pictures introduce the passing of time as acts in a stage play and the scenes show the different ages of Earth beginning with life in the seas, shores, and swamps down to our current time period. In the book, each prehistoric era becomes one scene in an act in Earth's life story that happens "on stage" in the illustrations. Several text narrators tell the story—an astronomer, paleontologist, historian, grandmother, and the author. To draw the students into the story and emphasize that the "stage" belongs to the students, the author says the story is "your life story" and it is "you" who plays a leading role.

In a fifth-grade class, a teacher read Mary Adrian's *The Mystery of the Dinosaur Graveyard* (Hastings House, 1986) and the students listened to the adventures of two children who discovered an almost-complete dinosaur skeleton. Another read-aloud choice, Caroline Arnold's *Dinosaur Mountain: Graveyard of the Past* (Clarion, 1989), told the students about the National Dinosaur Monument in Utah and ways that life in the Jurassic age currently are being uncovered. The book showed how cooperation among paleontologists helps in their discoveries. After a discussion of the books, the class members invited a resource person from a nearby museum to talk about additional information on dinosaur finds. When the classroom speaker arrived on a scheduled date and talked to the students, they showed displays of what they had learned about dinosaurs to their visitor and discussed the projects they completed. Some students told about their work and others reported on paleontology, fossils, and dinosaurs with bones as long as a bus. Still others presented original lyrics in songs, books, and other items in a classroom museum they called a *dinosaurium*. The students' studies resulted in a large collection of materials that they discussed with the museum's representative.

Computer Simulations

The power of computers and software was brought to the attention of third-grade students through a simulated dinosaur hunt, *The Dinosaur Discovery Kit* (First Byte), a favorite with primary-grade children. The girls and boys kept individual records of what they discovered through this simulation (and others) as they studied dinosaurs. Often, the children met together as a group and shared the information they gathered with one another. They discussed dinosaur discoveries further with two books by Dougal Dixon, *Be a Dinosaur Detective* (Lerner, 1988) and *Be a Fossil Detective* (Derrydale/Crown, 1988). With facts from these books, both the teacher and students talked about ways to identify dinosaurs by their skeletons, ways to match them to the food they ate, and ways to deduct the identity of a dinosaur from the prints it left. As the children interacted with software, kept their own records, and discussed with others what they learned from books, they became aware of their own growth in learning.

Displays

In another third-grade classroom, the teacher organized a display table with dinosaur fossils and other items brought back from a trip to Utah's National Dinosaur Monument. (During the first week of school, the teacher surveyed the students' parents about recent trips and knew which parents to contact for information and items to add to the dinosaur display.) On a book cart, the teacher arranged a selection of informational books, poetry, and fiction. On the inside back cover of these books were cardboard pockets and in the pockets were several cards with different questions, activities, and lines of inquiry.

Reading Card #1: WHAT'S HATCHING FROM DINOSAUR DINAH'S EGG?

Read Lee Lorenz's *Dinah's Egg* (Simon & Schuster, 1990) to discover the humorous situations that happen when Dinah's egg rolls out of her nest.

1. With a friend, reread the story *Dinah's Egg*.
2. Draw (dictate, write) an event from the story (losing an egg from the nest, egg rolls away, funny things happen, and so on).
3. With your friend, reread parts of the story a third time to get more words and ideas you want.

Talk about your drawings and words with a friend. Sign your work and give it to your teacher.

After preparing cards, the teacher placed them in books for students to consider. Selecting their own books, the girls and boys chose a question, activity, or line of inquiry from one of the cards inside the books and followed up the topic with supplementary reading and study. Doing this, boys and girls accepted ownership of their work as they freely interacted with items on a display table, read about the items, and then self-selected a direction for study.

Following a line of inquiry means that students use books as resources related to the theme. Interested students find the reading selections to support their inquiries from a class book corner, a school library collection, and other sources. For instance, an inquiry about dinosaurs, both meat gulpers and plant snatchers, takes a reader to several sources (e.g., to books with information and activities, to humor, and sometimes, to fanciful stories). On this topic, the range of books is a wide one and includes Patricia Lauber's *Dinosaurs Walked Here and Other Stories Fossils Tell* (Bradbury, 1986) as well as Millicent Selsam's *Tyrannosaurus Rex* (Harper & Row, 1978). Selsam's book explains how to build a tyrannosaurus rex from fossil bones, whereas Lauber's book tells what information fossils give us. For example, a fossil of a hind foot of a baby duckbill, 4 inches wide, is compared to one toe of an adult duckbill, 8 inches wide. Lauber's book also shows students the similarities between some of the creatures of the past and creatures of the present—the horseshoe crab, birds, and fishes. To use what the children learn about ways the dinosaurs and other creatures moved, they may develop a bulletin board and suggest a title such as "Ways Prehistoric Creatures Got Moving!"

Learning Centers

In a fifth-grade classroom, a teacher engaged students in a learning center to build interest in the theme. These students made their own fossils to bury in a classroom dig in the school ground, hoping that someone will find their modern fossils at a later time. The materials for making fossils were on a classroom table labeled "Fossil Center" where the girls and boys write the steps they will use in the process of making fossils. Later, they described these steps to other members in their study group and discussed the materials they used for the fossils.

One resource, Aliki's *Fossils Tell of Long Ago* (Crowell, 1990), tells students how to create a one-minute fossil from a clay imprint of a hand and what to do with it—dry it and then bury it for someone to find a million years from now. With clay, plaster of Paris, leaves of plants, and other objects, the students make their own fossil-like imprints. With other information from Aliki's book, students may discover the way dinosaur tracks are cast in mud, how insects trapped in tree sap harden into amber, and why fossils of tropical plants show up in very cold places. Interest in the topic continues as girls and boys read about fossils that have been found, make fossil prints, and then talk about what they have learned with others.

Newspaper Articles

A sixth-grade teacher introduced a unit with a news article about a recent discovery of a new type of small dinosaur. After reading the article, the students discussed the importance of the new findings. When this current discovery of paleontologists was read about in the newspaper, the students realized that observations about dinosaur discoveries were real. The discoveries were meaningful and important enough to reporters to investigate and put in the news for adult readers, and by implication, important for the students, too.

As a reference, Dougal Dixon's *Hunting the Dinosaurs* (Gareth Stevens, 1987) provided a time line for the students and showed the chain of life and the development from one-cell animals to other animals. Susan Carroll's *How Big Is a Brachiosaurus? Fascinating Observations about Dinosaurs* (Grosset & Dunlap, 1986) and Mary Lou Clark's *Dinosaurs* (Childrens, 1981) described different dinosaurs, what came before them and after, why they disappeared, and how we learned about them.

Reading News Articles

The teacher selected some readings from other newspaper articles and discussed the importance of other recent findings with the students. These were "New Type of Small Dinosaur Discovered" (The *Sacramento Bee*) (Reproducible 1), "Piecing Together Bones of 'T Rex' " (Wilford, 1990b) (Reproducible 2), and "This May Be the Biggest Dinosaur Ever" (The *Sacramento Bee*) (Reproducible 3). To focus on the findings, the teacher used an overhead projector, a transparency of the articles, and duplicated copies. First, the teacher and students read one article together, discussed it, and then took time to study what was learned with partners and complete an activity of writing questions about the article. The students worked cooperatively, read other articles together, and signed their work of written questions. When finished, they placed their work in their dinosaur portfolios (folders used for teacher assessment [see Chapter 9]).

Ranking Discoveries

After the students discussed the articles, they analyzed the material in each article and evaluated the importance of each discovery. They ordered the discoveries in ranks as the most important finding (rank 1), fairly important (rank 2), and not too important at this time (rank 3). As a guide for this, the teacher distributed a ranking sheet (Reproducible 4) and discussed the process of rank ordering with the class. In their discussion groups, the students analyzed what they read in the news articles, expressed their criteria, developed a rank order, and gave reasons for determining the ranks.

Paintings

A thematic unit can also play an important role in helping children develop a receptive attitude toward expressive art. To foster this, a second-grade teacher introduced a unit with a mural from the pages of Scully's *The Great Dinosaur Mural at Yale: The Age of Reptiles* (Abrams, 1989). The tall narrow pages were unfolded into a full-color illustration nearly 60 inches long. The teacher also showed the reproductions of paintings in a calendar, *Album of Dinosaurs* (Barnes

& Noble) and the National Geographic paintings in Kathryn Jackson's *Dinosaurs* (National Geographic Society, 1972). The teacher gave one illustration from the calendar to each pair of student partners in the room and invited them to talk about their observations and then to write their thoughts about what they saw. Joining together as a total group, the partners talked and read their thoughts aloud and contributed questions for a board list of questions about dinosaurs. Related questions were grouped together into a question map. The question map guided the inquiries of the children on other days of study and led them to books such as Jean M. Craig's *Dinosaurs and More Dinosaurs* (Scholastic, 1973) with its life-like dinosaur illustrations, Helen Roney Sattler's *Dinosaurs of North America* (Lothrop, Lee & Shepard, 1981) with its illustrations of 80 dinosaurs found in North America, and Janet Riehecky's *Dinosaurs* (Childrens, 1989) with its information about the creatures' unique physical traits. Beginning the thematic unit with an introduction to a mural and reproductions of paintings, the children observed the artwork of others and asked questions about what they saw. Their questions led to further research about the topic and recognition of ways artists depict prehistoric life in their books.

Problems

With a sandtable simulating a dig in the room, a fourth-grade teacher started with a problem related to the dig. The dig was marked off in squares with string and a student probed the sand with a probing stick as others waited to see when the stick met some resistance and struck something hard. The students thought carefully about what they saw and then drew a picture of what they *thought* was beneath the probe. They showed their drawings, talked about their ideas, and wrote their predictions on a chart. Some students told about the "finds" they once had made in other places and others talked about the tools they used to dig for different objects.

For reference use, data sources with illustrations and observations about fossils were on a nearby table. One was Byron Barton's *Bones, Bones, Dinosaur Bones* (HarperCollins, 1990), which enabled the girls and boys to read about the activity at a dig and see the ways scientists dug, wrapped, packed, and assembled what they found. In another book, David Lambert's *The Dinosaur Date Book* (Avon/Diagram Group, 1990), the students got information about the size and features of the large animals. Useful as an alphabetical reference, it has over 1,000 entries from A to Z, with information about individual dinosaurs and their color, size, and speed. The book also lists fossil discoveries continent by continent and names of the world's best dinosaur museums. Another source by Lambert, *The Field Guide to Prehistoric Life* (Facts on File, 1985), has a record of which creatures lived at what time in prehistory and some observations about the latest scientific discoveries. As a cross-check reference for these discoveries, more information about origins and investigations of fossils are found in Lampton's *Dinosaurs and the Age of Reptiles* (Watts, 1983). All ideas from the dig, the data sources, and the discussions were used to stimulate the students' writing.

With fifth-grade students unable to visit an actual dig because of the district's financial restraints, a teacher gathered students around a Gobi (sand) table and introduced them to tasks related to the time-consuming work of a paleontologist. At an actual dig, a paleontologist uses a collection of tools from dynamite to toothbrushes, and the teacher wanted the students to realize that it takes about 15,000 hours to dig out a large dinosaur fossil and about 90 days to reconstruct a dinosaur egg fossil.

Buried in the classroom dig at the Gobi table, and unknown to the students, were several fossil replicas—interlocking replicas of dinosaur bones (Child-craft)—covered before the start of the school day by cooperating students from another classroom. When found, the interlocking pieces were used by the girls and boys to reconstruct different dinosaur shapes and then to research and write information about the assembled dinosaur. For a self-check and a partner-check, the teacher marked lightly all of the ends of the bones of one type of dinosaur with a colored marking pen (red indicates one type, blue another). Cooperatively, all students worked with other student "bone diggers" at the classroom dig and in their discussion groups.

Several questions were asked by the students about their classroom dig: Why was the digging area marked off the way it was? Why did the sections have letters on the sides of the sandtable and numbers on the ends? What were they for?

Seeing the tools, a student asked, "What are those things for?" The tools were used by girls and boys working at the sandtable and included a journal, storing tray, magnifying glass, spray bottle of water, brush, and (for a gentle probe) clear straws. The hands-on activity elicited more questions. Who wanted to probe the first section? Who would record the letter and number of the section explored first? Who would show a way the tools could be used? Additional questions continued the discussion: When the probe struck a hard object, what tool(s) would take away the sand carefully? Which tool(s) could be selected to clean the object? Relating to the work of the paleontologist, the students discussed how they would use the water, storing tray, magnifying glass, and other tools.

The students' questions led the direction of the activity, and the girls and boys "read" the locations of the objects they found by identifying a square and calling out its corresponding letter and number. Then they discussed a use for the blank mural sheet on the wall. Some students used rulers to mark off the mural sheet to represent squares on the sandtable and then drew their sketches of "found fossils" in the appropriate grid square on the paper. The sketches showed the fossil replicas as they were uncovered. This visual display became an information record for everyone in the classroom and by using the sketches as a reference, all students could see the way the classroom dig was proceeding and what findings were discovered each day.

During the study, the girls and boys worked daily at the table and, after digging, they wrote observational notes and drew sketches of the found objects in their journals. They discussed the importance of recording where a fossil was found and indicated the location of each fossil with a grid letter and number. The students recorded each discovery in their journals and on the mural sheet that was the "wall record." The comments of the fossil finder's thoughts also were written in his or her journal.

This hands-on approach was deemed by the teacher to be more effective in generating student interest than if the teacher had used an approach of assigning textbook reading about fossils. The procedure launched inquiry by the students, for the girls and boys inquired into the problem, thought about possible responses, talked about ideas, and discussed predictions with one another. Through children's literature related to the topic, the teacher also provided data sources for the students' examination. Everyone had an opportunity to present what was learned through discussions, journals, and the record on the wall.

Questions

Student inquiry does not always need to begin with tools for a simulated dig, a Gobi table, or any other collection of items gathered by the teacher. Indeed, a unit's beginning often does not need to be developed by the teacher, for the girls and boys will ask their own questions and introduce a line of inquiry in the classroom. If interested in dinosaurs, students might select responses to some of their questions from the question-answer format in Darlene Geis's *The How and Why Book of Dinosaurs* (Grosset & Dunlap, 1960). Geis's format has information about the creatures, their size, eating habits, habitats, and behavior. Together, the teacher and students can decide on what other data they need, organize in teams to gather information, and meet together to talk about the results of their work in study groups.

Replicas

One morning, some third-grade children arrived in their classroom and saw a five-foot long green stegosaurus (Nature Company) in the center of the room. The large replica quickly became the focus of their questions and discussion, and the teacher told the children that a few pages from a book would be read to them about this dinosaur and where its fossil was found. Reading the pages, the teacher facilitated the learning about the stegosaurus and led the children toward discovering dinosaurs as a content of study by focusing their discussion on the large replica. A nearby table had a display of books that included *Creatures of Long Ago: Dinosaurs and Animals Showing Off* (National Geographic Society, 1988) opened to show its pop-up pages, Douglas Norman's *Factfinder: Dinosaur* (Stoddart, 1989), and Douglas Norman's *When Dinosaurs Ruled the Earth* (Stoddart, 1988). In *Factfinder,* an index led the students to material arranged in one-page chapters. *When Dinosaurs Ruled the Earth* had charts and maps that elaborated on information about evolution and new fossil finds. Several dinosaur models-to-scale were passed around, handled by the students, and measured: a 20-inch apatosaurus/brontosaurus, a 15-inch triceratops, and a 16-inch tyrannosaurus rex. Large and small, the dinosaur replicas fostered the students' interest in the prehistoric creatures and led to further reading and writing.

Resource People

After discussing the content of their study with a natural science specialist from the community, the third-grade girls and boys realized the importance of the work done by people living near them, as well as the importance of the related study they did in the classroom. Indeed, a visit by the specialist allowed for additional insights to be developed and encouraged the students to interact with a community resource outside the school. Visits by people from the community were continually encouraged in the classroom and the teacher did not overlook the possibility of each child's parent or relative being a resource person for a particular topic of study. For any given topic of study, the teacher believed it was possible that at least *one* child in the class would know an adult whose work related in some way to the study. Meeting with resource people who were invited to the class was important to the students; during these meetings, the students connected their lives at school with their relatives, adults in the home, and workers in their community.

Roleplaying

Roleplaying can also lead students into a thematic unit because it develops a context for a related investigation and establishes a need for research. For example, a unit about discoverers of fossils of prehistoric animals began when students in a combined fifth- and sixth-grade class were assigned the roles of dinosaur fossil hunters who made fossil discoveries. Before playing their roles, the players needed additional information about dinosaur fossil hunters and found what they needed in data sources. The roleplayers read about certain events in the lives of the hunters, located names of authentic fossils found by past hunters, and acquired information about ways the discoveries were made.

To begin their research about fossil hunters, some students reviewed the portraits of paleontologists in John Wilford's *The Riddle of the Dinosaur* (Knopf, 1985) and others read parts of John Gilbert's *Dinosaurs Discovered* (Larousse, 1979) and located facts they needed about the discoveries of the first fossil in 1706 and later findings in 1979. Kate McMullan's *Dinosaur Hunters* (Random House, 1989) also gave other students several anecdotes about Mantell, Cope, Marsh, and other discoverers of fossils. Using this information, the students discussed what fossils were found and where. The teacher then asked the students to cross-check the information they found. For example, they were asked to cross-check the information in the first paragraph of McMullan's book with information in other books to verify the accuracy of the statements.

To see evidence of worldwide interest and support for this study from other scientists around the world, the students determined which of the paleontologists were from countries other than the United States. Before playing the roles, students listed additional questions they wanted answered and then they searched further for information. Their questions included Who were some other hunters? and What did the hunters find? They also wanted to know what the hunters used to uncover fossils and the ways the hunters identified what they had found. These questions took the students on a search for facts before playing their roles and became a base for future inquiries as they explored references to find information about the hunters of fossils. At a later time in the study, roleplaying again introduced other scientists, important events in their lives, and their contributions.

Data for Roleplay

As examples of roleplaying situations about fossil findings, the following two situations were developed for older students from observations by John Ostrom (1978), the discoverer of a meat-gulping dinosaur, the deinonychus.

Situation #1

When John Ostrom discovered the fossil of the deinonychus (die-on-nike-us), he had some surprises. Ostrom found a huge sickle-like bone more than three inches long on one toe of each foot of the dinosaur, and he determined the bone was a weapon used to kill prey. He guessed the claws, when not in use, were carried in a retracted position so as not to be damaged. Ostrom also guessed this dinosaur was very fast and agile and used its foot talons against an enemy or victim—perhaps it even jumped from one foot to another while kicking out at its prey or attacker with its free foot. Ostrom further maintained that this quickness was not associated with the image of a cold-blooded dinosaur but rather with a large flightless warm-blooded bird like an ostrich.

Its hands and arms surprised Ostrom. Its long hand had three powerful fingers with large sharp claws designed for grasping. The wrist joints enabled the hands to turn toward each other so the dinosaur could grab prey and work both hands together—something only humans and certain other mammals can do.

To the student in the role: In what ways do you agree or disagree with Ostrom's guesses (deductions)?

Situation #2

In Montana, John Ostrom found a few fossil parts of a single plant-snatching dinosaur along with several specimens of the meat-eater, deinonychus. Ostrom guessed the plant snatcher was the prey animal but it was six times larger than the meat-eating attackers. He asked, "How could the smaller meat eaters attack a larger plant eater with success?" Ostrom's hunch was that the smaller meat-eating dinosaur hunted in packs, and the predator fossil specimens found along with the larger plant-eating prey appeared to be the victims of the prey's final struggle.

To the student in the role: In what ways do you agree or disagree with Ostrom's conclusion? What other hunches (predictions) do you have?

Social Actions

"The more learners can actively participate in decision-making activities and work on self-selected problems beyond the classroom," writes Bennett (1990, p. 307), "the more likely they are to increase their feelings of personal and political effectiveness." To show how some students participated in a decision-making activity beyond the classroom, one fourth-grade teacher selected Mary Elting's *The Big Golden Book of Dinosaurs* (Golden, 1988) and read aloud the book's dedication. Elting's book was dedicated to the fourth-grade students of McElevain Elementary School in Denver, who lobbied to make a stegosaurus the official state fossil of Colorado. Lacking an official state fossil in their state, too, some of the girls and boys were interested in writing to the students now enrolled in the McElevain Elementary School to find out more about how the fourth-grade class accomplished this project. "Project Letter Writing" began and Elting's book interested a few students who reread the dedication and browsed through the pages. Two other books by Elting became study references: *Dinosaurs and Other Prehistoric Creatures* (Western, 1988) and *The Macmillan Book of Dinosaurs and Other Prehistoric Creatures* (Macmillan, 1984).

Then the fourth-grade teacher read to the students a fictional version about the successful social action of the class who lobbied to make a stegosaurus the official state fossil of Colorado. Listening to Barbara Steinger's story, *Oliver Dibbs and the Dinosaur Cause* (Four Winds, 1986), read aloud over several days, the students had an ongoing discussion about the problems (including an interfering bully) and the solutions in the story before Will Dibbs and his classmates succeeded in making the stegosaurus Colorado's state fossil. The students predicted some of the problems they thought they would face in proposing legislation in their state. They discussed their predictions about problems associated with passing a law in their state and talked about the ways they might react to some of the problems.

Equally important to knowing the social action in the story was knowing about the current social action of others. Wanting to keep current, the students read the newspapers and listened to news reports and documentaries on television and radio that related to the topic. They discovered something was going on in Colorado's famous Morrison Formation and read about it (Reproducible 5). Southwest of Denver, a group that called themselves "Friends of Dinosaur Ridge" designed a project to protect an outcropping of dinosaur fossils at the Morrison Formation and proposed a Dinosaur Ridge Park, a mile long and 200 feet wide, to be built. The students discussed the proposed park and the value of its purposes—to be an outdoor education laboratory and a "hands-on science, ecology, natural history park" (Loew, 1990).

To further expand a social action component of this thematic unit into the community, the teacher located a community member—an environmental manager with the state's highway department—whose work related to the unit and invited him to the classroom to meet and talk with the students. Additionally, the teacher looked for places for students to visit in the community that were related to the theme, and then, with the students, identified concerns in the community to address through the unit.

Classroom Update

- Teacher and student attitudes toward literature-centered programs are positive ones (Zarrillo, 1988).
- A long-term literature program affects students since they demonstrate significantly more positive attitudes toward the concept of the teacher reading to students and talking about books in school. Furthermore, students gain in literary knowledge and maintain reading achievement levels comparable to students who receive traditional reading instruction (Swinger, 1975).
- Students with little interest in books show gains in their responses to literature from in-depth discussions since the discussions create interest in particular books and genres which are not always popular (Wilson, 1975).
- The amount of reading children do greatly affects their growth in reading (Clark, 1976; Fader, 1982).

Topic B: Planning a Unit Further

To plan a thematic unit further, you should link together a content curriculum and a literacy curriculum and identify the connections between the two. These connections can be a framework for the unit as the students learn the expressive arts of language and construct their own knowledge bases about content. The unit can provide for self-selected lines of inquiry so a student can pursue his or her learning interests. As the students follow their own interests, the unit will expand into the study of different topics. For example, a dinosaur unit may expand into a study of other reptiles and amphibians, endangered species, or the earth's ecosystem. In the unit, a sense of ownership of inquiry emerges as the girls and boys suggest their original plans and activities or engage in variations suggested by you. A sense of ownership begins for you, too, as you take the opportunity to engage in a line of inquiry that you are interested in pursuing. Your unit should include an opportunity for students to work alone, in pairs with a learning partner, and in groups or whole-group situations (see Chapter 4). With this arrangement, you can promote a conducive risk-taking environment for students where their errors are accepted and where they can discuss processes and display products representing their work.

Features of a Thematic Unit

Interested in the development of thematic units, Dr. Victoria Jew (1990), Project Coordinator of a recent Title VII Curriculum Improvement Project at a major western mainstream university, works with preservice and inservice teachers and provides them with this description:[2,3]

Thematic Unit

Integration. A thematic unit consists of a group of lessons that are planned around a specific theme. Since a theme can be carried through a variety of subject/content areas, the thematic unit lends itself to the integration of the different areas of the curriculum. By planning through a theme across different subject/content areas, a thematic unit also allows for an in-depth study of a specific topic.

Theme. The theme for a thematic unit can be a specific topic or a concept. For example, topics such as stars, ocean, dragons, or flight can be themes that allow for investigations in a variety of subject/content areas. However, themes that deal with concepts such as justice or injustice, prejudice and discrimination, or freedom also can be explored through different content areas of the curriculum. Naturally, some themes lend themselves to a greater variety of content areas while others are obviously more suitable and focused in one or two content areas with limited spin-off lessons into other areas.

Organization. A thematic unit can be organized to take up every period of the instructional day over a period of time. With such an organization, one activity period merges into the next with little attention to the time boundary of separate subjects during a school day. The teacher, however, aware of the subject areas involved in these activities, plans a unit to include the different subject areas and provides the balance between the various areas within the total unit.

Time Periods for Specific Subjects or Theme. Another way to organize a unit can be through one or two time periods designated for specific subjects. For example, a unit on stars can occupy the science period four days a week over a three week period. However, the same theme goes on simultaneously in language arts, social studies and art one day, math and physical education the next or just science on yet another day depending on the sequencing of the content or the specific plan to achieve an effect or to provide for a specific experience.

A third way to organize a unit, particularly for student teachers who are working under restrictions unique to a specific placement, can be through one or two time periods designed for specific subjects. During the designated period(s) the theme may be carried out through activities that involve different subject areas. For example, a unit on mythical beings can be housed during the reading/language arts period for three weeks. The majority of the activities are through reading about mythical creatures and through writing a skit that is acted out. Another period may compare some of the creatures with animals previously studied in science using categorization from science. Yet another lesson can compare similar mythical creatures from different cultures.

Structure. Since a thematic unit occupies a long period of time, it is desirable to build in activities that can create excitement at different points in a unit and activities that build connections between different activities in different subject content areas. Some possibilities could be: a most dramatic or spectacular event to initiate a unit, an action bulletin board that students are involved in constructing that continues to focus the class on the theme in a visible way, or a summation activity that puts many of the sub-themes together into a culminating activity.

Topic C: Exploring Literature-Based Study with a Core of Structure[4]

A Core of Structure Implements Literature-Based Instruction

When students are going to interact with children's books around a theme with your class, you will want to consider your own list of possibilities for guiding an in-depth study through books. To begin an in-depth study in your classroom, you should consider the components in the Core of Structure to Implement a Thematic Unit in Literature-Based Instruction and the chapter that relates to each component. Interested teachers find the Core of Structure helpful as a design for planning a unit for the classroom. Of course, the information in the components for your unit will differ from the information needed by the teacher in the next classroom. The ideas you select related to the components in the Core will be based on the interests, skills, and concept knowledge of your students. The information and ideas another teacher selects will be based on the skills and knowledge of students in his or her classroom.

Using your knowledge of children's books, state curriculum frameworks, district curricula, teaching techniques, and class organizational plans, you will rely on this information to initiate your unit. Other information you need will come from the resources you select to implement a unit and from ways you decide to meet the diverse needs of students in your classroom. Still other pieces of information will come from the techniques you want to use to assess and evaluate the progress of your students, as well as your awareness of the findings of research that supports literature-based instruction. Developing a thematic unit relies on all of these components and the way you integrate the information that is represented by the components in the Core of Structure.

Extensions for Chapter 1

1. *Conduct an interview with a group member.* Team up with a partner in your study group and interview her or him about favorites in children's literature. Write the information you get from the interview on the large paper sheet given to you by the group facilitator. Display your interview sheet as you make the introduction, and introduce your partner to the others in your group by using the information on the sheet.
2. *Bring an article up to date.* Find a research article such as Koeller's review "25 Years Advocating Children's Literature in the Reading Program" in *The Reading Teacher* (February, 1981, pp. 552–556). Bring the topics of research discussed in this article up to date with some recent studies you find. To what extent do the findings of the recent studies support the point of view that the amount of reading done by a student affects growth in attitudes, reading, and reading comprehension? Report what you found to others in your group.
3. *Survey the book.* Look at the front cover and the title page of this book and tell a partner what you learned from looking at those pages. Refer to the copyright page and tell the additional information found there. Look at the Table of Contents and tell your partner how the book is organized (the topics discussed, the importance of topic compared to the number of pages allotted in the book, and the most significant subject from your point of view). Preview each chapter of the book and read the headings and the subheadings. Would you use what you just did with elementary students? Why or why not? In which grades?

Endnotes

1. P. Hubbell in B. Hopkins (Ed.), *To look at every thing* (New York: Harcourt Brace Jovanovich, 1978).
2. *Core of Structure to Implement Thematic Unit in Literature-Based Instruction* was developed by V. Jew and P. Roberts (California State University, Sacramento, 1990) and designed as a visual organizer for the guidebook by A. Jew (1990–91).
3. Developed by Dr. Victoria Jew, Project Coordinator of a recent Title VII Curriculum Improvement Project at California State University, Sacramento (1990).
4. The Core of Structure is related to the implementation model of CSIN (the California Science Implementation Network, California State Department of Education), which emphasizes using in-depth, hands-on, process-centered units as the elementary science curriculum. CSIN recommends a unit-planning process for the new Science Framework and calls for units to be planned to "tell a story" and refers to a unit planning team as "storyboarders." Units in the model are designed around a few key questions and teachers

teach 3 to 5 units per year, as opposed to teaching general surveys of science currently promoted by textbook-dominated science instruction (C. Hasegawa, California State University, Sacramento, 1990). Similar suggestions are made in *A Guide to Curriculum Planning in Science* (Wisconsin Department of Public Instruction, 1987), *Gifted Talented Science, Grade 6* (Anne Arundel Public Schools, Annapolis, MD), and other educational guides.

Resources

Barnes & Noble. 126 Fifth Avenue, New York, NY 10011. Reproductions of paintings in *Age of Dinosaurs* calendar.

Casual Living U. S. A. 5401 Hangar Court, PO Box 31273, Tampa, FL 33631-3273. Fossil kits of apatosaurus/brontosaurus and tyrannosaurus.

Childcraft. 20 Kilmer Road, Edison, NJ 08818. Fossil kit with a 70-million-year-old dinosaur fossil bone.

Films, Inc., distributor. 5547 Ravenswood, Chicago, IL 60640-1199. Video: Baker's *Where the Forest Meets the Sea* (Film Australia).

First Byte. 3333 E. Spring Street, Suite 302, Long Beach, CA 90806. Software: *The Dinosaur Discovery Kit* (Pre–1). Also five-foot-long inflatable stegosaurus or tyrannosaurus rex.

Nature Company. 750 Hearst Avenue, Berkeley, CA. Replica.

Smithsonian Institution. Dept. 0006, Washington, DC, 20073-0006. Triceratops Kit 6001.

Texture Films. 1600 Broadway, New York, NY 10019. Video: *Evolution*.

Troll. 100 Corporate Drive, Mahwah, NJ, 07430. Models-to-scale from Carnegie Museum.

Readings

Bennett, C. I. (1990). *Comprehensive multicultural education: Theory and practice.* 2nd ed. Boston: Allyn and Bacon.

Clark, M. M. (1976). *Young fluent readers: What can they teach us?* Portsmouth, NH: Heinemann.

Fader, D. (1982). *The new hooked on books.* New York: Berkley Publishing.

Goodman, K. (1986). *What's whole in whole language?* Toronto: Scholastic-TAB Publications.

Jew, V. (1990). *Thematic unit for preservice teachers in a multicultural center.* Unpublished paper, California State University, Sacramento, CA.

Loew, P. (1990). Dinosaur capital USA: 113 years later, Morrison Formation continues to startle scientists. The *Sacramento Bee*, Tuesday, April 10. Frontiers, p. D6.

National Council for the Social Studies (1989). *Charting a course: Social studies for the 21st century.* Washington, DC: National Council for the Social Studies.

Ostrom, J. (1978). Extinctions. *National Geographic* (August).

Pehrsson, R. S., & P. R. Denner (1989). *Semantic organizers: A study strategy for special needs learners.* Rockville, MD: Aspen Publishers.

Rohter, L. (1990). Another jungle in jeopardy. The *Sacramento Bee*. Monday, August 6, p. A9.

The *Sacramento Bee* (1985). This may be the biggest dinosaur ever. Saturday, August 9, pp. A1, A24.

The *Sacramento Bee* (1986). New type of small dinosaur discovered. Friday, December 19, p. B11.

Swinger, A. K. (1975). *The effects of a long term literature program on the participating grade six students and their teachers.* Ph.D. dissertation, Ohio State University, DAI 36: 7192A.

Wilford, J. N. (1990). Piecing together bones on T rex. The *Sacramento Bee,* November 7, p. D6.

Wilson, R. R., Jr. (1975). *In-depth book discussions of selected sixth graders: Response to literature.* Ph.D. dissertation, Ohio State University, DAI 36: 7195A.

Zarrillo, J. J. (1988). *Literature-centered reading programs in elementary classrooms.* Ph.D. dissertation, Claremont Graduate School. AAD88-11932, DAI 49/06A: 1366.

Chapter 2

How May I Infuse a Literacy Curriculum in a Literature-Based Classroom?

Teacher Reflections for Chapter 2

Chapter 2 responds to your interests about:

- A literature-based classroom and sustained silent reading and writing
- Choices for inquiry/activities for students and reading aloud
- A story presentation to students and reading-writing connections
- A literacy curriculum infused with content
- The component in the Core of Structure to implement a literature-based thematic unit: Select literature base—Infuse a literacy curriculum

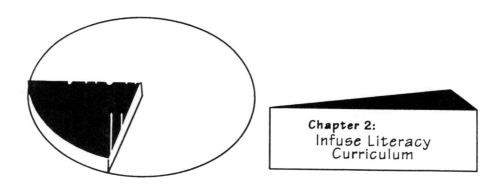

Component in Core of Structure to Implement a Thematic Unit for Literature-Based Instruction: Select Literature Base—Infuse a Literacy Curriculum

Vignette in Fourth Grade: A Green Dinosaur Day

"Brontosaurus,[1] diplodocus, gentle trachodon . . . ,"[2] chants one student to herself as she walks toward her fourth-grade[3] classroom to start her school day and a study about dinosaurs. For an informational reminder, a large sign in English and Spanish is on the classroom door and announces "Today Is a Green Dinosaur Day." This means the focus for the day will be literature-based instruction and the activities will be centered on content about dinosaurs as the teacher and students experience language together. Another teacher-prepared poster is a large green paper stegosaurus with the words, *Today Is a Green Dinosaur Day: How did we find out about dinosaurs?/Como descubrimos los dinosaurios?* Sometimes, the visual cue for literature-based instruction takes other shapes. The cue is a banner, cartoon, illustration, hanging mobile, or long paper streamers in bright colors that hang from the top of the door frame to the floor. The schedule for the day is devoted to the brontosaurus (apatosaurus), gentle trachodon, and other prehistoric creatures.

Schedule for a Green Dinosaur Day

8:20	Read about terrible lizards: Sustained silent reading
8:25	Discussion/introduction of new concepts/skills
8:25–35	Free writing in journals: Sustained silent writing
8:35–45	Read aloud Kroll's *The Tyrannosaurus Game*
9:00	Recess
9:20	Reenact a story game
9:40	Tell and write a pass-it-on story
10:00	Recess
10:10	Teacher tells story, *How I Captured a Dinosaur* by Schwartz
10:30	Students tell stories they have read
11:00	Recess
11:10	Dialogue and dictation: Introduce new concepts/skills
12:00	Lunch with a story
12:30	Display story words on paper shapes
1:00	Visualizing, categorizing, referencing
1:30	Recess
1:40	Measure objects with dimensions similar to a small dinosaur
2:30	Build word map
3:00	Prepare for cross-age reading to kindergarten
3:20	Class meeting to discuss the academic day; book talk time
3:30	Dismissal
4:00	Teacher reads journals, writes comments, records assessment notes, adds to portfolios, and plans for the next day

Topic A: Reading about Terrible Lizards: Sustained Silent Reading

Sustained silent reading (SSR) begins this study of the content about dinosaurs. Entering the classroom, the young girl, along with her friends, sees the visual cue and knows what to do because all had agreed the afternoon before that this day would begin with silent reading about dinosaurs. Large posters from the *Dinosaur Poster Book* (Courage Books, 1990) decorate the room and provide historical information about each dinosaur and show different ways artists interpret the prehistoric creatures. One dinosaur poster (International Reading Association, 1990), which shows two dinosaurs reading books, says, "Read. Avoid Extinction." On a monthly calendar, some students write their names in the date squares to show they want to talk about a book during "Book Talk" time, a show-and-tell about literature. Students see a display of books on the theme that includes *Los Dinosaurios* (Troll, 1976) and its English version, *More About Dinosaurs* by David Cutts; *Giant Dinosaurs* (Scholastic, 1975) and its Spanish version, *Dinosaurios Gigantes* by Erna Rowe; *Dinosaurio en Peligro* (Permabound, 1977) by Sharon Gordon; and *Dinosaurs and Their Young* by Russell Freedman.

Yesterday's read-aloud by the teacher, *Dinosaur Dig* (Morrow, 1990) by Kathryn Lasky, is the photo-documentary on display. In the story, the children heard of a family's adventure in Montana, searching for dinosaur bones with a paleontologist. In the photographs, the children saw what the family discovered by following a river's "ghost" and traveling over it in a pickup truck, by walking down slopes inhabited by rattlers, and by digging with a trowel to find a dinosaur rib about 65 million years old. Near the book are large charts with the names of fossil discoverers and early fossil finds from cultures around the world. To emphasize the contributions of discoverers from other countries (currently, about 30 full-time dinosaur paleontologists work worldwide), the charts bring the lives of these people into the study:

Discoverers of Dinosaur Fossils Around the World

In the United States

- 1676 *Eastern United States:* Reverend Robert Plot and others in Massachusetts (1802) discovered fossil bones.
- 1877–1890 *Wyoming:* In Como Bluff, Othaniel Marsh and his men found a stegosaurus skeleton.
- 1900s *Western United States:* Othaniel Marsh and Edward Cope together discovered over 135 new dinosaur types.
- 1964 *Montana:* John Ostrom uncovered deinonychus fossil.
- 1977 *Colorado:* Jim Jenson uncovered important fossil sites in Dry Mesa quarry and found the bones of the largest dinosaur ever known (with shoulder blades 8 feet long), pterosaurs, and other fossils.

In Other Countries

- 1822 *England:* Mary Ann Mantell found fossil teeth; Dr. Gideon Mantell (1824) found first fossil of iguanodon; in Oxford, Reverend William Buckland (1824) found a fossil jawbone with blade-like teeth; and Sir Richard Owens, anatomist (1841), named the animals *dinosauria* (terrible lizards).
- 1800s *France:* George Cuvier, a naturalist, collected fossil bones and now is recognized as the founder of paleontology, the study of ancient living things.
- 1965 *Mongolia:* An expedition to the Gobi Desert by Ostrom uncovered arms (almost 8 feet long), hands (almost 2 feet long), shoulders, and rib fragments of a giant carnivorous dinosaur named deinocheirus (terrible hand).
- 1971 *Mongolia:* Zofia Kielan-Jaworowska, paleobiologist, discovered skeletons of a protoceratops and a velociraptor who had died fighting each other.

Selecting Preselected Books about the Content of Dinosaurs

During sustained silent reading, the students choose from a preselected group of books in the classroom book corner. (The teacher uses findings from research to guide teaching, and a recent finding indicates students who read from preselected sets of books read more pages than students who hear only book talks or who select books individually [Lawson, 1983].)

With this collection, the students' interests and wide range of reading skills are met, so the books about dinosaurs make reading available for every boy and girl regardless of his or her abilities in recognizing words, reading sentences, and getting meaning from the printed page. The collection provides for those who are beginners in reading (emerging in literacy), those who are beginning to read independently (developing in literacy), and those who read confidently and competently (fluent in literacy). The books offer students both poetry and prose, fiction and nonfiction. Examples of informative writing, humorous readings, and rhymes are in the collection, too, to support the study. From the classroom book corner, an interested reader selects books about dinosaurs that have information, offer humor, and show creative stories and artwork of authors and artists.

To offer a menu of projects related to the literary curriculum for interested students, "Choices" (Reproducibles 6, 7, and 8) are available. Titles of books useful for reference material are provided on the pages that can serve as guides to books for a searching student. Specifically, in Reproducible 6, a student reviews such projects as locating a figure of speech and explaining it in writing, selecting a quote for elaboration, or listing words in a story that tell action—what the dinosaur did. In Reproducible 7, a student may elect to make a small study book about dinosaurs, write beginnings to a basic sentence stem, *A dinosaur is . . . ,* or elaborate and turn brief sentences into longer ones. With Reproducible 8, a student explains something to others and elects to tell some of the causes of the dinosaurs' extinction or the ways small dinosaurs compare with others, or elaborate on classes of dinosaurs.

Topic B: Discussing Reading

After sustained silent reading, the students join their literature partners and participate in paired oral retelling, talking about what was read to one another. While they do this, the teacher watches their interaction and observes the girls and boys as they review facts, use pronunciation guides, and interact with books in several ways. The teacher sees which children are reviewing facts, using word guides, finding unusual features in books, and reading further.

Reviewing Facts

Reviewing facts about dinosaurs, two partners are absorbed in one of the books. Their focus is a book of time periods beginning millions of years ago that shows when the first plants, birds, and bony fish appeared. Using the index to find some dinosaurs they want, they talk about what they find, the dinosaurs' habitats and feeding habits. Another student is reading Michael Berenstain's *The Day of the Dinosaur* (Random House, 1989) and two others look at another time chart featuring the age of the dinosaurs and the age of humans. They have *Dinosaurs* (Simon and Schuster, 1981) by Mary Packard and point to a map in the back of the book to find a geographic location for a dinosaur. Using a world map, a student points out the locations of different countries in the world where fossils have been found. Further, he infers the tyrannosaurus lived mainly in the United States, the brontosaurus in Australia, and the diplodocus in South America. A question-and-answer format in the book has such questions as What was the world like? How big did they get? and Why did some have bony plates on their backs? This question-and-answer arrangement is a popular one with the two students, and they take turns asking questions of one another, responding and talking about the information from the pages.

Using Pronunciation Guides

"Umm, umm, o sawr," is what the teacher overhears from another student as he reads pronunciation guides in *The Littlest Dinosaurs* by Bernard Most (Harcourt Brace Jovanovich, 1989). The text compares small dinosaurs to familiar similar-sized objects; for example, Most points out that a 10-foot long dravidosaurus (dra vid o SAWR us) would fit in a bus shelter of today and a 4-foot-tall lesothosaurus (less o tho SAWR us) could wear children's clothing. An illustration shows a student that if a 20-inch micropachycephalosaurus (my' crow pack e sef' a lo SAWR us) spelled its name with wooden alphabet blocks, its name would be longer than the dinosaur itself.

Emerging readers in the room are not neglected, for several books offer easy-to-read texts. Joyce Milton's *Dinosaur Days* (Random House, 1985) has three lines of text with pronunciation guides on each page. Searching for a book about dinosaurs that shows an author's creative sense of story, a beginning reader finds Syd Hoff's *Danny and the Dinosaur* (Harper & Row, 1958), a story about a day of play by Danny and a museum dinosaur. The student moves the book up and down in imitation of a rolling ride on the back of a dinosaur as the dinosaur gives Danny's friends a ride on his back and plays hide-and-seek. As the day ends in the story, the dinosaur goes back to the museum and leaves Danny with his memories of the day of fun with his prehistoric friend.

Locating Unusual Book Features

Features deemed different and unusual by the students are found in some books. The students develop insights about information—facts are found in lists, material is arranged in alphabetical order, and content is elaborated in picture captions. In particular, one feature, an alphabetical arrangement of articles about 100 dinosaur species, makes information about an ancient animal easy to locate in Ron Wilson's *The New Dictionary of Dinosaurs* (Barnes & Noble, 1988). Looking closely at prehistoric scenes that include creatures of long ago in exhibits, another student finds names of museums with dinosaur exhibits in Carla Greene's *Before the Dinosaurs* (Bobbs-Merrill, 1970).

Reading Further

A book about the topic with suggested readings can lead an interested student into further reading. For a fluent reader, such a book is Edwin Harris Colbert's *The Year of the Dinosaur* (Scribner's, 1977). With a setting in an area currently part of Texas, a reader follows a year in the life of a brontosaur as it marches through swamps, builds its nest, and escapes a flood. Another student reads about possible causes for the dinosaurs' extinction in *What Happened to the Dinosaurs?* (Crowell, 1989) by Franklyn M. Branley. Branley mentions that the extinction could have been caused by animals devouring dinosaur eggs; by a change of the earth's temperature; by fires, ash, and dust caused by a comet; or by a scarcity of dinosaurs' food sources due to comet showers. Pondering such information, a student asks, "Why did dinosaurs became extinct and other animals survive?" With the teacher's guidance, this question leads the student into further inquiry as the teacher suggests Susanne Miller's *Prehistoric Mammals* (Messner, 1984), a book with information about ancestors of today's animals—bats, beavers, and elephants.

To bring the search for dinosaur fossils into the classroom, *The Dinosaur Hunter's Kit* (Running Press, 1990) is placed at a project table for a hands-on approach to learning about fossils. This kit contains field notes from a dig, simulated dinosaur fossils in a block of clay, and excavation tools for digging them out. The students' interest in dinosaurs takes them to the hunter's kit and to more study of animals—the ones that lived in the ancient seas as well as the ones that appeared after the dinosaurs died out. At the end of William Wise's *Monsters of the Ancient Seas* (Putnam, 1968) is a list of key words useful for developing a reader's word association map about sea-dwelling animals. Another book, Michael Berenstain's *After the Dinosaurs* (Random House, 1988), shows some of the early mammals from a rat-like triconodon (tri CON oh don) to mastodons (MAST oh dons) that appeared after the giant reptiles died out.

Topic C: Writing in Journals

After a discussion of what they had read, the students wrote their thoughts in free-writing journals (spiral-bound notebooks). Free writing (silent sustained writing, SSSW) was nonthreatening and encouraged the students to consider their thoughts (Pyle, 1990; Allington, 1975; Bromley, 1985). The girls and boys focused on what the day's content topic was about—dinosaurs—and wrote their flow of words and thoughts about their reading. They wrote words in whatever order the words came—and without a worry about punctuation. However, the teacher found that some students wrote in a chronological or sequential order about what they had read, which improved their fluency with words. Others mentioned the extent to which reading was interesting or uninteresting and then said if they were going to find another book about dinosaurs. Still others asked questions and recorded some of the ideas they had. One student was not writing and nudged the teacher with, "I don't know what to write." The teacher nudged back with, "Why not write about, 'I can't write right now because . . .' or 'Talk to yourself on paper about what your read,' or 'Jot down a great mess of words or phrases.'" At the close of the school day, the students gave their open-ended journals to the teacher, who will write brief comments without grading or evaluating the mechanics, structure, or spelling. The free-writing journals provided insights to the teacher about the students' thinking, the problems that would need attention, and the future focus of instruction.

Topic D: Hearing Students' Sounds of Language

"Last Saturday, as I was eating breakfast, a tyrannosaurus. . . ." Reading the first line, the teacher showed the students *The Tyrannosaurus Game* (Holiday House, 1976) written by Steven Kroll. She sat with the students in a story circle and, before reading further, began with a story opener. To lead into Kroll's story, the teacher had several openers from which to choose:

1. Students imagine the dinosaur in the story's title and talk about what they can visualize (see in their minds) about tyrannosaurus rex. The words that describe the dinosaur are listed on a writing board.
2. Students "sit on the tail of the dinosaur"—that is, they think about riding along with the dinosaur and visualize the actions the dinosaur might do in the story. More descriptive words and actions are listed.

Turning back to Kroll's story, the teacher asked the students to use their own sounds of language for story associations and introduced the story events that would need sound effects during the read-aloud. The teacher invited the girls and boys to make sounds for Kroll's story actions when a tyrannosaurus crashed through a window, a tryannosaurus got stuck on the stairs, a tyrannosaurus sneezed, and a tryannosaurus plopped down on a seesaw.

Topic E: Demonstrating Reading Aloud: A Fanciful Dinosaur Story

In Kroll's story, Jimmy was in his classroom on a rainy day and began a pass-it-on story. As the students listened to the story of Jimmy, they were anxious to see if any of their thoughts (imaginings) from the story openers came true. The action started when an imagined tyrannosaurus crashed through Jimmy's kitchen window and continued when Jimmy turned the plot of his story over to a friend with the words, *and Peggy said.* . . . Peggy verbally picked up the plot line and added something new to the story. Each student contributed to the plot as the tyrannosaurus caught a bus, played on a seesaw, and rode a roller coaster. When the story reached Phillip, the last student, he neatly ended Kroll's story with the words " . . . but then the tyrannosaurus was gone."

During the story, the teacher maintained student interest by incorporating some of these story-related activities:

1. The teacher individualized the story when it was appropriate. For instance, the teacher related a story event to an event in students' lives or to an event in the community. In *The Tyrannosaurus Game,* the students played a game inside the classroom on a rainy day—something the girls and boys in class had done—and the names of Kroll's students were changed to students' names in the room.
2. Further, the teacher invited students to participate: They added sound effects, listened for certain information page by page, answered questions about each page or illustration, and made remarks about the story.

When Kroll's story ended, the teacher returned to the selected story openers and discussed the openers again to end the story session. With this connection, the story openers became story enders:

1. Which student's ideas (pictures in the mind) about tyrannosaurus rex came true? The teacher pointed to the listed words on the writing board that described the dinosaur and the students discussed any words predicted and added words not mentioned.
2. Which student "sat on the tail of the dinosaur" and imagined the dinosaur actions? The students discussed the words about actions listed on the board.
3. Which students found out if any of their story thoughts (imaginings) came true? What came true? The students discussed words on the board related to the story.

Prepare Before Reading Aloud

A teacher uses certain techniques when preparing to read aloud. For example, a teacher prereads a story (Plan A) before presenting it to the class, practices reading it aloud, determines which words need clarifying, and, in case the first story is uninteresting to the students, has a followup story (Plan B).

Prereading

In prereading, a teacher determines which long parts to delete (or summarize) and works on pitch and dialogue of the characters. When the story is short, it is

read in one time period. When the story is long, a teacher selects the best place for stopping each day to set up the listeners' anticipation for the next day's reading. In case the story turns out to be uninteresting to the class, a teacher also plans a brief one- or two-sentence summary to bring the story to a quick close. When a teacher's personal copy is read aloud, the teacher cuts narrow strips from self-adhesive address labels and places them in the gutter margins between the pages to separate them just enough to be able to turn the pages easily. Page separators made from index cards or strips of cardboard work for school and library books.

Reading Aloud

Ready to read aloud, a teacher arranges the students close to the book so they can see the illustrations. She or he gives information about the title, the author, and the artist. The teacher holds the book to one side so each page is easily read (and seen) and looks up at the end of sentences to look into the eyes of the listeners.

Clarifying

A teacher inserts clarifying words when needed: "The tyrannosaurus plays on a seesaw—(and to clarify) that is, a teeter-totter—a balance board that children ride up and down on the playground." To further clarify when needed, stick figures are drawn on the board or prepared on a picture card and shown to the class to illustrate a word. As an example of clarification with another book, *What Happened to Patrick's Dinosaurs* (Clarion, 1986) by Carol Carrick, a teacher adds meaning to the term, *asteroid,* with these words, "Maybe an asteroid—that is, a small, rocky ball in space—hit the earth and covered it with dust." Other words in Carrick's story receive clarification: *cave men* (this means women and children, too, who lived in natural hollow places under the ground or in the sides of mountains thousands of years ago) and *invented* (to create something new or to think of something for the first time). Like Carrick's work, almost every book will have a word or two that needs clarifying for one or more of the children.

Assessing

A teacher assesses continually to determine the interest the listeners have in a story. If students show little interest, a teacher quickly summarizes the rest of the story in one or two sentences, puts the book away, and selects a more interesting book (Whitehead, 1968).

Topic F: Reenacting a Story Game about Dinosaurs

After reading *The Tyrannosaurus Game,* the teacher invites the students to reenact Kroll's game from the book and starts another version of this dinosaur story. The storyline passes from one student to another in the classroom. Here is the story model:

1. *First student:*   "Last Saturday, I was eating breakfast, when all of a sudden, a tyrannosaurus came crashing through the window. And (name of next student in the classroom) said. . . ."
2. *Next student:*   The student who was named by the previous student continues the story with one or two sentences. When her or his addition is finished, the student passes the story along to the next student in the classroom by saying, "And then, (name of student) said. . . ."
3. *Story-telling challenge:*   Students may include the names of their peers

(who previously told story parts) in the current story line when it is their turn to participate.

Topic G: Passing It On: A Fanciful Dinosaur Story

The students' oral telling of Kroll's story becomes a written pass-it-on story as they use the story model further and transform it from a retelling to a written narrative. The girls and boys are placed randomly in small heterogeneous groups. To get in groups, each selects one index card with a dinosaur sticker on it. All students holding the cards with an apatosaurus sticker in blue are in one group, those holding a card with stegosaurus in pink are in another group, those with a protoceratops in orange in still another group, and so on. Each student has a selected title or a sentence to start a story. Within a one-minute period (sometimes measured with a timer) and with or without help from another group member, each student finishes a sentence and gives his or her beginning to someone else. Each receiving student silently reads what has been written and continues to write the story from that point. After another one-minute time period, the paper is again passed along to another student. Writing continues until each contributes to the story. The last student ends the story and selects a partner to help read the story aloud to others. Thus, the language activity with Kroll's book is an extended, repetitive one that includes a first reading by the teacher, an oral retelling, a written retelling, and a rereading by the students.

Topic H: Telling Fanciful Dinosaur Stories for Models

Using Original Words: Dinosaur Voices, Dinosaur Stories

Using original words to tell Schwartz's fanciful story about a dinosaur, the teacher begins, "Once there was a little girl who was fascinated by dinosaurs. On her birthday, she found a live dinosaur in the desert." As Schwartz's story is told, the teacher takes a title card from a nearby container—a card with the words: *How I Captured a Dinosaur* (Watts, 1989)—and clips the card to the frame of a story mobile hanging overhead. The teacher tells about Albert, the Albertosaurus, and how he became the girl's animal companion, found a new home, enjoyed watching mud wrestling on television, and visited school. As the story continued and unbelievable events happened, card after card (to represent events) was added to the story mobile. When the story was over, the mobile was filled with cards relating events of the story.

Retelling a Story

To introduce a story retelling, a call for volunteers went out to retell Schwartz's story and to take down cards from the story mobile as all events were mentioned again. After the cards were used in the retelling, the cards and the mobile were taken to the classroom book corner for the students to use when they retold the events in their own words on other occasions. On subsequent days, the teacher used alternative ways of introducing story retelling:

1. *Dramatic roles.*   Students reinterpreted the story with creative drama.
2. *Character roles.*   Students took different roles of characters and retold the story.
3. *Setting associations.*   For each illustration, a student responded to, "If you

were near this setting (desert, mountain, house), what might you see? What might you hear?"

4. *Plot retellings.* Students retold the plot with "Who can retell . . . ?" To do this, one student (or the teacher) began the story with one of the characters. At a selected point, the story line was turned over to another student with, "And now, (student name) will tell more of this story."

5. *Story retellings on a chart.* Students dictated a telling of the story in their own words for a language experience story on a chart.

6. *"Dinosaur moves along."* These were words that selected the next reader or teller. During a reading or telling, the teacher or student said, "Time for the dinosaur to move along" as a signal for the teller to choose the next teller.

Classroom Update

- Students of different reading levels can and will sustain silent reading over a given period of time (Wittreich, 1984).
- Students who read from preselected sets of books read more pages than students who hear book talks or select individually (Lawson, 1983).
- Literature is a necessary component of writing context since it is a source of authentic experience for students (Burton, 1982).
- Talking together fosters comprehension of what was read, provides a time for sharing why the reader enjoyed a story, and promotes titles of books to interest other readers (Lesser, 1990).
- Listening to literature read aloud plus discussion of stories facilitates the composition of stories (Coleman-Mitzner, 1981).
- Reading aloud, combined with direct teaching, supports large gains in academic achievements of third-grade students (Lopez, 1986).
- Organizational complexity of students' narrative writing increases with age (Anthony, 1981).

Topic I: Telling More Dinosaur Stories: Teaming Up with Others

Still other retellings of stories—events that could or could not have happened—take place in literature teams. In a team, each student tells a selected story, either realistic or fanciful. First, each member engages in mumble reading and tells it to herself or himself alone in a mumble fashion. Then each student joins with a peer and the pair tell their stories to one another. One student enjoys the jokes in the humor of his selection entitled *Dodosaurs: The Dinosaurs That Didn't Make It* (Crown, 1983) by Rick Meyerowitz and Henry Beard and tells about the events from a fanciful time period, the Dodozoic era, when dodosaurs lived on a small island continent called Thingamagaea. The student enjoys the author's creative names for the dinosaur inhabitants who were not equipped for survival on the island: attackadactyl (who resembled a P-38) and titanicasaurus rex (who was a sinkable dinosaur). In a project related to the humor of *Dodosaurs*, the teacher asked the students to consider a dialogue format through dictation, a cooperative project for students in writing teams of two.

Topic J: Engaging in Dialogue: Dinosaur Dictation

To engage in a dialogue format through dictation in a cooperative manner, the girls and boys dictated humorous sentences for dialogue between dinosaur characters. The sentences were written on the board. After a list was reviewed, with the students reading the parts, each team of two wrote original sentences (or selected sentences from the list), used quotation marks, and included the marks with the dialogue in a written conversation called "Daffy Dialogue with Dinosaurs." Here are some of the contributions: "I hurt my ankle," cried anklysosaurus. "I'll take all of you!" claimed allosaurus. "I have a tall tale to tell you," tyrannosaurus tooted. "I'm especially spiny," said spinosaurus. "My plates are flat," stegosaurus whined. "I can honk my horns," hooted triceratops. "I need to lose weight," apatosaurus wheezed. "I'm way up here!" hollered brachiosaurus. "Come, fly with me," pteranosaurus said.

Topic K: Lunching with a Story: Dinosaur Hunt

"We're going on a dinosaur hunt . . . " chanted the girls and boys together. With a family member's permission, each student (who wanted to do so) remained in the classroom at noon for a fact-and-fiction lunch. While the students ate lunch, they listened to selections from an informational book about plant-eating and meat-eating dinosaurs and to a dinosaur story read by older sixth-grade students who had agreed to be readers. The students called their lunch "The Green Dinosaur Picnic" and placed a green dropcloth on the floor. To prepare for this, they had sent invitations to several older students and asked them to be their guest readers. For their guests, the students decorated paper place mats and napkins with dinosaur drawings. At lunchtime, they gathered around with their lunches, sat down for their picnic on the cloth, and ate as they listened to read-alouds.

To end their lunch period, Rosen's *We're Going on a Bear Hunt* (Macmillan, 1989) was turned into a dinosaur version accompanied with hand movements. In the dinosaur version of this familiar story, the setting for the hunt was the prehistoric times, the Age of the Dinosaurs, and the students followed a dinosaur (not a bear) verbally through oozy mud, cold swamp water, a thunderous storm, quicksand, and, finally, into a dark cave. At the climax of this telling, the girls and boys repeated the events with hand movements and knee slapping, and finished with the closing promise to never go on a dinosaur hunt again. Returning to their studies after lunch, the students wrote thank-you notes to their guest readers and told them their thoughts about the Green Dinosaur Picnic.

Topic L: Displaying Dinosaur Story Words on Shapes

After writing thank-you notes, the students had a wonderful conversation about what they heard at their fact-and-fiction time at lunch. They cut original shapes of dinosaurs for word cards, wrote words and phrases from what they heard on their dinosaur-shaped cards, and displayed the cards in the room. On a subsequent day, to retell what they had learned, the students used the cards as memory notes and referred to them in their discussion. Thus, remembering what was heard at the Green Dinosaur Picnic became a connection to another wonderful conversation.

Topic M: Moving from Dinosaur Fancy to Facts

To review the content heard at lunchtime, the teacher reread a descriptive paragraph from the information book the students had heard at noon and asked them to sketch what they imagined from listening to the words again. Using their sketches as resources, the students reflected (visualized, imagined), categorized, and referenced.

Visualizing

After they listened to the descriptive words and their sketches were finished, the students showed their work and talked about it, and the teacher read the paragraph again as a verbal adjunct. The teacher asked all to study their sketches for a visual check: Did they use any descriptive words they had heard as information to make their sketches? The students reviewed their work in pairs and helped one another with their sketches and visual checking.

Categorizing

The students' illustrations also became a resource for categorizing. The teacher announced there were two mystery categories the class was going to discover after studying the pictures of dinosaurs they all had drawn. (The teacher predetermined silently and mentally that the sketches would be categorized into plant eaters and meat eaters.) After seeing the sketches, the teacher asked some students to sit on the right side of the room (sketches of plant eaters) and other students to sit on the left side of the room (sketches of meat eaters). (Of course, the teacher did not tell the students the mystery categories because the teacher's purpose was for the students to use clues from the drawings and from the class discussion to make their predictions to determine, guess, or predict the categories.) The teacher asked each student to show his or her drawing and tell about it.

1. After each student presented a drawing, the teacher mentioned that the student was showing some clues in the drawing that would help the class determine one of the mystery categories.
2. According to the predetermined (unmentioned) categories of dinosaur plant eaters and meat eaters, the teacher directed each student to return either to the left side of the room or to the right side.
3. After each presentation, the teacher asked class members to look at the sketches of students sitting on the left side of the room and at sketches of students sitting on the right side of the room to see if anyone could determine a name of either of the mystery categories from studying the pictures. After each drawing was shown, the teacher asked, "Who thinks they have a name for one of the mystery categories?" The students who thought they had determined a mystery category whispered their prediction(s) in the teacher's ear and kept it a secret until all the pictures had been shown and the categories were announced to all.

Referencing

After the sketches were presented and the mystery categories identified, the teacher invited students to "Stump the Teacher" and ask questions about dinosaurs. This activity gave the teacher an opportunity to show students different ways to use reference materials when an answer to a question is not known. The students gathered around the teacher. Turning to a pile of reference books stacked on the floor, the teacher demonstrated ways to find information about each question asked, and in doing so, showed the girls and boys the values (and uses) of such tools as the table of contents, index, glossary, and picture captions. When appropriate, the teacher read excerpts and showed information from maps, graphs, and diagrams, too. Sometimes the teacher was stumped and said so. For example, "What color were the dinosaurs?" was answered with Harvey's *The World of the Dinosaurs: A Question and Answer Book* (Lerner, 1986) and the teacher used the question-and-answer format in the book to respond to other questions by students. Using many books, the teacher demonstrated other ways to find information about the students' questions and read aloud excerpts from other sources for additional queries (e.g., What were the last dinosaurs? What was the biggest?).

Topic N: Comparing and Measuring Objects: Dinosaurs and Math

Another question was "Do we call it a brontosaurus or an apatosaurus?" and the answer was in Dave Petersen's *Apatosaurus* (Childrens, 1989), a book about the dinosaur with two names who weighed as much as 20 of today's cars. The teacher pointed to a visual and verbal comparison (metaphor) where Petersen compared a huge apatosaurus to a slender-necked giraffe. Pointing out this comparison, the teacher suggested the students create oral compositions using *like–not like* in beginning sentences such as "An apatosaurus is *like* a giraffe because . . . " and "An apatosaurus is *not like* a giraffe because. . . . " All were encouraged to tell other comparisons.

Another comparison was considered with Most's book *The Littlest Dinosaurs,* and one of the types, the protoceratops, who was 2 1/2 feet high and 6 feet long. Supplied with rulers, the students measured things in the room and discovered objects the same height or width as the dinosaur. Students made labels and marked objects with word cards that said: "as high as the proto" or "as long as the proto." They repeated this measuring activity with the dimensions of the compsognathus (comp SOG na thus) who was only as big as a goose.

Topic O: Building a Dinosaur Word Map

To build a word map about what they knew, the students used word cards and two pocket charts. The students first told and then displayed in writing what they knew about dinosaurs. The students' prior knowledge was shown graphically on sentence strips in two pocket charts placed side by side. The words, *dinosaurs, dinosaurios,* were written on a circle cut from green art paper and placed in the center of the two pocket charts. As words and phrases about dinosaurs were mentioned by the students, they were written on sentence strips and cards made from green art paper or poster board and went in slots in the pocket charts. Labels (headings to categorize information) on cards were placed in appropriate locations in the pockets. Lengths of green yarn were fastened with tape from the green circle in the center and went outward from the circle to the labels. With two pocket charts side by side, the students had additional space and could move information around. Doing this, the students saw the way a schematic map was built: The green circle announced the topic, green cards showed key words and phrases, and green yarn lengths led from the topic word outward to the labels to show relationships. Moving the cards around, the students categorized words under different headings and connected relationships between ideas and concepts in the headings. This colorful semantic map showed what information the students knew.

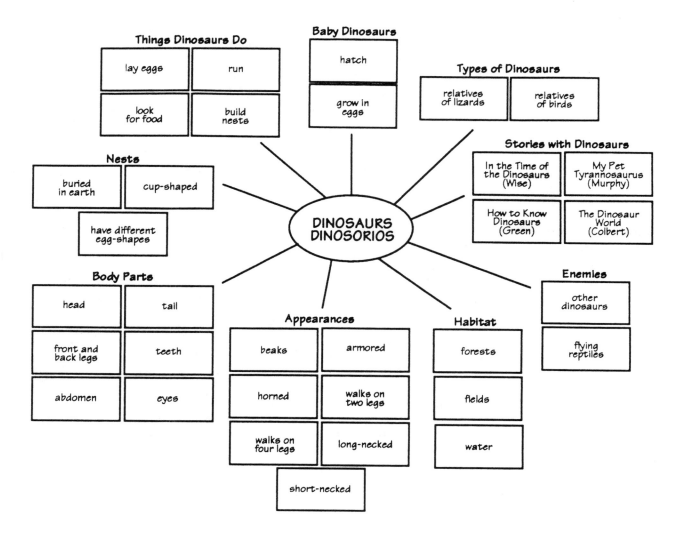

After recording initial observations about what was known about dinosaurs, each student began individual research and read with a personal goal of adding to the word map something she or he knew. As the students read to add information to the map, they used a personal copy of the word map and identified where each piece of information would go. After personal research and recording additional information, the students got back together as a whole group, reported their findings, discussed what they found during their research time, and decided where the information went in the pocket charts.

Classroom Update

- Children, ages 4 to 8, have a limited understanding in distinguishing literal and intended meaning of messages (Webber, 1988).
- Reading affects children's narrative writing and readers see themselves as writing longer and better stories and enjoying writing more (Nielsen, 1980).
- Story telling, hearing stories read aloud, and watching storytellers on videotape are all valuable for developing listening skills (Young, 1988).
- Children's memories for stories have been influenced by structure of narra-

tive with well-formed versions eliciting quantitatively and qualitatively superior recall more often than did poorly formed stories (Brennan, 1982).

- Fourth- and fifth-grade students articulated their ideas of meaning in literature study groups but changed their ideas when they heard articulate views (Edds & Wells, 1988).
- Literature read aloud affected aspects of narrative writing of fifth-graders with literary quality improving most in writing of lowest readers who heard sophisticated literature (Dressel, 1986).
- Dialogue journals have been effective in eliciting engagement responses about literature for fifth-graders (Danielson, 1987).
- Primary-grade children selected books on the basis of illustrations, length, content, genre, and their familiarity with a book (Carter, 1988).

Topic P: Preparing for Cross-Age Tutoring

Additional minutes of the school day were spent in more silent reading as the students prepared to read to young boys and girls in kindergarten. *Danny and the Dinosaur, What Happened to Patrick's Dinosaur?,* and other titles showed on covers of books the students had selected. Later in the afternoon, they visited a kindergarten class and read books to small groups of students. Reading to children in small groups offers as much interaction as one-to-one readings and appears to lead to greater comprehension than the whole class or one-to-one readings (Morrow & Smith, 1990). To introduce her book with a tune that summarized an event, one girl used a song pattern from "Yankee Doodle." On a previous day, the teacher had demonstrated a way to summarize a short story by putting words into the rhythm of selected music. Remembering this, the girl found an event from Carrick's *What Happened to Patrick's Dinosaurs?* and matched the words to the rhythm of "Yankee Doodle." She sang it to her kindergarten group: Curious Patrick/asked big Hank,/"How fast did dinos go?"/Hank gave up/when Patrick said,/"Their spaceship/was quite slow."

All of the fourth-graders showed the storybooks they selected from the school library and the classroom book corner to the kindergarten children. After the reading session, the fourth-graders returned to their own class and discussed which books they liked and which books they thought the kindergarten children liked, and talked about the illustrations with one another. They spent additional time rereading their selected books to each other in pairs and suggested ways they could improve their reading to the kindergarten children in future weeks.

Topic Q: Closing with a Class Meeting

After their talk about what they could do better to improve their next reading-aloud session, the students participated in a whole group meeting. During this meeting, the teacher demonstrated the discussion of a book title, said a few words about an appealing feature of the book's format (or genre), and gave an interesting fact about the author. Responding to the discussion needs of the students, the teacher demonstrated a way to stop at different places in a story to allow for predictions to be made, relating what was happening in a story to a personal experience, and allowing time for the kindergarten children to talk about why a particular character might act in a specific manner.

Explaining New Words to Others

The teacher mentioned ways students could be direct and clarify words for the younger children. She gave examples of the different ways the meanings of new words could be explained and called them "Story Thickeners." To demonstrate ways to clarify words, the teacher showed the following:

1. First, give a descriptive definition in another sentence after the word. *Story Thickener:* "The pteronodon (te RAN on don) lived in prehistoric times." To clarify *pteronodon:* "The pteronodon was a gliding reptile that had a body no larger than a turkey's with wings that stretched more than 25 feet for gliding over the sea. It had a long tail for steering and probably would dive into the water and snatch up fish for food." To clarify *prehistoric times:* "About 65 million years ago."
2. Second, follow a new word with a short restatement. *Story Thickener:* "The pteronodon—it was a gliding reptile with wings—lived in prehistoric times."
3. Third, use another statement, synonyms, or rephrasings for the unfamiliar word. *Story Thickener:* "The pteronodon (the largest was rhamphorhynchus [ram foe RING cuss]) had wings that stretched to more than 25 feet and lived in prehistoric times."

Students who read their selected stories and clarified the words they read to kindergarten students developed their own reading fluency and focused on comprehending the story. By reading to others, they read repeatedly, saw demonstrations of reading by their peers and their teacher, and became more effective readers themselves (Cohen, Kulik, & Kulik, 1982).

Extensions for Chapter 2

1. *Consider the component in the Core of Structure—Infuse a literacy curriculum.* With your elementary students, determine topics of interest from the content areas and then integrate those topics in the unit as the students write, read, listen, and communicate orally about content. What literacy activities related to these topics might you infuse into the curriculum?
2. *Identify text features in the books that you want the students to discover.* For example, in *The Last Dinosaur* (Scholastic, 1989) by Jim Murphy, the author uses a background of facts for a fictional story. With this story, students can consider the possibility of the end of the dinosaurs with this scene: One female triceratops is looking for the others in her herd and is unaware that they are no longer alive.
3. *Start dialogue journals with elementary students.* The first day students meet together as a class, they can introduce themselves to the teacher in writing. After the writing time is over, the teacher may read his or her written introduction and introduce an "author's desk" or an "author's chair" (Graves & Hansen, 1983). For the first 10 minutes of each subsequent day, students may write in their free-writing journals.

Endnotes

1. The correct name for the giant plant eater is *apatosaurus*. This is an interesting misconception (the original skeleton on which the brontosaurus was based was a mistake caused by mislabeled boxes during transportation, resulting in two sets of bones being mixed) that was clarified in the past few years and

brought to the attention of a science instructor at a large western mainstream university by the instructor's six-year-old nephew (interview with Dr. C. Hasegawa, California State University, Sacramento, 1990).

2. Verse by P. Hubbell in B. Hopkins (Ed.), *To look upon a thing* (New York: Harcourt Brace Jovanovich, 1978).

3. Fourth grade is the example here; however, other grades may have other beginnings.

Resources

The Dinosaur Hunter's Kit (1990). New York: Running Press. Has field notes, replicated dinosaur fossils in clay, and excavation tools. All ages.

International Reading Association. 800 Barksdale Road, PO Box 8139, Newark, DE 19714-8139. 22″ × 34″ dinosaur poster.

Readings

Allington, R. (1975). Sustained approaches to reading and writing. *Language Arts,* 52 (September): 813–815.

Anthony, P. J. (1981). *Examining children's written narratives: The relationship between writing ability and logical thinking during the period between concrete and formal operations.* Ann Arbor, MI: University Microfilms, 87-09-316.

Brennan, A. D. H. (1982). *Children's story recall as an effect of structural variation of text.* Ed. D. dissertation, University of Kentucky. UMI/CD-ROM 83-0000 *DAI* 43: 3860A.

Bromley, K. (1985). SSW: Sustained spontaneous writing. *Childhood Education,* 62 (1): 23–29.

Burton, F. R. (1982). *The reading-writing connection: A one year teacher-as-researcher study of third-fourth grade writers and their literary experiences.* Ann Arbor, MI: University Microfilms, 82-0032.

Carter, M. A. (1988). How children choose books: Implications for helping develop readers. *Ohio Reading Teacher,* 22 (3) (April): 15–21.

Cohen P., Kulik, J. A., & Kulik, C. (1982). Educational outcomes of tutoring: A meta-analysis of findings. *American Educational Research Journal,* 19, 237–248.

Coleman-Mitzner, J. (1981). *Oral story making experiences to improve the oral language proficiencies and "sense of story" of fourth grade remedial reading students.* Ann Arbor, MI: University Microfilms, 81-26-483.

Danielson, K. E. (1987). *The effect of the dialogue journal process of fifth grade students' written responses to literature. Dissertation Abstracts International,* 48, 1111A. Ann Arbor, MI: University Microfilms International 87-17, 249.

Dressel, J. H. (1986). *Listening to children's literature read aloud: Its effect on selected aspects of the narrative writing of fifth-grade students. Dissertation Abstracts International,* 47, 3307A. Ann Arbor, MI: University Microfilms International 87-00, 460.

Edds, M., & Wells, D. (1989). Grand conversations: An exploration of meaning construction in literature study groups. *Research in the Teaching of English,* 23 (1) (February): 4–29.

Graves, D., & Hansen, J. (1982). The author's chair. *Language Arts,* 60: 176–183.

Lawson, M. A. (1983). *The effects of placement and advertisement of books on the amount and nature of reading done by fourth-grade students.* Ann Arbor, MI: University Microfilms, 84-05157.

Lesser, J. H. (1990). USSR + USA. *The Reading Teacher,* 43 (6) (February): 429.

Lopez, J. G. (1986). *The relative impact of oral reading with direct teaching methodology on reading comprehension, listening, and vocabulary achievement of third grade students.* Ann Arbor, MI: University Microfilms 87-05139.

Morrow, L. M., & Smith, J. K. (1990). The effects of group size on interactive storybook reading. *Reading Research Quarterly* (Summer): 213–219.

Nielsen, B. F. (1980). *Effects of reading on children's narrative writing.* Ed. D. dissertation, Brigham Young University. UMI/CD-ROM 80-16081. *Dissertation Abstracts International* 41: 99A. Ann Arbor, MI: University Microfilms International.

Pyle, V. (1990). SSRW—Beyond silent reading. *Journal of Reading,* 33 (5) (February): 379–380.

Webber, L. S. (1988). *The development of the ability to distinguish between literal and intended messages. Dissertation Abstracts International.* Ann Arbor, MI: University Microfilms, 49, 09A.

Whitehead, R. (1968). *Children's literature: Strategies of teaching.* New York: Prentice-Hall.

Wittreich, Y. M. (1984). *An analysis of the effects of sustained silent reading in fourth grade on an intact group of children as well as six individuals within the group.* Ann Arbor, MI: University Microfilms, 84-18142.

Young, Y. E. (1988). *The effects of storytelling on children's listening skills.* M. S., University of Oregon. AAD13-35240 MA:27/03: 323.

What Literature Base Is Available for My Thematic Unit?

Teacher Reflections for Chapter 3

Chapter 3 presents ways to:

- Explore a theme
- Get acquainted with a literature base about dinosaurs
- Select from over 100 choices available for students' projects generated from books
- Introduce a paleohistory about dinosaurs through children's literature, grades 5–6
- Consider the component in the Core of Structure to implement a literature-based thematic unit: Select literature base

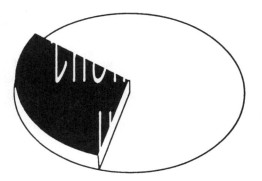

Chapter 3:
Select Literature Base

Component in Core of Structure to Implement a Thematic Unit for Literature-Based Instruction: Select Literature Base

Vignette in a Multigrade Class: Age of Dinosaurs

Recently, on Potowatomi Indian Reservation, Michigan, at Hannahville Indian School, "Project Me" infused a literacy curriculum with content and integrated language naturally into thematic content (Dooley, 1990). Traditional Indian values and their teachings were integrated. Also, the students' learning styles were an important part since Downing's 1975 study had suggested students learned faster when teaching began with a concrete approach and then moved to an abstract one (Downing, 1977). The "Age of Dinosaurs" was studied in a unit and the students made wall charts of what they knew and what they wanted to know about dinosaurs. They read and wrote reports, as well as created original books and illustrated them. Spelling and vocabulary lists each week provided the focus for phonetic and structural analyses. To infuse the theme with art, students created papier maché models of dinosaurs for a display and used shoe boxes and other materials to construct dioramas to show scenes about prehistoric creatures. To integrate math, the students made wall murals and used mathematical scales. To infuse social studies, they used a globe and maps to locate places where fossils were discovered. As an example of their social action and community interaction, students talked with a fossil collector who visited and showed her collection.

For a final activity, the students planned a Dinosaur Party and invited parents and friends. The students wrote and illustrated their guests' invitations. They followed directions in recipes and made dinosaur gelatine shapes and snacks. At their party, the students displayed dioramas and murals and, to entertain their guests, they read dinosaur books and the stories they had written. Later, supported with community contributions, the students went on a field trip to the Milwaukee Museum of Natural History. After this unit, the students followed their interests with individual choices of study and some chose to study reptiles and amphibians.

In another class—a primary class with limited English proficient students—a theme of dinosaurs linked the content areas of natural science and literature with expressive skills related to math, music, and art, all integrated into the children's study (Sommer, 1990, p. 206). Connections linking content areas and the expressive skills of language and mathematics were taught with the content (Cecil, 1990). This curriculum infused content about dinosaurs with a variety of projects that included:

1. *Art.*   Incorporating art, students read directions and created dinosaur pictures. In their cooperative learning groups, they painted pictures of dinosaurs, and using a cut-and paste-technique, constructed dinosaur environments in pop-up books.
2. *Art/Natural science.*   Linking art to natural science, the students constructed fossil replicas with plaster of Paris, leaves, rocks, and shells.
3. *Literacy.*   In groups, students composed questions about dinosaurs based on their research. They answered questions in a game-show format. To compose a class book about dinosaurs entitled *The Important Book,* the girls and boys worked in groups, researched facts, and recorded facts about dinosaurs on a fact map. They wrote a story using a guide: "The important thing about _____ is _____. It _____. It _____. It _____. But the important thing about _____ is _____."
4. *Math.*   Incorporating math, the students solved math problems involving facts about dinosaurs. They drew pictures based on descriptions and predicted and measured a scale model of a brontosaurus using their bodies—a shape they renamed bodysaurus.
5. *Music.*   Music led students to songs such as "Tyrannosaurus Rex," "Thunder," and "Did You Know the Stegosaurus?"
6. *Poetry.*   The students used a story starter *"If I were a dinosaur, I would*

be . . . " to write a paragraph and mount in a pop-up book, a book similar in format to Tanner Ottley Gay's *Dinosaurs and Their Relatives in Action* (Aladdin, 1990). They brainstormed adjectives and described dinosaurs for a class word association map. They used this pattern to compose a poem: "I like dinosaurs. _____ dinosaurs. _____ dinosaurs. _____ dinosaurs. _____ dinosaurs. I like dinosaurs."

Topic A: How to Find a Literature Base for a Unit

There are many ways to develop successful literature-based instruction in a classroom. For instance, in a literature-based environment, students will expand their writing as they work in groups, with partners, or independently. As they do this, students will make connections from one curriculum area to another and from one skill to another. Not all units will be about dinosaurs—some will be about the concepts of justice or equality, the environment (oceans), symbols across cultures (dragons), or language (alphabet books), and to support the theme, you will want to look at books *about* children's books that list titles of children's literature by subjects. For a listing of the books in print about a particular topic for a unit, select *Subject Guide to Children's Books in Print* (Bowker), *Children's Catalog* (H. W. Wilson), *Children's Books in Print,* or *Best Books for Children* (both published by Bowker). You can get ideas about introducing children's books on a theme from Leonard's *Tied Together: Topics and Thoughts for Introducing Children's Books* (Scarecrow, 1980) or you can select high-interest books for students who are developing their reading skills in *Easy Reading: Books: Series and Periodicals for Less Able Readers* (International Reading Association, 1979) by Graves, Boettcher, and Ryder. Also, you can find reference books to support the children's interests and reading levels and locate these books by subject in *Reference Books for Children* (Scarecrow, 1981) by Peterson and Fenton. Further, Chapter 7 has additional resources and other book selection aids to help you in your search.

How to Choose Your Own Books

Of course, not all of these books (or many others written about dinosaurs) are classics. Some of them meet criteria for quality literature for children and others do not. To determine quality literature, Sutherland and Arbuthnot (1986) and Huck, Hepler, and Hickman (1987) suggest criteria for different genres and these criteria are yardsticks that help a teacher and the students see if different genres measure up to the use in the classroom. Using criteria is easy—it is something students do every day and something a teacher can review with them. For example, a student uses criteria when ordering a hamburger just the way he or she wants it at a local hamburger franchise. Each student has criteria for ordering a hamburger—lettuce, tomato, onion, special sauce—and each orders that item with those things on it. Similarly, the following criteria let a student (or teacher) judge books to see if they are the "literary hamburgers" he or she wants before selecting them in the classroom.

Guides for Selecting Books

Biographical fiction: Stories of People. (1) Is it authentic? (2) Objective? and (3) Documented? (Sutherland & Arbuthnot, 1986).

Fanciful fiction: Plausible imaginings. (1) Does it have a well-constructed, creative, consistent plot? (2) Convincing characters? (3) A worthwhile theme? (4) Appropriate style? and (5) Believable fantasy? (Huck, Hepler, & Hickman, 1987).

Historical fiction: Reality of the past. (1) Is it honest and accurate? (2) Are characters realistic? (3) Is there a strong sense of time and place? (4) A judicious use of dialogue and dialect? and (5) Is there a universal theme? (Sutherland & Arbuthnot, 1986).

Informational nonfiction: Exploration of observations. (1) Is it accurate? (2) Current? (3) Is it in sequence logically? (4) Is the subject limited in scope and suitable for the intended audience? (5) Absence of stereotyping? and (6) Is it clearly and interestingly written? (Sutherland & Arbuthnot, 1986).

Poetry: Seldom-discussed friend. (1) Does it have melody and movement? (2) Does it use words or sounds that are evocative? (3) Imagery? (4) Does it concentrate on a mood, an emotion, or an experience? (5) Is the effect striking? and (6) Does it stir our imagination or reach our senses or move us deeply or provoke us to laughter? (Sutherland & Arbuthnot, 1986).

Realistic fiction: Slices of life. (1) Does it tell a good story? (2) Does it center on a child's basic needs? (3) Do characters grow and change in the story? (4) Is there an important idea? (5) Are ideas expressed clearly? and (6) Do actions move in a logical sequence to a logical outcome? (Sutherland & Arbuthnot, 1986).

Some of the books about dinosaurs mentioned in this chapter have only temporary value for the purpose of a study. However, the books foster a student's growing recognition of problems related to endangered species, the ecological health of our planet, and the problems scientists are working on, which, in turn, show a student how this all affects humans. These books about dinosaurs create an interest and an awareness and, in most cases, provide a sound informational base for a reader. This interest promotes scanning, browsing, and reading further on the topic. The books also show various ways a particular author or artist interprets the theme of dinosaurs. Some students will notice, that for young children, several authors use personified dinosaurs as the characters or warp the time periods by putting humans in the age of the large creatures.

Topic B: A Look at Dinosaur Book Duos: From Book to Book to Increase Listening, Reading, and Writing

Dinosaur book duos are books, fact or fiction, about dinosaurs that can be used together to become book partners. These book partners can show different fictional approaches to the topic; present riddles, jokes, and word play; or provide variety in nonfictional information. Sometimes, they can be "just for fun." Several titles to consider are given here.

Different Approaches to a Topic

Facts about dinosaurs can be determined from the illustrations in *The True Book of Dinosaurs* (Childrens, 1955) by Mary Lou Clark. To see variants of informational books on the same topic, students of all ages can compare illustrations in this book of the 50s with books published in the 60s, 70s, and 80s, such as *Dinosaurs, The Terrible Lizards* (Golden Gate, 1969) by Rosalie Davidson, *Dinosaurs* (Osbourne, 1977) by Anne McCord, *Dinosaurs* (Random House, 1977) by Sy Barlowe, *Dinosaurs* (Gloucester Press, 1979) by Kate Petty; Boney's *Dinosaurs* (Price Stern Sloan, 1988), or Fuchshuber's *From Dinosaurs to Fossils* (Carolrhoda, 1981). After students compare illustrations from two of the books, the teacher may collect anecdotal remarks (e.g., From which illustrations did the student observe the most information? How did the student verify this information?). Second-graders and older can learn how to use a glossary with *Dinosaurs and Other Prehistoric Creatures* (Modern Pub./Unisystems, 1988). They may explain its use to someone else, or discuss with a partner the observations in *Dinosaurs of Land, Sea, and Air* (Modern Pub./Unisystems, 1988) and put what they learned into use to create a Dinosaur Trivia game to present to a classmate at home with an illness and give the student an idea of what is being studied.

Just-for-Fun Approach—Fanciful Dinosaur Stories

To enjoy the fun and fantasy of the idea of imaginative dinosaur stories, students can select *Dinosaur Chase* (HarperCollins, 1991) written by Carolyn Otto or *A Dinosaur for Gerald* (Carolrhoda, 1990) by Helena Clare Pittman. In the first story, dinosaur robbers are involved in a jewelry theft and dinosaur police in cars chase them past palm trees and tall buildings. In Pittman's book, Gerald takes care of his sister's classroom iguana over the summer and it becomes his "dinosaur" as he imagines a prehistoric rabbit with stegosaurus-like plates along its back and other dinosaur-like animals.

Word Play, Jokes, and Riddles

Riddles from David A. Adler's *The Dinosaur Princess: And Other Prehistoric Riddles* (Holiday, 1988), Jeffrey Nelsen's *My Favorite Dinosaur Jokes & Riddles Books* (Macmillan, 1988), and *Why Didn't the Dinosaur Cross the Road? and Other Prehistoric Riddles* (Whitman, 1990) by Joanne E. Bernstein and Paul Cohen introduce humorous questions to ask of others. In *The Dinosaur Princess,* the students find plays on words such as "How did cave men and women discover the sun?" (It just dawned on them.) After seeing riddles from the books on an overhead transparency, girls and boys (grade 2 and older) can sharpen their deductive reasoning skills by making connections from the riddle questions to possible answers before a student volunteer reads the answers from the pages. Older students may write original riddles questions and ask for possible answers.

Topic C: A Selection of Over Eighty Book Projects about Dinosaurs

Myers (1989) maintains that a teacher should think of classroom lessons as invitations for students to seek connections between ideas and contexts they encounter in a classroom and their world. As inquirers into their classroom world, the girls and boys should take responsibility for their own learning, ask questions they want to answer about any personal (or group) doubts, and search for information and experience they need in order to add to their knowledge. Doing this, the students learn something because the learning satisfies the students' inner curiosity about a topic. Studying the topic of dinosaurs, certain concepts can be emphasized during students' lines of inquiry, such as (1) We have made our observations (understandings) about dinosaurs from fossils, (2) From fossil observations, we understand that dinosaurs had a variety of features, (3) Not all dinosaurs lived at the same time, (4) Other animals and plants lived in the world with dinosaurs, and (5) Dinosaurs are now extinct—they no longer exist or are alive.

How to Provide High-Interest Projects: Ideas in Book Pockets

A wide variety of children's books leads to different lines of inquiry and allows girls and boys to choose their own paths of study. Providing choices, a teacher encourages alternatives in activities to foster self-direction in students, which correlates to positive self-concepts and school success (Novak, 1985). In this correlation, a student makes choices that lead to a contribution in class, which develops a student's self-concept. This, in turn, leads to more risk taking in future choices and more learning experiences. To provide choices, a teacher suggests possible inquiries, distributes some ideas in writing, and records suggestions. To offer suggestions, idea notes can be placed inside a book's front cover or typed on index cards and placed in book pockets (library card pockets) inside a book's back cover. When a student browses through a book, the student sees the suggested idea (which may trigger an original one) and determines what project to select a choice for his or her learning activity. Often, a suggestion in the book serves as a springboard as a student mentally jumps forward with his or her own inquiry and thoughts.

If desired, a teacher shows students (grade 4 and older) examples of lines of inquiry (Reproducibles 9 and 10 both list informational items/books in which inquiries are found). Reproducible 9 asks students if they want to learn more about the dinosaurs' extinction, the dark star (nemesis) theory, or how to build a dinosaur skeleton. Reproducible 10 asks if students want to locate books with information about such things as pronunciation guides, grouping dinosaurs into categories, and drawing different types. As a part of self-selected learning, a teacher can also suggest additional activities and write a contract for a student to include individual interests (e.g., perhaps a student will want to learn more about the ways authors and artists represent dinosaurs in books they write and illustrate).

Topic D: A Look at Books Suitable for Readers, K–2

A wide range of materials about dinosaurs makes up the collection of books suitable for kindergartners and first- and second-graders. The informational books tell about fossil findings and facts; some contain activities and others show different ways authors and illustrators present dinosaurs in stories.

Books with Information

Behavior

1. Martha Dinsmore's *What Really Happened to the Dinosaurs?* (Master Books, 1988) and *Dinosaurs and Monsters* (Watts, 1984) and *What Really Happened to the Dinosaurs?* (Dutton, 1977), both by David Cohen, offer broad overviews to engage a student with charting what is based on observations and what is based on conjecture. To do this, students (grade 2 and older) select pictures that they think are based on actual fossil finds and then search for information on the pages to support their opinions.

2. With its simple text and illustrations, *Dinosaur Alphabet Book: ABC Adventures* (Troll, 1985) by Pat Whitehead introduces characteristics of various dinosaurs along with letters of the alphabet, key words, and key sentences. The text provides a model for writing an alphabetical story (Roberts, 1984, 1985, 1990a) and leads to further inquiry with its conclusion, "There are no more dinosaurs in the world. They are extinct. But there are many other interesting animals today. Do you know where? They are at the zoo. Some of these animals even look like small dinosaurs from long ago." *Strange Creatures that Really Lived* (Scholastic, 1987) by Millicent E. Selsam mentions that some creatures of long ago looked like fish, others like lizards, and still others like turtles with long necks. Animals familiar to today's students are shown on the last page of Whitehead's book—the turtle, lizard, and salamander.

Coloring

3. Pastel illustrations in Anthony Rao's *Dinosaurs* (Putnam, 1979) show another way of looking at dinosaur colors and may lead to students' experiments with the use of pastel colors for coloring dinosaurs in artwork.

Eating

4. *What Did the Dinosaurs Eat?* (Coward, 1972) by Wilda Ross, *Dinosaur Dinners* (Watts, 1991) by Sharon Cosner, and *What Big Teeth You Have!* (Crowell, 1986) by Patricia Lauber discuss prehistoric meals. Ross identifies the plants a plant-eating dinosaur could find for food during the Mesozoic era, Lauber tells ways dinosaur teeth become clues to the food a dinosaur ate and to ways it caught or gathered its food, and Cosner mentions adaptations that helped the animal digest its food. With partners, younger students may "read" the illustrations to restate the information, and older students (grade 2 and older) may look in other sources to verify the information.

Classifying

5. Students may study groups of dinosaurs and ways to tell them apart with Joanna Cole's *Dinosaur Story* (Morrow, 1974). *A Look Around Dinosaurs* (Willowisp Press, 1988) by David Duffee, and *The New Dinosaur Library* (Garth Stevens, 1990) by Douglas Dixon and Jane Burton. Other titles in the library series include *The Very First Dinosaurs, When Dinosaurs Ruled the Earth,* and *The Last of the Dinosaurs.* Each book describes the appearance, habitat, eating habits, and prehistoric cousins of the reptiles. After listening to excerpts read aloud, the students may talk about the illustrations of the parallel hip bones in the bird-hipped group and the nonparallel hip bones in the lizard-hipped group, and discuss "If you were a dinosaur fossil hunter and wanted to place the dinosaur fossils you found into groups, how would you use the information about the bird-hipped group and the lizard-hipped group?"

Dinosaur Young

6. Maida Silverman's *Dinosaur Babies* (Simon & Schuster, 1990) reports facts about nine different dinosaur hatchlings, where they lived, their behaviors, and what they looked like, and Richard Cremins's *Pop-Up Baby Brontosaurus* (Dial, 1989) reports on one type. *Baby Dinosaurs* (Lothrop, Lee & Shepard, 1984) by Helen Roney Sattler shows pictures of dinosaur eggs of various sizes found in different nests. Some egg fossils are the size of potatoes, others are the size of basketballs and softballs. As study options, students can recall information about dinosaur babies, determine a way to draw the eggs life-size and then to scale, or predict the events that could have happened during one year in the life of a baby dinosaur by using monthly headings of January, February (or Monday, Tuesday), and so on.

Pterosaurs

7. A study can be extended for an interested child with Helen Roney Sattler's *Pterosaurs, the Flying Reptiles* (Lothrop, Lee & Shepard, 1985) and John Kauffman's *Flying Giants of Long Ago* (Crowell, 1984), both books with information about all kinds of flying marvels—from a pteranodon who flew along at 30 miles an hour, to a ctenochasma whose jaws were filled with hundreds of needle-like teeth. Partners may list some characteristics of flying reptiles and discuss the following with the teacher:

    a. How do you know which of these characteristics really *are* characteristics of the pterosaurs? What can you do to find out?

    b. If the information listed as characteristics in the book are really characteristics of the pterosaurs, what would you expect to see in illustrations of fossils of pterosaurs in another book?

    c. What would you write (dictate) as behaviors/actions/features of pterosaurs you would want to see in the illustrations of another book?

    d. After looking carefully at the illustrations in another book of your choice, what are some characteristics about flying reptiles you found and wanted to see as evidence to confirm what you thought?

    e. What are characteristics you found that you *had not entered* on your list?

    f. What are characteristics on your list you *did not see* in the illustrations?

    g. What did you see in some illustrations that *contradicted* something on your list?

Q and A

8. After reading a question-and-answer format in *New Questions and Answers about Dinosaurs* by Seymour Simon, girls and boys in groups of four may discuss what was learned: Were dinosaurs smart? Did dinosaurs have families? Which dinosaur had the most teeth? After discussing each question, students in groups of four agree on a response, write it cooperatively, and sign their work.

9. Ways the asteroids, comets, meteor showers, and a nemesis (dark star) could have caused the disappearance of the creatures are found in Daniel Cohen's books, *What Really Happened to the Dinosaurs?* (Dutton, 1977).

10. One source about lizard-hipped sauropods—six of the largest dinosaurs that ever lived—is Seymour Simon's book, *The Largest Dinosaurs* (Macmillan, 1986). As students understand the meaning of the term, *lizard-hipped,* they can explain it to their partners. If students find outdated observations (e.g., the "longest dinosaur" is diplodocus), they may bring the text up to date with information about the recent findings of supersaurus, ultrasaurus, and others.

Books with Activities

The books that follow have built-in activities for observing, punching out, folding figures, and learning the alphabet. Some have word play possibilities with jokes and riddles, and others have pages for coloring, tracing, and connecting the dots.

Coloring and Activity Pages

11. Students interested in activities may select Jim Razzi's *Fun with Dinosaurs* (Scholastic, 1987) and *My First Coloring Book of Dinosaurs and Prehistoric Animals* (Grosset & Dunlap, 1988), or punch out and fold full-color dinosaur figures with *Dinosaurs,* or play with *Planet of the Dinosaurs Adventure Kit* (Harper, 1988) both by Stephanos Attalides. With no need for glue or scissors, children can assemble prehistoric figures for scenery and enact their own stories.

12. Those interested in additional projects can turn to *Dandy Dinosaurs: Fun Projects for Kids to Do* (Meredith Corp., 1989) for instructions for planning a dinosaur party, baking dinosaur-shaped cookies as a gift, and assembling a cardboard stage for a puppet show.

Oversized Books and Posters

13. *The Great Big Book of Dinosaurs* and *Timescape* poster (both Gareth Stevens, 1980) by Mitsuhiro Kurokawa are suitable displays. Dr. Ikuo Obata, paleontologist (Natural Science Museum of Japan), supervised Kurokawa's work and his contributions from the scientific community should be noted.

Observations

14. Demi's *Find Demi's Animals: An Animal Game Book* (Greenwillow, 1989) requires observation skills and engages a reader in finding a small dinosaur and other animals somewhere in the illustrations of large animals. Black-and-white answer keys are in the back as a self-check.

15. The idea of silliness (to contrast with what is not silly) in seen in Fortey's *The Dinosaurs' Alphabet* (Barron, 1990). Children can discuss what is in the print or pictures: "Is it silly/not silly for a yangchuanosaurus to say, 'I polish my teeth in the morning'?"

Word Play, Jokes, and Riddles

16. Students interested in word play might choose Bernard Most's *A Dinosaur Named After Me* (Harcourt Brace Jovanovich, 1991). In Most's book, the short stories feature a child and a dinosaur who are linked by their names. For example, Greg, a football player, dresses in protective gear and is seen with a stegosaurus who is wearing plates on its back for protection. The stegosaurus "shares" its name with Greg and is renamed Gregosaurus. Children can discuss the idea of sharing a name with a dinosaur by either finding a child's name in the dinosaur's name or by changing part of the creature's name to rhyme with the child's name.

Books with Stories and Rhymes

Stories and rhymes about dinosaurs are readily available for young students in kindergarten through second grade. Some of the stories have personified dinosaurs as characters and others have dinosaurs or related objects that come to life. Some educators and scientists become very agitated when these kinds of "cutesy" books are introduced to children in an educational setting. However, when a fanciful story elaborates on facts, there is no need to ignore the information, especially if the fanciful story adds to the facts rather than detracts from them. Further, when a teacher chooses to read one of these books because a child requests it, a teacher has the opportunity to discuss the idea of a fanciful story and mention an author's privilege to create fancy in tales and talk about such questions as, "Why do you think the authors who wrote these stories about dinosaurs chose to make dinosaurs human or put humans in the story? Or bring objects 'to life?' What ideas (themes) are the authors showing us?" Several of the stories that follow are humorous ones and a teacher can show the author's craft and ways authors/poets use words or engage in word play.

Stories

17. *Professor Curious and the Mystery of the Hiking Dinosaurs* (Crown/Clarkson N. Potter, 1991) by Yvonne Gil introduces the mystery of dinosaur footprints on the top of a mountain in the Alps and asks the question, "How did the footprints get there?" Readers may help solve the mystery as they learn how continents collided millions of years ago and see ways the collision placed rocks and beaches where the mountains are today.

18. With the students, a teacher may discuss the brevity in *Tyrannosaurus Wrecks* (Crowell, 1979) by Noelle Sterns or the lengthier actions in *Prehistoric Pinkerton* (Dial, 1987) by Steven Kellogg and suggest a retelling with the pattern of "I know . . . I wonder . . . If . . . " (Masaryk, 1990). The teacher may demonstrate the pattern with the story of Young Pinkerton, a Great Dane who is teething: *I know* that no object, from small to large, was safe from his chewing and gnawing. *I wonder* if the young girl should have taken him along on her class

visit to see dinosaurs at a museum. *If* Pinkerton keeps chewing away on the dinosaur skeleton display, then . . .

19. The series, *Annie K's Theater,* presents a play to perform in *The Dinosaur Tooth: Annie K's Theater #1* (Bantam, 1991) by Sharon Dennis Wyeth. In the story, Annie K, a 9-year-old playwright, gets her friends together and puts on a play about an archaeological dig, an evil museum curator, and a dinosaur. Two friends become rivals as they look for a dinosaur tooth and the rivalry leads to a disastrous dress rehearsal. To foster students' awareness of the visual differences in the formats of a play, a poem, and a story, a teacher may introduce the printed shapes of Annie K's play and the printed forms of a brief story and poem and discuss the terms *drama* (play), *poetry* (poem), and *prose* (story); what the written shapes look like on the pages; and some of the conventions related to capitalization, punctuation, and the way sentences are written in the different formats.

20. A teacher may read aloud a passage from Mary Carmine's *Daniel's Dinosaurs* (Scholastic, 1991) and select words to describe young bespectacled Daniel or his bedroom decorated with a pterodactyl mobile, dinosaur lamp shade, and clothing printed with dinosaurs. As children listen, the teacher may ask them to sketch their version of what they hear in the words that describe Daniel and his bedroom.

21. A surprise ending in Dahlov Ipcar's *The Wonderful Egg* (Doubelday, 1958) can lead students into predicting when they retell the story with a pattern of "I think the writer wanted me to know . . . because . . . " (Masaryk, 1990).

22. With an audience, students can retell Mordecai Richler's fanciful tale *Jacob Two-Two and the Dinosaur* (Knopf, 1987) or Scott Taylor's *Dinosaur James* (Morrow, 1991) to recognize episodes. In the first story, Jacob Two-Two gets away when unscrupulous adults threaten the life of his mysterious fast-growing lizard. In the second, James is fascinated with dinosaurs and earns his nickname as his unnamed sister tells the story of his encounter with Muggins Malone, a bully, and his rescue by a dinosaur. Students (grade 3 and older) may explore the use of synonyms and tell or write a brief nonrepeating story about James, using each word only once to tell the events.

23. Showing the special bond between a child and an animal companion, Hiawyn Oram's *A Boy Wants a Dinosaur* (Farrar, Straus, Giroux, 1991) tells a fanciful story of Alex, who wants a dinosaur for a friend. When Alex brings home Fred (a female massospondylus from the Dino-Store), difficulties begin. Fred eats all the food, gobbles up the laundry, and chews the wooden furniture. Causing trouble on an outing, Fred makes Alex face a decision of what to do next. Students may tell the story with a pattern of "The important thing about . . . is . . . " (Masaryk, 1990).

24. De Paola's *Little Grunt and the Big Egg: A Prehistoric Fairy Tale* (Holiday House, 1990) and Sundgaard's *Jethro's Difficult Dinosaur* (Pantheon, 1977) set off into fantasy as the books mix the Age of the Dinosaurs with an inaccurate concept of a boy living in the age and end in final surprises. In the first story, Little Grunt, searching for breakfast, finds a large egg. It hatches into George, a dinosaur that grows and grows. Because of his size, trouble sets in and George is banished. When George rescues Little Grunt and his cave people after the eruption of a nearby volcano, George is welcomed back. In the second, a young boy, Jethro, finds a special egg containing a dinosaur. Before finishing Jethro's story, a student may predict what will hatch from the egg and draw an illustration of the prediction.

Objects Come to Life

25. In the wordless *Dinosaur Dream* (Putnam & Grosset, 1988) by Robin Michal Koontz, Shane is disappointed when it is time to put his stuffed triceratop away and go to bed. His disappointment vanishes when he dreams he is carried away by a real apatosaurus. Riding on the dinosaur's back, Shane sees a world from the past. Facing danger, Shane's dinosaur friend hides him in a tree when a fierce tyrannosaurus challenges them. Then rescued by a triceratops (that looks like his toy), Shane finds himself at home in bed. To add text, a student can write original sentences on adhesive-backed yellow notes and affix the notes to the pages to tell the story (Roberts, 1990b).

Personified Dinosaurs

26. In Liza Donnelly's *Dinosaur Garden* (Scholastic, 1990), T. Rex and his dog, Bones, decide to plant a garden for dinosaurs. Suddenly, their garden becomes a jungle of roaming dinosaurs. After T. Rex finds an egg under some plants, the hatching begins, and an irate mother dinosaur appears. A pterodactyl flies into the next picture, rescues T. Rex and Bones from the protective mother dinosaur, and takes them home where T. Rex finds another egg. This ending becomes a beginning for another story as this egg cracks and a reader wonders what it will be. Other personified characters include a young dinosaur who searches for a playmate in Leslie McGuire's *Who Will Play with Little Dinosaur?* (Random House, 1989), a dinosaur who moves into a new penthouse apartment in New York City in Norma Klein's *Dinosaur's Housewarming Party* (Crown, 1974), and a naughty dinosaur in *Dilly, the Dinosaur* (Viking, 1987), *Dilly Visits the Dentist* (Puffin, 1987), *Dilly Tells the Truth* (Viking, 1988), and *Dilly & the Horror Movie* (Viking, 1989) by Tony Bradman. In the first, Dilly's intention to keep his jaw shut tight is changed when his dentist starts him laughing. In *Dilly Speaks Up* (Viking, 1991), Bradman has Dilly win out over his bossy older sister Dorla, and in *Baby Dot: A Dinosaur Story* (Clarion, 1990), Margery Cuyler gives human characteristics to Baby Dot, who is somewhat spoiled, throws a temper tantrum, and doesn't cooperate at school. When younger children suggest books like these be read aloud, a teacher may want to record them on an audiotape for the listening center.

27. Comic situations are found in Lisa Donnelly's *Dinosaur Day* (Scholastic, 1990), a story of a young boy's vivid imaginings about dinosaurs hiding under snowy clumps on the streets; in Donnelly's *Dinosaurs' Christmas* (Scholastic, 1991), where a hieroglyphics-talking dinosaur takes Rex and Bones to the North Pole where Rex and seven other dinosaurs help Santa fly the sleigh with the call of "Now Plateosaurus! Now Pteranodon"; and in Robin Pulver's *Mrs. Toggle and the Dinosaur* (Four Winds, 1991), a daffy teacher thinks a new student is going to be a dinosaur. To stretch imaginations, a student may be the caller of actions and others become silent actors. The caller announces situations and the actors enact the actions with silent motions, for example: "You are the first to see the dinosaurs come to town " (from Dom Mansell's *If Dinosaurs Came to Town* [Little Brown, 1991]); "You are the one who finds dinosaur eggs" (from Francis Mosley's *Dinosaur Eggs* [Barron, 1988]); and "You are the one who notices the dinosaurs on Halloween" (from Lisa Donnelly's *Dinosaurs' Halloween* [Scholastic, 1987]).

Poetry

28. *Erni Cabat's Magical World of Dinosaurs* (Great Impressions, 1989) by Erni Cabat draws a reader into exploring full-color, full-page illustrations as well as into reading 26 poems by Lollie Butler. To promote the display of poetry, some

students may be interested in making oversized dinosaur tracks and writing lines of a poem inside the tracks.

Topic E: A Look at Books Suitable for Readers in Middle Grades, 3—4

In nonfiction books for children in middle grades (grades 3 and 4), girls and boys find information about fossils, scientists' theories, activities, and different ways authors and illustrators present dinosaurs. In some of these books, fancy enhances facts. For example, the "Prehistoric Who's Who" (glossary) in Alice Dickenson's *The First Book of Prehistoric Animals* (Watts, 1954) is a lighthearted fanciful touch in a book of facts. For another, Bernard Most adds a touch of fanciful speculation without distorting facts in *Dinosaur Cousins?* (Harcourt Brace Jovanovich, 1987) and offers humor when he compares modern animals to dinosaurs. In this section, you will find books for middle-grade students to add to the children's books mentioned in other chapters.

Classroom Update

- Related to a whole-language program for a child's literacy acquisition, research findings suggest early reading-related skills arise across a preschool period that facilitates acquisition of analytical reading-related skills (Weir, 1989).
- Studies support the success of literature-based approach to literacy with many types of students—limited English speakers, stalled readers, those who have failed after decoding, and beginning readers who have a profile that will make failure likely (Tunnell & Jacobs, 1989).
- Story mapping has a positive growth effect in the development of story schema for second-grade students (Fountas, 1984).
- Students categorized as high imagers showed superior capacity for story retention and recall than did students identified as low imagers (Kane, 1984).
- Recent analyses of listening studies show that meaningful use of language through listening to stories, talking about experiences, and using puppets affects significant increases in reading achievement as well as language development (Hillerich, 1990).

Books with Information

Finding Fossils

1. In *Dinosaurs* (Morrow, 1954), Herbert Zim explains ways fossils are formed, discusses how scientists determine what dinosaurs looked like, and compares dinosaur skeletons with those of animals students know. To get more information about the creatures who ruled the earth millions of years ago, were world travelers, and felt at home in desert heat, arctic chill, or lush warmth, the students may select *Dinosaurs* (Doubleday, 1985) by Jean Zallinger, *Dinosaurs* (Random House, 1978) by Peter Zallinger, *Let's Look at Dinosaurs* (Watts, 1987) by Constance Milburn, or *Dinosaurs: Matter of Fact Books* (Putnam, 1982) by Donald Wolf and Margot Wolf. For reference use, J. Zallinger offers a pronunciation guide, an index of key terms, and an illustrated timetable.

2. Michael Foreman's *Dinosaurs and All That Rubbish* (Crowell, 1972) provides models for imaginative illustrations and poetic words. Interested students may write favorite quotations from the book to show characteristics of dinosaurs from fossil finds and add this information to their learning logs to keep a record of the content they are learning.

Habitat

3. Girls and boys find out what the world was like when protoceratops, triceratops, and other dinosaurs lived, as well as the reasons why they became extinct in *Dinosaurs and Their World* (Grosset & Dunlap, 1988) by Steve Parker. Reporting to the whole group, students can relate what it was like to "grow up as a dinosaur."

Movement and Travel

4. Picture maps and facts are in William Lindsay's *The Great Dinosaur Atlas* (Messner, 1991), and students may rewrite the information learned in their own words (Shugarman & Hurst, 1986).

5. Students see a dinosaur family tree in David C. Knight's *Dinosaur Days* (McGraw-Hill, 1977) and get information about how dinosaurs moved and traveled. Tracks show how they moved and traveled and are the focus of *Let's Go Dinosaur Tracking* (HarperCollins, 1991) by Miriam Schlein.

Relationships to Other Animals

6. After reading Peter Zallinger's *Dinosaurs and Other Archosaurs* (Random House, 1986), John Kauffman's *Little Dinosaurs and Early Birds* (Crowell, 1977), or *The Dinosaurs Who Lived in My Backyard* (Viking, 1988) by B. G. Hennessy, students may discuss the belief about little two-legged carnivorous dinosaurs (theropods no larger than a cat) that became birds and find sources with more information about theropods (Ostrom, 1978). If interested further, a student may write a letter to one of the authors at a publisher's address and ask further questions.

7. After reading *How Did Dinosaurs Live?* (Lerner, 1990) by Kunihiko Hisa and correlating the information with a picture globe of dinosaurs (The Nature Company), girls and boys may conference with the teacher and hypothesize about the following:

a. Would you hypothesize (guess/not guess) that if dinosaurs came back, they would live close to lots of water?

b. If your guess is true, then in what parts of your country would you expect to find large concentrations of dinosaurs?

c. After looking at the globe (The Nature Company) imprinted with locations of fossils finds in different countries and pictures of dinosaurs, where do you find large concentrations of dinosaur fossil finds? According to your guess about dinosaurs needing water, where *should* you find large concentrations of dinosaur finds but cannot? How do you account for this difference? Where do you find large concentrations of fossil finds that you did *not* expect? How would you account for this?

Types

8. Angela Sheehan's *Tyrannosaurus* (Rourke, 1981) offers information about the lives of carnivores. Some careful readers may question the mentioned time era for the dinosaur (there is a 25-million-year discrepancy with other sources). Students may cross-check the information with other references and, in a study group, discuss: "My hunch about the usefulness of the front feet of this dinosaur is . . . . About the size of the front feet, I would guess . . . . I would say they

were too small (not too small) to be useful because . . . . The two claws and toes on each foot would be useful because . . . . With information about an animal of today and the way it uses its short front legs, I would predict that a tyrannosaurus rex used its front legs to . . . ."

Young

9. Students may be interested in authoritative observations about recent discoveries in *Discovering Dinosaur Babies* (Four Winds, 1991) by Marian Schlein. A discussion of dinosaur parenting behavior can be initiated with "How did dinosaurs care for their young? Protect them?"

Flying Reptiles

10. For girls and boys who want to study flying reptiles, Kauffman's *Flying Reptiles in the Age of Dinosaurs* (Morrow, 1976) is suitable for cross-checking by students to see if the information is up to date. When discovering a book with out-of-date information, students may elect to write a letter to a librarian, stating why/why not a particular book should/should not be kept in a library.

How Life Began

11. Students will find colorful pictures of prehistory that begins with the earth's formation and shows prehistoric creatures in an informational picture book, *How Life Began* (Dillon Press, 1991) and *Stranger than Fiction: Dinosaurs* (Avon, 1990) by Melvin Burger. Burger discusses scientific theory with the text set off in boxes, includes pronunciation of scientific names, and has an index for research use.

Dinosaur Survey

12. The question "Is the dinosaur the biggest animal that ever lived?" is answered in Seymour Simon's book, *The Dinosaur Is the Biggest Animal That Ever Lived and Other Ideas You Thought Were True* (Harper & Row, 1986). The question from the title can become a basis for a quick survey for students who ask the question of friends and report the results to their study group.

Books with Activities

The books that follow offer multiple activities related to the study of dinosaurs, single projects that include folding original dinosaur shapes from paper, and word play in the form of jokes and riddles.

Multiple Activities

13. The scope is broad in *The Fossil Factory: A Kid's Guide to Digging Up Dinosaurs, Explaining Evolution and Finding Fossils* (Addison-Wesley, 1989) by Niles Eldredge, Gregory Eldredge, and Douglas Eldredge. Students find information about locating dinosaur remains as well as directions for building a Grand Canyon in a jar, making a plaster of one's own prints, raising tadpoles to see the changes when an animal evolves from a water animal to a land animal, and other activities. To present what is learned to others, students may explain directions for projects to other students and mention the materials needed to complete the work.

Single Craft or Skill

14. In *Fold Your Own Dinosaurs: 12 Challenging Models to Make* (Auckland, 1988) by Campbell Morris, students get directions for making basic folds—reverse fold, rabbit fold, and bird-base fold. After practicing, they may follow directions for folding an armor-plated stegosaurus, a swift running tyrannosaurus,

or other dinosaur. To explain the process to another, a student may select one of the basic folds, discuss the steps with others, and demonstrate/teach peers a basic fold.

Word Play, Jokes, and Riddles

15. With partners, students may select jokes to tell from Jeffrey S. Nelsen's *Dinosaur Jokes and Riddles* (Macmillan, 1989), Joseph Rosenbloom's *The Funniest Dinosaur Book Ever!* (Sterling, 1987), or *Fossil Follies! Jokes about Dinosaurs* (Lerner, 1989) by Rick and Ann Walton. In a group, students may discuss ways to write riddles and jokes (anything that makes you laugh), select situations (a setting an audience can relate to), and deliver punch lines (humorous lines that have surprises). For example, one student asks another, "What do you call a dinosaur at work?" (rep-toil) "What do you call the end of a reptile?" (rep-tail). "And a quiet dinosaur?" (a docile fossil). If interested, students can join with partners to write a humorous short story—perhaps a dinosaur comedy—and use one or more of the jokes from the books.

16. Authors Peterson and Kricher use present-day knowledge to suggest colors for different dinosaurs in *A Field Guide to Dinosaurs Coloring Book* (Houghton Mifflin, 1989). Students will find color illustrations in the front and back of the book and can locate numbers identifying dinosaur colors in black-and-white drawings of dinosaurs. Students may use the illustrations to divide dinosaurs into two groups based on a characteristic (attribute) they choose. After doing this, they can divide each of the two groups into two more groups of dinosaurs by using another characteristic they select (and so on). Students should record the characteristic that was selected to divide the first groups, the second groups, and so on, and then report their findings to the class.

Books with Stories and Poems

Stories

17. Dinosaurs who talk like humans—a fanciful behavior—are introduced in a realistic setting in *The Fantastic Dinosaur Adventure* (Simon and Schuster, 1990) by Gerald Durrell and support a discussion about the author's craft: How does the author make the dinosaur characters seem real when they speak their dialogue? Do the children seem real when they name the dinosaurs? What do students think of the children in the story using the dinosaurs to endorse products on television?

18. Students read *Camp Haunted Hills #3: The Dinosaur That Followed Me Home* (Minstrel/Archway, 1990) by Bruce Coville, sketch an outline of the main character, and consider the feelings expressed by the character followed by a dinosaur. Students show the order in which the feelings were shown by the character and see if they recognize any of the feelings they may have had at one time.

19. Students can discover elements in a mystery and find out the way a young boy, Nate, locates some missing dinosaur stickers and solves the case in *Nate the Great and the Sticky Case* (Coward, McCann, Geoghegan, 1978) by Marjorie Sharmat. Before a retelling, students can suggest alternative titles to rename the episodes (e.g., *The Sticky Case, Nate Sticks to the Case,* and *The Case of the Missing Dinosaur Stickers*).

20. Logic in a fanciful story carries a reader and a plot along as the student chooses a way to end Edward Packard's *A Day with the Dinosaurs: A Choose*

Your Own Adventure Story (Bantam, 1988) or R. G. Austin's *Brontosaurus Moves In* (Bantam, 1984). To update Austin's story, students may change a part (update name to apatosaurus) to suit his or her writing purposes and then create a story ending in a journal and read it to others. As an option, students may write the ending of the story first and then keep going backwards to figure out different events to create an original story.

Rhymes and Verses

21. Students read *Dinosaur Dances* (Putnam & Grosset, 1990) by Jane Yolen to discover silliness in rhymes (e.g., "When the allosaurus/Does a rhumba/ Does she lumber?/ Is she limber?"). The teacher may discuss with students the different dances and music they recognize from the descriptive words in the poems and can invite them to search through the illustrations to find images that interest them (e.g., a T. Rex drawn as John Travolta). Before making a visual display of poetic words that evoke images, the teacher may ask the students to talk about poems they most enjoyed. To begin a visual display of poetic words, a large circle may be drawn in the center of a sheet of paper with the heading, *Dinosaur Dances*. From the circle, lines are drawn outward and smaller circles drawn at the end of each line. In each small circle, students write names of poems they liked and then draw more lines from each small circle to place the words they liked best in each poem. Students may keep the display to use as a resource when they want to write poems independently. If interested further, they can compile poetry word collections from poems of other published authors as well as from poems of classroom authors.

Classroom Update

- Picture books are appropriate for older students and contribute to their literary and aesthetic awareness and language and their reading development (Driessen, 1984).
- Creating graphic material such as word maps or visual diagrams enhances comprehension and learning (Flood & Lapp, 1988; Heimlich & Pittelman, 1986); helps readers identify important issues in books (Cleland, 1981); and serves as an alternative to directed reading activities (Bromley, 1988).
- Creating graphic material helps students understand main ideas and supporting details (Flood & Lapp, 1988); enriches basal reading lessons (Freedman & Reynolds, 1980); and enhances understanding and appreciation of literature (Reutzel & Fawson, 1989).
- Rewriting brief paragraphs, highlighting major points, and elaborating enhances reading skills (Shugarman & Hurst, 1986).
- Preadolescents' responses to literature indicate the developmental link between a student attaining formal operations and a student imagining and accepting alternative realities in literature (Galda, 1980).

Topic F: A Look at Books Suitable for Readers in Upper Grades, 5–6

For this age group, a sufficient number of trade books is available to support a study of paleohistory about dinosaurs. In this section, books about dinosaurs give information on dinosaur fossil hunters, fossils, findings, and theories. Suggested activities, stories, and poems to engage a reader are included.

Books with Information

Dinosaur Paleohistory

To investigate dinosaur paleohistory, students may examine lives of dinosaur fossil hunters and what they have found through time; doing this, they learn something of the science of paleontology—its language, rules, and views—and become aware of findings and the relationships with other findings. They become aware of the modern setting—the current mysteries and theories. Unfortunately, there are gaps in this area (e.g., a lack of recent accounts of modern research expeditions, a lack of descriptions of current laboratory experiments, and a lack of current biographies of fossil hunters). The students can fill in these gaps with their writing in self-published books for the classroom book corners or the school library. Further, students may send their books to publishers interested in updating their material about dinosaur controversies, personalities of paleontologists, and fossil findings. To begin the students' investigations of a paleohistory of dinosaurs through children's literature, a four-lines-of-inquiry model[1] for older students follows.

Line of Inquiry I: A Search for Hunters of Dinosaur Fossils

Focus: Acquiring knowledge about dinosaur fossil hunters.

This inquiry, "A Search for Hunters of Dinosaur Fossils," includes reading literature about dinosaur fossil hunters (i.e., autobiographies, biographies, and biographical sketches). To keep a record of this inquiry project, a "Paleohistory of Dinosaurs" map integrates the study with reading and language arts. The map enhances reading presentations by linking nonfiction material to geographical locations (social studies). A display is placed on a bulletin board and in the center is a world map. After a narrative about a dinosaur fossil hunter is read, the teacher and students discuss the setting and the discovery. For example, a teacher points out the location of the Gobi Desert, the scene of the discovery of a stegosaurus's nest. The names of the fossil hunters are recorded on cards and placed around the map. Students use yarn to connect a card to the location of the dig and fossil discovery on the map. The map becomes an evolving bulletin board that serves as a reminder for all who want information about the digs and fossil finds that the students read about during the study. This map expands the students' knowledge of world geography as they think about different locations, identify map markings, talk about climate and terrain, read map legends, and discuss their interpretations of anecdotes. In this line of inquiry, the students share, discuss, and summarize any generalizations they can make about dinosaur fossil hunters and their work.

Early Fossil Discoveries

1. An account of what happened in lives of early fossil discoverers is told in *To Find a Dinosaur* (Doubleday, 1973) by Dorothy Shuttlesworth, in Christopher Lampton's *Dinosaurs and the Age of Reptiles,* and in *The Dinosaur Hunters: Othaniel C. March and Edward C. Cope* (McKay, 1963) by Robert Plate. Lampton gives readers descriptions of explorations and investigations. Plate's book, a dual biography, gives information about the beginning of two of the best collections of dinosaur fossils in our world today: Cope's collection of over 1,000 fossils was given to the American Museum of National History and Marsh's fossils were contributed to the Peabody Museum of Yale. Older students may review Plate's book as an example of a dual biography and create original dual stories of famous people of their choice.

2. Observations about a dig are in the chapter "The Spade Digs On" in Estelle Freedman's *Digging Into Yesterday* (Putnam, 1958). After hearing or reading this chapter, students may compare Freedman's information about the workings

at a dig with current information in a recently published book and report back to the group on how our understanding of this aspect of science has changed and unfolded since the 1950s.

3. Students see photographs of fossils of a fern, eggs, archaeopteryx, and 2,000 dinosaur tracks in the trackway at Rocky Hill (Connecticut) State Park in *From Living Cells to Dinosaurs* (Watts, 1986) by Roy A. Gallant. After reading or hearing the chapter, "Fossil Bridges to the Past," students interested in fossil sites can write and request information from the state capital or the local chamber of commerce. For places outside the United States, they can contact the country's embassy, which has offices in large cities in the United States. A nearby library will have the address of an embassy nearest the students.

Modern-Day Fossil Hunters

4. *Supersaurus* (Putnam, 1982) by Francine Jacobs is a straightforward account of the way Jim Jensen uses data, collects information, and reports his methods and results. For further discussion, the teacher may invite the students to contribute their thoughts about:

a. *The size of supersaurus:* 50 feet high, weighed 100 tons (15 times that of a bull elephant), and ate as much as 15 elephants each day

b. *The body temperature of the supersaurus:* cold blooded or warm blooded (Ostrom, 1978)

c. *The idea of Jim Jensen as a hero:* discuss Jensen and others who are admired for their outstanding qualities or great achievements

Line of Inquiry II: Journeys without Maps to Find Fossils

Focus: Fossils, studied by scientists, are found in layers of rock; paleontologists can tell what sort of plants and animals lived during each period in the earth's history; after study, plants and animals can be classified by scientists; and a paleontologist uses fossils to trace the ancestry of living animals back through geologic time to their origins.

This inquiry, "Journeys without Maps to Find Fossils" includes acquiring information about dinosaur fossils and findings through informational books. In this line of inquiry, students review the concept of dinosaurs by brainstorming as many words as they can think of about dinosaurs to link their prior knowledge about the topic to their current study. Categorizing these words, students can find words that are similar (that have something in common with other words) and place similar words in groups. They may label groups with headings such as *What Dinosaurs Looked Like, What Dinosaurs Ate, What Dinosaurs Did,* and so on. Students use this graphic aid about dinosaurs to help explain any new information (data) they find in other references as they search for information related to the headings of their labeled groups in other sources. This graphic aid represents the students' concepts about dinosaurs and becomes a guide to analyze information found in other books, computer programs, or audiovisual materials. The students are encouraged to find as many sources as possible about specific dinosaurs or about specific regions of fossil finds. Doing this, they get involved with multiple data sources to identify findings and cross-check observations about fossils and other findings.

To initiate cross-checking information, a teacher may engage students in questioning any information found in a text or in illustrations. On the cover of Geis's *The How and Why Wonder Book of Dinosaurs* (Grosset & Dunlap, 1960) is a deimetrodon, and the teacher asks if the animal should be there and if it should be classified as a dinosaur. To show cross-checking, the teacher shows the finned heat-absorbing dimetrodon in *Dimetrodon* (Bancroft-Sage, n.d.) and mentions that the book points out that this creature was *not* a dinosaur. For instance, in Moseley's *Dinosaurs: A Lost World* (Putnam, 1984) are illustrations of a plesiosaur and archaeopteryx; the teacher asks, "Are these dinosaurs? Should they be in a book about dinosaurs?" To demonstrate cross-checking, the teacher shows the text about the creatures in the book that points out they were reptiles. The teacher continues with, "Is it true the plesiosaur (marine reptile) and the archaeopteryx (birdlike reptile) were/were not dinosaurs? How can we find out?"

In *Tyrannosaurus* (Rourke Pub.), an illustration shows tyrannosaurus rex fighting an almosaurus. To suggest cross-checking, the teacher asks, "Was almosaurus a dinosaur that did/did not live in rex's time or its geographic area? How can we cross-check this?" *Tyrannosaurus* also gives an age for rex's time era, and the teacher may ask, "Is this age accurate or inaccurate? How can we check on this?" In another source, the students read that triceratops had the largest dinosaur skull, and the teacher may ask, "Where could we find information to verify this?" When a student finds information in another book comparing the skull of torosaurus with that of triceratops, the student can announce that it appears that torosaurus had the largest dinosaur skull. The teacher invites the students to research this informational item and others in data sources and to prepare a "Dinosaur Blooper" video about some of these unsupported "facts."

What Fossil Hunters Observed

5. *The New Dinosaur Dictionary* (Citadel Press, 1982) by Donald F. Glut alphabetically lists places where fossils were found, and *Fossil* (Knopf, 1990) has illustrations of trilobites, plants, leaves, and bones. In a related study about dinosaur bones, paleontologist Armand de Ricqles (University of Paris) found that bone tissue of various dinosaurs was similar to that of many living mammals but quite unlike the bone tissue of most modern reptiles. Observations about creatures of the past and sources that discuss this further are found in Keith A. McConnell's *Dinosaurs from A to Z* (Stemmer House, 1988), Darlene Geis's *Dinosaurs and Other Prehistoric Animals* (Putnam, 1982), *Before and After Dinosaurs* (Morrow, 1959) by Lois and Louis Darling, and *The Rise and Fall of the Dinosaurs* (Michael Friedman, 1989) by Joseph Wallace. In Wallace's Chapter 6, students find out how a scientist observes and determines the information about the size, weight, and eating habits of a dinosaur. With partners, students may discuss the extent of the reliability of the deductions that scientists acquire from dinosaur fossil bones after reading Chapter 10 of in *The Big Book of Dinosaurs* (Bison Books, 1988) by Dougal Dixon.

6. In "Reading the Fossil Record" in *All About Strange Beasts of the Past* (Random House, 1956), Roy Chapman Andrews suggests that students' thoughts roam in many different directions to get information from the fossil record:

a. From the shape of dinosaur teeth, a scientist determines if it is a _____ (carnivore, herbivore).

b. From a dinosaur's length, a scientist determines _____ (weight, height).

c. From the construction of a dinosaur's "hands," a scientist determines if the hands were used for assistance in_____ (walking. feeding, defending).

d. From its skeleton, a scientist determines if a dinosaur belongs to a suborder of _____ (type, species of dinosaurs).

e. From the overall skeleton, a scientist determines the way a dinosaur _____ (walked and ran).

f. From the skeleton of its tail, a scientist determines the use of the tail as a _____ (balance or weapon).

The Dinosaurs' Young

7. With *Dinosaur* (Knopf, 1989), students get a close-up look at a dinosaur nest and eggs, a 120-million-year-old skull, and dinosaur skin. In groups of four, students may read and record facts they find about the fossils. For a review of content, they can write their own questions and answers and engage in "Stump the Specialists" with a peacemaker (arbitrator) or a class president to lead a question-and-answer period. To be the specialists, one group takes a question from another group and cooperatively decides on an answer by using their books, notes, questions, or other sources. If the group members answer correctly, they take another question from another group. If the group answers incorrectly, the group retires and another group comes forward to be the specialists.

Classifying Fossils

8. Dinosaurs are classified (grouped) in the Diagrams Group's *A Field Guide to Dinosaurs* (Avon, 1983), and specific as well as general information about 300 species of dinosaurs is found in David Lambert's *Collins Guide to Dinosaurs* (Collins, 1983) and *The Age of Dinosaurs* (Random, 1987). All three books give students an opportunity to look at a scientist from four points of view (explorer, inventor, judge, and contributing activist). Students may discuss these views in groups. *View 1:* When new information is needed, how does a scientist become an explorer as he or she searches for information? *View 2:* When a new idea/tool/relationship is needed, how does a scientist show that he or she is creative? *View 3:* When it is time to decide the extent to which a new idea/tool/relationship is worth implementing, in what way does a scientist become a judge? *View 4:* When a scientist decides to put his or her idea into action, in what way does a scientist become a contributing activist?

Recognizing Tools of a Paleontologist

9. The tools a fossil hunter needs are discussed in Michael Benton's *The Dinosaur Encyclopedia* (Simon and Schuster, 1984). Students may list the tools that Benton discusses and then examine another data source to make a list of tools mentioned in the second source. For example, *The How and Why Book of Dinosaurs* (Grosset & Dunlap, 1960) by Darlene Geis also shows the tools of a paleontologist: brush, magnifying glass, tongs, and others. Both lists may be compared and results written in journals after students discuss the following questions: Which of the lists describes best the tools you think a fossil hunter would need? Why? How are the two lists different? Why do you think they are/are not different? How have you changed your mind about which tools would be used by a paleontologist? Why? What do these lists tell you about the study of fossil hunting? How would you decide which list was the most accurate?

Types of Dinosaurs

10. Students may focus on a specific dinosaur with Elizabeth Sandell's *Ankylosaurus: The Armored Dinosaur* (Bancroft-Sage, 1989). From skeletons, scientists know it was covered with spikes and bony armor, and that flat bones joined into large pieces. To extend information from the book, students may use writing starters (e.g., "From the fossils of . . . (skeletons, teeth, tail, head, eggs, baby dinosaurs), scientists believe that . . .") and write the responses in their journals.

11. Tables of time periods, dates, and life forms add to the informational metaphor in Alan R. Warwick's *Let's Look at Prehistoric Animals* (Whitman, 1966). Some students may not agree with Warwick's metaphor that compares a fairy tale to the story of the earth's beginnings about long-dead ancient animals and its ending with prehistoric humans. An included visual time line shows the earth's beginning with volcano activity and continues with the behavior of humans and mammoths. For discussion: Do students agree/disagree with the metaphor? Why

or why not? Other helpful books on this topic are *Discovering Prehistoric Animals* (Troll, 1989) by Janet Craig, *Dinosaurs* (Prentice-Hall, 1985) by Jasper Diamond, and *Prehistoric Life* (Silver Burdett, 1981) by Michel Cuisin.

12. When students select Helen Roney Sattler's *The Illustrated Dinosaur Dictionary* (Lothrop, Lee & Shepard, 1990), they may use alphabetical order to look up information about a favorite dinosaur. After doing this, each student may explain to a partner the way to use the ABC arrangement, and later write the directions for using the dictionary on an index card and place it with the book for others to read.

13. Clear information about the structure, behavior, and habitats of the tyrannosaurus rex family is in Helen Roney Sattler's *Tyrannosaurus Rex and Its Kin: The Mesozoic Monsters* (Lothrop, Lee & Shepard, 1989). To extend what is learned from the book and to review content, students can engage in a Thinkathon with other students to pass along information about these creatures to others. As examples of Thinkathon activities, students can show others how to make a comparison; mention synonyms and antonyms that could be used in discussing dinosaurs; give examples of using words carefully to say what is meant; classify dinosaurs; and discuss the location of dinosaur habitats in the world.

14. Ways scientists read clues about dinosaurs is explained in two survey-type books, *Dinosaurs from A to Z* (Stemmer House, 1988) by Keith A. McConnell and *Tyrannosaurus Rex and Other Dinosaur Wonders* (Messner, 1990) by Q. L. Pearce. Both texts offer conversation topics—a dinosaur speed demon, a fishing dinosaur, and the possibility that tyrannosaurus rex was a scavenger rather than a fierce predator. When writing about a specific dinosaur in their journals, students should be encouraged to give the dinosaur an authentic characteristic gleaned from an illustration and mention such things as a protruding jaw, a sideways squint, or an overbite.

Relationship from Past to Present

15. In John Sibbick's *Creatures of Long Ago: Dinosaurs* (National Geographic, 1988), movable features may be shown by one student to another and then the paper-engineering discussed. In writing, student partners may compare the features of dinosaurs in Sibbick's book with other paper-engineered books.

16. Portrayals of other dinosaur family trees that may show discrepancies to discuss with the total class are in Joseph Rosenbloom's *Dictionary of Dinosaurs* (Messner, 1981), David Knight's *Dinosaur Days* (McGraw-Hill, 1977), *The Dinosaur Family Tree* (Lerner, 1990) by Kunihiko Hisa and Sylvia A. Johnson, and David Lambert's *Dinosaurs* (Rourke, 1982). Under the category of *bird-hipped*, Lambert shows armored dinosaurs (stegosaurus), horned ones (triceratops), and bird-footed ones (iguandon). Under *lizard-hipped* are sauropods (brachiosaurus), carnosaurs (tyrannosaurs), and deinonychids (compsognathus). All four books may be reviewed and discussed before students create their own versions of a dinosaur family tree. Hisa's text tells about flying and swimming dinosaurs and their link to birds, and suggests that shifting plates in the earth's crust may have caused the extinction of the dinosaurs, an idea that will be new to many students. Illustrations should be observed carefully, too (i.e., Should the sauropods have their nostrils by their mouths or do the nostrils belong on top of their heads?). A version of a dinosaur family tree might look like this:

Version of a Dinosaur Family Tree

Ornithischian	*Saurischian*
horned (ceratopsions)	meat eaters (theropods)

plated (stegosaurs)   plant eaters (giant sauropods)
armored (ankylosaurs)
duck-billed (ornithopods)

Dinosaur Life

17. Students can consider the possibility of different colors for different dinosaurs along with the idea of a pink pterodactyl after reading Robert Bakkers's *The Dinosaur Heresies* (Morrow, 1985). In another source, Llyn Hunter's *Dinosaur ABC Coloring Book* (Dover, 1990), dinosaurs are shown in ABC order in natural surroundings of millions of years ago, and the author's notes on dinosaur colors point out ways scientists make guesses about the colors by comparing fossils with present-day animals that have similar habits. For instance, a scientist knows that many hunting animals of today have spots to keep them concealed in foliage until they are ready to attack. This suggests that a hunting dinosaur, such as deinonychus, may have had camouflaging marks, too. Students may make their own hypotheses about the coloring of dinosaurs, discuss their views, and then write about their thoughts in letters to the authors. They can sketch a pink pterodactyl in their journals and write why they agree/disagree with Bakkers's idea or design colors of textured scales for a pterodactyl and other prehistoric creatures of their choice.

18. Observations about giant and tiny reptiles from 135 to 190 million years ago are in Dougal Dixon's *The Jurassic Dinosaurs* (Gareth Stevens, 1987). In the index, a student finds that when a dinosaur name begins with a capital, it means the name refers to a *type* of dinosaur, (e.g., Stegosaurus); and when a dinosaur's name begins with a lowercase letter, it means the name refers to a *group* (such as crocodiles). The use of the index—and the difference between *type* and *group*—can be explained by one student to others. For individual projects, students can consider reading further about some unsolved mysteries of the Stegosaurus. The extent of the mobility of its spiked tail could lead to experimenting with different degrees of mobility for a model of its spiked tail. Students may also discuss the possible use of the bony back fin of a Stegosaurus as a heat-loss fin that had a network of canals with large blood vessels, a discovery made by James Farlow, Carl Thompson, and Daniel Rosner (Yale Engineering Department).

19. Ways the asteroids, comets, meteor showers, and a nemesis (dark star) could have caused the disappearance of the creatures are found in Daniel Cohen's *Dinosaurs and Monsters* (Watts, 1984). With information from these sources, students can respond to the question "Did comets kill the dinosaurs?" After discussion, they might write their private thoughts to DEAR LANRUOJ (*journal* spelled backwards), tell why they think the way they do, and begin their entries with "At this moment, I . . . " or "Here I am thinking about. . . . "

20. If curious about creatures that did not die out when dinosaurs did, a student may select Russell Freedman's *They Lived with the Dinosaurs* (Holiday, 1981) to find a skeleton of diplodocus, similarities of certain fossils related to creatures of today (crickets, horseshoe crabs, sharks), and pronunciation guides in the picture captions. In a literature group, a student can explain why he or she thinks the author believes these animals lived with dinosaurs and make a list of these creatures for the group.

Size Relationships

21. The illustrations give a sense of size and size relationships in Mary Elting's *Dinosaurs* (Western, 1987) and show a full-sized youth sitting in a claw of a

deinocheirus and a penny placed next to a mouse-like mussaurus (moose SAW rus) fossil, one of the smallest reptiles found by scientists. Labels of dinosaur names—a plant-eating diplodocus, titanic apatosaurus, three-horned triceratops, and others—are found in the full-colored pictures.

Line of Inquiry III: Expeditions of Paleontologists
Focus: Work of a paleontologist.

During this line of inquiry, students develop considerable understandings about dinosaur fossil hunters, fossils and their meanings, and dinosaurs and their habitat. Students realize fossils are found in layers of rock, are studied, and are used by paleontologists to tell what sort of plants and animals lived during each period in the earth's history. These plants and animals are then classified. Further, fossils are used by paleontologists to trace the ancestry of living animals back through geologic time to their origins. To develop these understandings, the students read, analyze, and cross-check related nonfiction and evaluate it as to authenticity, credibility, and the author's style. To evaluate their informational books, students meet periodically in response groups and consider the following: In what ways are the facts accurate? How do facts support the general ideas? How can we tell this? How is the author qualified to write this? How can we tell? How is the material up to date? How can we tell? In what ways is the writing clear? In what ways is the writing organized with tools of reference?

Restoring Replicas
22. Girls and boys find large illustrations of museum restorations of dinosaur replicas and their environment in *Life Before Man* (Thames & Hudson, 1972) by Zdenek V. Spinar, *Life Before Man* (Time-Life, 1972), and *In The Time of Dinosaurs* (Scholastic, 1968) by William Wise. Students can predict to others what a visit to an actual museum exhibit would be like after seeing the full color illustrations in *The London Museum of Natural History Eyewitness Book: Dinosaur* (London Museum of Natural History, 1987). In their explanations, the students should be encouraged to use colorful words and vigorous twists of language about the 160-million-year-old dinosaur puzzle with words that *describe dinosaurs* (i.e., giants of all the ages, creatures with husky skeletons, bones as long as a subway car, nasty company, and dinosaur tormentors); *describe dinosaur behavior* (i.e., long-distance travelers, bumpy ground navigators, sand storm survivors, and refuge seekers); *describe dinosaurs and their young* (i.e., living in herds like wildebeasts, surviving in fossil nests, living in family scenes from the past, huddling together as hatchlings, and growing up together as young dinosaurs) and *describe setting* (i.e., the lush world of the Cretaceous period compared to empty desolate canyons).

Speaking the Language of a Paleontologist
23. With a friend, each student may discuss the terms used by a paleontologist and pronounce the dinosaur names in *Those Mysterious Dinosaurs* (Western, 1989) by Gina Ingoglia. Each can explain the use the pronunciation guides of names inserted right in the text, a helpful device that eliminates the task of turning to a pronunciation guide in the back. To focus on what prehistoric life was like, students may review information related to prehistoric time periods and design questions using the information for a whole-group review (including tie-breaker questions) for a prehistoric quiz bowl for the classroom.

Line of Inquiry IV: Observations and Rise and Fall of Theories

Focus: What we know/don't know about dinosaurs.

This line of inquiry includes reading literature about current mysteries and theories. The students begin to understand ways different authors present remaining fossil mysteries that are unsolved, as well as the ways they present their theories to explain certain happenings (a collection of scientific "why" tales). Students consider the following: How did the dinosaurs behave? Why did they act this way? and Why did the dinosaurs disappear?

Extinction

24. Students can read further about a "dark star" theory (an explanation based on the best observations available) in several books: *The Dinosaurs and the Dark Star* (Macmillan, 1985) by Seymour Simon, *Dinosaurs* (Greenhaven, 1987) by Peter and Connie Roop, Isaac Asimov's *Did Comets Kill the Dinosaurs?* (Gareth Stevens, 1988), *The Dinosaurs and the Dark Star* (Macmillan, 1985) by Robin Bates and Cheryl Seman, and Franklyn M. Branley's *Dinosaurs, Asteroids, and Superstars: Why the Dinosaurs Disappeared* (Crowell, 1982). In Simon's book, students find observations about Muller's nemesis theory, and in the Roops's book, they discover other hypotheses (and rebuttals) of scientists. As the students separate facts from opinions, the teacher may point out that there really isn't a scientific *fact*—just direct observations—and everything else is deduction and inference. Thus, science theory does not really claim to be a "fact," for the process of science is really a process of falsification. This means if no one can prove a theory wrong, it stands. Discussing this, a teacher should encourage students to think of theories as models of explanation *that may change as additional observations are presented* and to "clear up" any misconception that "science proves facts." For further study, a student and an adult in the home can prepare a read-aloud audiotape of the book. To do this, the student makes arrangements to check out a tape recorder, blank tape, and the book from the teacher and agrees on a date to return these materials to the classroom listening center for others to enjoy.

25. With a partner, a student may discuss the examples of persuasive writing and one of the theories of dinosaur extinction (e.g., Alvarezes' theories, Muller's nemesis theory) in *Dinosaurs: Opposing Viewpoints* (Greenhaven, 1988) by Peter Roop and Connie Roop. The partners may consider possible causes of the extinction of the dinosaurs sudden severe cold weather, shifting of the earth's plates or the spreading of continental masses, withdrawing of seas, supernova explosion, and survivors. In groups, older students may discuss the scientists' hypotheses about dinosaurs and analyze arguments. To do an analysis, students may choose one hypothesis and rebuttal to focus on during a discussion. They can identify elements in the argument and determine the strength and weakness of each element in the argument. Younger students may find another issue for debate in Roops's *Opposing Viewpoints Juniors* (Greenhaven, 1989) and study the charts, cartoons, graphs, and photographs before making a final choice.

Books with Activities

Introduction to Volcanoes

26. Students can explain to others how to make a chemical volcano after reading Alan Kramer's *How to Make a Chemical Volcano: And Other Mysterious Experiments* (Watts, 1989). They can list steps on a chart for all to see and include any warnings listed at the end of the experiment.

Drawing Dinosaurs

27. Students can learn one way to draw a dinosaur with Michael La Placa's *How to Draw Dinosaurs* (Troll, 1982). Each student draws one and shows what was learned about drawing to a partner. With the whole group, a teacher may review the importance of reading the entire set of directions carefully (get meanings of any words you do not know; reread to find out *if* you need to collect materials [tools, utensils, ingredients] and *what* you need to collect).

Dinosaur Observations

28. Students may use "Fun Facts" pages in Melvin Berger's books, *Stranger than Fiction: Dinosaurs* (Avon, 1990) and *Prehistoric Mammals: A New World* (Putnam, 1986) to make a dinosaur observations game to be used to review the content learned. Students discuss what facts will be needed to create the game, participate in making the game board, and explain the rules of the game to others before it is played.

Art Extensions

29. Suitable for discussion and an art extension, the pop-up spreads in Tenner Ottley Gay's *Dinosaurs and Their Relatives in Action* (Aladdin, 1990), in Stewart Cowley's *The Mighty Giants* (Warner, 1989), and in Rupert Mathews's *The Great Dinosaur Pop-Up Book* (Dial, 1989) show paper-engineered dinosaurs. Students can compare differences in illustrations in these pop-up books with *The Giant Dinosaurs: Ancient Reptiles that Ruled the Land* (Troll, 1979) by Douglas Eldridge.

30. To make paper figures, students may follow step-by-step instructions for wet folding in John Montroll's book, *Prehistoric Origami* (Dover, 1990). They can create a volcano, prehistoric tree, seagoing elasnosaurus, or land creatures. After the figures are finished, the students may use poster board and write explanations of how the figures were made and place the explanations beside the figures for a display.

Books with Stories and Poems

Dinosaur Search

31. A reader can examine the elements of writing a mystery and tell others what made the "case" a mystery in *The Case of the Disappearing Dinosaur* (Minstrel/ Archway, 1990) by Laura Lee Hope. To examine the element related to the character, the reader evaluates the main character and responds to an open-ended sentence: When_____(name of character) was_____, I thought she/he was being_____because_____.

32. A student may examine the writing of science fiction and travel to another time and place on a search for dinosaurs with David Bischoff's *Search for Dinosaurs* and Peter Lerangis's *Last of the Dinosaurs* (both Bantam/Doubleday/Dell, 1987, 1988). The reader is given rules of time travel, a dossier of facts, and makes plot choices based on information supplied in the book. To search for dinosaurs, the reader follows a path of historical accuracy and content learning. When an inaccurate choice is made, the reader is sent to another more dangerous period of history.

Baby Duckbill

33. To read about a life of a baby duckbill, a student may select *Dinosaurs and Their Young* (Holiday House, 1983) by Russell Freedman and *Maia: A Dinosaur Grows Up* (Running Press, 1987) by John Horner and James Gorman. Partly fiction, Horner and Gorman's expository writing gives information about the

importance of recent discoveries about dinosaurs, and Freedman's text suggests girls and boys learn more about ways some duck-billed dinosaurs cared for their young. For a whole-group discussion, the teacher may invite the students to question some of the names of the dinosaurs with "Since ducks lived *after* the dinosaurs, why do we call some types the 'duck-billed' dinosaurs? Why don't we call ducks the 'dinosaur-billed' birds? What other animals have characteristics of dinosaurs that we could rename?"

Digging Up the Past

34. Related to fossil discoveries, students may read about the techniques of modern archaeology in Carolyn James's *Digging Up the Past* (Watts, 1990). Damien and his friend Joe find a piece of blue glass in the woods and Damien's mother, an archaeologist, tells him the glass is old. The boys find more objects and begin a dig. Along with other techniques, Damien's mother shows them how to lay out the grid for the digging, explains terms (*datum point* and *strata*), and assists the boys as they excavate their dig and discover that it is a rubbish dump used by a nineteenth-century farm family. Students may write letters to others in the class to tell what they learned from the story about techniques of archaeology. To build a library of read-along tapes with this book and others, they record the story (and other stories) during a read-aloud session. Placed with the books, the recordings become tapes for the listening center. The students should not worry about any comments, questions, interruptions, or statements made during the taping. These remarks will not be distractions for future listeners; the remarks will be heard as elaborations and will add to the listening experience for many of the girls and boys (Preece, 1990).

Dinosaur Narrator

35. After reading *We're Back! A Dinosaur's Story* (Crown, 1987) by Hudson Talbott, a student can pose as Rex, the dinosaur narrator, and retell a part of the science-fiction story about seven dinosaurs who get smart on Brain Grain, go to outer space, and then return to a holiday parade in New York City. Descriptive words (*good, brave, happy, old, young*) about the character may be written on the board on lines around the name and used when the student introduces the character(s) in the story.

Poems

Mumble Poetry

36. Students will find poems about dinosaurs, nature, and seasons in *Til All the Stars Have Fallen: A Collection of Poems for Children* (Viking, 1990) selected by David Booth. With a poem, the teacher can introduce students to Mumble Poetry. The teacher reads a poem selected by students aloud several times and then, in a rereading, selects different lines to mumble. When they hear mumbling, they chime in and say the words they know.

Choral Reading

37. For a choral reading, students can update the poem "I Saw a Brontosaurus" in *Something Big Has Been Here* (Greenwillow, 1990) by Jack Prelutsky, and change the word *brontosaurus* to *apatosaurus*. The apatosaurus gives the narrator a ride through the streets in town and the fields in the country. Students can suggest different ways to interpret the poem by adding sound effects, clicks of the fingers, toe taps, and other features for several rereadings.

Extensions for Chapter 3

1. *Consider the component in the Core of Structure: Select a Literature Base.* List all of the books as well as the book activities, ideas, projects, and line(s) of inquiry about your theme that the books can support. Select a book such as *Thunderfeet—The Story of Alaska's Dinosaurs* (Paws IV Pub., PO Box 2364, Homer AK 99603) to read to children and plan one inquiry/ activity project for a book of your choice.
2. *Give a report or panel discussion.* Present an individual report or join with others to give a brief panel discussion on one of the related readings from the list for this chapter.

Endnote

1. This model was developed by the author and has evolved since 1975 while trying different approaches in presenting literature for children through units related to science and in evaluating literature with preservice teachers, graduate classes, and inservice teachers.

Resources

Lodestar/E. P. Dutton. (1989). *The great dinosaur timescape. III.* New York: Lodestar/Dutton. All ages.

Houghton Mifflin (1989). *Dinosaur's Playhouse kit, Parts 1 and 2.*

Readings

Bromley, K. (1988). *Language arts: Exploring connections.* Boston: Allyn and Bacon.

Cecil, N. L., ed. (1990). *Literacy in the '90s: Readings in the language arts.* Dubuque: Kendall/Hunt.

Cleland, C. (1981). Highlighting issues in children's literature through semantic webbing. *The Reading Teacher,* 34 (6): 642–646.

Dooley, M. C. (1990). Rice cakes, rattlesnakes, and rock n' roll: A thematic approach to teaching language arts and social studies. In Nancy Lee Cecil (Ed.), *Literacy in the '90s: Readings in the language arts.* Dubuque: Kendall/ Hunt.

Downing, J. (1977). Concepts of language in children from differing socioeconomic backgrounds. *Journal of Educational Research* (May–June): 277–281.

Driessen, D. Z. (1984). *A description of a select group of six fifth grade students' response to picture books. Dissertation Abstracts International* 45: 1668A. Ann Arbor, MI: University Microfilms International, 84-18934.

Flood, J., & Lapp, D. (1988). Conceptual mapping strategies for understanding information texts. *The Reading Teacher,* 41 (8): 780–783.

Fountas, I. C. (1984). *An investigation of the effect of a story mapping program on the development of story schema in selected second grade students. Dissertation Abstracts International* 41: 6844A. Ann Arbor, MI: University Microfilms International, 84-16844.

Freedman, G. & Reynolds, E. (1980). Enriching basal reading lessons with semantic webbing. *The Reading Teacher,* 33 (6): 677–684.

Galda, S. L. (1980). *Three children reading stories: Response to literature in preadolescents. Dissertation Abstracts International* 41: 2438A. Ann Arbor, MI: University Microfilms 80-27440.

Hillerich, R. L. (1990). Making music of language: From research to practice. In Nancy Lee Cecil (Ed.), *Literacy of the '90s: Readings in language arts* (pp. 56–63). Dubuque, IA: Kendall/Hunt.

Heimlich, J. E., & Pittelman, S. D. (1986). *Semantic mapping: Classroom applications*. Newark, DE: International Reading Association.

Huck, C., Hepler, S., & Hickman, J. (1987). *Children's literature in the elementary school* (4th ed.) New York: Holt, Rinehart and Winston.

Kane, E. M. (1984). *Storyreading in second grade: Exploring physiological rhythms and retention of high and low imagers in three classroom settings. Dissertation Abstracts International* 45: 408A. Ann Arbor, MI: University Microfilms International 84-12460.

Masaryk, J. (1990). Good ideas for teaching language arts: Patterned retellings. *The California Reader,* 23 (2): 26–27.

Myers, J. (1989) ERIC/RCS: Making invitations that encourage active learning. *Journal of Reading,* 32 (6) (March): 562–563.

Novak, J. M. (1985). *Invitational teaching for mere mortals.* Paper presented at the American Educational Research Association annual meeting, Chicago. March 31–April 4. Ed 258 969.

Ostrom, J. (1978). Extinctions. *National Geographic* (August).

Preece, A. (1990). Literacy and the listening center. *Reading Today,* 8 (2) (October, November): 12.

Reutzel, D. R., & Fawson, P. C. (1989). Using a literature webbing strategy lesson with predictable books. *The Reading Teacher,* 43 (3): 208–215.

Roberts, P. L. (1984). *Alphabet: A handbook of ABC books and activities for the elementary classroom.* Metuchen, NJ: Scarecrow Press.

Roberts, P. L. (1985). *Alphabet books as a key to language patterns.* Hamden, CT: Library Professional Publications.

Roberts, P. L. (1990a). Alphabet books: Activities from A to Z. *The Reading Teacher,* 44 (1) (September 1990): 84–85.

Roberts, P. L. (1990b). Learning about text structure through the wordless book-writing connection. *The California Reader,* 24 (1) (Fall): 9–11, 24.

Shugarman, S. L. & Hurst, J. B. (1986). Purposeful paraphrasing: Promoting a nontrivial pursuit for meaning. *Journal of Reading* 29 (February): 396–399.

Sommer, S. B. (1990). Putting the pieces back together: Integrating the language arts. In N. L. Cecil (Ed.), *Literacy in the '90s: Readings in the language arts.* Dubuque, IA: Kendall/Hunt.

Sutherland, Z., & Arbuthnot, M. H. (1986). *Children and books* (7th ed.). Glenview, IL: Scott, Foresman.

Tunnell, M. O., & Jacobs, J. S. (1989). Using "real" books: Research findings on literature based reading instruction. *The Reading Teacher,* 42 (7) (March): 470–477.

Weir, B. (1989). A research base for prekindergarten literacy programs. *The Reading Teacher,* 42 (7) (March): 456–461.

Chapter 4

What Teaching Techniques and Class Organizational Plans Are Available?

Reflections for Chapter 4

Chapter 4 helps you select and implement:

- Techniques for teaching
- Ways to organize the class
- Uses of the component in the Core of Structure to implement a thematic unit in literature-based instruction: Select Teaching Techniques and Organizational Plans

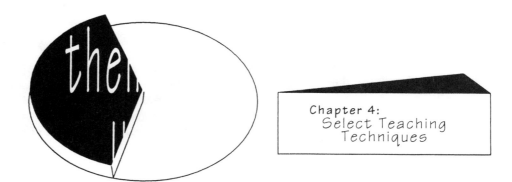

Component in Core of Structure to Implement a Thematic Unit for Literature-Based Instruction: Select Teaching Techniques and Organizational Plans

Vignette in Third Grade: Community of Learners

A third-grade teacher starts each school year with a theme called "A Community of Learners" (Schmidt, 1990) to set the stage for whole-language activities during the year. The teacher states his philosophy behind the theme and mentions that, as a class, the students need rules as they cooperate with each other to fulfill the purpose of learning in the class. The teacher and the students together are responsible for safety, leadership in academics, and meeting the academic guidelines set by authorities in the district/state. (See Chapter 5 for an example of an implementation of guidelines in social studies.) Using this theme, the students create a classroom Bill of Rights, develop a cooperative consensus model of decision making, and understand the teacher's responsibility of interacting with all discipline problems. The students get to know each other and understand each one's unique differences. Together, the students create a classroom alphabet book about themselves (*A* is for *Amos* who is unique because . . .). Daily, students respond in writing in their reflection/dialogue journals to sentence starters such as, "In our classroom community of learners, today was a . . . (great day, average day, terrible day)."

During the first week of school, the students discuss what to place in a time capsule to represent their community of learners. They bury the capsule in a school yard corner and retrieve it the last week of school to talk about what was done during the year and to make comparisons about what developed in their class community. In addition to other books about the Bill of Rights available for check out by the students, two books by Warren Coleman, *La Carta de Derechos* (*The Bill of Rights*) and *La Constitucion* (*The Constitution*) (both Childrens, 1989) are available in Spanish. They introduce the U.S. Constitution, discuss the meaning of the Bill of Rights, and emphasize the basic freedoms of citizens in the United States. With *La Carta de Derechos,* the first ten amendments written to support the concept of equality proclaimed in the Declaration of Independence are reviewed.

Topic A: Teacher Beliefs

Just as Schmidt's (1990) beliefs shaped a community of learners at the beginning of the school year, so does a teacher's beliefs about literacy shape the instructional practices in the classroom (Wells, 1988). A teacher's beliefs promotes connections between the classroom and the larger cultural context and between literacy events and the lives of the students. To promote this kind of connection through school conditions, Forehand and Ragosta (1976) indicate that benefits in integrated education include a multiethnic curriculum and assignments that avoid racially identifiable groups. Other benefits include extracurricular activities that are scheduled during the school day, biracial work and play teams among students, and student-focused human relations activities.

Classroom Social Status

To avoid racially identifiable groups and to provide equal status among students, a teacher should be aware of *expectation states theory* (Cohen, 1978, 1979). According to this theory, classroom social status affects a student's interaction, and the interaction then affects the amount of learning in a specific curriculum. Researchers de Avila, Cohen, and Intili (1981) advocate several ways of fostering equal status among students. From the results of their study, these researchers suggest that learning be across a broad front in the classroom. For example, in a

14-week period, students in nine classrooms in grades 2, 3, and 4 were exposed to a wide variety of science/math experiments and activities designed to improve cognitive, linguistic, and academic skills. In addition to a basic course of study, the students engaged in the activities for 30 to 60 minutes a day.

Special Instruction by Teachers

Based on the recommendations of Cohen and others, the teachers gave special instruction to lower achievers prior to their participation in small-group cooperative learning. The instruction reminded the girls and boys that many different abilities were needed for the tasks at hand; everyone was going to be *good* on at least one of the abilities in the group; students should ask anyone in their assigned group for help; students must help anyone who asked for help; and students should select a new group to work with when work in the first group was completed. With this special instruction, the lower achievers then made unique contributions to their group, which helped equalize their classroom status. Further, achievement and interracial friendships were enhanced. This enhancement included the improvement of students in linguistic proficiency as well as academic and cognitive gains. The improvement that was found took place regardless of whether the child was LEP (Limited English Proficiency) or FES (Fluent English Speakers). There were positive outcomes for both. It seems that both types of children learned in the same atmosphere and that learning for one group was not at the expense of the other group as long as certain requirements were met. The requirements included interaction—especially verbal interaction. Talking was a critical element. Also, there was a need for a social organization that supported certain types of interactions. These interactions included task-related talk, requests for assistance, and offers of assistance to others. Other interactions included nontask-related talk, talk to the teacher (or peers or aides), cleaning up, working alone (versus working in groups), observing others, waiting for directions, and transition (wandering).

Access to Resources

Also, there was a need for a wide variety of resources and access to them by the students. On worksheets to be filled out in English or Spanish (or other target language needed), the procedures were drawn (or written) and the results from students were drawn (or written). Inferences were called for and some of the written language was included. The information required for learning could be given without any written language (with drawings) and did not penalize a student who lacked either oral or written proficiency. In this study, the worksheet activity significantly contributed to the gains—particularly the scores of the students on the California Test of Basic Skills (CTBS). The related study sheets seemed to offer a powerful reinforcer to instruction in the basic skills areas.

Engagement Time

It appeared that there was a substantial relationship between the percentage of time that the students were observed talking about the tasks and their gains. Similarly, there was a strong relationship between the amount of time students spent reading and writing with the worksheets and their improvement in reading and math. Thus, it seemed that in order for new material to be absorbed into a student's working memory, it had to be discussed and talked about with others. Overall, the proficient bilingual student showed the most consistent improvements.

Community of Learners in Centers

From the work of de Avila, Cohen, and Intili (1981) comes ways for increasing classroom interaction and for providing status equivalency for students. To increase the classroom interaction, for example, a third-grade teacher established learning centers where students had access to information about a topic. To prepare the centers, the teacher developed information sheets and vocabulary cards, and included multisensory experiences with materials such as clay, markers, rolls of butcher paper, audiotapes for choral verse, and so on. The teacher began with an introductory day (Day 1) and introduced the topic from a library book. On Day 1, the teacher discussed the themes in the learning centers and related them to the topic of study. In this discussion, new vocabulary was presented and, with the students' input, semantic maps were created to represent the students' knowledge of the subject. With the students' dictated questions about the topic, a question map was developed and the students' expectations about what they want to know were listed. Rules of cooperation at the centers also were discussed. Three student guidelines (based on Cohen's work) related to cooperation were useful: You may ask anyone at your center for help; you must help anyone at your center who asks for help; and after you finish, you may choose a new center.

Cooperating with Assigned Roles

In roleplay situations, the students rehearsed skills of cooperative learning. They rehearsed asking questions, listening to others, helping another person, explaining to others, showing others how things work, and giving others what they need. The teacher assigned roles in the group that included the following: *facilitator* (a student who saw to it that group members got any help they needed); *checker* (a student who made sure that everyone finished their worksheets); *reporter* (a student who discussed what the group learned during the end session held each day); *supervisor* (a student who helped with clean up); and *officer of safety* (a student who oversaw the safety of all in the group).

Roles in the centers were rotated daily. Based on the research of de Avila, Cohen, and Intili, an orientation was given each subsequent day, which gave students time to discuss the idea that everyone should participate in the center activities. To promote status equivalency, the teacher reminded the students daily that everyone was going to be *good* on at least one of the abilities needed for the tasks in the center. In the cooperative group work, it became crucial for the students who did not understand what was expected of them to feel comfortable in asking peers for assistance. The teacher worked diligently at establishing this feeling of being comfortable with each student in the center.

Participating in Initial and Daily Orientation

After the orientation on Day 1, there were succeeding days (Days 2–7) where the teacher started a period of group work, beginning with about 15 minutes of orientation. The teacher used the daily orientation time to set the stage and presented some of the topic materials from the textbook, a related book, or another resource that were not placed in the learning centers. The teacher's orientation included anecdotes, library books with illustrations, information related to the topics, and sometimes a resource person. After each daily orientation, the girls and boys worked in the learning centers for 30 to 40 minutes, with the task of completing each center that day, and they finished the worksheet that accompanied the task.

During each orientation, the teacher, aware of status treatments that were used to change expectations for competence, would always say something related to this to the students. Each of the multiple ability tasks in the center was accompanied by a status treatment by the teacher that did something to change expectations for a student's competence. To do this, the teacher told the students that many different intellectual and problem-solving abilities were required for the tasks and that reading and writing were only two of the necessary skills. Here, the teacher stated clearly that no one would be good at all of these abilities but everyone would be good on at least one of the abilities (de Avila, Cohen, & Intili, 1981). Later, in each group at a learning center, each member had an equal opportunity to contribute.

Studying in Learning Centers

The learning centers were large cardboard boxes carried to students' desks or tables. In the boxes were direction sheets, books, activity sheets, question sheets, and other materials needed to carry out the activities—ones where students learned by doing something. Each learning center had a different focus with multisensory activities. Each day, the teacher rotated the learning centers among groups of students so that each student had the experience of different learning activities (auditory, tactile, visual, kinesthetic) as he or she gathered information and solved problems. While the students were in groups of 4 or 5 at each center, the teacher walked around the room and served as a facilitator for the learning during the time period. Each student was responsible for completion of the task and the worksheet at each center. Each day after the work in the centers, the teacher scheduled a debriefing (or a wrap-up/evaluating time). To do this, a reporter from each learning center read and answered one of the six questions from the worksheet. The students discussed the information in the context of the total group, and thus reviewed the learning of all of the students involved in the study.

Literature for Learning Center Boxes

In a learning center box, the written instructions and worksheets (in English and Spanish and with pictures in sentences) were related to the district's required literacy/mathematics skills. The students' tasks required different abilities, such as spatial and visual abilities, reasoning, roleplaying, and accuracy. Most valuable were the tasks treating social science/natural science/math concepts in different ways and with different media.

To develop learning center boxes around children's books, the teacher found the following books useful as a base for activities:

Learning Center Box # 1: To explore the concept of humor, the teacher read *Dinosaurs I Have Known* by Barry Louis Polisar and showed a video, *I'm a 3-Toed, Triple Eyed, Double Jointed Dinosaur and Other Songs for Young Children.* The students sang along and discussed the concept of humor (e.g., what it was that Polisar did that made words in the songs funny to them). In the center, the students reread the book, replayed the video, and read the words of the song together as they listened and found examples of humorous language.

Learning Center Box # 2: To improve their ability to draw dinosaurs, the teacher introduced the students to *Draw 50 Dinosaurs and Other Prehistoric Animals* (Bantam/Doubleday/Dell, 1985) by Lee J. Ames. In the book, the girls and boys saw how a few basic lines led them step by step to a final drawing of a dinosaur such as tyrannosaurus rex, brachiosaurus, and triceratops. They restated the steps to others and, after drawing the dinosaurs, they made a visual display for the book.

Topic B: Other Teaching Techniques

Strengthen the Program with Variety

Integrating a literacy curriculum with a topic from content, you should consider experience-centered projects, second-language learning, and independent study. You will want to find different techniques that actively involve students in jigsaw groups, mini-lessons, and team learning. Further, there are values in audio drafts, cross-age tutoring, guided imagery, and self-instructional packages. You can use a variety of prereading strategies, provide experience to augment children's background knowledge, use interactive strategies, and include group discussions (Maria, 1989). To show ways they did this, several teachers have written about their successful ventures to put variety into their programs, which are discussed next.

Connect Literature to Other Curriculum Areas

A first-grade teacher used literature to tie together science, writing, and poetry. After several weeks of study about whales and listening to books read by the teacher, the first-graders said that one of their favorite books was *There's a Sound in the Sea: A Child's Eye View of a Whale* (Scrimshaw, 1975) by Tamar Griggs. So, the teacher turned to other poems to give the children as much exposure as possible to the sounds of language beautifully used. Soon, the teacher noticed some poetic-sounding language appearing in some of the children's writing (Stephens, 1989). One day after lunch, the teacher sat with the children on the rug and said, "Let's write a poem together. What shall we write about?" The children called out their ideas for a line in the poem and the teacher wrote them down. The teacher reread the lines and the children told the teacher which lines they thought belonged together and in which order they should appear in the poem. (The children had talked about line breaks in past discussions of other poems and knew that it was the poet's decision as to where to divide the lines.) The children decided where the line breaks in their poem should go and arranged the lines. They illustrated the poem and published it in a small book that was placed on a reading table with other class-published stories. The next day during the writing period, several children began writing whale poems on their own.

Respond with Audio Drafts

Use of a tape dictation program helped a student with writing. First, a writer's thoughts were expressed fully on a tape recorder. Then, the student listened to the tape and wrote down notes for a revision. Sentence by sentence, the recorder was stopped and the student's ideas were written down on paper for a first draft.

Provide "Leads" for Writing

Stephens (1989), a first-grade teacher, explained to the children that writers use the word *lead* to tell the way a piece of writing begins. Then the teacher read leads from several books and the children talked about which ones they liked best and why. The list of leads was reviewed again and the teacher asked the children to think about leads the next time they started writing a new story or revising an old one (Stephens, 1989). The children accepted the idea of leads because writing a story with an interesting beginning made sense to them. Before long, *a good lead* was a phrase that came into their comments at sharing time.

Develop Self-Instructional Packets

A self-instructional packet can present a lesson (or series of lessons) with a small amount of material and allows a student to learn at his or her own rate (Johnson & Johnson, 1971). To prepare a packet, a teacher plans activities in sequence, writes the objectives, builds in feedback, and prepares questions that relate to the instructional objectives. These teacher-prepared packets, suitable for all ages, will assist a teacher in meeting the individual needs of the students, motivate their learning, and keep their interest on the topic. Different ideas for developing self-instructional packets on tape, video, computer disc, or in written form are found in *A Resource Guide for Elementary School Teaching: Planning for Competence* (Kellough & Roberts, 1991).

Provide Team Learning with Jigsaw Groups

To facilitate student team learning in the jigsaw group arrangement in a sixth-grade class, the content (story, chapter) was divided into the same number of parts as there were students on each team in the class. A story was divided into (1) setting and character introduction, (2) problem, (3) conflict, and (4) the way the problem was solved. Students on the teams who had the same content part studied together and became the experts on that part; they returned to respective teams to teach the material to others (Slavin, 1983, 1987).

Encourage Involvement by Parents

A teacher can introduce himself or herself to parents by letter, send home a monthly calendar of school events, or publish a monthly newsletter to keep parents informed. A teacher can create sessions to assist parents in helping children with assignments, invite parents to meet the authors of children's books who are visiting the school, and end the year with an evaluative questionnaire to parents asking how the school can better meet the needs of the children. Additionally, a teacher can make modifications based on the comments that strengthen the program (Valeri-Gold, 1990).

Classroom Update

- Language for young children is learned best through use, from the known to the unknown, and in low-risk environments such as a social event (Harste, 1990).
- Discourse competence of fourth-grade Hispanic students more accurately predicted academic achievement on a reading comprehension test than grammatical competence (Jax, 1988).
- Repeated readings (or multiple readings of connected text) is a useful instructional technique for improving reading ability for such students as young children, disabled or remedial readers, developmental readers in regular education classes, and mature adults (Dowhower, 1989).
- Cooperative learning teams achieve at higher levels of thought and retain information longer than students who work quietly as individuals (Johnson

& Johnson, 1986); members help one another with a sense that learning is important, valuable, and fun (Slavin, 1983, 1987).

- Fifth- and sixth-grade students in a cooperative group had positive attitudes and liked their social studies class more than competitive control group students (Wheeler & Ryan, 1973).

- In sixth grade, developing and writing compositions enhanced both transfer and memory and was beneficial for both good and poorer writers. Students who synthesized information through writing scored significantly higher than students using other types of learning activities (Smith, 1988, 1989; Copeland, 1985). Across the grades, there are trends of increasing story length, plot connectivity, and some increasing plot complexity (Vine, 1989).

- Key research in classroom management at the elementary level (Emmer, Evertson, & Anderson, 1980; Evertson, Emmer, Sanford, & Clements, 1983) and the secondary level (Evertson & Emmer, 1982) has indicated that effective teachers engage in specific behaviors at the beginning of the school year that promote desirable student behavior.

- Cooperative learning groups have positive effects on achievement, self-esteem, positive social interaction, and interpersonal attraction among children from diverse as well as homogenous backgrounds (Cohen, 1986; Johnson, Johnson, & Maruyama, 1983; Slavin, 1983).

- In research on effective questioning, it seems one technique for obtaining a high frequency of responses in a minimum amount of time is through group choral responses, an effective way to conduct guided practice. Effective teachers monitor the class and adjust instruction based on student performance (Rosenshine & Stevens, 1986).

Topic C: Establishing the Classroom for Thematic Instruction: Preparing Your Students for Learning

This section was written by Janie Low of California State University, Sacramento.

Implementing Strategies for Thematic Instruction

Preservice and first-year teachers approach the classroom with optimism about implementing the ideas and strategies learned in their teacher training program. To their dismay, these novice teachers discover that even with an exciting curriculum, problems with student behavior can and do occur. What can teachers do to make their initial years and subsequent years of teaching successful for themselves and their students?

Whether you choose to conduct your classroom in a more traditional style (i.e., teacher-centered discussions, lectures, individual competitive structures) or a facilitating style (i.e., student-centered discussions, problem solving, and cooperative learning structures), you need to plan and implement organizational and procedural structures that will enable students to be self-directed, productive, and responsible. If you want a classroom in which students focus on learning, you should:

1. Preplan to prevent problems from occurring.
2. Clearly delineate and communicate rules and procedures.
3. Teach to these expectations by providing specific directions, giving examples

and reasons, providing students opportunities to practice these expected behaviors, and giving feedback to the students on their performance.

4. Maintain maximum contact with your students the first few days of class and engage them in whole-group activities.

5. Be consistent in applying and enforcing established rules, procedures, and consequences.

6. Focus on particular students versus giving general criticisms.

Using Thematic Instruction: Rationale

Though thematic instruction can be and has been used in more traditional teaching-style contexts, thematic instruction lends itself well to a facilitating teaching style. Characteristics of a facilitating style (democratic, supportive, interactive) are discussed further in contrast to a nonfacilitating style (autocratic, confrontive, formal) in Kellough and Roberts's *A Resource Guide for Elementary School Teaching: Planning for Competence.* The authors show a teacher how to develop a profile on his or her teaching style, discuss review research contributions toward the development of a teaching style, and provide sources of learning style assessment instruments.

In thematic instruction, children may be organized in a broad range of teaching/learning formats that are child centered where curricular areas are interrelated. Among those formats are learning centers, independent work, teacher mini-lessons with one or several children, small-group activities partners, and whole-group lessons. However, this writer advocates cooperative learning groups for thematic-based instruction since this structure has been shown to have positive effects on students. For example, allowing students in small groups to make decisions about task procedures gives them a sense of self-control and provides opportunities for them to develop active citizenship skills—a major goal for a democratic society (Cohen, 1986). According to Graves (cited in Hoskisson & Tompkins, 1987), cooperative grouping also helps students become independent learners as opposed to learners who rely solely on the teacher as a source of knowledge.

Organizing Thematic Instruction: Guidelines

Guidelines for effectively organizing for thematic instruction are those that practicing teachers have found to be successful. These recommendations are consonant with basic principles of effective classroom management:

1. *Small/Cooperative grouping.* Students benefit from cooperative learning experiences (Cohen, 1986), and many educators and researchers, including Slavin (1983), recommend specific procedures to prepare students to work in collaborative groups. Though specific components vary depending on the goals of different structures, there are defined skills that students need to acquire in order to have a successful group work experience. Underlying successful group work is the need for:

    a. Clear guidelines for accomplishing the activity
    b. Clear expectations for behavior, which must be monitored and enforced
    c. A shared responsibility between teacher and students for the monitoring and enforcement.

The nature of the responsibility for varied roles that students assume in cooperative groups must be clearly understood. Therefore, whenever group roles change, you need to teach to those roles by engaging students in a discussion about the purpose of the roles and providing time for students to identify and practice behaviors that are crucial for each student's effective functioning in varying roles.

2. *Facilitating.* As a facilitator/leader, you, the teacher, are responsible for monitoring the groups to ensure that students are appropriately fulfilling their individual as well as group responsibilities. Initially, you need to provide specific feedback on a regular basis to the students to report how they are effectively fulfilling their responsibilities and either to suggest or elicit from the students ways that the students can be more effective in their roles. As the students become more proficient in their roles, sporadic feedback is recommended.

3. *Learning centers or stations.* Learning centers or stations are one variation of small-group learning and lend themselves well to thematic instruction. A variety of learning activities can be made available to the students across different content areas through learning stations. In a learning station format, students have increased opportunity to work with a range of materials and are exposed to diverse strategies for revisiting key ideas or concepts. Thus, students are more likely to learn the key concepts underpinning the theme (e.g., How does climate affect what we [or other animals] eat and how we live?) because of repeated exposure to knowledge and skills in novel and motivating contexts.

As with group work, students need to be prepared for the learning center experience. You can maximize your students' success with learning stations by careful preplanning. Cecil (1989) offers the following criteria when constructing learning stations:

    a. A learning station should have specific objectives.
    b. A learning station must be well equipped.
    c. A learning station should be colorful and attractive.
    d. A learning station must be functional.
    e. Activities in a learning station must facilitate self-learning.

Expectations for the activity at each center should be clearly delineated and clear guidelines and procedures for accomplishing the objectives should be provided. Further, expectations for behavior should be well established and consistently monitored and enforced. Scheduling for learning stations must be clear yet flexible in order to meet the needs of the entire range of children in the class. Cecil suggests two basic systems for scheduling students into stations: rotational and contractual. Procedures for rotating through the learning centers should be taught, including opportunities for student rehearsal of the procedures. Necessary materials must be prepared in advance and readily available for student use. Students need to know where to place and store their work as they progress through the centers and what to do when they finish the center activity before the allotted time expires or when they did not have adequate time to finish a learning station activity. Folders (or "mailboxes") clearly labeled for each student enable students to store and retrieve their own work. Students also need strategies for obtaining assistance when the teacher is unavailable. Designating specific students on a rotational basis as student assistants or assigning "study buddies" eliminates long periods of waiting for the teacher and facilitates positive student interaction.

Making Thematic Instruction Work

The procedures and structures for delivery of instruction is a function of both your teaching style and the needs of your students. Therefore, you should select the instructional and organizational formats that you feel will most effectively enable you to ensure that your students will develop and acquire targeted knowledge, skills, attitudes, and values.

Foundational to the success of instruction, regardless of your teaching style, is the establishment and maintenance of a successful system of classroom management. Although an effective system of classroom management may not ensure that students will learn, the ability to manage student behavior effectively is the initial step toward the more important goals that relate to cognitive and affective learning. Therefore, if your students know what is expected of them and if you provide fair, clear, and consistent guidelines for meeting those expectations, students will likely develop the skills and attitudes to make responsible choices. As a result of creating an optimal classroom environment, you will maximize students' learning and enjoyment of that learning. In the process, you, too, will experience the excitement and satisfaction that comes from knowing you have provided the experiences and leadership that will enable your students to become competent and confident learners.

Encouraging Responses by All

Before a fourth-grade teacher read aloud facts about a new species of dinosaurs, several purposes for listening were ·established. Some students listened for a description of the new species. Others listened to find out what the word *avaceratops* meant, and still others listened for the words about the new discovery site. In addition, everyone listened to find out how the world of the dinosaurs was similar or different from our world today. After the article, "New Type of Small Dinosaur Discovered" (Reproducible 1) was read aloud and discussed, the students considered the task of being a director of a dinosaur display at the Academy of Natural Sciences. As a writing extension, some students wrote to a director of a dinosaur display at a nearby museum and created pictures for a replica of this new type of dinosaur that could be displayed at the Academy.

After a news item was read, questions about facts were asked aloud by students. After each question was asked, they discussed it with partners, asked for help, and gave help to others. To respond, they gave answers in an oral multiple-choice manner. The "possible-answer #1" and the "possible-answer #2" were read aloud by the teacher and, after discussion with partners, the students responded. This gave LEP students an opportunity to ask for help or receive help· and focus on the content. For a variation, every student discussed the question with a study buddy and answered by holding fingers against the chest (not up in the air) for the number of the answer selected, or held small tagboard cards with the numerals on them and displayed one card in the air to indicate the response that was selected.

Responses with Answer Fans

Another response activity asks students to identify with an identification number (1, 2, or 3) a specific word from among words that sound alike: *to* (1), *too* (2), and *two* (3). To identify the correct use of these homonyms, the students listened to one sentence about dinosaurs (with one of the homonyms included) as it was read aloud. They selected the correct version of the word (*to, too,* or *two*) by selecting its identification number from small strips they had in front of them. The strips had numbers on them that corresponded to the words that sounded alike and the strips were fastened together to form an answer fan (narrow strips of tagboard or railroad board fastened with a paper brad). Students hid their answers against their chests until the teacher gave a the cue "Dinosaur Responses." With the cue, students held up the number they selected from their answer fans and the teacher scanned the room to see which students were responding and in which ways they were responding. Students were asked to provide an explanation to support their choices in selecting answers. The activity continued as other sentences were read.

Responses with Answer Boards

For other questions, students responded by writing their answers with yellow chalk on small (4″ × 4″) writing boards made of cardboard covered with black adhesive paper. Their answers were covered with their hands until the teacher gave a cue. With the cue, students held up their answer boards to show their responses. This gave the teacher another opportunity to make a visual check. To respond, students use chubby yellow chalk (it writes best on the dark adhesive surfaces) and paper towels (or tissues) for erasers. For a variation, large manila envelopes covered on the fronts with felt or flannel may be held on the lap to display response cards. The envelope provides storage for the cards.

Eliciting Responses during Prereading, Reading, and Postreading

Prereading

To assess prior knowledge in a prereading activity, fourth-grade students made "display" cartons of their knowledge. To make a display carton of knowledge, the sides, top, and bottom of a small milk carton were covered with art paper and labeled on each side with one of these headings: *who, what, when, where, why,* and *how*. In groups, students were responsible for writing information for one side of the carton. All teams contributed their information to make one cube.

During Reading

To respond during a reading activity, students searched for information in a book about dinosaurs. The information to look for was written on a search card placed in a cardboard pocket inside the back cover of the book. Messages on search cards included: Tell three facts you learned from reading this section. Can you find a quote you like from each page of this dinosaur book and write it in your dinosaur journal?

Postreading

To respond to a postreading activity, facts about the content the students learned from reading were displayed on clean, discarded milk cartons and prepared as a postreading activity. To do this, the students summarized and organized the information they learned, wrote paragraphs, and drew illustrations to glue to the cartons.

Eliciting Responses to Illustrations: Predictions Before, During, and After the Event

Students in all grades may predict events for before, during, and after the events found in pictures. Given illustrations about dinosaurs, teams of two can respond and make predictions before, during or after the event seen in the picture.

Before the Event

To make a prediction before the event in an illustration, the student teams looked carefully at an illustration and thought about what might have happened before the picture took place. They considered actions or events that might have taken place, where the dinosaurs might have been, and what the dinosaurs could have done to get to where they were in the illustration.

During the Event

To make a prediction during the event in the illustration, the students told about what is happening in the scene and made predictions about what was going on.

After the Event

To make a prediction after the event in the picture, the student teams predicted what could happen next. They discussed where the dinosaurs might go from the point they saw in the picture and predicted the next actions the dinosaurs could take.

Topic D: Using Community Resources

You will be interested in organizing instruction to include your available community resources. Community resource agencies and their personnel provide a rich set of experiences for students as they meet community workers who provide services for people in areas of food and health and safety. Locations in the area can be sites for outdoor lessons and visits to museums, parks, gardens, and streams can illustrate concepts.

Role models from the community should talk to students about their motivation and preparation for their careers as effective links between school and business and the technological world. Building involvement, you can introduce students to enrichment and extracurricular activities such as the district's science fairs, a local science exhibit, or such programs as California's Mathematics, Engineering, and Science Achievement (MESA) program, which support students who have an interest in technical careers. Further involvement can come from your interaction with the school's parent-teacher association, community action groups, a local university's incentive program, and after-school clubs dedicated to fostering students' healthy attitudes toward their chosen careers.

Topic E: Giving Final Reports

A message on the board is read aloud and announces to the class members that more is to come to close the day. This is the time when the students report on what they have learned. The reports are classroom experiences that are recognized by all. The students are encouraged to speak clearly, to think about what is said, to look at the members of the class as they interact with one another, and to be brief. The reports are in various forms:

1. *Scheduled individual reports.* During the previous week, three students volunteered for their turns to be reporters on dinosaurs. They make their reports to everyone in a study circle—a discussion to support the personalized study time. This is also a time for other student volunteers to explain something that has been studied during the day (or week) or give brief talks about a process, an idea, or a topic related to the study. Further, the reporters (or other students) tell any news about dinosaurs read in newspapers or magazines. The reporters of the class help keep all class members up to date with local and world news and tell of any recent happenings related to the study to the class. For example, a recent news article about finding a 20-million-year-old leaf in Clarkia, Idaho, is related to this topic, for scientists have found a DNA molecule in the leaf can be compared with a DNA molecule from a tree leaf presently growing. The changes seen will tell scientists the changes in the growth patterns of the species over millions of years. The students discuss why this is important, its link from the present back to the past, and how this present-day information could help scientists predict changes that happened in past plant and animal life.

2. *Spontaneous individual reports.* At the end of the scheduled reports, each student takes time to respond to one of the following, either in writing, by dictating

it to another, or by commenting on it to the group: Today I learned _____.
I need to _____. or This was my lucky day at school because _____.

3. *Round-the-room reporting.* Some students team up with others to teach what was learned or accomplished earlier in the day. At each of several tables, a team of two students reports to others seated around the table. After each team has reported, the listeners move to another reporting table. This means that each pair has to repeat their facts several times to different groups. It also means that listening students ask questions and talk about the ideas they heard or talk about ways to help the reporters clarify their presentations.

Topic F: Punching Up Reports

MacKinnon (1962) identified the characteristics of creative children as being original, resourceful, independent in their judgments, and having a sense of humor. To foster creativity in all children in the classroom, creative ways for giving reports are encouraged by the teacher.

Alphabet Format. The alphabet can be the form of a report, with students writing 26 sentences about a topic beginning with *A* is for . . . and *B* is for. . . . Alphabet books are useful as models for reporting when they show facts about related topics (Roberts, 1984, 1992). Models to display are John Brennan's *A is for Australia* (Dent, 1984) and its information about animals such as the dingo, emus, and kangaroos; Elizabeth Cameron's *A Wild Flower Alphabet* (Morrow, 1983) and its dedication to her grandchildren, handwritten annotations about each flower telling its uses, and related stories for each flower; Jean Johnson's *Teacher A to Z* (Walker, 1987) and its informative paragraphs about teaching characteristics for each letter and a final section to foster greater awareness of the importance of teachers in every community. Observing the format in these and other ABC books gives students different ways to use the alphabet to report on content.

Author Report. Students may report on an author of books related to the topic. Authors who have made several contributions with dinosaur books are Issac Asimov, Ray Bradbury, Miriam Selsam, and Helen Roney Snyder.

Book Quotes. Students may print passages and quotes from books and display them along with illustrated scenes and mention them in the narrative of their reports. For example, a final page in George Ella Lyon's *A B Cedar: An Alphabet of Trees* (Orchard, 1989) tells readers, "Air and food/ Shade and wood/ Trees give us/ a stair to climb/ A place to look/ Even this book! /"

Catalog. Students can create a catalog related to the topic of study and refer to the catalog during the reports.

Choralspeak Responses. Students may give their reports by asking questions and letting peers answer in group choral responses as well as individually. Realizing there seems to be a considerable amount of support for a questioning strategy that uses a combination of choral and individual responding (Rosenshine & Stevens, 1986), a teacher encourages students to give their reports in this way.

Comparative Words. Students can find exciting words used by authors and prepare a chart with two columns with headings of *The Author Says This* and *I*

Say That. Displaying the chart, students may refer to it to review information learned on the topic while reporting.

Concrete Shape Poems. After students read and see poems in different shapes from such sources as Eve Merriam's *Finding a Poem* (Atheneum, 1970), students may write about the topic in free verse or write inside paper shapes that reflect the topic.

Contacting Others. Students may include in their reports what was learned by making a call on the telephone or writing a letter inquiring about a facet of their inquiries.

Crossword Puzzles. Students can report the information they gained through meanings of words in a crossword puzzle. Using a transparency shown on the overhead, students can show a crossword puzzle they developed and read the word clues to others as they fill in the puzzle on the transparency.

Debate. Students may report through a debate on an issue related to the topic.

Dialogue. Students may write a brief script with dialogue about the topic. Dialogue between two characters is developed, discussed, and written in a brief script about the topic. Students can perform the script to give information about the topic to others.

Dinoricks. Students may read *The Book of Pigericks* (Random House, 1983) by Arnold Lobel and listen to its accompanying read-along cassette for patterns for writing dinoricks (limericks about dinosaurs) that give facts in humorous ways.

Endings with Questions. Some students may end their reports by asking, "What did this make you think about?" and then lead the discussion that follows.

Found Poetry about the Topic. Students can give examples of "found poetry" (poetic words expressing a thought in prose) to add to a report. To do this, students may find phrases in favorite books about the topic and copy the phrases as free verse. The verses are read aloud, discussed, and included in a report.

Journals and Diaries. Students may read aloud a part of their journals and diaries to class members to emphasize points in a report.

Modern Fable. Students may review a fable and write a brief modern fable related to the topic of study.

News Reporting. Two students can prepare their reports the way news reports are done on a television show and be co-anchors. With colorful words and vigorous use of language, they can announce parts of the report as "news" with oral headlines.

Original Books. Students can make scrapbooks with all kinds of information. The books should include several sources: clippings about books on the topic; written reports from others; illustrations from favorite books; something about the authors and artists' original poems and stories; records of books read; book lists of books found; newspaper and magazine articles' duplicated material; and copies of letter(s) the students wrote to inquire about something or ask for information.

Original Dictionary.   A student can make a brief dictionary and present his or her own oversized book containing entries related to the study's content.

Pictorial Maps.   Students can select picture maps to show countries related to the topic. An individual map can show pictures to represent sites and, as a border, print the titles of books about the topic read by the students.

Pictures.   Students may report through pictures and display each illustration in turn to emphasize certain points in a report.

Survey.   Students may report on a survey of favorite books on the topic—what the titles are, who read them, what is found in the books, and so on.

Q and A Game.   Students may review what they learned through an original question-and-answer game. To do this, they make an original game about the topic with questions related to the unit's content, discuss the way the game is played, and review the questions related to the topic. A master sheet with the answers may be prepared and placed with the game.

Show Three, Report on One.   A student displays three books related to the topic of study, reports from one of the three titles shown, and asks others to predict which book it is after hearing the report.

Time Line.   Students may refer to a time line on a class wall to show a time period for certain events and use points on the time line as a structure for giving information.

Twenty Questions.   Some may report in the form of *Twenty Questions* and engage others in the class in playing twenty questions. They should ask for information about the unit's content studied by the students.

Topic G: Preparing Props to Go with a Report

Props such as visual aids or sound effects can add to the students' reports. As an example of an effective sound effect, a teacher may ask students to make a quick drum roll before announcing the name of a reporting student. When the teacher says, "Drum roll, please," the students slap alternate hands on their knees quickly (while silently counting up to 10, then stopping). Other sound effects and props that add "punch" to student reports follow.

Audiovisuals.   With an overhead, the transparent scenery goes by. With a prehistoric background, the student shows movement related to a report (e.g., a dinosaur going up one side of a volcano and down the other).

A Dinosaur Award.   When reporting on a favorite dinosaur story, a student creates a "Dinosaur Award" and tells why the book is worthy of the award.

Box Story.   A student writes text, draws illustrations, and then uses tape to fasten the pages together in an accordion format. The last page is taped to the inside of the bottom of the box and the first page is taped to the inside of the top of the box. The top of the box is the book's cover and is illustrated. The box story is opened and displayed as the students gives a report on the story. Variations on this activity include the envelope story, the container story, and the paper plate story.

Box Movie and Box Television.   A student may make a box movie and change the time of day (making nighttime pictures generated from daytime scenes in a book); write word balloons with dialogue for characters in a cartoon strip format; or sketch characters on maps.

Clay Dinosaur Models.   With models of dinosaurs made of clay, students can show the stance, posture, and characteristics of a specific type of dinosaur as each type is discussed in the report.

Dinosaur Figure for Overhead.   Facts may be reported on a selected dinosaur with the use of a dinosaur figure on an overhead. To make the figure, a student traces the shape of a dinosaur on heavy paper and cuts out the shape. The dinosaur shape is fastened to thin paper (tissue or onion skin) and bent out (or bowed out) from the paper. The dinosaur head is fastened with paste or a staple. The student should look at the shape from a side view to see that the dinosaur shape bends out from the paper. Next, the student moves the legs and feet closer to the head and then staples the feet. The thin sheet is pasted to a frame ($9'' \times 8''$) similar to one that is put on transparencies. When ready to report on the dinosaur, the student places the frame on the stage of the overhead. A friend turns on a flashlight and moves the light in a figure 8 over the dinosaur figure. This light movement will make the dinosaur **appear** to move as the student tells the facts about the dinosaur, discusses his or her research, and gives an explanation about why the light movement makes the dinosaur appear to move.

Dinosaur "Report Lines" and Sound Effects.   To make a dinosaur report line, a student uses a clothesline and clothespins to pin up cards that have written headings that sequence the report. Additionally, sound effects made by friends in the "right places" will enhance the report.

Diorama.   Students can make a diorama to show a scene from fiction, nonfiction, or poetry. As a variation, an oversized page made from cardboard with a circular or oval cutout opening may be placed in front of the diorama to reveal the scene. For contrast, two dioramas may be made to show the difference between the days of the dinosaurs and present-day life.

Flip Page Story.   Students may make a story with pages that are slit into several long narrow rectangles to "flip" (turn over) to reveal illustrations underneath.

Graphic Organizers.   Sketches, characters outlines, and other shapes may be drawn by students on the board and used to display written information about the topic.

Mobiles.   Mobiles with figures and paper shapes can be assembled to give the information that will be featured in a report.

Mural.   A student can add emphasis to a report with a mural that shows ideas. Three-dimensional effects made with cloth samples, yarn, and wallpaper samples will add texture and make the scenes effective. When the scenes are taped together with masking tape and rolled on a discarded paper tube from wrapping paper, a student can unroll the mural as the report progresses.

Stick Puppets.   Students may give reports with a stick puppet character as the narrator or with stick figures of dinosaurs and other prehistoric animals who give parts of the report.

Topic H: Teacher Reports

News Events.   Related to their topic of study, students and the teacher meet and the teacher retells a news event with characters for the flannel or felt board created with three-dimensional designs. The designs are made with fabrics, trimmings, and sequins to create textures on the characters. With the lights dimmed, the teacher reports on a news item and accents the report with the felt board figures. For a surprise ending, the last figures shown are painted with glow-in-the-dark paint that shines (Zauder Bros.).

Newspaper Articles.   As an option, when the teacher gives a report about some recent information found in a news article, he or she can emphasize the important findings with glow-in-the-dark writing (Childcraft). With the lights dimmed, the teacher may report beside a special writing board that is placed centrally so all can see and the teacher writes key words and phrases from the report on it with an inexpensive laser-light pen (Toys to Grow On).

Closing a Study.   To review information the students have gained from the study and to add variety to a presentation, the teacher may introduce a glow-in-the-dark fossil bone (fossil replica painted with glow-in-the-dark paint [Zauder Bros.]) that is handed from student to student as information is shared. With lights dimmed so the fossil will "glow," students know it is their turn when they receive the fossil and it is time to tell at least one piece of information learned during the day's study. To take turns, the fossil is handed along from one student to another.

After the reports are given, the students should discuss, "What did this day's study make you think about?" After a whole-group discussion, each writes three best things he or she learned from the day's study. With a partner, they read and discuss their selections. The rule is that at least one idea from the partner must be added to the student's learning journals and mentioned to others in the total class when all get together for a final meeting of the day to close the study.

"The dinosaurs disappeared about 65 million years ago, no trace of them can be found after that time," reads the teacher from *Dinosaurs: A Lost World: A Pop-Up Book* by Keith Moseley. The students see the pictures of allosaurus (a powerful runner more than 30 feet long), parasaurolophus (a dinosaur with a crest on its head that curved backward like a horn), and their corresponding dinosaur skeletons in three-dimension "pop-up" pages. The teacher concludes, "And so, too, will our dinosaur study disappear since the clock shows we are going to have to end our study today."

Extensions for Chapter 4

1. *Consider the Core of Structure.*   Select one of the components in the Core of Structure and begin a thematic unit with the information you have on that component. Just choose a place to start and do it! Identify one of the projects you listed for a starting point—the project should be the one you intend to use first to begin the unit—and plan a class schedule or a calendar time line for it. Remember, the students will suggest other projects requiring some modification of the time schedule.

2. *Volunteer.*   Volunteer for one small section of the chapter and be ready to explain the material and relate the key points to a small group. If a class is divided into groups, one member of each group will have the responsibility for one of the assignment sections and will explain it to the other group members. As a group, design a chart for writing the main ideas and terms from the group discussion. Would you suggest this approach for reviewing

information about what was learned to students in the elementary school? What grade levels?

3. *Initiate paired reading with parents.* Parents may read along with their children in a book of the child's choosing and engage in paired reading. Introduce parents to this idea and ask them to participate in paired reading with their children for 5 minutes each day for 3 months. Parents may adjust their oral participation according to the difficulty that the child experiences (e.g., in the text where the child reads with fluency, the parent switches to silent reading and allows the child to read orally alone).

Resources

Childcraft. 20 Kilmer Road, Edison, NJ 08818. Glow-in-the-dark board; dinosaur bone replicas. All ages.

The Nature Company. PO Box 2310, Berkeley, CA 94702. Dinosaur globe. All ages.

Rainbow Morning Music. 2121 Fairland Road, Silver Spring, MD 20904. Book: *Dinosaurs I Have Known;* video: *I'm a 3-Toed, Triple Eyed, Double Jointed Dinosaur and Other Songs for Young Children.* Grades 1–3.

Toys To Grow On. PO Box 17, Long Beach, CA 90801. Laserlight pen & board # 758. All ages.

Zauder Bros., Inc. 10 Henry Street, Freeport, NY 11520. Glow-in-the-dark paint. All ages.

Readings

Cecil, N. L. (1989). *Freedom fighters: Affective teaching of the language arts.* Salem: Sheffield.

Cohen, E. (1978). *Student influence in the classroom.* Paper presented at the annual meeting of the American Educational Research Association, Toronto.

Cohen, E. (1979). *Status equalization in the desegregated school.* Paper presented at the annual meeting of the American Educational Research Association, San Francisco.

Cohen, E. (1990). Continuing to cooperate: Prerequisites for persistence. *Phi Delta Kappan.*

Cohen, E. G. (1986). *Designing groupwork strategies for the heterogeneous classroom.* New York: Teachers College Press.

Cohen, E. G., Lotan, R., & Catanzarite, L. (1984). Treating status problems in the cooperative classroom. In S. Sharon (Ed.), *Cooperative learning: Theory and research.* New York: Praeger.

Copeland, K. A. (1985). *The effect of writing upon good and poor writer's learning from prose.* ERIC Document Reproduction Service NO ED 276 993.

de Avila, E., Cohen, E., & Intili, J. K. (1981). *Multicultural improvement of cognitive abilities.* Final report of Contract No. 9372. Sacramento: State Department of Education. NIE Grant No. NIE-G078-0158.

Dowhower, S. L. (1989). Repeated reading: Research into practice. *The Reading Teacher,* 42 (7) (March): 502–507.

Emmer, E., Evertson, D., & Anderson, L. (1980). Effective classroom management at the beginning of the school year. *The Elementary School Journal,* 80 (5): 219–231.

Evertson, C. M., & Emmer, E. T. (1982). Effective management at the beginning of the school year in junior high classes. *Journal of Educational Psychology,* 74: 485–498.

Evertson, C. M., Emmer, E. T., Sanford, J. P., & Clements, B. S. (1983).

Improving classroom management: An experiment in elementary school classrooms. *The Elementary School Journal,* 84, (2): 172–188.

Forehand, G., & Ragosta, M. (1976). *Handbook for integrated schooling* Princeton, NJ: Educational Testing Service.

Harste, J. (1990). Jerry Harste speaks on reading and writing. *The Reading Teacher,* 43 (4) (January): 316–318.

Hoskisson, K., & Tompkins, G. (1987). *Language arts content and teaching strategies.* Columbus, OH: Merrill.

Jax, V. A. (1988). *Narrative construction by children learning English as a second language: A precursor to reading comprehension.* Ph. D. dissertation, University of California, Los Angeles. AAD88-22895. DAI: 49/08A: 2133.

Johnson, D. W., Johnson, R. T., & Maruyama, G. (1983). Interdependence and interpersonal attraction among heterogeneous and homogeneous individuals: A theoretical formulations and a meta-analysis of the research. *Review of Educational Research,* 53 (1): 5–54.

Johnson, R., & Johnson, S. (1971). *Assuring learning with self-instructional packages.* Chapel Hill, NC: Self-Instructional Packages.

Johnson, R. T., & Johnson, D. W. (1986). Action research: Cooperative learning in the science classroom. *Science and Children,* 24: 31–32.

Kellough, R. D., & Roberts, P. L. (1991). *A resource guide for elementary school teaching: Planning for Competence* (2nd ed.) New York: Macmillan.

MacKinnon, D. W. (1962). What makes a person creative? *Saturday Review* (February): 15–17.

Maria, K. (1989). Developing disadvantaged children's background knowledge interactively. *The Reading Teacher,* 42 (4) (January): 296–301.

Roberts, P. L. (1984). *Alphabet books as a key to language patterns.* Hamden, CT: Library Professional Publications.

Roberts, P. L. (1992). *Alphabet: A handbook of ABC books and activities for the elementary classroom* (2nd ed.). Metuchen, NJ: Scarecrow Press.

Rosenshine, B., & Stevens, R. (1986). Teaching functions. In M. C. Wittrock, (Ed.), *Handbook of research on teaching,* (3rd ed., pp. 376–391). New York: Macmillan.

Schmidt, J. (1990, Fall). Start your year with a Bill of Rights. In *The Whole Idea Newsletter* (p. 1). San Diego: The Wright Group.

Slavin, R. (1983). *Cooperative learning.* New York: Longman.

Slavin, R. E (1987). Ability grouping and student achievement in elementary schools: A best-evidence synthesis. *Review of Educational Research,* 57 (3) (1987): 213–255.

Smith, C. B. (1988). Does it help to write about your reading? *Journal of Reading,* 32 (2) 276–277.

Smith, C. B. (1989). Learning through writing. *The Reading Teacher* (November): 172–173.

Stephens, D. (1989). First graders taking the lead: Building bridges between literature and writing. *The New Advocate,* 2 (4) (Fall): 249–258.

Valeri-Gold, M. (1990). Back to basics: Getting parents involved. *Reading Today* (December/January): 24.

Vine, E. W. (1989). *Plot units in children's writing: A study of the development of story structure.* Ed. D. dissertation, University of Massachusetts. AAD90-11813 DAI: 50/12A: 3877.

Wells, D. (1988). *Literacy in a third grade whole language classroom.* Ph. D. dissertation, Arizona State University. AAD89-07745 DAI: 50/01 A: 76.

Wheeler, R., & Ryan, F. L. (1973). Effects of cooperative and competitive classroom environments on the attitudes and achievements of elementary school students engaged in social studies inquiry activities. *Journal of Educational Psychology,* 65: 402–407.

Chapter 5

How May I Integrate Social Studies and Expressive Arts?

Teacher Reflections for Chapter 5

Chapter 5 helps you choose ways to integrate a literacy curriculum with:

- Visual and performing arts and the social sciences (anthropology, economics, geography, history, political science, sociology) as a foundation for social studies, the emphasis on people and their relationship(s) in their social and natural environment
- Children's literature to support social studies/sciences and visual and performing arts
- The component in the Core of Structure to implement a thematic unit in literature-based instruction: Integrate Social Studies and Expressive Arts

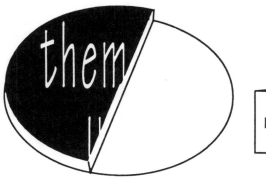

Component in Core of Structure to Implement a Thematic Unit for Literature-Based Instruction: Integrate Social Studies and Expressive Arts

Vignette in Combination Grade: All-Day Study

In this vignette, students in a fourth-fifth combination classroom use the content from science to recognize and evaluate data, generate hypotheses, draw conclusions, and make generalizations. The students are working in a social context (social sciences). Inquiry is a main focus as a teacher emphasizes the goals of developing knowledge and cultural understanding, developing democratic understanding and civic values, and developing participation skills related to effective citizenship and social action. Additional skills—study skills and critical thinking skills—related to the content and to the social context are also emphasized. Since specialists knowledgeable in the social studies/science disciplines are not always available in the classroom to answer students' questions, lines of inquiry provide them with ways to access information about a study topic. The following shows an all-day schedule of one way the students followed a line of inquiry.

All-Day Study

Period 1

Students' question: What were dinosaurs like?

Procedures (working in a social context):

- Students generate an hypothesis about dinosaurs in general. They refer to a dinosaur globe (Nature Company) to locate selected dinosaur fossil finds, discuss ways to find out about these animals, and study words used by paleontologists when they talk about dinosaurs.
- They write words about what they know (prior knowledge) from such sources as Kingdon's *The ABC Dinosaur Book* (Childrens, 1980) on the board: *reptiles, calm, gentle, fast, ferocious, variety, armor, crests, plant eaters, dinosaur eaters.*
- With a partner and the list of words, girls and boys discuss what can be inferred about dinosaurs from the words and then write three characteristics of dinosaurs (or about the life of these large creatures). They read aloud their characteristics to others. If interested, they illustrate their writing.

Period 2

Hypothesis: Students work in heterogeneous groups and write statement(s) describing what they think dinosaurs were like: "The dinosaurs were . . . ."

Procedures: Work in groups with roles of facilitator, peace maker, recorder, safety monitor, and others.

Periods 3 and 4

Testing hypothesis: Students identify evidence they would need to find if their guesses about dinosaurs are accurate.

Procedures: Working in groups, students consider: If you think dinosaurs are reptiles, then what evidence do you want to find to convince yourself that they really are reptiles? Ask yourself this same question for other characteristics about dinosaurs with: "If dinosaurs were . . . then I would expect to find evidence about. . . ."

• Given a filmstrip (video, film) about dinosaurs, students select one of their hypotheses to test, discuss what evidence they want to see in a filmstrip, and then look for evidence in the filmstrip.

• The facilitator projects the filmstrip slowly so students can comment on what they see. Sometimes the filmstrip is stopped so students can discuss evidence they observe. Notes about evidence are written and the filmstrip is reshown for checking purposes.

• After the showing, students discuss the hypothesis with others and determine evidence they have seen and what evidence they still need.

For discussion: "Were there any new characteristics found in the filmstrip that could become a new hypothesis for which one could find evidence?"

• Given a book about dinosaurs, students select another hypothesis to test, discuss evidence they expect to see in the book, and then look for evidence in other sources.

Period 5

Conclusion: Students read a newspaper article about dinosaurs and discuss anything they think might be inaccurate. They suggest ways to cross-check information.

Procecures: With other members, students suggest five characteristics of dinosaurs to write on the board. Students group similar characteristics together.

• They agree with others on a statement telling what dinosaurs were like and write a statement to tell major characteristics of dinosaurs and their way of life, such as: "From books and other sources I have read and seen, dinosaurs were . . . ."

Integrated math: Among the characteristics of dinosaurs the students discussed were the lengths and heights of the huge animals. Calling a "Ten-Minute Dinosaur Fact Hunt" before measuring lengths of dinosaurs on the school yard, the teacher asks each student to select a book and search further for information about sizes of dinosaurs or identified body parts. During the fact hunt, students read to discover lengths of dinosaurs, lengths and widths of body parts, and take notes on what they find. Students report their findings, go to the school yard, and measure lengths of string to equal some of the lengths, heights, and widths they have found in their reading.

Procedures back in the classroom: Students refer back to their measuring and to their original thoughts about dinosaurs they held at the beginning of the study.

• They discuss: How typical of all reptiles are dinosaurs? What can be done to find out more about this? What other groups of reptiles can be studied? They write reports about what was learned in pairs and tell what they recorded about their learning to others.

Integrating Social Sciences

Connecting Past to Present

Relating the prehistoric past to the present, students in the upper-elementary grades study some of the history of paleontologists and look at influences of fossil finds on human behavior and knowledge. Drawing from various disciplines, a unit on dinosaurs includes processes of learning from the social sciences and the areas of anthropology, geography, history, political science, psychology, and sociology. For instance, the students consider ways to preserve a dinosaur graveyard threatened by a new housing development or consider a related problem in their community (e.g., taking some social action to save an artifact location from being destroyed). In doing this, students see themselves and others as responsible citizens and part of a human community.

Topic A: Connecting with Disciplines

As the teacher, you will ask yourself questions about the way the unit is progressing to ensure that students have learned something from the different disciplines that support social sciences during their experiences. The following questions are examples to consider as you select activities and projects with students:

1. *Anthropology: How does a national or worldwide community of scientists organize and share information about fossil finds?*   To acquire information about fossil finds in a community, sixth-grade students visited a nearby museum of natural history. They prepared for a visit by looking at photographs of exhibits and people who work on them in *Auks, Rocks, and the Odd Dinosaur: Inside Stories from the Smithsonian's Museum of Natural History* (Crowell, 1985) and *Museum People* (Prentice-Hall, 1977), both by Peggy Thomson.

In class, students assembled dinosaur skeleton models, identified parts of the body in the model, labeled them, and discussed the skeletons with others. They researched information about the models. To recognize the country in which fossils of a particular dinosaur were found, they located sites of fossil finds with a dinosaur globe (Nature Company) then wrote descriptions of their work; labels were in English-Spanish and other languages used by the students. Using English-other language dictionaries, such as *Longman English-Chinese Photo Dictionary* (Longman, 1989) by Marilyn Rosenthal and Daniel Freeman, they worked with a primary English or a secondary English language partner. They shared ways information about dinosaurs was recorded in other languages. On a chart, they identified and wrote dinosaur words in languages of paleontologists from other countries. For example, in *Longman Photo Dictionary/Edicion Bilingue en Espanol* (Longman, 1990) by Rosenthal and Freeman, full-color illustrations showed numbered items above vocabulary lists in English/Spanish to assist the students, such as tooth/*diente;* mother/*madre;* tape measure/*cinta metrica;* brush/*brocha;* desert/*desierto;* rock/*piedra;* and egg/*huevo.*

2. *Economics: What kinds of work are done by others to bring us information we need about our topic of study?*   With the question, How could we find out which states have state dinosaur fossils?, students in a fifth-grade class divided into study groups named for different kinds of dinosaurs (e.g., protoceratops Andrewsii, named in honor of Roy Andrews who first discovered nests of protocer-

atops). They discussed the kinds of work done by others to bring them information they needed about the topic. They talked about parts of the economy related to the topic—jobs held by workers in museums, sculptors, designers of exhibits, and manufacturers of vehicles, tools, camping supplies, equipment, products, and clothing used by paleontologists—and recorded what they found.

3. *Geography: How has geography influenced what we know about fossils?* "You don't have to travel far to find books that will help prepare students for a geography bee," writes Roberts (1989). To get ready for a geography bee with a focus on fossil finds, fourth-grade students read references and other resources, studied maps, and looked at illustrations and photographs. On the hunt for facts about past worlds, they consulted *Hammond Past Worlds: The Times Atlas of Archaeology* (Hammond, 1988), an atlas that covers a time period from 16 million B.C. to the mid-1800s and includes pictures of reconstructions of ancient buildings on ancient sites. Continental drift, the idea of continents creeping across the earth's surface after being together in a super continent called Pangaea, authentic maps, diagrams, and numbered small inserts as keys were found in John Stideworthy's *The Day of the Dinosaurs* (Silver Burdett, 1986) and small world maps showing animal habitats, facts, and figures were located in *Kenneth Lilly's Animals: A Portfolio of Paintings* (Lothrop, Lee & Shepard, 1988). For answers to current questions about the United States, the third edition of Sue R. Brandt's *Facts about the Fifty States* (Watts, 1988) was selected. These books and others were of value to the students because questions in the bee required knowledge of names of countries, places where fossils were found, and regions. During the bee, students identified by name the places shown to them on unlabeled maps and in books, slides, and posters. Interested in showing what they had learned, the students organized a local competition in their school and invited other classes to join in. For another project, the students wrote for maps of states from the American Association of Geologists (PO Box 979, Tulsa, OK 74101). Some of the states recognized dinosaurs: Colorado had a stegosaurus as a state dinosaur; Nevada had an ichthyosaur; and Massachusetts honored its dinosaur tracks.

To relate a *sense of place* from a map to the literacy curriculum, the students also engaged in the five I's: imaging, interacting, introducing, innovating, and illustrating. When *imaging,* students first thought of a sense of place found on a map, imagined it, and listed objects and actions they thought they imagined. When *interacting,* they talked with partners about their word lists and imagined ideas. When *introducing* ideas through writing, they discussed choices for leads—opening sentences for writing. When *innovating* their ideas, they composed a description of an imagined place. When *illustrating,* students turned their stories into a book format and completed their publications about geography with illustrations, cardboard covers, proofreading, and final editing.

To demonstrate map skills, the students showed their ability to recognize a symbol's use (Reproducible 11); demonstrated their ability to recognize the use of a nonpictorial symbol (Reproducible 12); and used a key for map reading (Reproducible 13).

4. *History: How has a community changed over time in ways we receive information about the past?* Students in a third grade interviewed elderly people they knew and traced the history of ways people received information in the time of their grandparents and compared what happened then with ways people receive information today.

5. *Political science: How does a scientific community organize itself to study prehistoric life and to provide information about that time period?* On a trip to a nearby library, sixth-grade students found telephone books from other cities and located needed information by looking through them. They located names

and addresses of regional museums and exhibits so they could send written letters of inquiry.

At the British Natural History Museum, scientists have provided information about relationships among animals in the book *Dinosaurs and Their Living Relatives* (British Museum of Natural History, 1985) and observations about present-day animals for a reader to use to work out relationship(s) among dinosaurs. Interested in this, some students wrote to the museum for permission to take slides of the illustrations to display how dinosaurs were related to other animals, living and extinct. A pre-show discussion took place before the slides were viewed and the students classified each of several dinosaurs as either *bird hipped* or *lizard hipped*. After the students did this, they viewed the slides and discussed what was seen so that the problems that scientists have in classifying prehistoric animals were reviewed. With the information they got from the slides, the students talked about ways their thoughts changed about the paleontologist's work and ways animals were typed from fossil finds. Relying on the information from the slides, the students saw a method for working out relationships among animals and used their knowledge about present-day animals to work out hypothesized relationship(s) among the dinosaurs. To engage in this further, the students grouped similar living things together and considered animals that shared a common feature. Using this grouping arrangement, they assumed that animals in a group were related through a common ancestor. And of course, the students' questions led to further searches in other informational paragraphs, bibliographies, glossaries, indices, and other features of reference books.

6. *Sociology: What community groups operate to bring us information about fossils?* Students in a fifth grade considered several projects: they could write to state parks and exhibits for free information about dinosaurs; they could write to DINAH (Vernal, UT 84978) and send a legal-sized self-addressed stamped envelope to get a Dinosaur (fossil) Hunting License; or they could invite a resource person to class (a ranger from a park or an area where fossils have been found) to discuss dinosaurs of the past and endangered animal species of the present. To emphasize findings in countries other than the United States, they could correspond with paleontologists such as Phil Curry, Don Brinkman, and Dale Russell (Tyrell Museum, Alberta, Canada) and Dong Zhiming (Beijing, China).

7. *Social action view: In what way can students participate to resolve a real problem in the community?* To engage in social action, sixth-grade students considered an action related to their community and to their points of view. They could:

a. Write to a legislative representative to ask for a dinosaur as a state fossil.

b. Discuss a current endangered species and the problems encountered, and suggest social actions.

c. Discuss the problem of our environment and suggest social actions.

d. Participate to resolve a real problem in the community and learn about some available community services.

To start a discussion about this, a teacher showed a video of ethnic children talking with a young female ranger in *Exploring the Forest* (Alfred Higgins Productions, 1989) about caring for forests, logging, and the importance of trees to early settlers. For students interested in ideas and efforts to save rain forests, excerpts from *Jungle Rescue: Saving the New World Tropical Rain Forests* (Atheneum, 1991) by Christina Miller and Louise Berry were read aloud. This book told of the plight of Central and South American rain forests and had sources for future study. The teacher engaged students in using green toothpicks arranged to scale on a styrofoam base to represent a certain number of trees to an acre. As the teacher introduced causes of destruction to a rain forest (e.g., clearing one acre by bulldozers), students removed the number of toothpicks equivalent to an acre to see the effects.[1]

Topic B: Connecting with the Community

1. *Recognizing available community services.* How will students learn about available community services? A way to introduce students to services in the community is to relate the content being studied to resources and workers in the community (libraries, parks, natural history museums). In a study of dinosaurs, a fourth-grade teacher invited each student to adopt a dinosaur and its habitat (woods, stream) and explore and study the selected animal by contacting some community services in the study:

a. Students were introduced to a children's librarian who discussed a variety of dinosaurs and their connection with birds in nonfiction works. They discussed parts of a book, the value of each part, and ways to get information. Taking notes from their reading fostered the students' study of dinosaurs and their habitat.

b. After writing their notes (reminders about what they have read) about habitat, the students talked with a scientist in the area about an animal's adaptation to its habitat. To follow up on the information about an animal's adaptation, each wrote a dinosaur's name on a chart, located information about the dinosaur, and made hypotheses about the ways the animal adapted. Students' reports included information about the topic and information about the selected illustration process—collage, crayon drawings, watercolors, and finger painting.

For information purposes, some students selected Tweedle's *The World of Dinosaurs* (Weidenfeld & Nicolson, 1977) and Troll's illustrated series with titles of *The Giant Dinosaurs, Last of the Dinosaurs, Flying Dragons,* and *Sea Monsters* (all Troll, 1980). For elaboration about taking notes for reports, *How to Write a Great School Report* (Lothrop, Lee & Shepard, 1983) by Elizabeth James and Carol Barkin was used as a reference. James and Barkin's matrix format shows students ways to record notes about warm-blooded dinosaurs, draw conclusions, and develop an outline about "Were Dinosaurs Warm-Blooded?" The students illustrated their individual reports with their own illustrations or with illustrations from newspapers and magazines. Students were encouraged to place titles under illustrations to show they knew how to use captions as a way of giving additional details to readers.

c. To integrate their study with processes of art, the students wrote to a paleontologist and asked about ways the scientist used art in his or her work. They created their own invented and imagined equipment needed by a present-day dinosaur fossil hunter, made a exhibit of tools and invented some for the future, and created a dinosaur and fossil hunter museum.

d. A dinosaur assembly was the culmination for the study. Students suggested resource people to visit the classroom: an expert on paleontology, a librarian, an artist, and a photographer to show pictures of fossils. The students discussed ways these individuals should be contacted and other preparations for the visit(s).

2. *Meeting elected officials.* How will students meet elected officials willing to work with students to solve problems? To arrange a meeting, fourth-grade students considered what would be needed to start their own class campaign to ask their state to honor a state dinosaur fossil. Questions for their group discussions included: What would they need to have before selecting a fossil? Who were specialists to write to, talk to, and get advice from about this matter? In what way did a bill become a law? Who did they want to invite to class to tell them about

this process? Who were their state senators who could introduce a bill? Who else could students write to or call about this interest? What other arrangements or contacts with the community could be made? How could they find answers to these questions?

Topic C: Connecting in the Classroom

To reinforce ideas about the study to students, engage in activities related to understanding others, such as the following:

1. *Communicating feelings to others.* How will students learn ways to communicate their feelings to others? Although an activity of point and counterpoint might occur at any grade, most teachers begin to introduce debates in fourth grade. In a sixth-grade class, debates were one communicative approach the students used to communicate their feelings. During a study, they considered these topics: Birds and archosaurs *are* related versus birds and archosaurs *are not* related, and Birds and crocodiles *are* related versus birds and crocodiles *are not* related.

2. *Understanding people and events of other times.* In what ways can people, places, and events of other times become real to the students? To make events of other times become real, exciting dramas can unfold about time periods, fossil discovery, and the fossil hunters. In a third-grade class, a form of drama often used was pantomime, where the students silently acted out various actions from scenes on pantomime cards. Another form was roleplay, where the students discussed the information they needed before they played roles of fossil hunters such as Jim Jensen, Robert Owen, Mary Ann Mantell, and others.

3. *Reading biographies.* Fictionalized biographies, autobiographies, or biographical narratives make events of other times real and lead to reading and writing. To assist students in writing biographies, a fourth-grade teacher read aloud from material about dinosaur hunters every day for one to two weeks. Then for a two-week period, the students studied the life of a selected dinosaur hunter as a topic. They independently read material about the hunter (sometimes from the sources the teacher used) and recorded their reactions in their journals. As a project, they wrote their own original fictionalized biographies about the hunter. Using writing as a way to learn more about dinosaur hunters and paleontology, the teacher scheduled several activities:

a. Seeing filmstrips of their choice, students worked with partners and took notes on what they learned.

b. Creating original questions and answers from material in filmstrips and other sources, the students wrote in journals. Gathering into study groups, they asked their questions of other members.

c. Reading about his or her topic of interest, each student wrote sentences about it, revised the writing with a partner's help, and then prepared a final copy.

d. After seeing other films, filmstrips, or videos on the topic, each student wrote a descriptive paragraph, used notes, and checked information with others in the class.

e. Each student wrote a question he or she wanted answered and researched the answer in classroom and library materials. Each wrote a paragraph to fully answer the question.

f. A last draft was proofread by another student for spelling, punctuation, and capitalization.

g. For a final project, the written work, illustrations, and models were displayed in the classroom on a day called "Dinosaur Fossil Hunter Day."

4. *Thinking critically.* How do students show they think critically, have their assumptions challenged, formulate questions, and generate opinions? To generate opinions, third-grade students experienced things as well as learned about things as they went outside the class. They engaged in reading, writing, speaking, and listening opportunities and developed oral histories of fossil finders. They interviewed people at a nearby science exhibit/museum, reported real-life research about beliefs held by community/school members, and published their collections of materials. They became reporters, question askers, and agents, gathering information as they approached their community. They observed, explored, questioned, collected, analyzed, and took notes about their study.

To assist the students as they began to distinguish between observing data and drawing inferences, the teacher challenged the students' assumptions and introduced the terms *bird hipped* and *lizard hipped*. The teacher asked students for their responses about the terms and then wrote on the board characteristics of each type of dinosaur suggested by the students. Students also wrote this information in their learning logs. Then a book (filmstrip, slides) about types of dinosaurs was shown to see the extent to which information contradicted or supported students' opinions. A selected book was Lambert's *Dinosaurs* (Rourke, 1982) that included a dinosaur family tree with bird-hipped examples (stegosaurs, triceratops, iguandon) and lizard-hipped examples (brachiosaurus, tyrannosaurus, compsognathus). Others were *A First Look at Dinosaurs* (Walker, 1982) by Millicent E. Selsam and Joyce Hunt and *The Largest Dinosaurs* (Macmillan, 1986) by Seymour Simon. In the first, skeletons and hips with parallel bones were shown for the bird-hipped group and nonparallel bones shown for the lizard-hipped group. In the second, the focus was six lizard-hipped stone-swallowing saurapods. Notes were taken as students saw and heard information from the books' presentations. In a follow-up discussion, the students were involved with deduction: "The dinosaur fossil you found had small parallel hip bones. Since you know that some dinosaurs had parallel hip bones (bird-hipped group) and others had nonparallel hip bones, you predict that this dinosaur fossil must be related to the bird-hipped group." Observed by the teacher, the girls and boys showed they were thinking critically as they talked about the contradictions they found in the content material.

5. *Categorizing words.* How may students categorize words? Second-grade students categorized words about the topic and built a word resource, "Categorizing Words," for word choices to use during their writing (Reproducible 14). Students imagined a "Dinosaur Word Dig" as a sand dune filled with words about dinosaurs. They filled in the dune with words they chose. At any time, students could "dig in" and get words for their writing. To show this visually, students designed sand dunes on art paper for individual "Word Digs" and wrote in the words in any arrangement and made as many categories as they wanted. Resources they used included the *Rourke Dinosaur Dictionary* (Rourke, 1989) and *The Illustrated Encyclopedia of Dinosaurs* (Crescent/Crown, 1985).

6. *Looking for main ideas.* How may students look for main ideas? With their teacher, third-grade students looked at a large illustration and offered the main idea of the illustration. After discussing the main idea, they looked for details in the picture that supported the idea. For instance, when Illustrations from *Dinosaurs: A Lost World* were shown, students saw one double-page spread showing the relative size of a brachiosaurus when it was compared to a giraffe, rhinoceros, elephant, and hippopotamus. As students looked at the picture, they suggested a main idea and the details they saw. After showing the illustration on an opaque projector, the teacher passed the book around to give students an opportunity to see the illustrations more closely and then asked students to write in their choices for a main idea and details that supported it (Reproducible 15). Other dinosaur

illustrations were shown and the main idea and supporting details found in each illustration were discussed. Using students' words about each illustration, the teacher recorded students' words in a format on the board to show the main idea/supporting details.

Main Idea:_____

Supporting Details:

1. _____

2. _____

3. _____

As students' suggestions for a main idea and supporting details were written by the teacher, they also wrote their ideas in their social sciences journals. Later, they divided into teams of two, selected their favorite dinosaur books from their desks, and turned to an illustration in one of them. Their team task was to look closely at it and to determine the main idea and some supporting details for the illustration. One team member was a facilitator and safety helper; the other was a recorder and materials' helper. When the main idea and details were recorded for this illustration, the team members selected a second illustration, then a third, and so on. When the students regrouped, each team showed one of the illustrations to the rest of the class and announced the main idea and supporting details determined by the team.

7. *Analyzing and outlining information.* How may students analyze information and outline it? Before a study, fifth-grade students prepared semantic maps to show their knowledge about dinosaurs prior to the study. Using one of the maps, the teacher mentioned that grouping information was as easy as knowing the ABCs. Using the concept of an *A* group, a *B* group, and a *C* group of related ideas and words, the teacher encouraged students to identify related ideas by marking on the semantic map on the board any words and phrases related in some way with *A* (or *B*, or *C*). Students made decisions aloud about the relationships and followed along with a teacher's demonstration about using all the *A* words and ideas (*B* words and ideas, *C* words and ideas) to prepare an outline (with Reproducible 15). The outline became a reference for writing paragraphs as a whole group.

8. *Organizing ideas for writing.* How may students organize ideas for writing? When some third-grade students needed assistance in organizing ideas for nonfiction writing, they used a compare-contrast organizer, a Venn Diagram, to help them organize information. In two overlapping circles (circle *A* and circle *B*), students wrote notes about observations they had gathered from two different books (book *A* and book *B*). Observations that were the same in both books were written in the overlapping area (intersection) of the circles. Observations from book *A* that were *different* from book *B* were recorded in the remaining portion of circle *A;* observations from book *B* that were *different* from book *A* were recorded in the remaining portion of circle *B*. This compare-contrast organizer was used as a reference tool when the students wrote their nonfiction paragraphs about what was different and what was similar in books *A* and *B*.

9. *Summarizing material in writing.* How may students summarize material in writing? Sixth-grade students summarized their study with a discussion around this focus question: What possible roles could students take when writing from a viewpoint other than their own? This meant each student would summarize the

unit from one of several points of view. Thus, a summary was written to someone other than the teacher, was about the topic of study, was in another interesting format (e.g., a conversation among two or more people, a newspaper article, a travel brochure, a long telephone conversation, a script of a play, and so on). When discussing this, a teacher allowed plenty of time for students to talk about different possibilities.

a. Should one write from a dinosaur's viewpoint? From a view of a tree in the Age of Dinosaurs? From a view of a scientist living today? From a view of a farmer who discovers a fossil?

b. Who could students write to? What aspect of the topic of dinosaurs could be selected?

c. In which format do students want their writing to take place—friendly letters, news articles, outlines, reports?

When decisions were made, the students developed their writing from a viewpoint other than their own point of view, they wrote to someone other than the teacher, and they used a form different from the usual paragraph.

10. *Summarizing end of a lesson.* How may students summarize at the end of a lesson? At the end of a class period emphasizing the content, sixth-grade students listed three interesting (or important) ideas about the lesson and then joined with another student to discuss their entries on the lists. After discussion, each partner added one idea from the other's list to his or her own list. Returning to the total group, each student reported which idea was added to her or his list and the reason why the idea was added.

Topic D: Connecting with Topics in Social Sciences

Topics[2] such as the ones that follow can be centers of a social sciences curriculum integrated with a literacy curriculum. Specific sections of literature and other resources (films, computer software, audiovisual materials) will enrich the study. Learning includes the participation of students in civic activities, community service, debates, developing individual or local histories, mapping activities, roleplaying, simulations, and cooperative learning activities. In the following section, guidelines from a curriculum guide[3] are selected to show how the topics could be implemented through a selected theme in a literature-based classroom:

Primary Grades

Kindergarten: *Families at work now and long ago.*   To build sensitivity toward others and to become aware of cultural diversity, students may be introduced to rhymes, tales, and stories that show values and conflicts from times in the past and in working together now.

Books: *Activity:*   Ask students to discuss the dilemma of working/ not working together in Guy Gilchrist's *Thanks a Lot, Tricerator: A Tiny Dinos Story about Helping Others* (Warner, 1988), a Children's Choice selection. While Tot plays, Rex rakes leaves. In return, should Rex help Tot later when a purple baboon occupies Tot's space? Discuss the idea that the author has personified the dinosaur character by asking, "What does the author want to tell us?" Encourage the students to substitute the name and personality of a real child into the story and discuss what happens when children don't work together.

Activity: To see similarities in stories, ask students to compare "The Tortoise and the Hare" found in *Aesop's Fables* (Viking, 1981) by Heidi Holder with Guy Gilchrist's *Plateo's Big Race: A Tiny Dinos Story about Learning* (Warner, 1988). In the story, a plateosaurus loses a foot race because he cannot read road signs.

Activity: Invite students to write a story about Plateo's race with a pattern from Judith Viorst's book, *Alexander and the Terrible Horrible No Good Very Bad Day* (Atheneum, 1972). Use this pattern: At the start of the race, Plateo_____. Plateo could tell it was going to be a Terrible Horrible No Good Very Bad race. In the middle of the race, Plateo_____. Plateo could tell it was going to be a Terrible Horrible No Good Very Bad race. At the end of the race, Plateo_____. Plateo could tell it was going to be a Terrible Horrible No Good Very Bad race.

First Grade: *Children in time and space.* To build sensitivity to the neighborhood and to community services such as a natural history museum, students may be introduced to realistic fiction and nonfiction that shows values in neighborhood and community services working together now in the United States and other countries.

Books: *Activity:* To find out ways exhibits and collections in natural history museums are designed, ask students to listen to *Dinosaurs, Dragonflies, and Diamonds: All about Natural History Museums* (Four Winds, 1988) by Gail Gibbons. Ask students to explain some of the information they heard to their literature group.

Second Grade: *People who make a difference.* To build sensitivity to people who supply our needs, to our ancestors of long ago, and to people from many cultures who have made contributions, students may be introduced to stories that show values and contributions from times in the past and in current times.

Books: *Activity:* After reading Mary Brooke Casad's *Bluebonnet at Dinosaur Valley State Park* (Pelican, 1989), students retell to others some of the ways Bluebonnet, a bonneted armadillo, tries to keep visitors in Dinosaur Valley State Park from discovering a prehistoric armadillo ancestor.

Third Grade: *Continuity and change.* When do we continue our traditions and when do we change our traditions? To build sensitivity to our past and our traditions and to meet everyday folks as well as heroines and heroes, students are introduced to biography, folktales, legends, songs, and realistic stories.

Books: *Activity:* Introduce students to 80-year-old Julia Creath Summerwaite in Conrad's (1989) *My Daniel* (Harper & Row, 1989). Summerwaite shares memories of her brother's work with her grandchildren when she flies to New York to visit her son's family.

Intermediate Grades

Fourth
Grade:

Our changing state.   To bring state history and geography to life, students focus on regional geography of the state; its people and their ethnic, racial, and cultural diversity; and its past and its current status. Students may be introduced to fiction and nonfiction that show cultural diversity from times in the past and in current times.

Books:

Activity: To interest students in map functions, introduce *As the Crow Flies* (Bradbury, 1991) by Gail Hartman or *One Day in the Tropical Rain Forest* (Crowell, 1990) by Jean Craighead George, a story of Tepui, an Indian boy. Tepui leads a scientist to find a previously unknown butterfly and helps stop destructive bulldozers attacking a forest on Venezuela's Orinoco River.

Fifth Grade:

Our nation's history and geography.   To develop awareness of our nation's development, students may be introduced to fiction and nonfiction that show our nation's development from times in the past and in current times.

Books

Activity: *Basics of Geography* (United Learning), for grades 4–8, is reviewed with filmstrips, a teacher's guide, and blackline masters for students to learn: (1) differences between maps and globes and ways to locate places with *Places and How to Find Them;* (2) observations about living patterns (housing, occupations) affected by water and climate; (3) effects of water and climate on people from *Water-Climate and Patterns of Living;* (4) land types and their effects on people, along with pro-con arguments of humans' use of natural resources in *Land Forms and Patterns of Living;* and (5) observations related to the concept of global interdependence and the world as regions to help better understand our world's people and places in which they live in *Organizing by Regions.*

Sixth Grade:

Our world's history and geography.   To understand people and events leading to major Western and non-Western civilizations, students may be introduced to fiction and nonfiction that show people and events related to major Western and non-Western civilizations. For example, hunting for fossils of dinosaurs is an event continuing today in *Dinosaurs Down Under: And Other Fossils from Australia* (Clarion, 1990) by Caroline Arnold with its introduction to fossils (amphibians, birds, dinosaurs) exhibited in a museum's show, "Kadimakara: Fossils of the Australian Dreamtime," displayed at Los Angeles Museum of Natural History in 1988.

Books:

Activity: To discover what vertebrate fossils have been found, read aloud Caroline Arnold's *Dinosaurs Down Under: And Other Fossils from Australia.* Ask students to each select a fossil to draw and write about in their journals. They tell what they have learned about vertebrate fossils.

Activity: To get acquainted with various field guides before visits to a nearby museum of natural history, students review Diagram Group's *A Field Guide to Dinosaurs* (Avon, 1983), a book that groups dinosaurs by their scientific classification and tells how to find out what creature lived when and Halstead's *Collins Gem Guide: Dinosaurs and Prehistoric Life* (Collins, 1989), a small-sized guide with observations from fossil records that fits in a pocket.

Activity: Students can link back to the past with *Discover: Mysteries of the Past and Present* (Kids Can Press, 1990) by Katherine Grier and learn what scientists and historians do through cleaning skeletons of small chickens and doing other projects.

Activity: For a version of dinosaurs' family tree, students may study Lambert's *A Field Guide to Dinosaurs: The First Complete Guide to Every Dinosaur Now Known* (Galahad, 1982) and compare the dinosaur family tree with another they find. What is different? Alike?

Audiovisuals   *Activity:* To establish relationships with places, students (grades 4–6) view videos *Finding Your Way: Using Maps and Globes* (Rainbow Educational Video), *Mapping Your World* (National Geographic), and *Using Maps, Globes, Graphs, Tables, Charts, Diagrams: A Video-Based Unit of Study* (United Learning); and filmstrips, *Themes of Geography I and II* and *Using a Classroom Atlas, Location, Place, Relationship within Places, Movement, and Regions.*

Integrating Expressive Arts

In an integrated literature-based unit, composing processes in expressive arts can be powerful meaning-making vehicles when processes engage children in dramatizing, creating music, singing, reading and writing poetry, story telling, drawing, painting, and sketching.

Through a study of content, a teacher is concerned with the students' abilities and sensitivities about creating art forms, understanding expressive arts, making judgments about the arts, and appreciating the work going into expressive art forms. Students can use a variety of art forms to read, write, speak, listen, visualize, and think creatively. This variety includes recognizing artworks by portrait painters and landscape painters since such works can be used as starting points in writing poetry, building character sketches, and writing in journals. Further, the artworks help students in building vocabulary and in researching the use of a symbol (such as the dragon) that can be found in art and literature from several countries. Students may visit museums to tie art to writing and reading of literature.

As an example of infusing expressive arts in a second-grade class,[4] a unit began with a talk about fossils (what they are and what they mean to humans) and a field trip to the school yard to find replicas of dinosaur fossil bones (Childcraft) that had been buried by older students from another class the previous day. The unit continued with a study of dinosaur objects collected from the environment. For instance, from an offer on the back of a well-known cereal box, dinosaur skeletons were collected by the teacher and students. The skeleton diagrams (with the numbering of all of the bones) were used as puzzles for students to put together.

Basic observations about fossils and where the fossils were found were discussed after listening to *Come with Me* science audiotapes. First, the girls and boys heard one tape about a dinosaur type. They then brainstormed the observations they heard and wrote them on the board. They listened to other observations read aloud and then added the additional information they had heard during listening time.

Infusing reading with music, the children listened to a song about the dinosaur being studied. The teacher displayed sentence strips with the words of the song. The teacher used sentence strips of colored paper of purple, red, black, and green because the sentences on different colors alerted the students to the totality of each sentence. Students listened and read the word-strips together. Then they added sound effects (such as repeats of thunder), sang the song again, and kept the rhythmic beat by tapping with their hands and fingers.

As an introduction to publishing, the students prepared their own dinosaur-shaped books. The students prepared their own pages and wrote observations on the pages. Before illustrating their pages, they reviewed the steps for a directed drawing from the *Come with Me* science material. To draw a brontosaurus, they read:

Step 1: Draw a circle for the body and a circle for the head.
Step 2: Draw the neck and tail.
Step 3: Draw the legs.
Step 4: Finish the body.
Step 5: Draw the features.
Step 6: Draw something about the habitat.
Step 7: Put it in your original book and add a sentence.

Two of their favorites—tyrannosaurus rex and triceratops—did not have drawing directions in the science material, so the teacher wrote the steps for drawing these dinosaurs for the students to follow.

For independent study, the students looked at the question-and-answer arrangement in *Dinosaurs* (Doubleday, 1987) by David Cohen. They each selected one question and answer to read aloud to someone. Several questions-answers were recorded on an audiotape. One student was encouraged to be a tape technician—to push the record button and turn the tape over when needed and to label the tape and place it with the book in the listening center. After a week, the student erased the tape and the students used it to record more questions and answers.

Five dinosaurs were studied. After the last one had been read about, sung about, and talked about, the unit was culminated by making dinosaur mobiles. To make dinosaur body shapes for the mobile, students cut shapes from colored felt and punched the felt edges with a one-hole paper punch to make holes for lacing. Filled with plyfill material (one bag filled 30 shapes), the shapes were decorated and laced. Clay models of dinosaurs were also made. The models were glazed and fired in preparation for Open House—a night when parents and children visit the school to talk to the teacher, discuss the learning of the children, and look at displays of the children's work. For Open House, each student's "homework" was to bring an adult from home to the classroom and to tell what he or she was learning at school to that person. When the students arrived with their "homework," they walked back to the classroom book corner, showed the pages of their original books, and talked about the trade books they liked. They looked at the pictures in *The Berenstain Bears and the Missing Dinosaur Bone* (Random House, 1976) by Stan and Jan Berenstain and in Daniel Cohen's *Dinosaurs*—two of the teacher's read-alouds. They told their visitors about their experiences in finding bone replicas in a school ground dig, listening to audiotapes about dinosaur observations, and their other activities.

Topic A: Creating, Understanding, and Appreciating Art Forms

Several books about dinosaurs have illustrations by artists who are paleontologists or who have worked closely with paleontologists. For example, Patricia Lauber, in *The News about Dinosaurs* (Bradbury, 1988), selected up-to-date paintings and drawings of dinosaurs by paleontologists and their close associates and included the works of Gregory S. Paul, Douglas Henderson, Mark Hallett, John Gurche, and Robert T. Bakker. The works of Hallett, Gurche, and Paul are also seen in the Los Angeles Museum of Natural History. Laurence Pringle, in *Dinosaurs and Their World* (Harcourt Brace Jovanovich, 1968), included illustrations from other museums and the illustrations show the art of Charles R. Knight, his restoration work, and an early painting, "Notice of the Iguanodon" by Gideon Mantell (1825). Edward Radlauer, in *Dinosaur Mania* (Childrens, 1979), selected full-color pictures by Mary Butler, an illustrator for the Natural History Museum in Los Angeles. All of these paintings extend and clarify an elementary student's understanding of the topic and can be integrated into a unit. Further, with the book *What Were Dinosaurs?* (Lerner, 1991) by Kunkhiko Hisa and Sylvia A. Johnson, an analogy can be made between dinosaur artists and paleontologists to show both are people who interpret fossil evidence in different ways. The analogy is an interesting way for students to review current information and visualize facts. As examples of expressive arts, museum paintings and exhibits are valuable sources to engage the students in reflecting about artworks. To assess students' understanding of art forms, a teacher may consider the following:

1. *Recognizing selected works.* To recognize selected artworks on the topic of dinosaurs, these reproductions can be shown (McKean, 1986):

a. "Protoceratops" by artist Bill Stout shows a family scene from the past with a dozen six-foot long dinosaurs sleeping together under the stars.

b. Mark Hallet's composite scene of some long-distance travelers—an allosaurus and various other Australian dinosaurs from different times—is titled "Australian Dinosaurs."

c. "A Clash of Bones" by Mark Hallet shows aggressiveness with two pachycephalosaurus fighting and charging with their helmeted heads.

d. "Tryannosaurus" by Gregory Paul shows an open-jawed beast traveling rapidly over marshy land.

e. "Maiasura Peeblesorum" by Gregory Paul is a fossil nest—a maisaura hatchery.

To further understand the use of color and lines by the above artists in creating powerful paintings, students can engage in the following activities.

Students in a second grade are shown Bill Stout's painting of dinosaurs sleeping together under the stars and Mark Hullet's composite scene of the allosaurus and other dinosaurs. Ask students to predict which one is the night scene. Call attention to the use of colors. Have students place objects from the room in daylight and in shade to find out ways the colors change. Then, based on their observations about color, ask students who chose the painting of the dinosaurs under the stars as the night scene to support their selection based on what they have observed.

Show students "Clash of Bones" and ask them to comment on the appearance of the two pachycephalosaurus and respond to the question, "Why do they look so long?" Point out the band of horizontal lines used in the painting. Also draw attention to the extension of the two bodies to the edge of the painting.

Show students "Tyrannosaurus" by Gregory Paul and ask them to comment on the size and the movement of the large dinosaur. Ask, "What does the artist tell us about the movement of the huge creature? Is it moving quickly or slowly?

What makes you think so? Is it a large dinosaur? How did the artist make to look so large? What did he do to make it look like it is moving?" Draw attention to the proportion of the dinosaur to the total painting. Help the students observe the use of horizontal lines in the horizon, the plants, and the clouds.

Remind students of the use of horizontal lines, proportion, and use of colors as they draw, paint, and create original artworks such as murals and collage composition.

2. *Exploring characteristics of an artist.* How will students develop a knowledge of art history? Students in grades 5 or 6 listen to excerpts from *Looking at Beasties* (Childrens, 1977) by J. Behrens or from *Just Imagine: Ideas in Painting* (Scribner's, 1982) by R. Cummings. They view *The Magic Gallery* (EVI) to explore characteristics of an artist or a movement with representative works, and later, create art objects in that genre (grades 2–6). For a further emphasis on elements of art with explanations of how paintings, sculptures, prints,and drawings are made, students react to Lippincott's *Art for Children* series (1990) by Ernest Raboff. To discuss works of great artists, students read *Getting to Know the World's Greatest Artists* series (Childrens, 1989) by Mike Venezia. With this, students get acquainted with such artists as da Vinci, Picasso, and Rembrandt. Further, the *Art Play* series (Abrams) offers single-book versions focusing on a single painting or artwork. This series includes *Kandinsky: Sky Blue* (Abrams, 1990) by Max-Henri de Larminat; *Picasso: The Minotaur* (Abrams, 1988) by Daniele Giraudy; and *Delaunay: The Eiffel Tower* (Abrams, 1988).

3. *Customs, costumes, music, and dance come together in an artistic work.* How will students write scripts? Compose music? Design sets? Stage and produce? To see one way a country's customs, costumes, music, and dance come together in an artistic work, invite students in the primary grades to review a video, *Billy Goat's Bluff* (Beacon Films, 1989). With voices of Vesnyvka Girls Choir adding to the presentation, this Ukrainian folktale begins when a father agrees to purchase a frisky goat, Ivan, for his son Peter. Ivan is ill mannered and runs away to Sister Fox's house when faced with punishment. Hungry, Ivan gobbles Easter treats and creates havoc in the house. Returning, Sister Fox turns to other animals for help and they want to punish Ivan, but Peter arrives in time to plead for Ivan by using an Easter theme of forgiveness (grades 1–3).

4. *Seeing symbolic language in dance.* How will students explain symbolic language of dance movements? Invite students to see a video, *Songs and Dances of the Nisqually* (Diogenes Foundation) where explanations of symbolic language of each dance movement is shown in a pow-wow held by the Nisqually. To transfer what was learned from this video back to a dinosaur topic, students can locate music that represents movements of large creatures and plan body language that has meaning to go along with the music (grades 3–8).

5. *Creating classroom bulletin boards.* How will students identify a good display and plan an overall design for the classroom? After seeing a video, *Creative Bulletin Boards* (American School Pub.), ask students to discuss ways to identify a good display, plan an overall design by selecting colors and shapes, and prepare artwork related to their study (grades 4–6).

6. *Seeing artists' works.* How will students transfer their knowledge of design to developing a project to present to the class? Invite students to look at illustrations by Arnold Lobel in *Dinosaur Time* (Harper & Row, 1974) by Peggy Parish and the way some pictures break their frames and go right into the text. For example, on a right-hand page, the long turning neck of a brontosaurus breaks a black line of the border as the animal hungrily chews leaves and its tail leads back to the left-hand page to twitch under a last line of text on the page. In

another book, fanciful wishes about dinosaurs of a young boy are shown in *If the Dinosaurs Come Back* by Bernard Most. In hypothetical situations, the purple, red, and yellow dinosaurs "help build skyscrapers" and "rescue kittens stuck in very tall trees" and do other helpful things. With examples of ways illustrators show dinosaurs in these books and others, engage students in designing projects such as making an informational diorama of a scene with a selected animal whose background has been researched, writing and drawing about a favorite animal, illustrating an original booklet to show their observations, or dramatizing certain events in an animal's life (grades 4–6).

7. *Recognizing theme in music.* How will students develop theme recognition skills in music? After listening to one of the videos in *Adventures in Listening* series (Merit Audio Visual) with the titles of *Debussy, Danse Macabre,* or *Peter and the Wolf,* ask students to discuss theme in a musical composition. With available rhythm instruments, engage students in working together to compose a brief rhythmic selection and then discuss with others the way they tried to keep to their theme (grades 4–6).

8. *Exploring musical elements.* How will students become aware of musical elements? To become aware of musical elements such as rhythm, melody, harmony and interpretation, students may engage in learning about pitch, rhythm, movements, and interpretation by using instruments improvised from pencils and towel rolls after hearing *Making Musical Things* (Scribner's, 1979) by A. Wiseman or *Musical Adventures* (Musical Munchkins). To further explore these elements, students may observe a video series, *Elements of Music* (SIRS), to become aware of musical elements through analogies between space exploration and music about rhythm, melody, form, tone color, interpretation, and harmony and dynamics (grades 4–6).

9. *Identifying musical instruments.* How will students become aware of musical instruments? Introduce musical instruments to students with the video, *Peter Ustinov Reads the Orchestra* (Mark Rubin Prods./Alcazar) (grades K–3).

10. *Recognizing information through songs.* How will students recognize that information is introduced through songs? Invite the girls and boys to start a school day by singing the message in the "World Pledge Song" from *Barley and Reindeer Milk* (People Records). "World Pledge Song" is based on Peter Spier's book *People* and has a message of caring for earth, sea, and air "with peace and justice everywhere" (all ages).

11. *Engaging in choral conversations.* How will students become aware of people's rhythmic patterns of language and music? Invite students to participate in a call-and-answer technique of choral conversations with cassettes in *Beats: Conversations in Rhythm for English as a Second Language* (Educational Activities) (grades 2–5).

12. *Understanding ways artists have been influenced.* How will students understand ways artists have been influenced by visual arts and why they became committed to the world of art? Students may select several artists and write to them to inquire about ways they have been influenced by visual arts. Artists who have focused on the prehistoric age are Eleanor M. Kish, a Canadian artist, whose paintings appeared in *A Vanished World—The Dinosaurs of Western Canada* (Canadian National Museum of Natural Sciences, 1985); Charles R. Knight, an American artist of prehistoric life and creator of nearly 1,000 works of art, whose paintings and murals are in leading natural history museums in the United States; and Rudolph F. Zallinger, a Pulitzer prize recipient, who produced an outstanding mural, *Age of Reptiles,* now in the Peabody Museum of Natural History at Yale, and who teaches drawing and painting at the University of Hartford and is artist-in-residence at the Peabody Museum (grade 4 and older).

To show students the ways several women artists were influenced by art and became committed to visual art, *Inspirations: Stories about Women Artists* by Leslie Sills (Albert Whitman, 1989) can be introduced. Artists include Georgia O' Keefe, Freda Kahlo, Alice Neel, Faith Ringold, and others. A biography series, *American Women of Achievement* (Chelsea House, 1989), focuses on women whose actions and ideas were crucial in shaping American history, several of whom are artists: Mary Cassatt, Georgia O'Keefe, Grandma Moses, Louise Nevelson, and Margaret Bourke-White (grade 4 and older).

13. *Recognizing artists' techniques.* How will students recognize some techniques used by artists? To discuss examples, show students the black-and-white illustrations of the styles of 19 different masters in *Famous Old Masters of Painting* (Dodd, 1951) by Roland McKinney. To focus on one artist, read to students *Meet Edgar Degas* (Lippincott, 1989) by Anne Newlands or *Linnea in Monet's Garden* (Simon and Schuster, 1987) by Christiana Bjork and Lena Anderson. Reproductions of Monet's paintings are found in Bjork and Anderson's book; Newlands's book includes letters, notebooks, and other materials selected by Degas, discusses his allegorical works of the 1850s, and shows his later scenes of Paris life (grade 3 and older).

14. *Recreating dinosaurs through sculptures.* To show the way two artists create realistic dinosaur sculptures, read excerpts from *My Life with the Dinosaurs* (Minstrel, 1989), a dual biography by Stephen and Sylvia Czerkas. Black-and-white photographs of their work show the animated models of dinosaurs the Czerkas create to put in scenes for exhibits. Discuss photographs of the scenes (e.g., what do the students learn from the scenes about the way some dinosaurs hunted? Searched for food?) (grades 5–6).

15. *Sculpting with "invisible" clay.* Ask students to pretend to have invisible dinosaur playdough or clay. With this invisible material, they pound and shape it into something related to the theme. With pretend motions, they make something out of it and then show how they would use it to a partner. If the partner understands the actions and guesses the object's name, then the partner receives the invisible material and makes another object. The partner demonstrates its use and the other student guesses the name of the object (all ages).

16. *Understanding ways heritage influences compositions.* How will students understand ways heritage brings cultural and musical influences to compositions? Invite students to see composer Alexina Louie's desire to convey her inner spirit through her work in the video, *The Eternal Earth* (Rhombus Media/Bullfrog Films, 1987). From Vancouver's Chinatown, Alexina Louie expresses her East-West sensitivities and integrates traditional Chinese instruments and themes into her symphony about the earth. Alternating between scenes of a street celebration in Chinatown and the Toronto symphony performing her work, Louie intersperses comments and shows her musical notation methods with her use of a ruler and French curve (grade 5 and older).

Topic B: Integrating Expressive Art Forms with a Literacy Curriculum

Drama

Using Body and Facial Expressions

"For a character to live," writes Todorov (1977), "they must narrate. Thus, the first narrative subdivides and multiplies into a thousand and one nights of narratives." To bring a character to life, kindergarten girls and boys looked for characters in stories who might have tales to tell another character, and then brought a story to life by telling those tales. The students found ways to show emotions of characters through body and facial expressions in still enactments after the original tales were told. Further, when the students created a group story, a teacher invited dialogue that went along with action with discussion probes such as, "What do you think this character would say?" and "What story could this character tell?"

Using Reader Scripts

With the readers' script, *The Dinosaurs' Dinner* (United, 1990), a first-grade teacher read the story aloud while the students made sounds effects and chimed in on repetitive lines. In this script, a little girl met a brontosaurus who wanted to come to breakfast and others who wanted to come to lunch, tea, and dinner. The little girl was delighted but could not find a meal for them when they turned down hot dogs and cold cuts. When she woke them from their nap, she discovered they were vegetarians and, finally, knew what to feed them.

Using a Story

Verriour (1990) suggests that stories discovered in a story of a drama can deepen students' understanding of the meaning of the present time period in a drama. For example, during a second reading, a second-grade teacher stopped a story at a certain point and allowed the children time to create a cooperative image of the setting. Imagining their own images of the setting gave them ownership of the context. At another point in a story, the teacher engaged the children in roles as fossil hunters and asked them to talk among themselves in small groups just as the·real fossil finders would do. Of course, the teacher joined a small group, too. The "fossil hunters" talked about troubles of the explorations. When the group talk faded, the teacher asked students to pretend and remember what life was like at the digging site. Specifically, students pretended to do something they did before the expedition (before they left to search for fossils). Staying in small groups, girls and boys participated in silent enactment scenes and posed in actions to show what life was like at a dig. As students pretended to dig for fossils, one stepped out of the scene and told other class members what was going on.

Using a Commercially Prepared Play

Some fourth-grade students rehearsed a commercial play from *The Great Dinosaur Pop-Up Book* (Dial, 1989) by Rupert Mathews and gave information about dinosaurs to an audience of friends from another class. Instead of using puppets, the students used the press-out paper models of a stegosaurus, a triceratops, a one-foot-tall Tyrannosaurus Rex, and others, which were on pages of the book. Inside was a script for *Return to the Forest of the Dinosaurs* and the students' talked about ways to present the play. Additional dinosaur cutouts for other characters were made by students and the performance was reviewed. A favorite song was selected to open the play and accompany the script. Further, the students discussed needed accents in an opening scene, action in other major scenes, and then listed props they would use. They talked about:

1. Paper plants "growing" right on stage as they were pulled from seeds into giant trees and plants; trees scented with squirts of pine or evergreen air freshener spray; and eyes of characters, moon, stars, and constellations glowing in the dark
2. A cloud narrating background information; mists of fog (made with baby powder) through which a dinosaur character traveled; and hurdles of hot streams or bubbling pots of steam made with air-scent sprayer
3. A dinosaur hatchling who played hide-and-seek, tug-of-war, and races with another; one dinosaur who scared another or who scrubbed another's back

or tail; a dinosaur "teenager" who caught a pine cone or other object; and gluing a large seed on an end of a clear plastic straw and moving the straw back and forth between two playful dinosaurs (giving the appearance of dinosaurs throwing a seed back and forth)

Creating Settings

Students considered settings and other suggestions: Would dog biscuits shaped like bones serve as fossil findings? Could rope or heavy string be used as vines hanging from trees? Should certain items (such as extra tree leaves chewed by a hungry dinosaur) be hung on nylon thread or fishing line from bars across the top of the theater? One student thought an egg carton would make "bumpy ground" and another suggested a cardboard tube to use as the center inside of a volcano. Floating clouds, shooting comets, a rising sun, and flickering fire flames from a lava flow of a nearby volcano were discussed as possible additions. Another student said seeds with velcro backing could be added to trees or bushes so dinosaurs could pull them off when eating. Still another wanted to add prehistoric birds, clouds, raindrops, and snowflakes to the scenes. They talked about ways scenery could move and suggested that the sun and moon could move in an arc in the sky and show time was passing. Additionally, they talked about ways these props could be made and who would volunteer to make them.

Creating Actions

To the students, the interactions between characters and scenery were important because they moved the story along and the actions became the focus of more discussion. One boy wanted a tree to be a hiding place for a young dinosaur, and another thought a mound would be the right spot from which a young dinosaur could "pop up" out of an egg and surprise another. Still another student suggested a path of rugged rocks for a dinosaur to walk through and said that if one scene was near water, an ocean wave could splash and scatter a group of little dinosaurs playing on the beach.

Some ready-made dinosaur puppets and stuffed toys were available and were considered as characters. The students "performed" with them (moved them around) in the group and talked about which ones could be possible additions to mix and match with the others they created.

Creating Sound Effects

The students also thought about different sounds for the various dinosaurs and planned demonstrations of the sounds of certain objects brought from home. The following were some of the demonstrations they did in their group:

1. Students crumpled cellophane with their hands and crumpled paper stuffed into a plastic bag and listened to the sounds to see if the effect made the sound of fire in a forest. One student blew hard through a straw placed in water to see if the effect made the sound of water flowing in a prehistoric creek. Swirling a few dry beans in a shallow pan gave students the effect of pounding, howling wind and rain.

2. Two students tapped tops of two inverted wooden bowls and experimented with the sounds to see if this was the effect wanted for "galloping" dinosaurs, and all stamped their feet to get the effect of animals fighting. The opening and closing of pliers was the sound the students wanted for a dinosaur chewing. And one student suggested a whirring hand-turned egg beater for the sound of a flying pterodactyl, while another suggested sprinkling small amounts of white confetti for the effect of snow.

3. They talked about what they could use to look like lava moving from a volcano: A strip of red cardboard or red sponge to look like a long, billowing

lava stream? A red strip of cloth pulled from a fissure in a volcano and down the side?

4. A white discarded egg-shaped container (originally containing hosiery) and a white balloon popped with a pin were suggested for an egg that cracked. With either prop, a baby dinosaur hatchling could appear from below stage as if it had hatched.

5. Could a red balloon—topped with red confetti or small red glittery pieces of metallic paper—be hidden inside a volcano crater? When air was blown through a straw attached to the opening in the balloon, the balloon could explode and send confetti and metallic paper flying, creating a reddish display resembling the fire of a volcano explosion.

6. Wind-up toy insects (oversized) were suggested to bring life to a prehistoric scene. Using a party horn blower as a tongue, a prehistoric reptile could have an extra long tongue when air was blown through the party horn, and seeds could slowly extend up from the ground to their full height as prehistoric ferns when pushed with a stick. For research for other kinds of plants for the scenes, the girls and boys looked in reference books to find shapes of gingko seeds and leaves and other plants that grew in the Age of Dinosaurs.

7. Bristles cut from an old hairbrush, paintbrush, or toothbrush contributed just the right covering for some creatures. Small pieces of fake fur added realistic touches on a prehistoric pterodactyl, and dark green and copper sequins caught the light and gave a glittering effect to the bumps on the plates of the animals.

Using Shadow Puppet Theater

The sixth-grade students discussed ways to present information with a shadow puppet theater. The students used a contrast of light and dark and moved shadows across a stage. A white sheet hung from the ceiling and a light was placed behind it. Black paper was used to create the figures. Clear plastic straws supported and moved the figures. Students thought of tall and short (fat and thin) dinosaurs and used bases made from discarded plastic butter tubs, boxes of different sizes and shapes, and tall plastic bottles for different sizes of dinosaurs. For some figures, brass paper brads were placed at the joints of animals' paper legs, arms, and tails to make them movable.

Using Audience Participation

The students wanted the audience members to be involved in a drama's telling and to repeat rhymes, chant, or sing songs. Students talked about ways the audience could add to the presentation. At a certain signal, the words from Hubbell's verses "Once upon, upon" could be chanted by audience members, or names of characters could be said in unison at certain points in the story. Refrains could be repeated when a dinosaur character appeared. They considered the idea that, in a fanciful situation, audience members could verbally "help" (give warnings) to dinosaur characters in danger. "Cheering" words or actions chanted by the audience would provide support for a character when needed. For instance, a sleeping mother dinosaur, unaware of a predator, could be called to action to wake up and protect her hatchlings. New words could be sung to a familiar tune (e.g., the mother dinosaur could be sung awake with words sung to "London Bridge Is Falling Down": "Mother dinosaur, please wake up, please wake up, please wake up/ Mother Dinosaur, please wake up/ Rex is coming"). Audience members could wave their hands, clap, or click their fingers in appropriate places.

Further, the students talked about songs to be sung at the beginning and ending of the presentation. For example, an original version of "Have you ever seen a dinosaur?" could be sung to the tune of "Have You Ever Seen a Lassie" to open the show. They talked about other favorites that could be selected, and mentioned "Yankee Doodle Went to Town" as a tune for different words about dinosaurs: "Mother dinosaur went to drink, watching side to side. . . . . "

Using Original Plays

Kutiper (1988) suggests using a resource, *Writing Your Own Plays: Creating, Adapting, Improvising,* to help students turn their stories into plays. Topics include ways that plays differ from stories, ways to select an appropriate or personal story to turn into a play, and ways to write a play. To support the use of drama in the classroom, Bidwell (1990) suggests:

1. Play a drama game of acting out behavior of a character's name drawn from a container and asking others to "Guess the Character."
2. Play roles of characters; complete a brief research project related to stories with historical settings before preparing a skit or play about an historical event.
3. Create a skit or play for a different ending for a story that has been read.
4. Videotape any skits and plays created by students and ask them to evaluate performances and suggest improvement to be made.
5. Select a section from a story for Reader's Theater to prepare a script. Stories to be considered related to a dinosaur theme are:
   a. Grades 1–3: K. Brandt's *Case of the Missing Dinosaur* (Troll, 1982); M. Cohen's *Lost in the Museum* (Dell, 1983); F. Crozat's *I Am a Big Dinosaur* (Barron, 1989); E. Curran's *Home for a Dinosaur* (Troll, 1985); M. Donnelly's *Squeak the Dinosaur* (Toy Works, 1987); and A. Lavie's *The Dinosaur's Cold* (David & Charles, 1988)
   b. Grades 4–6: *Dinosaurs Beware! A Safety Guide* (Little, Brown, 1982) by M. Brown and S. Krensky; L. Cauley's *The Trouble with Tyrannosaurus Rex* (Harcourt Brace Jovanovich, 1988); and K. Dolby's *The Incredible Dinosaur Expedition* (EDC, 1987)

Preparing for a Performance

The girls and boys designed and wrote invitations, addressed envelopes, and agreed to send thank-you notes to those who attended. Tickets were printed for members of the audience. Feedback (evaluation) sheets about the performance were made for attendees. An advertisement was designed for a class newsletter and a class bulletin board displayed the news. Volunteers visited other classes, announced the play, and invited other students. Refreshments were served at intermission, and napkins, cups, and placemats were designed and decorated. After the performance, the group's drama critic(s) (student volunteers) wrote an article for the class or school newsletter. Performers also wrote letters to the editor of the newspaper and explained their points of view about the show.

Music

Connecting Music to Literature

"Probably the most practical approach to integrating literature with musical content into the curriculum is the thematic studies approach," writes Linda Leonard Lamme (1990). "Musical theme studies using picture books might include the study of musical instruments, singing, performing, dance, or how music makes one feel." Using a theme, students can study science (sounds and instruments), social studies (cultural songs and dances), math (rhythms), language (lyrics), and reading (books of music). Using the theme of dinosaurs, students certainly can relate music to reading.

"Oh, Stella Stegosaurus was built like a tank," sang the children as a second-grade teacher incorporated reading through singing. The girls and boys were singing "Stella Stegosaurus" along with music on an audio cassette (Caedmon, 1985). Students listened for information they heard through the music and the words of the song. They learned that this dinosaur had a "double row of plates that ran down her back," was "twenty feet long," and "weighed maybe two tons or more." After the sing-along, a student walked among class members as all repeated the chorus and sang the words, "Oh, Stella, Please tell us . . . what was the world like in one hundred million B.C.?" When the singing stopped, so did the student—who then pointed to another class member. The identified student responded to the musical question, "What was the world like in one hundred million B.C.?" and contributed any information he or she knew about the Age of Dinosaurs. The responding student became the next one to walk among the others and identified another informational contributor as the chorus was repeated.

On cassettes of *I Wish I Was a Dinosaur* and *Dinosaur Rock* were more original songs about dinosaurs that were played for a class sing-along. A favorite was "Tyrannosaurus Rex" (Caedmon, 1985) with its warning of "The jungle land is overgrown/ You mustn't go there all alone . . . ." Additional observations about this dinosaur were heard: "He couldn't fly/He couldn't swim/His teeth were sharp/A live one has never been seen."

To begin a reading-music connection, students' interest in the song was motivated by a picture of dinosaurs (other motivators could be a filmstrip, questions, story, or guest speaker). Along with the song, the teacher included reading, and each word judged to be difficult (triceratops, ankylosaurus) was introduced. The teacher set a purpose for listening to the song and the words of the song were read orally by the teacher and students. The teacher led the song while the students sang along and then questions about the song were asked (Why has a live one never been seen?). The song was repeated and vocabulary and word attack skills were incorporated into a post-song discussion. The song was sung again and accompanied by motions suggested by the students.

Connecting Familiar Songs to New Words

The girls and boys listened to more songs on records and tape recordings and continued to sing their favorites on subsequent days. For some of the songs, students reviewed words as they were projected on an overhead projector. After each review, students sang the words. In addition, familiar songs about related topics were featured. A ballad "On Top of Old Smoky," became a dinosaur story-song when the students' dictated different words for it and changed its title to "On Top of the Crater." On subsequent days, students contributed other words to fit rhythmic patterns of other songs such as "Dem Bones, Dem Bones" ("Them bones, them bones, them dino bones . . ."), "Frere Jacques" ("Are you sleeping, dinosaur?"), and "Old MacDonald Had a Farm" ("Mother dinosaur had a nest").

Connecting Music to Content

In a first-grade class, young children changed well-known finger plays with their contributed dinosaur words. While they were thinking about some words to contribute to songs, the teacher read from *Kites Sail High: A Book about Verbs* (Grosset & Dunlap, 1988) by Ruth Heller: "And here is a sentence with verbs galore . . . Lizards LEAP and PILE in a heap/ and SLITHER . . . and CLIMB and SPLASH and CREEP/ and SWIM and CAVORT and FALL asleep." The verbs reflected some of the behaviors of dinosaurs. Heller's book was left open at the page and displayed in the book corner. The children did movement exploration to musical selections and selected music as background to listen to their favorite dinosaur poems or stories. They selected music for a background for choral-speak situations and made their own instruments for a background accompaniment. They listened to sounds of familiar and unfamiliar tools and related the sounds to their predicted expectations of sounds made by dinosaurs. They collected song lyrics and changed the words to relate to the dinosaur topic. Doing this, young students were introduced to the process of reading through songs.

To infuse the study of dinosaurs with music and art, the girls and boys in a fourth-grade class translated sounds they heard into block prints, collages of leaves and grasses, inkings, and placed "found objects" on a hanging. Some students selected a familiar tune and experimented with a recorder to discuss tones that reminded them of dinosaurs and created a painting of a local scene and then did another to show the scene as it might have been in a prehistoric time period. Other students looked at the video of Baker's book and listened to musical interpretations of a primordial forest and then created their own music with instruments. During a rereading of Baker's story, some interpreted the story with the sounds of instruments they had selected. Other students drew sketches of the fossils they had found in their studies and created their own fossils with clay. Still others recorded key events about what they had learned and painted them on clay tiles.

Classroom Update

- A program of music-poetry language arts produces cognitive results for a low achiever as well as positive student and parent responses (Hudspeth, 1986).
- For fourth-grade students identified as low achievers, music with poetry activities led to gains in language mechanics and total language development (Hudspeth, 1986).
- For fifth-graders of high, middle, and low ability, popular songs used as musical poems promoted positive attitudes toward poetry (Demetrales, 1986).
- Combining poetry and drama has been most successful in fourth grade, and combining art and poetry is a favorite area enjoyed by all of the students (McCall, 1979).
- Classroom environment, teacher attitude, and poetry activities relate to Rosenblatt's theory and support the point of view that reading and listening to poetry should be an aesthetic experience (Whitin, 1984).

Poetry

Chanting a Refrain

"Tyrannosaurus raised his head and . . . ." Back in the circle again with the students, the third-grade teacher read the first two lines from Patricia Hubbel's verse, "When Dinosaurs Ruled the Earth," and suggested the girls and boys listen to the rhythm in the language as other verses about dinosaurs were heard. The words were from a collection of poems in the book, *To Look At Every Thing*, poems selected by Lee Bennett Hopkins. In one poem, Hubbell included a rhythmic refrain summarizing her introduction to dinosaurs and everyone chimed in to chant the lines ending with "dabbled in the muds of time,/Once upon, upon."

Predicting Meaning

Before Hubbel's poem was heard totally, the teacher introduced a poetry word prediction procedure and led students in a search for meanings of some words they would hear in the poem. This prediction procedure focused the students' attention on poetic word choices. Poets, like other writers, always seek the best words—the words that relay a thought the best way—and sometimes the word presents a comparison to the reader. To predict what some of the words in Hubbel's verse might mean, students divided a sheet of paper with a three-way fold. Words with multiple meanings from the poem were selected: *time, bared, bid, company*. Students wrote the words in the left-hand part of the folded paper. They wrote their predictions for the meaning of each word in the center area of the paper. Then they listened to the poem for these words with multiple meanings and determined what each word meant in the poem's context.

After listening to the teacher read the poem and then looking at the poem's lines containing the words shown on an overhead transparency, the students marked a check in the third area of their papers if the definition each of them selected/wrote was similar to the definition gained from the oral reading of the poetic lines. If a student's predicted definition did not make sense in the poem, the student and a partner wrote a more appropriate definition and put it in the third column of the paper. Together, the students discussed key words from the poem that helped them decide to change or to keep their definitions for the words. Here are some multiple meanings the students discussed from Hubbel's poem:

time: Which meaning was best for the word *time*? Does the word mean a measurement in hours, days, years? Does it mean the moving of a clock's hands? Does it mean a certain point in the past, present, or future (e.g., the *time* was millions of years ago)? Does it mean a period of history (e.g., human beings were not known in the dinosaurs' *time*)? Does it mean an occasion that had a certain purpose (e.g., it was *time* for the dinosaur's nap)? Does it mean a number of occasions where something happened (e.g., that was the third *time* the baby dinosaur had fallen into the water)?

bared: Which meaning was best for the word *bared*? Does the word mean to reveal feelings (e.g., he *bared* his feelings)? Does it mean to uncover something else (e.g., the mother dinosaur *bared* its teeth when the pterodactyl startled the hatchlings)?

bid: Which meaning is best for the word *bid*? Does the word mean a greeting (e.g., the injured dinosaur *bid* the others a greeting by lifting its head)? Does it mean an order or command? To offer a certain price for something? An attempt to obtain something (e.g., with a challenging roar, the dinosaur made a serious *bid* to be the leader of the herd)?

company: Which meaning was best for the word *company*? Does the word mean a group of animals who joined together (e.g., the *company* of dinosaurs moved across the river)? Does it mean someone or some animal who visits (the hatchlings were waiting for the *company* of other young dinosaurs)? Does it mean companionship (e.g., the hatchling was a friendly dinosaur who enjoyed the friendship and *company* of others)?

Interpreting Orally

The girls and boys thought again about the verse and dinosaurs and suggested ideas for an oral interpretation of the words. They contributed their ideas about ways they wanted to say some of the words. Ideas students mention included stretching out the word *long* to *l-o-o-n-g* in "long and yellow teeth"; and making a sharp staccato sound while saying "eating without delay" and "happenings of the day." They suggested other ideas for the verse about the allosaurus who was "taller than a building" and "taller than a tree." Each time the students' ideas were used and the verses were repeated. Each verse was interpreted orally with the suggestions of the listeners and the girls and boys always concluded their oral interpretations with the refrain "dabbled in the muds of time,/Once upon, upon."

To further consider the meaning of the lines, the students talked about the senses that come to mind with the poet's words, *dabbled in the muds of time*. The students and the teacher asked questions about some words in the phrase: What does it mean to dabble? To splash in and out of water? To do something a little (but not in a serious) way? What might be felt when one's hands or feet touch the mud? Is it wet? Soft? Sticky? What would we see? Dirt that is wet? What would we hear? Squishing?

Keeping the Rhythm

During another recitation of this poem by the teacher, the girls and boys joined in with a finger-tapping accompaniment and maintained the rhythm of the verse by striking two fingers of one hand on two fingers of the other hand. Those who wished to do so said any remembered words along with the teacher. When the verse was completed, the teacher turned to the youngsters on one side of the circle and asked, "Will you be the ones to say the words, *muds of time*? As we repeat some of the lines of verse, will you keep chanting *muds of time, muds of time, muds of time*?" The teacher demonstrated the suggestion (the refrain's chant sounded like a musical round—a familiar arrangement to all who have sung "Row, Row, Row Your Boat") and asked the students to act this out in a roleplay situation before the actual repetition began. Beginning with, "Brontosaurus, diplodocus, gentle trachodon," the verse was repeated and the students on one side of the circle chanted the phrase, *muds of time*, as a verbal accompaniment similar to that of a round. Before repeating the lines again, the students discussed what body action could be added in pantomime style to show some of the meaning of the poem. Some of them decided that rolling their eyes and baring their teeth in an intimidating way would be just right to go along with Hubbel's words about the fierceness of the tyrannosaurus. So, several students said the lines of the verse and kept the beat with their tapping fingers while the others in the refrain group repeated the words, *muds of time*, and still others made the motions.

Joining in a Rhythmic Round

Next, the teacher turned to students on the other side of the classroom—members of another refrain team—who suggested another motion (gnashing of teeth) to accompany other words, *Once upon, upon, Once upon, upon, Once upon, upon*." The class repeated the verse again as members of one side of the circle rolled their eyes and chanted *muds of time* and the members of the other side gnashed their teeth and chanted *Once upon, upon*. Several class members joined with the teacher and repeated the words of the now very familiar verse and kept the beat of the rhythm of Hubbel's language about roaming dinosaurs with their tapping fingers.

Creating a Poetryscape

With different purposes, students listened again to Hubbel's poetic words read by the teacher. Different students listened for:

1. Words they thought were interesting (*dabbled, pygmy brain, awed his foe*)
2. Words that rhymed (*trachodon, upon; eye, bye; day, delay; tree, company; time, slime*)
3. Words that made a picture in the listener's mind (*swamp-filled world*)
4. Words that made noises (*roamed, gnash*)
5. Words that would help the student paint a picture about the poem (*taller than a building, taller than a tree*)
6. Words that would help a student choose colors when drawing a picture about the poem (*muds, yellow teeth, tree, building*)

After reading, the students received lines of the poem cut into strips and worked with partners to reassemble the poem by rhyming it. Once assembled, the poem was orally interpreted with suggestions by the group for a choral speaking arrangement. The teacher asked for ways to show reactions to the poem's words and the students discussed their ideas:

1. *Art:* "We could cut out a magazine picture that shows what the poem is about or draw pictures of what's in the poem. We could listen to music while we painted pictures of dinosaurs. We could put our pictures on the bulletin board."
2. *Dramatic play:* "We could act out the poem or make puppets to do the acting. We could move our hands and feet to do the actions."
3. *Listening:* "We could use the tape recorder and record the poem."
4. *Music:* "We could listen to dinosaur music."
5. *Oral interpretation:* "We could make noises to go with the words."
6. *Writing:* "We could write the poem and put in on the bulletin board."
7. *Book publishing:* "We could make our own book of dinosaur poems."
8. *Speaking:* "We could say it again with different noises and grind our teeth again."

After hearing these verbal responses, written reactions by students were invited and displayed on the board where a copy of the poem was shown—an initial contribution to the class's poetryscape bulletin board.

Searching for Real or Fanciful Behemoths

For creative writing in a fourth-grade class, students' interest in huge creatures led them on a search for other large (real or fanciful) behemoths—dragons—and ways they were shown in stories of different cultures. The students discovered that dragons, a name given to large creatures of the ancient world, were usually shown with a body like a large crested snake with claws. They had wings like those of great bats, breathed fire and smoke, were found in legends and myths, and were strangely like other actual creatures that lived in the prehistoric past. In fact, Eldridge introduced the pteranodon and other creatures that flew in prehistoric times by calling them "flying dragons" in his book *Flying Dragons: Ancient Reptiles that Ruled the Air* (Troll, 1980). Looking at the book, the students saw that dragons were much like the great flying reptiles that existed long before humans appeared on earth. In a discussion, they considered how the idea of dragons came about. One student thought humans might have found the bones of the gigantic flying reptiles (or of dinosaurs) and thought they were dragon's bones. Another student thought some humans started the idea of fire-breathing dragons when they saw the great tongues (colored pink and yellow) of the Komodo dragon and believed it was flashing fire.

The students discovered that almost every country had dragons in its myths. In western countries, the tales told of dragons as terrifying scaly creatures; some had wings and flew while others slithered like snakes. In some of the countries, the dragon was a symbol of evil. In other countries, the symbol of the dragon was very important (in Wales, the dragon is on the national flag). In eastern countries, the dragons lived high up in the sky and were rich, wise, and powerful. They had the neck of a snake, the claws of an eagle, and the horns of a stag. Sometimes, they fed on swallows that glided in their kingdoms. Often, the dragons were benign (or neutral) and could take human form. In China, for example, the dragon was a kingly emblem and was once thought of as a god.

The students discovered many stories that feature dragons and found that in Greece, dragons were slain by Hercules, Apollo, and Perseus. In legends from Norway, Germany, and England, dragons were killed by Sigurd, Siegfried, and Beowulf. One book, *Dragons and Other Fabulous Beasts* (Grosset & Dunlap, 1980) by R. Blythe, had stories of different dragon personalities from both East and West, tales the teacher read aloud. In "Sigurd and the Dragon Fafnir," Sigurd used the sword of Odin (his father) and slayed Fafnir, the great gray dragon, whose blood poisoned and killed humans. In slaying it, Sigurd won the elf-gold the dragon guarded. In "The Terrible-Tempered Dragon," Chen-Tang, the red dragon, lost his temper when he discovered his favorite niece (the dragon king's daughter) had been mistreated. He rescued her from her ill-treating husband and returned her in her human form to the king, The Chief Dragon of All China. In "The Fire Dragon of the Burning Mountain," a dragon was the keeper of the volcano fire and made flames, fiery flashes, falling rocks, and dreadful booms. Trapped by fallen rock, he was freed by a brave little girl, and, in return, he kept the volcano silent and did not destroy the village and fields.

Two other stories were favorites. In *Eyes of the Dragon* (Lothrop, Lee & Shepard, 1987) by Margaret Leaf, a magistrate of a Chinese village summoned the greatest dragon painter to decorate the mighty wall around the village with a portrait of the Dragon King. The portrait was so skillfully painted that it seemed almost alive, and when the eyes of the dragon were painted in (due to the magistrate's demand and over the painter's objections), the portrait came alive and the dragon crumbled the wall into pieces on the ground. In *Saint George and the Dragon* (Little, Brown, 1984) by Margaret Hodges, Saint George rescued the king's daughter and used his lance to kill the vicious dragon of Selena, a creature whose tail "swept the land behind him for almost half a mile" and whose huge jaws "gaped wide, showing three rows of iron teeth."

Involving Students

Investigating dragons from the literature of many countries helped the students learn a great deal about different countries and the people. The study increased multicultural understanding and fostered positive attitudes toward people in cultures different from the students' cultures. This was noticed by the teacher when the students were hearing and discussing Chinese tales of dragons and China was featured in the nightly television news reports. As they read about the dragon who broke his promise in "The Cock and the Dragon," a student decided that the person who told a story like this wanted to explain a natural happening. In the story, a dragon flew into a Chinese farmyard, borrowed the rooster's horns, and promised to return them but never did. Each subsequent morning, the rooster shouted out to the sky, "Bring back my horns!" The rooster's descendents have still not given up, for they still make a noisy shout in the morning. The students realized the story was an explanation of why a rooster crowed in the morning and a student said he would shout, too, if someone broke a promise to him. The teacher pointed out the similarity—the storyteller had something in common with the student—the determination to "shout out" when someone broke a promise.

During their discussions of other dragon legends, the students commented that countries such as Greece, England, and Norway showed dragons as evil, but in China, there was both a benign dragon ("The Golden Sheng, The Kind Dragon") and an evil dragon ("Dragon Thieves of Peking"). Some of the poems compiled by Laura Whipple from *Eric Carle's Dragons Dragons & Other Creatures That Never Were* (Philomel, 1991) were read aloud, and, with the insight gained, the students talked about what they had decided (i.e., that authors created stories and poems about their people's beliefs in dragons—good and evil).

Extensions for Chapter 5

1. *Consider the component in the Core of Structure:Integrate Social Studies and Expressive Arts.* List books, activities, ideas, projects, and lines of inquiry to connect your theme to this component.
2. *Create mental pictures.* In a letter to the editor in the *School Library Journal*, Myra Cohn Livingston (1987) states that teachers should encourage students to make their own mental pictures instead of showing them an illustration for "every set of words today." Why do you agree or disagree with Livingston's point of view about the use of realistic pictures in poem picture books?
3. *Emphasize that adults write, too.* Emphasize that adults write expressively and read poetry related to the theme to the students. Related to the topic of *How Did We Find Out about Dinosaurs*, Alice Mackenzie Swaim wrote about fossils and ranked first in the poetry category in the 1988 Writer's Digest Writing Competition. With students, discuss Swaim's final words about touching a fossil: "but in my hand I hold the shape of life, preserved in ancient rock, still pulsing through the chambers of my reverent heart."

Endnotes

1. This idea was contributed by Dr. Victoria Jew, Professor of Education, California State University, Sacramento, 1991.
2. From *History-Social Sciences Framework*. Sacramento, CA: State Department of Education, 1989. Integrating the language arts with curriculum areas is a focus in *A Guide to Curriculum Planning in English Language Arts* edited by Ellen Last, Supervisor, English Language Arts (Wisconsin Department of Instruction, 1989) and various other state guides.
3. Ibid.
4. Kristie Darras, primary-grade teacher, Elk Grove Unified School District, Elk Grove, California, contributed the classroom activities.

Resources

AIT: Agency for Instructional Technology. Box A, Bloomington, IN 47402. Video: *Art History II: A Survey of the Western World.* Grade 4 and older.

Alcazar Mail Order. Box 429, Waterbury, VT 05676. Video: *Peter Ustinov Reads the Orchestra.* Grades K–6.

Alfred Higgins Productions. 63050 Laurel Canyon Blvd., N. Hollywood, CA 91606. Video: *Exploring the Forest.* Grades 1–6.

American Schools Pub. Box 408, Hightstown NJ 08520. Video: *Creative Bulletin Boards.* Grades 4–6.

Barnes & Noble Booksellers. 126 Fifth Ave., New York, NY 10011. Antique maps. Grade 4 and older.

Beacon Films. 930 Pitner Ave., Evanston, IL 60606. Film: *Billy Goats Bluff.* Grades 1–6.

Bullfrog Films. Oley, PA 19547. Video: *The Eternal Earth.* Grade 6 (advanced) and older.

Childcraft. 20 Kilmer Road, PO Box 3143, Edison, NJ 08818-3143. Book series: *Art for Children* 189670. Grades 2–4.

Clearvue, Inc. 6465 Avondale Ave., Chicago, IL 60631. Filmstrips: *Looking for America* Series. Grades 4–6.

Colman Communications/United Learning. 6633 W. Howard St., Niles, IL 60648. Video unit: *Using Maps, Globes, Graphs, Tables, Charts, Diagrams: A Video-Based Unit of Study.* Grades 4–6.

Current/Rutledge/New Day Films. 121 W. 27th St., New York, NY 10001. Films. All ages.

Diogenes Foundation. 30300 110 Place S. E., Auburn, WA 98002. Video: *Songs and Dances of the Nisqually.* Grades 3–8.

Educational Activities. 1937 Grant Ave., Baldwin, NY 11510. Cassette: *Beats: Conversations in Rhythm for English as a Second Language.* Grade 4 and older.

EVI: Educational Video, Inc. Box 740, Holland, IL 60473. Video: *The Magic Gallery.* Grades 2–6.

Gessler Publishing Company. 55 1224 13th Street, New York, NY 10011. ESL supplementary materials. All ages.

GCT Inc. 314-350 Weinacker Ave., PO Box 6448, Mobile, AL 36660. Books: *Creative Dramatics for Children; The Good Apple Guide to Creative Drama; Reader's Theater* by C. & C. Cornett; *Discovering Anthropology* by N. Crosby & E. Marten; *Discovering Archaeology* by G. McCarthy & M. Marson; *The Map Corner.*

Kapco Adhesive Products Company. PO Box 626, Kent, OH 44240-0626. Self-adhesive book covers.

Merit Audio Visual. Box 392, New York, NY 10024. Video series: *Adventure in Listening.* Grades 4–6.

Musical Munchkins. Box 356, Pound Ridge, NY 10576. Video: *Musical Adventures,* Grades 1–3.

The Nature Company. PO Box 2310, Berkeley, CA 94702. Dinosaur globe.

Nystrom. 3333 Elston Ave., Chicago, IL 60618. Filmstrips: *Fundamental Themes of Geography I and II.* Grades 4–8.

People Records. 8929 Apache Dr., Beulah, OH 81203. Record: *Barley and Reindeer Milk.* All ages.

Rainbow Educational Video. 170 Keyland Court, Bohemia, NY 11716. Video: *Finding Your Way: Using Maps and Globes.* Grades 4–6.

Raintree's Children's Encyclopedia (1988). Milwaukee, WI: Raintree. Book series: *Famous Men and Women.* Grades 3–5.

Random House Home Videos. 400 Hahn Rd., Westminster, MD 21157. Video: *The Berenstain Bears and the Missing Dinosaur Bone.* Grades K–2.

SIRS: Social Issues Resources Series. Box 2348, Boca Raton, FL 33427. Video: *Elements of Music.* Grade 4 and older.

Society of Visual Education. 1345 Diversey Pkwy., Chicago, IL 60614. Filmstrips: *Economics in Our World* with *Producers and Consumers, Money and Exchange, The Government and Economic Systems.* Grades K–3.

Tinto, Pinguino. *El Libro de la Escritura.* New York: Teachers and Writers Collaborative, 1988. Workbook: Creative writing in Spanish. Grades 4–6.

Troll Associates. Mahwah, NJ. Book series: *Our Planet.* Grades 4–6.

United Learning. 6633 W. Howard St., Niles, IL 60648. Filmstrips: *Basics of Geography* series. Grades 4–8.

Universal Dimensions/Altschul Group Corp. 930 Pitner Ave., Evanston, IL 60202. Video: *Strategies for Teaching At-Risk Students.* For teachers.

University of California Extension Media Center. 2223 Fulton St., Berkeley, CA 94720. Video: *Poetry Is Words that Sing!* For teachers.

World Almanac Education. 1278 West 9th Street, Cleveland, OH 44113. Almanacs: *The Kids' World Almanac of the United States, The Kids' World Almanac,* and *The World Almanac Infopedia: A Visual Encyclopedia for Students.* All ages.

Readings

Bidwell, S. M. (1990). Using drama to increase motivation, comprehension, and fluency. *Journal of Reading,* 34 (1) (September): 38–41.

Curriculum Task Force of National Council for the Social Studies (1989). *Charting a course: Social studies for the 21st century.* Washington, DC: National Council for the Social Studies.

Demetrales, P. (1986). *Effects of a musical poems teaching approach on fifth grade students' attitudes toward poetry.* Ed. D. dissertation, Lehigh University. *DAI* 47: 2061A AAD86-16158.

Hopkins, L. B. (1978). *To look at every thing.* New York: Harcourt.

Hudspeth, C. C. (1986). *The cognitive and behavioral consequences of using music and poetry in a fourth grade language arts classroom.* Ann Arbor: MI: University Microfilms. No. 86-26486. *DAI* 47:2884A.

Kutiper, K. (1988). Finding the story in each of us through instructional media. *English Journal* (March): 76–77.

Lamme, L. L. (1990). Exploring the world of music through picture books. *The Reading Teacher* 44 (4) (December): 294–300.

Livingston, M. C. (1989). Birches: Letter to the editor. *School Library Journal,* 36: 60.

McCall, C. J. H. (1979). *A determination of children's interest in poetry resulting from specific experiences.* Ph. D. dissertation, The University of Nebraska–Lincoln. *DAI* 40: 4401A.

McKean, K. (1986). Dinosaur dynasty. *Modern Maturity* (October-November): 68–76. .

Roberts, P. L. (1989). Preparing for a geography bee. *Teaching K–8* (October): 56–57.

Servey, R. E (1981). *Elementary social studies: A skills emphasis.* Boston: Allyn and Bacon.

Todorov, T. (1977). *The poetics of prose.* Ithaca, NY: Cornell University Press.

Verriour, P. (1990). Storying and storytelling in drama. *Language Arts,* 67 (2) (February): 144–150.

Whitin, D. J. (1984). *Poetry as an aesthetic experience: The literary theory of Louise Rosenblatt and its implications for teaching poetry in grades K–3.* Ed. D. dissertation, Indiana University. *DAI* 45: 2759A.

Chapter 6

How May I Integrate Mathematics and Science?

Teacher Reflections for Chapter 6

Chapter 6 helps you choose ways to integrate a literacy curriculum with:

- Mathematics and natural science
- Computer software and related audiovisual materials
- The component in the Core of Structure to implement a thematic unit in literature-based instruction: Integrate Mathematics and Science

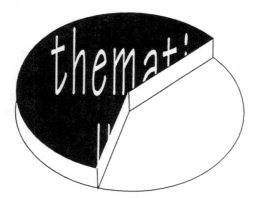

Component in Core of Structure to Implement a Thematic Unit for Literature-Based Instruction: Integrate Mathematics and Science

Vignette in Second Grade: Green Dinosaur Unit

As an example in a second-grade class, graphing was introduced as a means to review the lessons on dinosaurs that the children had studied and to survey the favorite topics of study. A graph was built in front of the students as each one drew a favorite dinosaur and contributed it to the graph. The students used their own individual graph copies to record what was added to the graph and marked an *X* with markers in the appropriate places. After the class graph was finished, the students read it and discussed the information they found. In addition to graphing, other activities to integrate science, reading with music, drawing, and publishing original books supported the unit.[1]

Integrating Mathematics

"The mathematics program of the elementary school must . . . provide children with the knowledge, attitude, and skills they will need to be mathematically literate," writes Leonard F. Kennedy, author of *Guiding Children to Mathematical Discovery* (Wadsworth, 1984). Kennedy maintains that children can search for patterns among numbers and can develop an awareness of how patterns are useful in organizing and synthesizing ideas about numbers. He states, "Rather than the teacher or a textbook presenting generalizations of mathematics, children can be guided to formulate them, using their own thought patterns and expressing generalizations in their own words." Studying a topic of interest motivates the girls and boys to learn and to keep a positive attitude as they explore content-related situations and remember observations. In doing this, students develop skills of literacy and numeracy and acquire knowledge related to the content.

When guiding children toward mathematical discovery in your elementary school mathematics program, you will see that some of the following topics are suggested in your district's material and are appropriate for the students in your class. The math topics usually found in a math program are numbers and operations, measurement, geometry, some use of statistics and probability, functions and graphs, logical thinking, and problem solving. These topics may be introduced as new concepts/skills and math topics from your class textbook through learning centers, or you may introduce mini-lessons into the unit, but you should avoid asking the children to follow the material about a particular concept from the "first page to last page" in the math text. Your textbook may have useful supplementary materials that will provide information required by your school/district/state (e.g., a beginning-of-the-year inventory, sets of achievement tests that cover the mathematics content, or end-of-the-year mastery tests). The findings from these materials may help you plan for your mini-lessons and the learning centers. Important to both instructional approaches, you will want to plan your instruction around student discussions and provide learning materials, your demonstrations, and guided practice for the students. Through small-group or whole-group instruction, you will want students to see that math is a form of communication and expression that lends itself to content study and is useful in describing the scientific or social environment. Examples from different grade levels are given in the following section to show ways that math can be used to express information about the topic of dinosaurs.

Topic A: Numbers

With rhymes, songs, finger-play activities, and counting books, young children in kindergarten count and "learn more than numbers" (Roberts, 1990) as they focus on the topic of dinosaurs. With Nancy Blumenthal's *Count-a-Saurus* (Four Winds,

1989), the girls and boys count numbers one to ten and begin the count with one stegosaurus standing in the sun, two compsognathus always on the run, and end with ten hadrosaurids sporting funny hats. The young students chant the repetitive refrain of "This is how we count-a-saurus!" and, with the teacher, pronounce the dinosaur names with the pronunciation guides in the book. To encourage vocabulary growth and the creative use of language, the teacher shows them the "Append-a-saurus" at the end of the book and reads some of its unique observations about each type of dinosaur. The teacher mentions the book's verse can be used as a jump-rope rhyme and chanted with others while jumping rope outside.

In a first-grade class, the children listen to counting verses from Beverly Randell's *Ten Big Dinosaurs* (The Wright Group, 1986) and the teacher reads aloud the verses about one to ten big dinosaurs.

After listening to *Four and Twenty Dinosaurs* (Harper, 1990) by Bernard Most and seeing the colorful pictures, the children move the dinosaur replicas around, arrange and rearrange them in groups, and count up to twenty-four. The replicas are categorized (those that walk on four feet or on two feet, those with armor and without armor) and arranged in order of relationships from largest to smallest (or little to big). The children write numerals for the numbers of replicas they have and copy numerals or trace numeral patterns. With Richard Armour's book, *A Dozen Dinosaurs* (McGraw-Hill, 1968), they learn another term for the number twelve. They also learn ordinal uses of numerals to classify order—the order of a position of the first, second, or third dinosaur in a row as well as the order needed to identify a museum address or the date of the year a fossil was found.

With small replica models of dinosaurs, the young boys and girls count the number of dinosaurs heard in the verses, add and compare numbers of dinosaurs in groups, and learn the patterns of one-more-than and one-less-than. With beans glued to tongue depressor sticks, some students learn values of one-to-ten and ten-to-one, and the meaning of place value. After discussing some of the animals in Moody's *100 Prehistoric Animals from A to Z* (Grosset & Dunlap, 1988), students count to 100, make a 100 number chart, and to see number use, refer to the book to find the size and weight of a particular animal.

Topic B: Operations

Addition

In first grade, children join together two or more groups of objects for addition and assign a sum to a pair of numbers. They respond to addition situations (How many do you have? How many red? How many green?), join groups of familiar objects (types of dinosaurs or other markers) and identify the number in each group. They also join felt or flannel pieces and recognize the signs for + and =. They add with fossil replicas or dinosaur models or beads, checkers, marbles, and pebbles; they add fossil replicas to containers; they select Cuisenaire rods to represent fossils and add groups together; and they write mathematical sentences in the vertical and horizontal format to show what went on.

Differences

Reviewing illustrations in *Dinosaurs Are Different* (Harper, 1986) by Aliki, dinosaur differences are discussed by some second-grade students. In line drawings, Aliki shows the differences in hip and jaw bones and teeth of dinosaurs and gives observations about the ruling reptiles, the saurischian group, and a second group related to birds, the ornithischians. These observations were useful and students wrote them on a class informational chart to point out differences between the two groups. Books in the classroom that had/did not have further information about the two groups were selected by the students, discussed, counted, and the numbers in each category for "Had Information" and "Did Not Have Information" were placed on a bar graph.

Subtraction

Differences were discussed further when the second-grade students considered subtraction in different situations. Using some model replicas, the girls and boys considered the situation where they knew the number of dinosaurs in a large group; then a number in a subgroup was removed (16 dinosaurs − 8 dinosaurs). Next, they considered what the difference in sizes of two individual dinosaurs replicas (ounces, pounds) would be: Dinosaur model replica *A* weighed 10 ounces and dinosaur model replica *B* weighed 5 ounces. How much smaller was dinosaur model *B* than dinosaur *A*?. How much larger was Dinosaur *A* than Dinosaur *B*? Third, students considered the subtraction situation of "How many more?" with problems similar to this one: Carlos was preparing his dinosaur diorama and wanted 12 different dinosaurs in the scene. Carlos counted and found he had 5 dinosaurs. How many more did Carlos need to finish the scene?

To see differences in another way, the students used the idea of one of the smallest dinosaurs jumping along a number line. A number line was drawn on the chalkboard to illustrate mathematical sentences such as 12 − 7 = _____ and 12 − 5 = _____. The movement of the small dinosaur along the line demonstrated the related sentences of 10 + _____ = 16 and 6 + _____ = 16. Other mathematical sentences were illustrated in this way.

Using a wide variety of materials and procedures at a learning center, the children will need brief activities that further develop their understanding of the addition and subtraction operations and that present the basic facts. For example, they can group addition and subtraction facts into a family of six (where all math sentences for the sum of six are grouped together) or into other families. In addition to a number line to learn facts, children may use markers, objects, addition tables, and charts to show they understand patterns of of sums up to ten and sums greater than ten.

Multiplication

Students in third grade may count the number of objects in two or more groups (e.g., 4 groups of 3 dinosaurs) and write a mathematical sentence that tells the number of dinosaurs in all of the groups: Four times three is equal to twelve (4 × 3 = 12). They complete other mathematical sentences for 2 groups of 5 dinosaurs, 2 groups of 7 dinosaurs, and so on. They use multiplication in story problems, such as: Everything the fossil hunter picked up went into the truck. Here are some of the things the hunter picked up: 5 groups of dirt picks, 2 picks in each group. How many picks? 5 small sacks of fossil bones, 5 fossil bones in each sack. How many fossil bones?

They may place objects (and symbols of objects) in rows and columns and write the math sentences that tell what is going on: Make four rows of shovels with six shovels in each row (4 × 6 = 24); make six columns of shovels with four shovels in each row (6 × 4 = 24); find the total number (product) of shovels in five columns with seven shovels in each column (5 × 7 = _____). They may make drawings of objects related to the content of study in rows and columns: Draw four objects (fossil bones, hunter's tools) in each of seven rows to find the total number (product).

Students may prepare a graph to show the number of books about fossils read by a group of children during the days of the week and use multiplication to determine the number of books read by student *A, B, C,* and so on.

Division

Seeing an array of objects related to the content of the study, students in third and fourth grade may discuss how many groups are seen in arrangements such as the following:

Arrangement 1   *Arrangement 2*
●●●   ●●
●●●   ●●
               ●●

In arrangement 1, they discuss "How many 3s in 6?" and the mathematical sentence 6 divided by 3 = 2. In arrangement 2, they discuss how many 2s in 6 and the sentence 6 divided by 2 = 3. Further, they can complete a table to find the number of small two-legged dinosaur fossils. To do this, they divide each number in the following table bv 2.

How Many Small Two-Legged Dinosaur Fossils?

Number of fossilized dinosaur feet	10	8	6	4	2
Number of dinosaurs					

They can complete another table to find the number of larger four-legged dinosaurs.

How Many Large Four-Legged Dinosaurs?

Number of fossilized dinosaur feet	20	16	12	8	4
Number of dinosaurs					

The students can consider the upright hypsilophodon (hip so LOFF o don), the "kangaroo of the dinosaurs," and discuss situations with this creature; for example: (1) When 10 fossilized legs are discovered—two for each dinosaur—how many hypsilophodons? (2) Where 16 hypsilophodons fossils are found on hills—two on each hill—how many hills? (3) When 8 dinosaur fossil hatchlings are found—4 in each family—how many families? (4) When 20 dinosaur fossils are found—5 in each group—how many groups?

Multiplication and division use can be combined further in situations related to content: Consider 5 groups of 6 dinosaurs. How many in all? Consider 30 dinosaurs separated into groups of 6. How many groups? The students can discuss what is going on and then write the two multiplication and two division sentences related to the three numerals, 5, 6, and 30. The sentences are $3 \times 8 = 24$; $8 \times 3 = 24$; $24 \div$ by 8 = 3; and $24 \div$ by 3 = 8.

Calculators, calculator games, and computer software also support activities for learning the facts basic to division, multiplication, subtraction, and addition (see Chapter 7).

Topic C: Properties

To provide an opportunity for some first-grade students to discover the commutative property as it applies to addition, a teacher guided the children to discover such equalities as 2 + 3 equals 3 + 2. As an example, one commutative activity required paper strips (8 1/2″ × 3″) and metal paper punches. Each student took a strip and, with a metal paper punch, placed a certain number of holes at one end of a strip and a certain number at the other end to represent the number in each of two groups of dinosaur models (3, 2) that the teacher showed. The holes were counted (3 at one end of the paper strip, 2 at the other) and numerals 3 + 2 were written on the strip to correspond with the number of holes punched. The strip was turned over and the students counted holes again (this time, the position of the holes was reversed and, after counting the holes, the students' writing showed 2 + 3). This procedure was repeated with other equalities. Other combinations of numbers were punched on other strips, which gave the students the opportunity to discover the commutative property of other numbers.

To provide an opportunity for students to see the associative property of numbers, the teacher asked the girls and boys to tell how they should group 8 small dinosaur replicas in three groups. As the teacher followed their suggestions for grouping the dinosaurs and showed the groups on the stage of the overhead projector, the students followed along, grouped their replicas in the same way, and counted the members in each group. Pushing group 1 and group 2 together on the overhead, the teacher then put group 3 with the other two groups. All of the replicas in the groups were counted and totaled. Then the teacher asked students to put the dinosaur figures back into the three original groups.

Demonstrating the associative property again, the teacher put groups 2 and 3 together first, then put group 1 with the other two groups. All of the replicas in the groups were counted and totaled. The teacher asked students to put figures back into the original three groups and to explain what was going on. The teacher wrote addition sentences to show the process on the board.

Topic D: Measurement

Measurement activities were also integrated into the literature-based unit. The first-grade students got acquainted with continuous materials (time) that could be measured. Working with measurement of time, individual calendars were made for one week and for the month. On the calendars, the children wrote in the sequence of numbers for days in the week and month to understand the measuring of time by days, weeks, and months. With scales, they discovered other continuous materials (weight of fossil bones) to measure.

Students in a second-grade class also got acquainted with discrete objects that could be counted and continuous material that could be measured. The teacher-led activities included the following:

1. Telling students about a 1983 discovery in Surrey, England, the teacher showed a picture of a dinosaur claw that was 30 cm long and used to hook fish out of the water. The teacher asked students to use metric rulers to measure off the length of the claw.

2. Seeing the model of the 30-foot-long apatosaurus in Aliki's *Dinosaurs Are Different,* the girls and boys estimated the length of its webbed fingers. With a photocopy of the dinosaur illustration, the teacher cut the copy apart and gave each student a piece of the dinosaur shape. Using rulers, students and their partners enlarged the piece they had by drawing it on a larger sheet of paper. When the piece measured one inch, the students enlarged it to ten inches. The enlarged pieces were cut out and assembled on the class wall to make an enlarged picture of the dinosaur.[2]

3. Listening to the story set in prehistoric times about a 50-foot long mother crocodile who defended her newly hatched eggs and her young from a tyrannosau-

rus rex in T*he Crocodiles Still Wait* (Houghton, 1980) by Carol Carrick, the students walked outside and measured the length of the mother crocodile and compared her size with that of a large dinosaur.

4. Looking at *A Gallery of Dinosaurs and Other Early Reptiles* (Knopf, 1989) by Peters and *The Rourke Dinosaur Dictionary* (Rourke, 1989) by Hincks, the students saw some of the 100 crested, horned, and spiked dinosaurs. In Peters's book, they were shown to scale and in relation to one another. The size relation of these creatures to humans was shown in dinosaur drawings placed next to five-foot-tall youngsters on the pages. An oversized dinosaur continued over three pages of the book, and seeing this, the girls and boys discussed ways to make their own oversized dinosaur to show to another class.

5. Discussing *Giants of Land and Sea: Past and Present* (Knopf, 1986) by Peters, the teacher showed a drawing of the largest dinosaur ever discovered, ultrasaurus, and compared its size to the size of an average human. The girls and boys were impressed by the hugeness of the ultrasaurus and the other oversized dinosaurs whose bodies continued over two and sometimes three pages that unfolded. They compared the illustrations with those in Jacobs's *Supersaurus* (Putnam, 1982). They talked about the large creatures and ways to show how large one of the dinosaurs would be compared to the size of someone in the class. They suggested using their feet as an arbitrary unit of measurement and walked off the length of the ultrasaurus on the playground.

6. Browsing through Simon's *The Smallest Dinosaurs* (Crown, 1987) and Dixon's *The First Dinosaurs* and *The Last Dinosaurs* (both Yearling, 1990), the students selected one of the small dinosaurs to use as a measurement. The boys and girls measured things in the room to discover objects that were the same height or length as the small dinosaur. They found and labeled several items the length of the cat-sized bone-headed microphachycephalosaurus (MY crow pack ee SEF uh low saw rus).

7. Measuring a distance of 40 feet on the school ground, the students got an impression of the length of one creature they found in a resource book—a giant diplodocus. On the playground, students walked forward the distance they measured—78 steps. They took turns with a meter wheel and marked off the lengths of dinosaurs they discovered in their reading. A few wanted to measure these: deinonyehus (2.5 m); hysilophodon (1.5 m); iguanodon (9 m); tyrannosaurus rex (12 m); and triceratops (7 m). Other students measured lengths of dinosaurs in feet with lines of string on the playground and ranked them from largest to smallest: brachiosaurus, 40; apatosaurus, 30; tyrannosaurus, 22; iguanadon, 18; allosaurus, 15; and stegosaurus, 11.

8. After measuring dinosaur lengths, the children recorded the information on the board in the class and then wrote the information in their math journals. The teacher placed a graph form on the overhead projector and projected the form on the board. The teacher encouraged the girls and boys to use the form projected on the board and to arrange their information from shortest to longest dinosaur for a class chart. The girls and boys had options, too: They could place the name of the dinosaurs in alphabetical order or in an order from largest to smallest. The names of the creatures could also be arranged in the order in which the dinosaurs appeared in the prehistoric period or in the order of a dinosaur family tree to show which ones are bird hipped and which ones are lizard hipped. Another arrangement could show dinosaurs with protective armor and those without. All were involved in developing a ranked list of some type.

9. Using a large graph laminated on poster board, some students made a picture graph and used one color block of paper for each meter measured to show the

lengths of selected dinosaurs. Plant-snatching dinosaurs were represented with one color of paper and meat-chewing ones with another color. To record further information, squares represented the lengths of dinosaurs that were measured with string, and circles represented lengths of dinosaurs measured with the meter wheel.

10. To introduce the concept of scale, the teacher reviewed the way the artist used scale in *Giants of the Lands, Sea and Air* (Knopf, 1986) by David Peters and demonstrated how to draw a five-foot dinosaur to scale on graph paper. The teacher drew two other dinosaur shapes on graph paper, cut them out, and arranged the shapes in order from small to large on a chart. Next, the students drew dinosaurs on graph paper and made a comparison chart of dinosaur lengths. The teacher walked around the room and monitored the progress of the students as they worked together.

11. Students considered the lengths of dinosaur footprints and looked at a diagram of the track of tyrannosaurus rex that was 28 inches long from back to toe, and they discussed ways to re-create it full-size in a drawing. They measured the length they would need for the outline and measured it again when finished. They drew outlines of other dinosaur footprints they found in references and measured the lengths and widths with rulers.

12. From photographs and observations in books about some of the discovered dinosaur footprints in fossilized dinosaur trackways, the students found that the tyrannosaurus had a 12-foot stride and the apatosaurus had a 13-foot stride, and they measured the distance of the strides from one footprint to another. They made footprints from paper cutouts and placed them on the classroom floor and on the playground. The distances needed between the footprints in the strides were measured by students. To further explore the concept of strides and the usefulness of mathematics to the paleontologists, the teacher encouraged the students to use a stopwatch and to measure the time it took for a student to run or walk that distance on the playground. When the students mentioned some of the behaviors of small dinosaurs, the teacher asked them to simulate the walk or run of a small dinosaur for a certain distance and then measure the time it took for them to do this. Using dinosaur "slippers" (The Lighter Side), students also made three-prong tracks in the playground sand and simulated a paleontologist discovering dinosaur tracks. They determined the distance of the stride and predicted what dinosaur could have made similar tracks.

13. Knowing that some scientists estimated that duck-billed dinosaurs probably traveled about five miles per hour, the students measured the distance and the time it took to run between a tyrannosaurus's footprints to predict out how fast and far it traveled in an hour.

14. Fastening a waist pack (that included a weight) around the waist to simulate the weight of a long dinosaur tail, one student made tracks in sand to see the difference the weight made in the footprints. Using rulers, the students measured the depth of the imprint of the footprint at different points in the track. In their notebooks, they drew diagrams of the tracks and labeled the drawings with measurements. To demonstrate this, the teacher showed them the way two scientists kept a list of field chronology activities in the back of Harner and Gowan's *Digging Dinosaurs* (Harper, 1988).

Carrying a weighted waist pack over the back to simulate the weight of a dinosaur's spiny neck plate, another student made the tracks and the others measured and observed the effect the placement of the weight had on the imprint of the tracks.[3] Another drawing of the tracks was made by the students and the measurements were recorded in their notebooks. The students made their own footprints in sand, measured them, drew them, and, in writing, compared their prints to the three-prong track of a tyrannosaurus rex. Relying on their drawings during discussion time in the room, the students talked about what fossil footprints can tell us.

15. To show what they had learned, the students discussed scale, measurement, and the materials that would be needed to make a mural to show the Age of the Dinosaurs. They agreed on the scale of one inch equals one million years. Moving from right to left on mural paper, the students marked an X as the starting point for the present time period and measured 100 inches to the left to show the beginning of the Cretaceous age, then 140 inches more to the left to mark off the Jurassic age, and then 210 inches further to mark off the Triassic age. To measure the passing of time for these periods, the scale was marked on the mural and it became a guide for the students as they located a particular place to put their illustrations and descriptive paragraphs about dinosaurs and prehistoric life.

Topic E: Geometry

Wirzup (1976) points out some of the research about students learning geometry by P. Van Heile, a Dutch mathematician, who indicated there were levels of knowledge through which students advance as they learned geometry. According to Van Heile, children in grades 1–5 first learn to recognize common shapes and then each shape's general characteristics (level I and II). At the end of grade 6, the students are able to classify figures according to their characteristics (level III). (The deductive study of geometry is level IV and occurs during the high school years.)

With a focus on van Heile's first two levels—recognizing common shapes and then each shape's general characteristics—illustrations of dinosaurs were collected, displayed, and observed as fourth-grade students looked for geometric forms in the forms and shapes of the large animals. For instance, the girls and boys saw the circular opening in the top of the skull fossil of the diplodocus and the triangular-shaped plates on the stegosaurus. They identified similar shapes—triangular shapes of dinosaur spikes, thumbs, and teeth. They also showed what they found in books—the triangular shape they saw in the spikes on the armor of the ankylosaurus, in the thumb spikes of an iguandon, and in the teeth of a tyrannosaurus. With the teacher's guidance, they talked about the inside and the outside of the closed curves they found in artists' drawings of the prehistoric creatures. When they created their original artworks, they pointed out the similarity of geometric forms and shapes to the objects they drew.

With Robin West's *Dinosaur Discoveries* (Carolrhoda, 1989), the students read step-by-step instructions and built models of dinosaurs and prehistoric plants with paper, scissors, and glue. Measuring, marking, and connecting some pencil dots before folding the required shapes (triangles, cylinders) gave students an opportunity to see the way geometric shapes were used in paper construction. They saw that circles and a triangle made a pair of eyes, rectangles made the teeth, and cylinders formed the body tubes. As students examined the paper models, they began to develop an understanding of what a two-dimensional or three-dimensional object was like.

The students compared the patterns in drawings of dinosaurs with the patterns found in present-day animals. For instance, the natural sculpture and symmetry in a reproduced shell of the Hawksbill turtle (Nature Company) was scrutinized as students discussed armor plates (shells) of dinosaurs and the possible similarities of a dinosaur's armor plates with the Hawksbill's shell.

Additionally, symmetry was seen in the natural design of skeletons of dinosaurs and in the designs of structures built by people. For example, a picture of a suspension bridge was placed beside an illustration of a skeleton of a diplodocus, a large plant-eating land creature. The students discovered the similarity: Just as a suspension bridge deck was hung from columns or piers placed side by side, the backbone of the large four-footed dinosaur was suspended between two pairs of legs (columns, piers). Just as bridge cables were strung downward from the bridge columns to the deck of the bridge, so were the muscles of the dinosaur sloped downward from the backbone and anchored in the legs. This arrangement allowed the large animal to carry its weight and to use its backbone as the main shock absorber for jolts and jars. To consider further the importance of the suspension of an animal's backbone, students looked at the design and symmetry of skeletons of the dinosaurs that walked on two legs and searched for structural designs developed by humans that were similar. Useful in the search was the resource *Bridges* (Dial, 1991) by Ken Robbins with its photographs of suspension, truss, and draw bridges.

After discussing the illustrations, the girls and boys saw ways an animal's backbone was suspended in other prehistoric creatures. For instance, students noticed the backbone of coelophysis (see OF e sis) and the way it was balanced with its long tail on one end and a long bird-like neck and short "arms" on the other. They saw the similarity of the backbone of the plesiosaur, a giant reptile of the sea, suspended between broad paddle-shaped legs with that of diplodocus whose backbone was suspended between thick stumpy legs. The teacher again compared the suspension of the large reptile's backbone with the suspension bridge and sketched both side-by-side on the board to show the similarities—both needed support, freedom to move, and ways to adjust to pressure and outside forces.

Related to the theme in a geometry center, students may make a series of plane figures that represent fossil digs. First, each dig will have three sides (isosceles, scalene, equilateral, right, acute, obtuse triangles) and then four sides (square, rectangle, parallelogram, trapezoid). Geoboards, pegs, and rubber bands can be used to make outlines of plane figures—common geometric shapes—and the diagonals. Paper covered with rows and columns of evenly spaced dots (dot paper) may be used by the students to copy the figures they form on the geoboards and the dot paper copies may be placed in a class book. In addition to handling and discussing solid models of such objects as a cube, pyramid, prism, and cylinder, students may use different lengths of yarn to enclose a "blob of space" on their desktop to make closed curves and discuss lines, segments, and rays, and follow up with drawings on the chalkboard or in individual books.

Topic F: Statistics and Probability

Work with statistics can begin as early as kindergarten and first grade as children make simple block graphs that represent colors or types of their favorite dinosaurs found in books. They organize and interpret information that relates to what they are learning. With graphs on the topic of dinosaurs, young students can record information about their favorite prehistoric animals of land and sea, animal colors, dinosaur babies, and stories they know. In the middle- and upper-elementary grades, students should work with data they gather from study projects or from people in the community in which they live. For example, a review of reference books and the information the books have about tyrannosaurus rex can provide data about whether tyrannosaurus rex the largest meat-eating animal that ever lived. A graph can indicate to the students which reference books have this information and which have facts about other meat eaters. For those who need a letter-writing extension, interested students may write to publishers of books that have any out-of-date information and ask for current titles of books that provide more accurate data.

Topic G: Functions

Students can learn about one-to-one relationship of numbers (function) through authentic classroom experiences. For instance, the relation of an early discoverer of fossils (Chapter 2) to a country can be expressed in writing as "Mary Ann Mantell was an early fossil discoverer from England." This relationship of one discoverer-to-one country can be shown by drawing separate lines from each name of the discoverer to the name of each discoverer's country. Doing this, students will see that the mathematical concept of function is not limited to math time but is at work in the language he or she uses. Mathematical relationships are found almost everywhere.

Topic H: Graphs

For a content study, students can complete tables and make bar, line, and picture graphs. Graphs will help young students compare, count, add, and subtract, and tables can keep a record for a daily count of something. For instance, graphs can compare types of dinosaurs, represent types of dinosaur fossils found, show the stories about a particular dinosaur type, and be devices for adding information or subtracting information found on subsequent days. Two ways one second-grade teacher integrated graphs are discussed next.

While reading, the girls and boys each kept a journal and recorded the types of dinosaurs read about in their selected stories. Each day, every child received a colored block for each type of dinosaurs read: a red block for each child reading about the lizard-hipped group, a blue block for each one reading about the bird-hipped group, and a yellow block for those whose reading covered both groups. The children stacked their blocks on a table and talked about the meaning of the number of blocks in each stack. Then, headings were written on a bar graph on chart paper and each child put a square of paper on the bar graph to make columns that showed the types of dinosaurs and the number of books read about them. Student book choices included Greene's *How to Know Dinosaurs* (Macmillan, 1966), Gabriele's *The Great Age of the Dinosaurs* (Penny Lane, 1985), Gerver's *Day of the Dinosaur* (Random House, 1986), and Granger's *Amazing World of Dinosaurs* (Troll, 1982). For emerging readers, Howard's *I Can Read about Dinosaurs* (Troll, 1972), Neilson's *Dinosaurs* (Troll, 1989), and Morris's *Dinosaurs & Other First Animals* (Harcourt, 1988) were available.

To make another graph, each child drew, colored, and cut out a small dinosaur shape to show the dinosaur in the story he or she was reading. The child pasted the shape to a chart that had names of dinosaurs on it. After putting the dinosaur shapes on the chart, students looked at the bar graph and discovered the patterns of types of dinosaurs that authors had written about in the stories. When the students contributed the information they found to their classroom graph and used these records to discover the types of dinosaurs found in stories, they began to see the graph as a useful device for collecting information.

In a fourth-grade class, the students noticed a certain feature of dinosaurs—armored plates—and recorded which dinosaurs did/did not have this feature. Books were read about extinction, habitats, behavior, and types of dinosaurs found in various regions or countries (Chapter 3), and were contrasted and compared on the graph. Other graphs showed the results of surveys that were conducted by the students. For example, bar graphs showed the ages in years of all of the students in the class studying about dinosaurs.

Organizing data with graphs was a way for the students to discover patterns, too. To assist in this, the teacher used permanent lines and spaces for a generic bar graph on an overhead transparency, and, when it was needed, projected the graph on the board so they could record information on the board for all to see. With the form projected on the board, the students discussed what was recorded and determined any patterns they found. Once the students knew how to measure degrees in a circle, understand percent and how to compute it, circle graphs were used, too. At that time, the teacher prepared a permanent circle for a generic circle graph on an overhead transparency and provided a large protractor and chalkboard compass for the students' use at the board.

Topic I: Logical Thinking

In a fifth grade, the students participated in activities that helped them think logically. To foster this, the teacher reviewed terms important to logic (e.g., *all, some, not, and, or,* and *if . . . then.* Involved in thinking logically about hypsilophodon, a small, speedy, bird-hipped, plant-eating creature, students engaged in dialogue with the teacher who asked: "Was the hypsilophodon a dinosaur? If you guessed (predicted, hypothesized, had a hunch) that it was a dinosaur, then you can use what you know about dinosaurs and say to yourself, '*If* the hypsilophodon was a dinosaur, *then:*

the hypsilophodon would have lived in the Age of the Dinosaurs.

the hypsilophodon would be a reptile that laid eggs.

the hypsilophodon would have died out millions of years ago.

the hypsilophodon would be cold-blooded and have backbones and dry, scaly skin.' "

These statements assisted students in a search for information that backed up their ideas that the hypsilophodon was a dinosaur. The students were encouraged to use statements to generate another point of view, too: *If* the hpsilophodon was not a dinosaur, *then:*

the hypsilophodon would *not* have lived in the Age of the Dinosaurs.

the hypsilophodon would *not* be a reptile that laid eggs.

the hypsilophodon would *not* have died out millions of years ago.

the hypsilophodon would *not* be cold-blooded or have a backbone or dry, scaly skin.

More if-then conditions were discussed by the students and teacher: "If you expected to find that it was a reptile, then you *would not* expect to find it gave birth to live babies. If you expected to find that it was cold-blooded, you *would* expect to find that it had skin with scales. You *would not* expect to find that it had skin without scales." To find further evidence about their hypothesis, the students read more about this creature who had toes like bird, a tail for balance, and a horned beak in *Hypsilophodon* (Rourke, 1984) by Ron Wilson. The if-then conditions were applied to two other dinosaurs after reading Redhead's *The Brontosaurus* (The Wright Group, 1976) and Oliver's *Memenehisaurus* (Rourke, 1986).

Other activities engaged the students in reading and writing about experiments, such as exploring the effects of different substances on fossils (and cleaned disinfected chicken bones). They wrote about experiments in journals, made up story problems, and discussed ways math was used in paleontology. For instance, size relationships were compared and expressed and proportions were calculated for displays. To do this, students used dinosaur-shaped crackers (alternatives were gummy dinosaurs, cereal shapes, goldfish crackers, oyster crackers) to set up ratios and proportions on their desks and follow the teacher's demonstrations on an overhead projector. Relationships between the sample and total number were described and discussed. After the discussion was over, they enjoyed eating the crackers and planned a mural to show layers of rock that were labeled for the Triassic, Jurassic, and Cretaceous periods. Working on the mural, the students participated in the following activities:

1. They affixed illustrations of dinosaurs to show their place in prehistoric life in the time periods. Along with other dinosaurs, the stegosaurus was placed in the Jurassic period, the triceratops in the Cretaceous period, and so on.
2. They classified each dinosaur as meat consumers or plant consumers. Students tallied meat-eating dinosaur fossils and plant-eating dinosaur fossils in the rock layers and determined a ratio of dinosaur predators to prey.
3. They determined ratios of dinosaurs that walked on all four legs to those that walked on two legs for the time periods. They tallied dinosaurs that walked on all four legs and dinosaurs that walked on two legs and determined a ratio.
4. They tallied flying reptiles and walking animals and determined a ratio of flying reptiles to walking animals. To determine another ratio, they tallied the dinosaurs with spiny plates and those without.
5. They discussed several points of view: "Could rock strata accurately show the different kinds of dinosaurs that lived together? Why or why not?" "If the ratio of predators to prey was very low, would we conclude that this was enough evidence to say that most dinosaurs were warm-blooded (endothermic)?" "How would this indicate that perhaps only predators were warm-blooded (endothermic)?" "What other evidence do we need?" "From what we know, what is the possibility that meat-eating dinosaurs were warm-blooded (endothermic) and that plant-eating dinosaurs were cold-blooded (ectothermic)?"

Other Comparisons

The students researched animals with similarities to dinosaurs and made comparisons (an activity suitable for grades 4 and older):

1. Ankylosaurus (ANG kul o saw rus), a walking tank, may have been like an armadillo because . . . .
2. Pachycephalosaurs (pack ee SEF uh low sahrs), the boneheaded dinosaurs, may have been like big-horn sheep because . . . .
3. When in danger, horned dinosaurs may have been like musk oxen because . . . .
4. Brachiosaurs (BRACK ee uh sahrs) may have been like giraffes because . . . .
5. Plant-eating sauropods (SAW uh pods) may have been like elephants because . . . .
6. Plant-eating dinosaurs may have been like caribou because . . . .
7. Coelurosaurs (see LURE uh sahrs) may have been like a desert roadrunner because . . . .

Topic J: Problem Solving

Sixth-grade students also used mathematics to solve the problems that were meaningful and relevant to them. They used mathematical sentences to express a problem situation (e.g., the number of students in class that day, the number not in attendance; the number eating lunch at the school cafeteria, the number bringing their lunches from home, and the number walking home for lunch; and the time on the clock, the number of minutes students have to work on their projects, and the time they predict they will finish). For projects related to problem solving the students engaged in:

1. *Listening.*   Listening to pages read aloud from *Dinosaur Discovery* (Bonjour, 1987) by Muller and Jacques, or reading pages with a partner and making up story problems related to what they heard, students wrote mathematical sentences such as: For a dinosaur discovery, the route of one discoverer was from Dinosaur Dig A (347 miles) to Dinosaur Dig B (701 miles) to Dinosaur Dig C (676 miles). What was the total distance of the route? Two-step problems were expressed mathematically, too: Getting ready for a dinosaur fossil hunting trip with her mother and father, Andrea's family bought 3 miniature flashlights for $1.49 each, 9 cans of soup for $.69 each, 9 cans of chili for $1. 59 each, bacon for $1.99, and crackers for $1.25. How much did the family spend?

2. *Using mathematical sentences and making a story problem for each.* Problems were generated from the text about the time periods in Man's *The Day of the Dinosaur* (Galahad, 1982), Kricher's *Peterson First Guide to Dinosaurs* (Houghton, 1990), Lammers's *Dinosaurs* (Sterling, 1990), Langley's *Dinosaurs* (Watts, 1988), and other sources.

3. *Using concrete materials, pictures, and diagrams.*   To do this, students drew pictures and diagrams for word problems. For an independent activity, one student added pictures and diagrams to the "Writing Suggestions for the Topic of Ancient Dinosaurs" in *Make Your Own Adventure Books* (Early Learning Book Club, 1990). It had reproducible pages and ideas for making books with pop-ups, flaps, wheels, and tabs. Another student selected Spizzirri's *Dinosaurs* and *Dinosaurs of Prey* (both Spizzirri, 1981), educational coloring books, as sources for dinosaur models.

4. *Using information from authentic maps to make mathematical problems.*   Some students used the information in Edwin Colbert's *Men and Dinosaurs* (Hammond, 1968) as a basis for story problems. Others found maps that showed the places of the field activities of two scientists, John Harner and James Gowan (1988) in *Digging Dinosaurs* (Harper, 1988) and made up math problems based on the information the two scientists wrote in their field chronology.

5. *Using imaginative creatures to solve problems.*   With fanciful creatures such as *Wollygoggles and Other Creatures* (GCT), the students considered Number Creatures, Word Creatures, and Figural Creatures. They looked for a pattern to establish a system for solving each problem and arrived at the rule for solving a related set of problems.

6. *Using dramatics to solve problems.*   With pantomime and creative drama, students acted out situations from Facklam's *And Then There Was One* (Little, Brown/Sierra, 1989), which provided events for drama.

7. *Using logic.*   Reviewing William Mannetti's *Dinosaurs in Your Backyard* (Atheneum, 1982), students learned how to use evidence from the past as well as the present to reach logical conclusions about such topics as (a) the descendants of dinosaurs in the backyard are birds, (b) small lumps of different sizes on fossil skin indicates different colors on the dinosaurs, and (c) the theory about the

dinosaur's known stance and intelligence is changing. Students also considered the use of analogies, matrix logic, fable logic, circle logic, syllogisms, and Venn diagrams with *Logic Anyone?* (GCT). *Wff'n Proof: The Game of Modern Logic* and *Logic in the Round* (both GCT) required use of symbolic logic. Further, *Logic in the Round* presented problems requiring the placement of objects or people in a circular situation (e.g., dinosaurs at a water hole).

8. *Using mental arithmetic for giving estimated and exact answers.* Students gave estimates as part of the problem-solving process. They rounded off numbers and then performed operations without pencil or paper. Estimations were followed by computed answers and checked against each other to see if the computed answers were reasonable.

9. *Using a story for more than one reading.* The students also focused on different aspects of a story that related to mathematics (Borasi, Sheedy, & Siegel, 1990). For example, one setting of a story was in the context of a city with an irregular pattern of streets that included diagonals (Euclidean geometry). Students looked for other relationships to mathematics, such as a city with a regular pattern of streets (non-Euclidean geometry); a map with the distance between home and school, home and the workplace, and home and a community building (mapping, distances, scales); numbers in home addresses (ways numbers are assigned); and ways a character thought about a problem, defined it, explored it, and evaluated solutions (insight into problem solving). Additionally, the students discussed any problems that had too little or too much information.

10. *Using a math center.* In math centers, the students experimented with hands-on approaches to numbers and recorded experiments in learning logs (e.g., "What did we discover this week in our math center?").

Classroom Update

- The time that students are engaged in relevant reading and mathematics tasks is positively associated with academic achievement (Borg, 1980).
- When teachers increased their emphasis on such functions as checking work, reteaching, proceeding in small steps, giving detailed instructions and explanations, and giving practice time, feedback, corrections, independent practice and weekly/monthly reviews, their students achieved more than students of teachers who did not emphasize these functions (Good & Grouws 1979).
- One of the differences between the effective and less effective teacher is the frequency of questions; effective teachers ask about three times as many questions as less effective teachers (Brophy & Good, 1986).
- Literature is a focus for interdisciplinary units that emphasize enjoyment of literary works and the aesthetic values in them. Literature stimulates a holistic learning situation. Third- and fourth-grade teachers report that students establish a bond with text in a nonstressful way that encourages them to take an active role in their own learning process, to take risks in exploring further, and to share with others what was learned (Austin, 1989).

Integrating Science

In *Big Old Bones: A Dinosaur Tale* (Clarion, 1989) by Carol Carrick, the third-grade students saw that Professor Potts in the story had a difficulty. He had many more dinosaur bones than he knew what to do with. The students helped the professor predict which bones were needed and which were not. This challenge showed the students some of the problems a scientist has as she or he works in sciencing. "Sciencing is what the scientist does; it is what elementary students should do when they study science," write Kellough and Roberts (1990). "We do not believe that you should teach children that there are 'steps to the scientific method.' To ask children to memorize steps in the scientific method is to imply that the process of sciencing is linear, and it is not! It implies that there is a beginning and an end which is final, and this is misleading. It implies to children, that for them, science is a repetition of the experiments, of memorizing the observations, and this is dull!" As a welcome contrast, sciencing includes data gathering, data organizing, idea building, and idea using. To gather data, students observe, measure, and verify; to organize data, students graph, classify, order, compare, and sequence; to build ideas, students explain, generalize, infer, interpret, make analogies, and synthesize; and to use ideas, students apply and control variables, define, hypothesize, build models, and predict—and all of these include hands-on experiences and processes.

Hands-On Experiences

Certainly, with hands-on experiences, science can become a part of an integrative approach in a classroom because:[4]

1. Hands-on science activities in elementary grades help students from diverse cultural/linguistic backgrounds develop experiential bases similar to that of their classmates. This is accomplished without coming in conflict with traditional mores of a child's native culture. A common set of experiences derived from science activities forms a basis for understanding concepts and using communication skills critical to all instruction.
2. Hands-on science activities where a child is able to see and assess his or her effect on a system helps a student develop a better sense of causal relationships and control over his or her destiny.
3. Learning process and problem-solving strategies of an activity-based natural science program helps a culturally diverse student learn to sort out the extraneous and focus on critical aspects of a situation. Training in observation and problem-solving skills helps children deal more effectively with the environment outside their specific culture. In addition, a natural science program assists students in developing a vocabulary appropriate to the mainstream population.
4. Science activities provide an opportunity for many students who are not visually academically oriented to experience success and gain confidence when their achievement does not wholly depend on their ability to read or write in English.
5. Activity-based science also provides a perfect opportunity for group work where social and communication skills are taught and practiced. Through activities, students have an opportunity to work in small groups extensively—a teaching strategy especially helpful to children with language differences.

Sciencing and its traits can be integrated with other areas as students' skills are developed in coordination with other curriculum areas. In this integration, the scientific patterns of change, stability, statistics, probability, logic, problem solving (Krulik & Rudnick, 1988), and critical thinking (Beyer, 1988) become curricular bridges from science into other areas. These curricular bridges are pathways that allow students to cross over from science into other areas. As an example, when the students' science investigations provide meaningful contexts for reading, writing, speaking, and listening, they cross over from science into the expressive arts (Thelen, 1984). Additionally, sciencing is easily integrated with history-social sciences since it is a human activity that relates to a certain time, place, and condition (see Chapter 5). Scientists and their work are achievements of people speaking diverse languages from diverse cultures—and can be included as an important part of history. Intellectual processes such as critical thinking, observing, analyzing, synthesizing, and expressive forms from the expressive arts (art, music, dance) cross over into scientific topics of light, sound, perceptions, scale, and structure, and link science with the arts. Students who draw and act can further enhance sciencing when they show artists' interpretations of what scientists do. Additionally, science makes contributions in areas of health and nutrition, psychological services, and physical education, and is integrated often in these areas.

Basic traits in sciencing are shown in Jean Rogers's *Dinosaurs Are 568* (Greenwillow, 1988). In Rogers's book, Raymond Wayliss is fascinated on his first day at school in first grade by a large illustration of a diplodocus on a classroom wall and his observant teacher takes him to the school librarian who shows him the dinosaur section, number 568. With this introduction to dinosaurs, Raymond begins his independent learning, reads carefully, and compares observations. Because of his careful reading, Raymond is able to point out an error about whales to an encyclopedia publisher. This results in a front-page newspaper story about him—a boy who satisfied his curiosities and followed through with his ideas—traits important in sciencing.

Topic A: Gathering and Organizing Data

"To find out what the dinosaurs looked like and how they lived, we must study the fossils of their bones, eggs, and footprints," read the teacher from *The ABC Dinosaur Book* (Childrens Press, 1982) by Jill Kingdon. "We also look at the fossils of plants and insects that lived in the Age of the Dinosaurs to learn more about life at that time." To infuse science into a thematic unit about dinosaurs with a literacy focus, the teacher read to the fourth-grade students and went through the writing process with them, from prewriting to publishing, for several days. Writing research reports was emphasized. To develop background information, the students studied dinosaurs (or other animals of interest to them) and the care of their young. To interact with a resource person in the community, a trip to visit the librarian at the public library was scheduled. Appropriate animal books were reserved for students at a nearby branch. With previous help from the teacher, librarians, classroom aides, and accompanying parents, the girls and boys chose and researched their selected animals through books, magazines, and other reference materials they found. Initially, students were encouraged to start their research by reading a specially chosen book about a selected animal.

For instance, if a student wanted to start research by reading about a particular dinosaur, *The ABC Dinosaur Book* (Childrens Press, 1982) by Jill Kingdon, as one of several books, was available and had dinosaurs entered in alphabetical order—an arrangement that made it easy for a student to find information about a particular one. Each student recorded information describing an animal, its habitat system, its interaction and care of the young, the adult animal, eating habits, and other information the reader found interesting.

Class demonstrations by the teacher became an important part of the unit. The teacher announced the name of the animal she was researching and used the overhead projector to show how information was selected about the animal's care of the young, its habitat, eating habits, and so on, from the book the teacher read. On subsequent days, the teacher showed students how to select relevant observations, how to place information in categories, and how to take notes (Aaronson, 1975). The teacher showed how to put notes in a paragraph form. She scheduled conferences with the students to discuss revising and editing. Parent volunteers were invited to the classroom to offer assistance to individual students as the reading and research project continued. When students had their first rough drafts, the teacher met with the students in groups, where the writers read their paragraphs and everyone listened and offered comments. The material was reread and the students took notes to give suggestions to the writer. Positive remarks, such as, "I liked the way you . . . ," were encouraged to support the writers. Using a colored pencil, each writer jotted down suggestions on his or her piece of writing to consider during rewriting. Having ownership in this way, each writer decided which comments would be included in the second draft.

When students had written, reviewed, and edited their second rough drafts, the teacher demonstrated how she added bibliographic information to her research report and discussed some of the mechanics of the editing process. Demonstrating the use of editing marks with an overhead transparency, the teacher encouraged students to use colored pencils to edit their writings. The final editing was done by the teacher (or classroom aide or parent volunteer). Then, illustrations were created and added to the report, along with a table of contents and a title page (Routman, 1988).

Topic B: Building Ideas of Science

Themes in Science

In a recent state science framework,[5] several themes were recommended for instruction: (1) energy, (2) evolution, (3) patterns of change, (4) scale and structure, (5) stability, and (6) systems and interactions. Themes such as these can direct the design of activities in the classroom.

1. *Theme of evolution: Do we see a mass extinction period today?*   Gathering information, some fifth-grade students realized that evolution was an organizing theory of biology and was an accepted scientific explanation of how animals and plants change over time and that it was no more controversial in scientific circles than the theories of gravitation and electron flow. With current information, the students saw that the theory of evolution was being modified as new evidence emerged. Theory about evolution was changing because scientists were now considering a new mechanism —the periodic occurrence of mass extinction—as a current subject of inquiry and debate. The focus of debate was this: If it is true that there were/are periodic mass extinctions on the earth and this turns out to be supported by all available evidence, this idea will modify the current history of evolution. Indeed, many scientists contend that today our planet is experiencing its greatest mass extinction in 66 million years, the time period when dinosaurs vanished along with 60 to 80 percent of other animal species (Gore, 1989). Some believe that we are in an extinction today that began 11,000 years ago when most of the large mammals (the saber-toothed cats, woolly mammoths, and huge ground sloths) were eliminated (Gore, 1989).

2. *What's fossil watching?*   Reviewing the theory of evolution provided observations, such as the ones Gore made, for the students in the classroom. As the students studied evolution as the history of natural things and their changes over time, they also studied patterns and processes from geology and biology that shaped history. They saw fossils as the marks of this evolving history (Jeffrey, 1985), and, through the study of two big ideas (themes) of science—evolution and patterns of change—the students learned that

a. Time provides the direction of evolution (e.g., what happens next depends on what has happened before).

b. Constraints come from influences such as chemicals, genetics, and physical environment.

c. Chance factors influence natural variation in what is possible. In a species there can be variation in characteristics, and living things progress through a life cycle that is characteristic of their species. This cycle begins with a new cell, continues through phases of growth and development to the adult form, and ends at death.

3. *Theme of change: What is a rainforest doing in the Rocky Mountains?* Indeed, the students became aware of present-day findings and fossils that were marks of evolving history through the daily news. Marks of history were reported in the newspapers when fossils of prehistoric palm fronds and other plants were found in Colorado during an excavation. The excavations for the construction of a new Denver airport (1990) revealed the prehistorical presence of a rainforest at the foot of what is now the Rocky Mountains. The discovered fossils showed prehistoric plants—signs that tell a part of the earth's history.

4. *Theme of stability: What is stable about a living fossil?* Recently in another part of the world, a living fossil was found. This gave students the opportunity to see the theme of stability working in the environment. Living fossils, stromatolites, were discovered in the shallow water of the eastern Bahamas by geologists from the Caribbean Marine Research Center. Stromatolites, whose fossils have been uncovered in rocks 3.5 billion years old, are living mounds of sticky blue-green algae that hold sand and sediments together on the ocean floor. They are living examples of the scientific idea/theme of stability. Still another living fossil was found that gave the students an opportunity to see another example of the theme of stability. Hans Fricke, a marine biologist from West Germany, discovered a living species of coelacanth (see LAH canth), a descendant of fish from the prehistoric age.[6] According to Fricke (1988), the fish had fins with muscular and skeleton systems, so it could rest with its fins braced (like legs) against the sea bottom. This living fossil provided a few mysteries for students to ponder: (a) the fish swam strangely—sometimes backward and sometimes belly up; (b) the fins were synchronized; the front right fin worked in tandem with the left rear and vice versa, giving it the same gait as a trotting horse; (c) the fish could rotate its flexible forward fins nearly 180 degrees, which let the fish scull along as it swam; and (d) the fin at the top of the tail waved as the fish drifted along the ocean floor.

Topic C: Sorting Data

Recognizing Dinosaurs by Attributes

To consider an understanding about reptiles that flew, a teacher in a fifth-grade class introduced *"Dinosaurs" that Swam and Flew* (Prentice-Hall, 1985) by David C. Knight and asked students to consider the idea that some dinosaurs were warm-blooded. Additional observations about this were read aloud from *The Warm-Blooded Dinosaurs* (Holiday, 1978) by Julian May. With these sources, and other books of their choice, the students gained information about evolution as a process of patterns and mechanisms and as a product of history. Emerging readers who asked for more information about scientists' discoveries and their theories about origins of dinosaurs were referred to *Why Things Change: The Story of Evolution* (Parents, 1973) written by Jeanne Bendick, and independent readers to *Before the Sun Dies: The Story of Evolution* (Macmillan, 1989) by Roy A. Gallant.

Studying a topic such as this from science, the girls and boys linked the topic to an area of expression—music. When the students integrated music into the topic, they realized that composers were creative with words and musical tones and used music as a way to pass along information and tell others about a topic. As an example of linking music and science in a fourth-grade class, the students sang their favorite dinosaur songs several times and were asked to think about what dinosaurs and their life would be like when they lived. Linking the information they gained from the songs back to a literacy curriculum, the students thought about some of the composers' words and the synonyms—other words that could be choices for composers. After singing a song about tyrannosaurus rex (Caedmon Records), they dictated selected words and phrases from what they heard: *slew the animals, awed his foe,* and *swamp-filled world.* With the aid of a classroom thesaurus, they wrote these words (and the synonyms) in alphabetical order on a chart of dinosaur words. Choosing synonyms to substitute for a composer's words, the song was reread aloud and the choice of the synonyms was discussed (e.g., Which words keep the meaning? The rhythm? The beat?). Here are some of the words the fourth-grade students discussed: *awe—shock, surprise, impress; foe—enemy, opponent, adversary; slew—destroy, put an end to, finish;* and *swamp—marsh, bog, slough.*

Further discussing the information they got from the song, the boys and girls talked about what dinosaurs in the past—herbivores as well as carnivores—might have to eat. While engaged in this, the teacher determined the extent to which the students realized that scientists can determine whether a dinosaur was a plant snatcher or a meat gulper from the shape of teeth and the texture of fossil bones. To assist in this, the teacher showed them illustrations of different-shaped fossil teeth from Aliki's *Dinosaur Bones* (Crowell, 1988). For some of the words the students heard in the book's passages, they found meanings in a dictionary and discussed them. To clarify, students consulted *The Lincoln Writing Dictionary for Children,* (Morris, 1988) and found that the word *dinosaur* came from two Greek words meaning "terrible lizard" and discovered it was a word used originally to identify the animals in 1841 by Sir Richard Owens, a British scientist. Believing dinosaurs were cold-blooded, ferocious meat eaters and related to lizards, Owens thought the Greek words fit the descriptions of all of these animals but some of the students believed some dinosaurs were warm-blooded, docile plant eaters, and not related to lizards, disagreeing with Owen's view. They wanted to search for other words to describe this group of dinosaurs. In talking together about this, the students and the teacher used words such as *bird hipped, plates, protective horns, reptiles, spikes,* and *weight* to describe their knowledge of dinosaurs. As they talked, they wrote the words on charts in the room. Looking up the meanings of other words and announcing them, the students added information to the topic. After looking up the meaning of *reptile,* they read the definition and said reptiles were cold-blooded animals that laid eggs, had backbones, and had dry, scaly skin. The teacher considered aloud some questions about the key words in the definition and asked, "How does this definition help us answer questions such as:

1. Were all dinosaurs cold-blooded? What meaning does this have for us?
2. What fossils of dinosaur backbones have been found? What does this finding tell us? What does the word *backbone* mean?
3. What fossils of eggs have been found? How do we know if it is true that all dinosaurs laid eggs? What evidence would we look for if this were false? If this were true?
4. Where did we get this information about dinosaurs? What are some of the ways we can get additional information about dinosaurs?"

These questions and others took the teacher and students back into books such as the *Hotblooded Dinosaurs* (Dial, 1976) by Adrian Desmond and *Dinosaurs* (Ladybird, n.d.) to search for the information they needed to pursue their lines of inquiry. Brief booktalks were given by the teacher about several sources: *Dinosaurs* (Raintree, 1990) had concepts of science to extend "you-centered" science narratives; *All New Dinosaurs and Their Friends from the Great Recent Discoveries* (Bellerophon, 1988) by Robert Long and Samuel Welles from the Museum of Paleontology at University of California, Berkeley, showed labels inserted in black-and-white drawings of recently discovered dinosaurs; and a science series, *Discovering Dinosaurs* (Lerner, 1990), was useful since it offered more than one book for students to use as reference material.

Topic D: Engaging in Research: Survey

Related to prehistorical animals, the students' discussion in a sixth grade led to a question, What do people believe about dinosaurs? To determine this, students wrote questions on a question map on the board that they wanted to ask friends, relatives, and classmates. Some questions were taken from *Dinosaurs* (San Diego Zoo Book) by John Bennett Wexo and included these: Do you believe that the first people and dinosaurs lived at the same time? That all dinosaurs were very big animals? That all dinosaurs had very small brains and were probably very stupid? That dinosaurs were just like lizards and other reptiles living today, only bigger? That all dinosaurs were clumsy and slow-moving animals?

The questions were printed on a survey sheet and reviewed by the girls and boys. The "Face-to-Face Survey" (Reproducible 16) was presented to the students to use as a base for discussion. Their discussion led to a way to keep a record of the answers the students received to their questions. They saw the importance of a tally mark in the right place on their survey sheet. They played out roles of the interview situations and asked questions of one another.

"I told you recess was the most important thing in school," said the teacher as the students went out to the playground in the afternoon and began their survey and asked their questions. Some used the time to visit areas in school and to interview the principal, office secretary, teaching aides, custodian, and cafeteria workers. After recess, the information was collected and the students counted the number of tally marks by each question. They wrote the sums on the board and talked about the meaning the survey had for them.

After the survey results were discussed, the students evaluated, discussed their experiences, and dictated what they wanted to say in a final report about their survey for a language experience chart. The criteria for their evaluation showed these questions on the chart:

1. What did we want to find out? (objective of the survey)
2. What steps did we take? (methodology)
3. Did we ask the right questions? (evaluation)
4. What did we find out? (results)

The teacher facilitated the discussion and asked, "From which grades in our school did the respondents come?" To show the value of knowing a respondent's membership in a grade, the teacher asked the students to consider other findings, such as: Did the second-graders believe fewer (or more) of the observations about dinosaurs than sixth-graders? Did this information tell us a relationship between the respondents' grade level and their beliefs about dinosaurs? In what ways did younger students believe (or doubt) more information about dinosaurs than older students? In what ways did older students believe (or doubt) more information about dinosaurs?

For the students who wanted to explore another type of survey research, the teacher suggested a panel technique where some of the respondents would be interviewed again at a later time to see if there were changes in the respondents' knowledge about dinosaurs. To increase the number of respondents, a survey in the future might include a questionnaire distributed to other students in the school (or family members). A telephone survey of the class members (with family permission to release a phone number) was suggested to collect further information about the questions.

Topic E: Publishing a Dinosaur Newsletter

After surveying their friends at school, the girls and boys discussed the items that most survey respondents believed and did *not* believe. To pass along to their friends the results of their survey and to record the information they discovered about prehistoric animals, the students took the information from the chart and published their final report about the survey on dinosaurs as a class newspaper. They distributed their paper to teachers and students in the other classes. They used their final report as the main article and included several other features in the paper. These features took them into different types of news writing: (1) informational writing with examples of dangers in the Age of Dinosaurs; (2) advertisement writing with samples of advertisements with words related to dinosaurs; (3) news writing with news stories about new fossils found; (4) persuasive writing with editorials about debatable points (e.g., building over fossils sites); (5) expository writing with ways to protect today's endangered species that could become extinct; (6) sidebar writing with information on charts and graphs; and (7) caption writing with illustrations and captions about imagined and yet-to-be-developed tools useful in locating fossils.

Topic F: Using Current Resources: Piecing It Together

Using *Science through Children's Literature* (Butzow & Butsow, 1989) as a resource, students were encouraged to read science activity books, newspapers, and magazines. Some magazines—*Discover, Nature, Science News,* and the teacher's copy of *Creative Classroom*—were read for current information not yet found in books and for creative ways to present information.

1. *What is the mystery of the fish that does headstands?* First appearing in the Devonian Age, today's coelacanths have muscular fins and are seen by some experts as a link to the state of evolution when a marine creature emerged from the water and walked or crawled on the land. The fish also has a strange headstand behavior, a mystery for students to consider. Fricke (1988) noticed the headstand behavior of the coelecanth and hypothesized that this strange behavior was connected to locating prey. Knowing that the fish had a feature in their skulls similar to the one that sharks used to detect weak electric fields given off by their prey, Fricke conducted an underwater experiment. He attached electrodes to the arm of the submersible submarine and located a coelacanth. The electrodes were extended to within an inch of the fish and the electric field around the fish was increased. Immediately, the coelacanth began to tilt and performed a perfect headstand. While performing the headstands, however, the fish did the unexpected and turned their heads *away* from the electrodes. So the mystery remains: In what way is this strange behavior of the fish connected to locating prey?

2. *What is the mystery of the fish that did not change?* Discussing the theme of stability, the students considered reasons why coelacanths have remained virtually unchanged for so many years. A comparison of the illustrations of the current species recently discovered with that of an ancient fossil showed students that the two were almost identical to one another. They discussed the environmental conditions that could have enabled these creatures to survive for about 30 million generations without being disturbed and made their own hypotheses about why the coelacanth might have had such strange behaviors. The teacher, too, contributed informational findings from Mike Wood's (1991) article, "Did Massive Volcanic Activity Do in Dinosaurs?" and other written materials. For additional activities, the teacher suggested Markle's *The Young Scientist's Guide to Successful Science Projects* (Lothrop, 1990) and *Breakthroughs* (Jones & Tinzmann, 1990). For emerging readers, *Science Predictable Storybooks* (DLM) were available and provided repetitive and predictable language. Fluent readers read a news article, "Piecing Together Bones of 'T Rex' " (Reproducible 2) and engaged in a writing extension "Writing to a Paleontologist about Piecing Together Bones of 'T Rex' " (Reproducible 17). The teacher asked the students to read the news article together as a group to find out about the latest fossil discovery of a tyrannosaurus and to determine which question(s) about this giant creature could be answered from the discovery. The teacher encouraged the students to write and ask the questions they had in a letter to Patrick Leggi, the paleontologist mentioned in the article.

Topic G: Debating: Pro and Con

Debating Dinosaur Mysteries

"Many scientists now believe that all dinosaurs were warm-blooded," read the sixth-grade teacher from Goodman and Elting's book, *Dinosaur Mysteries* (Platt & Munk, 1980). "Others say that some had inside heating and some did not. A few people still stick to the old idea that all dinosaurs were cold-blooded reptiles. Probably the experts will go on taking sides until more evidence for warm or cold blood can be found." Studying this further with O'Neill's *Dinosaur Mysteries* (Troll, 1989) and Penn's *Young Scientist Explore: Dinosaurs* (Good Apple, 1985), some students became "specialists" and took sides to prepare for a debate on *Dinosaurs were warm-blooded against the point that dinosaurs were cold-blooded.* Interested students chose their sides of the issue and read related sources and collected information about their points of view. To consider other points of view, the teacher showed "Debate Cards" (Reproducible 18) and asked other students to select a point of view they want to debate. Here are two some students considered:

1. *Debate: Insulation versus lack of insulation on types of dinosaurs.* Loris Russell (Royal Ontario Museum in Toronto) suggests dinosaurs were warm-blooded but they did not have any insulation such as hair or feathers and thus became extinct when the climate cooled (possibly from a supernova). Without insulation, dinosaurs could not keep their body heat in the longer, colder winters and so perished. *To student:* Find a source that agrees/disagrees with this view.

2. *Debate: Large dinosaurs were warm-blooded versus large dinosaurs were cold-blooded.* Some scientists think large-sized dinosaurs were probably warm-blooded and smaller kinds, like compsognathus and deinoychus, might have been cold-blooded (Ostrom, 1978). *To student:* If you agree, explain ways a large dinosaur would get all the food it would need each day to generate the heat it needed for its large body.

Topic H: Studying the Gingko and Other Trees: Descendants from Age of Dinosaurs

To develop a mural for their fifth-grade class, students referred to *Album of Dinosaurs* (Rand McNally, 1972) by Tom McGowen for background information. The book tells when each dinosaur was alive and their comparative sizes, as well as shows ferns, gingko trees, and other prehistoric plants in its marginalia. Bringing samples to class of plant leaves that were descendents of prehistoric plants, the students looked closely at the leaves of the gingko, willow, maple, and others on the overhead projector stage and with magnifying glasses. They completed a matrix, "Descendants of Prehistoric Plants: Features of Leaves" (Reproducible 19), and used their completed matrices as discussion notes as they reviewed "Talking about What You Observe" (Reproducible 20).

Topic I: Integrating Computer Software

Classroom Computer Center

Using a computer, a student develops literacy-numeracy concepts and applies his or her thinking skills during a study. The computer is more useful when it is integrated into the curriculum as a tool for learning to write and read than when it is used only as an isolated activity (Geisert & Futrell, 1990). In a computer center, students should take turns working on content software and selecting programs suitable for all in their group/team.

Grades K–2
Clifford's Big Book Publishing (Scholastic) invites young girls and boys to place text beside, under, or on top of any of the illustrations and to create one page at a time. To make original big books, pages print out in extra large (25.5″ × 33″) and large (17″ × 22″) sizes.

Grades 3–4
Dieting Dinosaur (Curriculum Applications) offers a hangman format to develop writing, spelling, and vocabulary skills. Hosted by a dinosaur who is on a diet, a prehistoric host eats only letters that fit into words to be guessed and teachers can replace the word bank with their own words and hints. Additional software useful for the content study are *More Dinosaurs* (Twin Tower Enterprises), *Pterodactyls—Alive?* (Twin Tower Enterprises), and *Isaac Asimov's Universe* (Clearvue). In *Explore a Story: What Makes a Dinosaur Sore?* (Collamore), students may continue a dialogue between a dinosaur and a present-day human, write their own text, or use existing stories and illustrate them.

Grades 5–6
Science Inquiry Collection: Fossil Hunter (Minnesota Educational Computing Corp.) has several topics for students with a wide range of skills. Girls and boys use tools seen on the screen to gather information about fossils in 10 different rock layers (Cambrian layer to Tertiary) in "Explore the Site." When a student commands his or her monitor partner to swing a pick at a rock layer, a fossil is shown on the screen and the student then uses other tools to gather information about the fossil. With "Graph," a student studies a horizontal bar chart of 10 geological time periods, finds the time span during which an organism lived, and then determines if the organism should be/could be a fossil in a specific rock layer. With "List," a student reads names of 40 fossils and locates a fossil in the rock layers to make a check mark appear on the list next to the name of the fossil.

With the command of "Read," a student receives a description of each fossil found, its category as to plants or animals, group (bird, reptile), and habitat. With "Review," the student reads the name of each fossil and the layer in which it was found. In "Find the Fossil," a student determines the geologic period in which the fossil existed; after the student finds a specific fossil, she or he returns to "Graph" to determine the period in which a specimen existed. "Identify the Period" is used when a student wants to determine the geologic period of a rock layer by analyzing the fossils. To do this, a student digs into an unlabeled rock layer and uses "Graph" to determine the time span when the organism lived, and thus eliminates other possible geological periods. With this program, students gather information, organize it, and analyze what is found—all important thinking skills.

Also for grades 5–6, *Dinosaur Blend* (Math Learning Center) supports integrated learning with topics of "Definitions and Vocabulary," "Field Research," "Information Research," "Classification," "Mathematics and Problem Solving," "Writing," "Social Studies," and "Arts and Crafts." Using this, students can select from a list of choices and teachers can choose a combination of tasks for them to complete. The noncomputer activities include determining if animals on a worksheet are dinosaurs, doing crossword puzzles, and reading a time line to determine time periods in which types of dinosaur lived. In *Designasaurus* II (Britannica Software) students can experiment with ways to help a dinosaur survive in prehistory and direct its movements and actions in one of seven time periods to eat, drink, and defend itself in order to survive. If any of four categories related to the status of the dinosaur—health, rest, food, water—fall below a minimal level, the dinosaur is sent back to a "laboratory."

All Grades

With levels of junior, senior, and expert, *Project Classify: Dinosaurs* (National Geographic Society Educational Services) has program disks, a student book entitled *The Time Traveler's Guide to the Age of Dinosaurs*, and activity sheets. On the junior level, students hear about a dinosaur and its characteristics and when it lived. Students choose to visit one of the time periods—Triassic, Jurassic, or Cretaceous—and identify the dinosaur from pictures. To develop problem-solving strategies, a more detailed picture appears and questions are asked. With the characteristics students identify, the program shows a second picture beside the first one. If students select the correct picture and enter the characteristic given by the paleontologist, the pictures match. If not, students reenter the characteristics or choose another dinosaur. With each correct match, more details about the dinosaur are given. For other options, students can return to the present to dig for fossils or select another dinosaur for another identification process. When digging for fossils, students see a map of the Western (or Eastern) hemisphere and three digging sites with the name of a province, state, or country. Students select one and move a marker on the map to the spot corresponding to the location. When they find the proper location, they discover the fossil remains of the selected dinosaur.

At the senior and expert levels, students identify dinosaurs with fewer clues and use reproducible activity sheets and the student handbook. The sheets are classification keys and clues to help students identify dinosaurs. Record-keeping capability is included for names of students, work they have done, and what work remains to be done.

Dinosaur Division (Continental Press) reviews basic observations and two-digit quotients. With this software, a student uncovers pieces of a dinosaur puzzle by answering 12 problems on each of six skill levels. *Dinosaur Days* (Highsmith) has word processing and graphics for developing original stories and pictures in creative writing for grades 2–5. Students can create stories with a data base of dinosaur observations and the graphics. To use this data base, a student reads information and then uses her or his observations to write stories and reports. Graphics of prehistoric days of dinosaurs can be selected to illustrate writing and used for bulletin board displays and class books. For those who need an idea to start a story, 20 story ideas and 100 scenes and graphics are available in *Story Stretcher* (Highsmith) and forms of poetry may be reviewed with *Poetry Palette* (Highsmith). This software includes explanations and samples of poetic forms, a rhyming dictionary, and graphics for illustrations.

Computers can help students develop an ownership of their learning. Keeton (1991) points out the value of computers in student writing, "Pupils . . . enjoy rewriting stories in their own words. When finished, the students read their stories aloud to the teacher or classmates. . . . After students revise the preliminary copy, the story is typed on the computer. As students watch their stories being printed, reactions are extremely positive. Their feelings of ownership and self-confidence increase, and they feel like real authors."

Topic J: Integrating Audiovisuals: Films, Filmstrips, and Television

Films and Filmstrips

In addition to computer software and televised stories, films and filmstrips are useful resources in the classroom. Before first-grade students see Hoff's fanciful story of *Danny and the Dinosaur/Danielito y el Dinosauro* (Weston Woods), the teacher sets a purpose and asks students to look for actions or listen for words describing the dinosaur. After the filmstrip, the girls and boys get in teams of two and use pretend telephone conversations to tell one another the story. In the dialogue, students take turns telling part of the story as they interpret and recall it and use some of the words to describe the dinosaur that they thought about during the viewing. When some students had trouble being brief and giving their partners their turns, one teacher used a one-minute egg timer to allocate time periods and to ensure that each would have a turn.

Grades 1–2

Dinosaur Tales and *More Dinosaur Tales* (Random House School Division) has four filmstrips/cassettes. In the first set, the stories are "Diplodocus Meets the First Bird," "Baby Horned Face and the Egg Stealer," and "The Last of Tyrannosaurus Rex." In the second, stories are "Iguanodon, the most Famous Dinosaur," "Styracosaurus and the Duckbills," and "Trail of the Brontosaurus."

Grades 3–4

Danger, Dinosaurs! (Centerstage Productions) has a cassette with a teacher's guide and book of educational lyrics/music about evolution and extinction of dinosaurs.

Grades 5–6

Related filmstrips are *The New Dinosaur Library* (Clearvue), *When Dinosaurs Ruled the Earth* (Society Visual Education) with accompanying worksheets, and *The Age of Dinosaurs* (National Geographic Society). *The Age of Dinosaurs* helps students understand the place of these large creatures in time and the concept of change as well as the methods used by paleontologists to gather more knowledge.

Advanced Grade 6 and Older

A Who's Who of the Prehistoric World (Films for the Humanities and Sciences) is a video that shows extinct lines of evolution and presents information about the evolution of Australia's animal life.

All Grades

A Magical Field Trip to the Dinosaur Museum (Aims Media) is a video that features Rosie O'Flannigan, a magical tour guide, and several children who visit a dinosaur exhibit at the Museum of Natural History.

Television: Reading Rainbow Program

Several television shows feature children's books. The Reading Rainbow program (PermaBound) has shown several selections about dinosaurs, which primary-grade children can review in the classroom:

1. Aliki's *Digging Up Dinosaurs* (Crowell, 1988) reviews the fossil finds from all parts of the world with information about some of the discoverers (e.g., Mary Ann Mantel in England; Dr. Gideon Mantell; and Dr. Richard Owens who named them *dinosauria*). On a video cassette (PermaBound), small dinosaurs as well as large ones are shown together in some of the illustrations. Thus, dinosaurs from two different periods are mixed and this invites students to cross-check the information (grades K–3).

2. The process of uncovering fossils is in Aliki's *Digging Up Dinosaurs* (Crowell, 1988): (a) uncovering the bones, brushing them with shellac, and numbering them; (b) drawing the fossil's position, taking a picture, wrapping it carefully; and (c) covering bones with wet tissues and then wrapping them in burlap and plaster before moving them (grades K–3).

3. Step-by-step directions about drawing dinosaurs are found in Michael Emberley's *Dinosaurs: A Drawing Book* (Little, Brown, 1980) (grades K–3).

4. The way a scientist solves a fossil puzzle is presented in Helen Sattler's *Is This a Baby Dinosaur and Other Science Puzzles?* (Harper, 1972). Students find evidence that in some of these domestic mother-baby scenes from the past, the types of egg shells range from elongated to round and from thick shells to thin (grades 1–3).

Topic K: Optional Activities

Where Are Fossils Found?

With the maps in a giant world atlas (Childcraft) in a book two feet high, the sixth-grade teacher and the students discussed different types of dinosaurs and where the fossils were found. Since the Mesozoic era was divided into three parts—Triassic, Jurassic, and Cretaceous—the teacher first presented the development of the Age of Dinosaurs with information about the Triassic period (225–190 million years ago) and placed yellow adhesive paper illustrations of early dinosaurs and their names on a displayed map in the big book atlas. Information books with additional facts were nearby and used as references during the discussion. This review provided a scope and sequence for the continued study of dinosaurs. For each placement of an animal on the map, an informational book was suggested by the teacher for further selective reading by an interested student (see Chapter 2).

To interest the students further in reading material related to a time line of dinosaur life, the teacher handed out several books and encouraged students to look through each book's table of contents to find an area of interest. Each student was invited to scan a selected chapter and then to turn to a partner and tell: (1) what the topic was, (2) one fact learned from the scan, and (3) one way this information would be helpful to others.

For further reading during a library visit, the sixth-grade students were given lists of books related to the time periods, animals of each period, and names of countries where fossils were found. Useful for their library searches, each reading list named animals in the sequence of animal development during the Age of Dinosaurs and gave appropriate book titles so interested students (teachers, parents) could readily find an informational source about a type of prehistoric animal. To present the list to students, the teacher duplicated "Reading Books about the Triassic Period" (Reproducible 21), gave brief book talks about a few of the books, and invited students to the school library to find some of the books on the list. When studying the other time periods, "Reading Books about the Jurassic Period" (Reproducible 22) and "Reading Books about the Cretaceous Period" (Reproducible 23) were introduced.

To use the information gained from reading and the students' follow-up discussion related to a dinosaur time line, the teacher introduced a globe (Nature Company; The Lighter Side) that showed dinosaurs and where their fossils were found. As the inflated lightweight vinyl globe was passed along hand to hand, each student located a dinosaur of interest, identified it, named the country in which its fossil was found, and told something about the dinosaur. To recall the geographical locations of fossil findings, a student led a recall activity and named a dinosaur (or asked where a particular type of dinosaur once lived) and then tossed the globe (which was light as a beach ball) to another class member. The receiver located the picture of the named dinosaur on the globe and the country where fossils of the named dinosaur had been found. Taking a turn, the receiver then named another dinosaur and tossed the globe to another student.

How Can People Identify Fossils?

In a third-grade class, students examined the bones in the Bones unit from the Elementary Science Study (McGraw-Hill). Using the unit materials, students worked in groups with others to identify some of the groups of bones. They measured and calculated the possible size of the creature whose bones were in the kit being studied.

What Have People Learned through Fossil Evidence?

To add to observations known about the dinosaurs, a second-grade teacher presented Byrd Baylor's *If You Are a Hunter of Fossils* (Scribner's, 1980) and Minelli's *Dinosauri e Uccelli/ Dinosaurs and Birds* (Observations on File, 1987) with its endpapers of colorful lines of evolution from the Triassic to the Cretaceous period. The teacher showed the numbers beneath animal names that indicated chapters in which to find further information (e.g., there are over 350 genres of saurischans). Another book, Pringle's *Dinosaurs and People: Fossils, Observations and Fantasies* (Harcourt, 1978), traced research on dinosaurs since the discoveries of fossils in Massachusetts in 1802. The teacher pointed out that Pringle tells about new ideas now being put forth about what dinosaurs were like.

To use their observation skills, the teacher engaged the students in studying the attributes of a set of numbered dinosaur replicas. Each small group (or team) of students wrote a detailed description of one of the replicas. Then the descriptions (and the replicas) were randomly mixed on desk tops and students were asked to identify each replica according to the written descriptions. Once identified, the replicas and descriptions were displayed for a classroom exhibit.

Who Can Predict Dinosaur Sounds?

Sixth-grade students read about "Parasaurolophus" in Moody's *100 Dinosaurs A to Z* (Grosset & Dunlap, 1987) and other references of their choice. One of the last dinosaurs of its time period, this plant eater was about 33 feet long and had a curved hollow horn inside a crest on its head. The long horn (tube) was 39 inches in length. The students discussed its uses: Was this a snorkel? Did it make noise? Was it a signal to others? Some scientists believe that the dinosaur trumpeted by forcing air in its chest up the throat, through the crest, and out the bill. Interested students bent plastic pipe in the shape of the long tube and blew on it to replicate the possible sounds made by parasaurolophus. Students then recorded the sounds made and placed the tape in a listening center for others to hear. Later, paragraphs about the dinosaur were written, read, and collected into a class book.

What Natural Causes Are at Work?

In a sixth-grade class, a teacher used teacher-developed dinosaur anecdotes to reveal natural causes at work with information from Vicki Cobb's *Bet You Can't* (Avon, 1980), a book that explains what happens in these situations:

- Could a small two-legged dinosaur jump forward on its toes if it held its toes with its front "hands"? The teacher tried it out with the students and asked them to hold their toes with their hands and then try to jump forward in that position. [Note: No, a small dinosaur could not jump forward on its toes if it held its toes with its front "hands" because the center of gravity of a small dinosaur (and a student's) maintains a balanced state and to go forward, the center of gravity must move ahead of the dinosaur's (student's) base. Holding onto toes prevents a student (and dinosaur) from making this shift in balance (and that's why a small dinosaur never held on to its toes).]
- Holding a long tree branch at the ends in its "hands," a small two-legged dinosaur kept another from pushing him backward into the nearby water. The larger dinosaur grabbed the branch in the middle and pushed with a steady pressure. The small dinosaur spread its arms out like wings and pushed upward slightly each time the other dinosaur pushed. How did the branch help the small dinosaur and keep the larger one from pushing him backward into the nearby water? [Note: The small dinosaur changed the direction of the force of the other dinosaur by flexing its arms out like wings and pushing slightly upward to divert any pressure or force.]
- A small dinosaur stepped into a pool of water that looked quite shallow but wasn't! The pool was deep and he fell in over his head. What made the pool of water look shallow to the little dinosaur? [Note: Light rays are bent as they pass from one transparent substance to another (water). This moves the image of the bottom of the pond upward and that's why the bottom of the pond seemed more shallow than it really was.]
- One small dinosaur tears large leaves from trees and bushes in order to find its food. With both "hands," the dinosaur crumples leaves into tightly packed balls. With only one "hand," it wrinkles up the leaf but is not able to compress it into a ball. Why can't the dinosaur make a ball of leaves with one "hand"? [Note: To compress a leaf into a sphere, pressure must be exerted over most of the surface, which requires both hands. One fully extended hand cannot cover enough of the surface of the leaf to make a sphere-shaped wad.]

How Do Paper-Engineered Dinosaurs Move?

In a fourth grade, the students discussed some of the mechanics of paper-engineering to determine ways objects could move on pages of books. A pop-up book, *Dinosaurs: A Lost World* (Putnam, 1984) by Keith Mosley, had dinosaurs that popped out in dark green scenes 65 million years ago. Pull-tabs made a stegosaurus move its tail, a triceratops move its enormous armored head, and an ankylosaurus strike out with its rounded club-like tail. When the students wanted to look closely at some of this engineering, the teacher showed them *The Genius of Lothar Meggendorfer* (Intervisual Communications, 1985). In the foreword, Maurice Sendak states that Meggendorfer is credited for turning the mechanical toy book and its movable paper parts into a work of art. Through a plastic window, the last page shows intricate levers hidden between pages that move the illustrated characters. Tiny metal rivets made of thin copper wire are fastened to the levers and a single pull-tab activates all of them, an arrangement that fascinates many students.

Extensions for Chapter 6

1. *Consider the component in the Core of Structure: Integrate Mathematics and Science.* Write your thoughts about the component in the Core of Structure and organize your plans or ideas related to math and science for the classroom. Record some projects that could be extensions of selected books.

2. *Teach rigorous science.* Since some scientific issues cause controversy, teachers are encouraged to support the teaching of rigorous science as a rational application to scientific and technological activities. Discuss this quote from the *Science Framework for California Public Schools Kindergarten Through Grade Twelve* (1990) and the extent to which you agree or disagree with it: "Science instruction should respect the private beliefs of students; on the other hand, the teaching of science cannot be suppressed simply because some individuals disagree with findings on religious or philosophical grounds" (p. 2).

3. *Develop a scientific understanding.* Teachers should make it very clear that, from a scientific perspective, evolution and other scientific topics do not bear on an individual's religious beliefs. As a teacher, do you agree or disagree with the following point of view: "Science is not theistic nor atheistic; it does not presuppose religious explanations. Science is concerned with the mechanics, processes, patterns, and a history of nature; it is neutral with respect to divinity, the supernatural, or ultimate causes. In fact, many of the scientists who have made important contributions to evolutionary biology, genetics, and geology, have been deeply religious persons from many different faiths who did not find a conflict between their religious beliefs and their scientific understandings. Teachers will realize that some people however, reject the theory of evolution purely on the basis of religious faith. . . . Concepts in the science curriculum should not be suppressed or voided on the grounds that they may be contrary to an individual's beliefs; personal beliefs should be respected and not demeaned. The way in which scientific understanding is related to religion is a matter for each individual to resolve; . . . there should be a clear separation between science and religion" (*Science Framework for California Public Schools Kindergarten through Grade Twelve*, 1990) (p. 24).

Endnotes

1. Kristie Darras, primary-grade teacher, Elk Grove, California, contributed this information.
2. This activity was contributed by Dr. Chris Hasegawa, California State University, Sacramento.
3. *Science Framework for California Public Schools, Kindergarten through Grade Twelve* (1990). Sacramento: California State Department of Education. This framework encourages thematic presentations (big ideas) of science concepts. Similar themes/suggestions are found in *A Guide to Curriculum Planning in Science* (Wisconsin Department of Public Instruction, 1987); *Gifted & Talented Science, Grade 6* (Anne Arundel Co. Public Schools, Annapolis, Maryland, n.d.); and other guides in other states.
4. Ibid.
5. Ibid
6. Years ago, in 1938, a commercial fisherman caught a coelacanth (*latimeria chalumnae*) off the coast of South Africa, which resulted in an extensive search for another one and a notice in three languages offering a reward by Rhodes University for its capture. In 1952, a fisherman in the Mozambique Channel near Madagascar caught a second one, *malania anjouanae* (*The Book of Popular Science,* Grolier, 1958).

Resources

Aims Media, distributor. 6901 Woodley Ave., Van Nuys, CA 91406. Video: *A Magical Field Trip to the Dinosaur Museum.* Grades 1–6.

Britannica Software. 345 Fourth St., San Francisco, CA 94107. *Designasaurus II.* Grade 6 and older.

Centerstage Productions. 1289 Bartlein Court, Menasha WI 54952. Software: *Danger, Dinosaurs!* Grades 2–6.

Childcraft. 20 Kilmer Road, Edison, NJ 08818. *World Atlas.* All ages.

Clearvue. 6465 N. Avondale, Chicago, IL 60631. Filmstrips: *The New Dinosaur Library* and *Isaac Asmiov's Universe.* Grades 2–5.

Collamore Educ. Pub. 125 Spring St., Lexington, MA 02173. Software: *Explore a Story: What Makes a Dinosaur Sore?* Grades 3–4.

Continental Press. 520 E. Bainbridge St., Elizabethtown, PA 10722. Software: *Dinosaur Division.* Grade 4 and older.

Creative Classroom. PO Box 53151, Boulder, CO 80321-51651. Magazine with activity sheets.

Curriculum Applications. Box 264, Arlington, MA 02174. Software: *Dieting Dinosaur.* Grade 3 and older.

DLM Teaching Resources. *Science Predictable Storybooks* (1986). Allen, TX: DLM Teaching Resources. Grades K–3.

Early Learning Book Club. 3000 Cindel Drive, Delran, NJ 08075. *Make Your Own Adventure Books.* All ages.

Elementary Science Study: Unit 43 (1974). New York: McGraw-Hill. Unit on Bones.

Films for the Humanities and Sciences. Box 2053, Princeton, NJ 08543. Video: *A Who's Who of the Prehistoric World.* Grade 6 (advanced) and older.

Films, Inc., distributor. 5547 N. Ravenswood, Chicago, IL 60640-1199. Video: *Pterodactyls—Alive?* Grades 2–4.

GCT Inc. PO Box 6448, Mobile, AL 36660. Games: *Wollygoggles and Other*

Creatures, Wff'n Proof: The Game of Modern Logic, Logic in the Round, and *Logic Anyone?* Grades 5–6.

The Highsmith Co. W5527 Hwy 106, PO Box 800, Fort Atkinson, WI 53538-0800. Software: *Dinosaur Days, Poetry Palette,* and *Story Sketcher.* All ages.

The Lighter Side. 4514 19th Street Court East, PO Box 25600, Bradenton, FL 34206-5600. Three-prong dinosaur slippers; inflatable globe with endangered species.

Math Learning Center. Box 3226, Salem, OR 97302. Software: *Dinosaur Blend.* Grades 3–8.

Mathematical Sciences Education Board of the National Research Council (1990). *Reshaping School Mathematics.* Washington, DC: National Academy Press. Framework for reform of school math.

Minnesota Educational Computing Corp. 3490 Lexington Ave. N., St. Paul, MN 55126. *Science Inquiry Collection: Fossil Hunter.* Grades 3–6.

National Geographic Society Educational Services. 17th & M St. N. W., Washington, DC 20038. Software: *Project Classify: Dinosaurs;* Filmstrip: *The Age of Dinosaurs.* Grades 4–6.

The Nature Company. PO Box 2310, Berkeley, CA 94702. Concrete sculpture of Hawksbill turtle shell 347187; *Dinosaur Hunter's Kit* 351965; inflatable globe with dinosaurs on continents. Grades 2–4.

PermaBound. Vandalia Road, Jacksonville, IL 62650. Books for pre-k: *Adventures of Big Bird in Dinosaur Days* by S. Roberts; *Amanda's Dinosaur* by W. Orr; *Curious George and the Dinosaur* by M. Rey and A. Shalleck; *Stanley* by S. Hoff; Video: *Digging Up Dinosaurs* by Aliki.

Random House School Division. 400 Hahn Road, Westminster, MD 21157. Filmstrips: *Dinosaur Tales* and *More Dinosaur Tales.* Grades 1–3.

Society for Visual Education. 1345 Diversey Parkway, Chicago, IL 60614. Filmstrip: *When Dinosaurs Ruled the Earth.* Grades 5–6.

Scholastic, Inc. 2931 E. McCarty St., Box 7502, Jefferson City, MO 65102. Software: *Clifford's Big Book Publishing.* Grades K–2.

Twin Tower Enterprises. 1235 Ventura Blvd., Studio City, CA 91604. Video: *More Dinosaurs.* Grades 2–4.

Weston Woods. Weston, CT 06883. Filmstrip in Spanish or English: *Danny and the Dinosaur (Danielito y el Dinosauro).* Grades K–2.

Whyte, M. (1988). *Undersea dinosaur action set. II* by D. Smith. Los Angeles: Price/Stern/Sloan. Activity set: *The second dinosaur action set.* Grades 1–6.

Readings

Aaronson, S. (1975). Notetaking improvements: A combined auditory, functional and psychological approach. *Journal of Reading,* 18 (October): 8–12.

Austin, S. R. (1989). *A field study assessing the role of children's literature in linking language arts, social studies and science as interdisciplinary units at the third and fourth grade levels.* Ph. D. dissertation, University of Pennsylvania. *DAI* 50/09 A: 2782. AAD90–4757.

Beyer, B. K. (1988). *Developing a thinking skills program.* Boston: Allyn and Bacon.

Borasi, R., Sheedy, J. R., & Siegel, M. (1990). The power of stories in learning mathematics. *Language Arts,* 67 (2) (February): 174–189.

Borg, W. R. (1980). Time and school learning. In C. Denham & A. Lieberman (Eds.) *Time to learn* (pp. 33–72). Washington, DC: U.S. Department of Education. National Institute of Education.

The book of popular science (1958). New York: Grolier.

Brophy, J., & Good, T. (1986). Teacher behavior and student achievement. In M. C. Wittrock (Ed.), *Handbook of research on teaching* (3rd ed., pp. 328–375). New York: Macmillan.

Butzow, C. M., & Butzow, J. W. (1988). *Science, technology and society as experienced through children's literature.* Paper presented at Science, Technology, Society Conference on Technological Literacy (3rd meeting). Arlington, VA. ERIC Document Reproduction Service No. ED 294141.

Butzow, C. M., & Butzow, J. W. (1989). *Science through children's literature.* Englewood, CO: Libraries Unlimited.

Fricke, H. (1988). Coelacanths: The fish that time forgot. *National Geographic* (June): 825–838.

Geisert, P. G., & Futrell, M. K. (1990). *Teachers, computers, and curriculum: Microcomputers in the classroom.* Boston: Allyn and Bacon.

Good, T. L., & Grouws, D. A. (1979). The Missouri mathematics effectiveness project. *Journal of Educational Psychology*, 71, 355–362.

Gore, R. (1989). Extinctions. Ill. by J. Blair. *National Geographic Magazine* (June): 662–699.

Jeffrey, D. (1985). Annals of life written in rock fossils. Photos by J. L. Amos. *National Geographic* (August): 182–191.

Jones, B. F., & Tinzmann, M. (1990). *Breakthroughs.* Columbus, OH: Zaner-Bloser.

Keeton, B. L. (1991). Computer printers and ownership of writing. *The Reading Teacher* 44 (7) (March): 527–528.

Kellough, R. D., & Roberts, P. L. (1990). *A resource guide for elementary school teaching: Planning for competence* (2nd ed.). New York: Macmillan.

Kennedy, L. M. (1984). *Guiding children's learning of mathematics* (4th ed.). Belmont, CA: Wadsworth.

Krulik, S., & Rudnick J. A. (1988). *Problem solving: A handbook for elementary school teachers.* Boston: Allyn and Bacon.

Ostrom, J. H. (1978). A new look at dinosaurs. *National Geographic Magazine* (August): 152–185.

Roberts, P. L. (1990). *Counting books are more than numbers: An annotated action bibliography.* Hamden, CT: Library Professional Publications.

Routman, R. (1988). *Transitions: From literature to literacy.* Portsmouth, NH: Heinemann.

Science Framework for California Public Schools Kindergarten Through Grade Twelve (1990). Sacramento: California State Department of Education.

Thelen, J. N. (1984). *Improving reading in science* (2d ed.). Newark: International Reading Association.

Wirzup, I. (1976). Breakthroughs in the psychology of learning and teaching geometry. In J. L. Martin (Ed.), *Space and geometry.* Columbus: ERIC Information Analysis Center for Science, Mathematics and Environmental Education.

Woods, M. (1991). Did massive volcanic activity do in dinosaurs? In *The Sacramento Union*, July 12, p. 1.

Chapter 7

What Resources Are Available to Me?

Teacher Reflections for Chapter 7

Chapter 7 helps you select resources for literature-based instruction by providing information about:

- Resources for a thematic unit including use of data base from Educational Resources Information Clearinghouse (ERIC), modeling materials for maps and scenes, audiovisual materials, award-winning children's books, bibliographies by theme, books by genres and types, and literature-based projects
- Resources for a specific thematic unit, *How Did We Find Out about Dinosaurs?*
  audiovisuals related to dinosaurs
  collections of dinosaur objects
  computer software related to dinosaurs
  dinosaur exhibits
- The component in the Core of Structure to implement a thematic unit in literature-based instruction: Select Resources

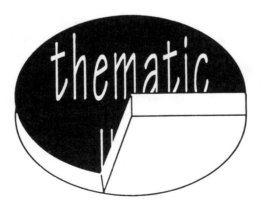

Component in Core of Structure to Implement a Thematic Unit for Literature-Based Instruction: Select Resources

Becoming Aware of Available Resources

"An important rule in planning," write Kellough and Roberts (1990) in their resource guide for elementary school teachers, "is to select learning experiences (for students) that are as direct as possible. That is, have them do that which you are teaching them to do." You'll be pleased to know there are many materials for you to consider as you plan thematic units, projects, and lines of inquiry. You will not be pleased to know that it takes time for you to locate, sort, select, and organize the materials you need. You should begin to organize file folders or computer lists by topics as soon as possible, so when you find a resource that relates to a unit theme, you can record information about it in your file. You may want to organize cardboard boxes by labeling them with the names of the themes and store the materials you collect for each theme in the separate boxes. For example, an object related to our nation's development found in June of one year will wait in its place until your unit on the development of our nation begins in March of the next year.

As an example of the variety of materials available on a specific theme, resources for items related to dinosaurs *not* mentioned in the other chapters are given in this chapter. You will find audiovisual materials, collections of dinosaur objects, computer software, and information about dinosaur exhibits. Catalogs of these companies contain resources useful for any thematic unit and should be ordered yearly to see what is current. Some of the materials will be found at your nearest teacher's exchange, educational outlets, or at local mass-market stores. Suggested reference books can be located in a nearby university library or may be ordered through a local bookstore. Since the availability and prices of items are subject to change, write for current information. You probably will want to use some of the following in your search for children's books on a particular topic:

A to Zoo: Subject Access to Children's Picture Books (3rd ed.) (Bowker, 1989), compiled by C. Lima and J. Lima, has more than 11,000 picture books for preschool through grade 2 classified by topics. Indexed by author, title, artist.

Adventuring with Books: A Booklist for Pre-K–Grade 6 (9th ed.) (National Council of Teachers of English, 1989), edited by M. Jett-Simpson, has nearly 2,000 recommended children's titles grouped by subjects. Subject index.

Books for Children to Read Alone (Bowker, 1988) by G. Wilson & J. Moss, has over 300 fiction and nonfiction books for preschool through grade 3. Analyzed with Spache and Fry Readability formulas.

Books Kids Will Sit Still For: The Complete Read-Aloud Guide (Bowker, 1990) by J. Freeman, has over 2,000 titles for preschool through grade 6 arranged by grade level lists. Indexes for subject, author, artist, and title.

Exciting, Funny, Scary, Short, Different, and Sad Books Kids Like about Animals, Science, Sports, Families, Songs, and Other Things (American Library Association, 1984) edited by Frances Laverne Carroll and Mary Meecham, has nearly 1,000 annotations for grades 2 through 5 arranged by such subjects as monsters, how to say things, and something to make me laugh.

Reading Ladders for Human Relations (6th ed.) (Council on Education and National Council of Teachers of English, 1981) by E. Tway, has subject areas and bibliographies related to children's self-knowledge and social awareness.

Tried and True: 500 Nonfiction Books Children Will Want to Read (Bowker, 1992) by G. Wilson and J. Moss, has books by grade level with subject-specific subsections. Indexes for subject, author, title, and reading level.

Topic A: Knowing a Literature Base for Unit, *How Did We Find Out about Dinosaurs?*

You may decide on several projects for inquiry/book extensions (activities and projects) to initiate the first exploration of the unit. To do this, you can ask each child to choose one (or more) of the projects and then to decide to work alone, with a partner, or with a small group. Hearing a child's choice gives you a guiding and teaching opportunity. For example, if a child chooses only to paint scenes of yards and houses as a followup or extension for a book, or if a child always plays with puzzles, you can suggest another activity or the use of those items to complete a related project (e.g., to make a book of the paintings with sentence captions or to create a set of completed puzzles with explanatory information on cards for a display). You have an interest in seeing that all children have an opportunity to engage in the arts of language for a variety of purposes with a wide range of resources. To assist you in becoming aware of this wide range, additional resources are mentioned here.

Topic B: Knowing Additional Resources for Unit, *How Did We Find Out about Dinosaurs?*

Audiovisuals

Alcazar Records. PO Box 429, Waterbury, VT, 05676. Cassette: *I Wish I Was a Dinosaur* (1989) by B. Dentino and K. Huber. Grades 3–4.

American Melody. Box 270, Guilford, CT 06437. Cassette: *Let's Clean Up Our Act: Songs for the Earth.* Grades 3–7.

Barr Films. 12801 Schabarum Ave., Box 7878, Irwindale, CA 91706. Video: *Fossils! Fossils!* Grades 4–8.

Caedmon Records. 1995 Broadway, New York, NY 10023. Cassette: *Dinosaur Rock.* Grades K–3.

California Academy of Science/Kay Productions. Box 1728, Sonoma, CA 95476. Cassette: *Dinosaurs.* Grade 6 and older.

CMS Records. 4685 Manhattan College Pkwy., # 120 Bronx, NY 10471. Cassette: *There's a Dinosaur in My Bed* by M. Bostick. Grades 3–7.

Coronet/MTI Films & Video. 108 Wilmot Rd., Deerfield, IL 60631. Video: *Storytelling.* Grades 1–6.

Educational Dimensions Group. Box 126, Stamford, CT 06904. Filmstrips: *Dinosaurs: From A to Extinction* with topics of "Building from Bones" (myths and clues from bones); "Reconstructing a World" (fossil clues that allow scientists to rebuild); "Doomed" (ways to read strata and find the point of dinosaurs' extinction); and "Extinction—How and Why" (importance of evolution and adaptation). Grade 6 and older.

Encyclopedia Britannica Educational Corp. 425 N. Michigan Ave., Chicago, IL 60611. Filmstrip: *Studying Across the Curriculum.* Grades 2–6. Video: *Literature, Literacy & Learning.* For teachers.

Films, Inc. 5547 N. Ravenswood, Chicago, IL 60640-1199. Video: *Where the Forest Meets the Sea* by J. Baker. Grades 1–4. Video: *Pterodactyls—Alive?* Grades 2–4.

Focal Point. PO Box 207, Pomfret, CT 06258. 4 filmstrips/cassettes with guide: *Dinosaurs: Some New Ideas* (1983) has topics of "Dinosaurs: What Were They?," "The Dinosaur Hall of Fame," "The Riddle of Archaeopteryx," and "Why the Dinosaurs Disappeared." 2 filmstrips/cassettes, posters, and guide: *Dinosaurs and Other Prehistoric Standouts* (1981) includes theories that dinosaurs were warm-blooded and succeeded by the birds. Grades 1–6.

Harper & Row. Keystone Industrial Park, Scranton PA 18512. Cassette: Aliki's *My Visit to the Dinosaurs*. Grades K–3.

Kimbo Educational. Box 477, Long Branch, NJ 07740. Cassette: *My Pet Tyrannosaurus*. Grades K–3.

Live Oak Media. Box 34, Ancromdale, NY 12503. Cassette & guide: *The Tyrannosaurus Game* by S. Kroll. Grades 1–3.

McGraw-Hill Educational Resources. Box 408, Hightstown, NJ 08529. Filmstrip & guide: *Dinosaur Travel*. Grades K–3.

Melody House. 819 N. W. 92nd St., Oklahoma City, OK 73114. Disc or cassette: *Dinosaur Cafe* has information about dinosaurs linked to etiquette, natural science, and self-esteem. Manners needed when inviting a dinosaur to lunch are discussed in "The Dinosaur Cafe," self-esteem is featured in "I Don't Want to Be Extinct," and observations of personified dinosaurs are given in "Cleo the Plesiosaurus" and "Sheriff Spike (Tyrannosaurus)."

Meridian Educational Corp. 236 E. Front St., Bloomington, IL 61701. Filmstrip & guide: *Developing a Science Fair Project*. Grades 4–8.

Nova: Public Broadcasting System. Alberta: National Film Board of Canada. Television documentaries edited by Alan Jensen: *The Hunt for China's Dinosaurs* (four-year exploration of the Gobi desert where paleontologists from China and Canada uncovered several rare species of dinosaurs); *The Case of the Flying Dinosaurs* (issue of birds that are and are not direct descendents of dinosaurs); and *T. Rex Exposed* (visit to actual dig in Montana during the extraction of the most complete skeleton ever found).

Vestron Video. 1010 Washington Blvd., Stamford, CT 06901. Video: *Dinosaur* narrated by Christopher Reeves. Scenes of museums, fossil digs, and a cat-scan of a dinosaur egg with embryo. Grade 5 and older.

Collections of Dinosaur Objects

AA Graphics. PO Box 75239, Seattle, WA 98125-0239. Rollagraph stamp system: print wheel and green ink cartridge of prehistoric animals 8RSR014.

Animal Town Cooperative Ventures. PO Box 845, Healdsburg, CA 95448. Game: *Dinosaurs and Things,* where players use the setting of prehistoric life on earth, learn about dinosaurs and early fish, amphibians, and reptiles. Grades 2–6.

Aristoplay. 100 Huron View Blvd., Box 7645, Ann Arbor, MI 48107. Game: *Dinosaurs and Things* with annotated bibliography of dinosaur books, museum guide, and instructions. Grades 2–3.

Babooshka. 1145 52nd Street, Brooklyn, NY 11219. Puzzles: tyrannosaurus or stegosaurus; dinosaur cookie cutter.

Bits & Pieces: The Great International Puzzle Collection. 1 Puzzle Place, Ridgely, MD 21685. Puzzle: Dinosaur that, when tilted, shows the movement of an erupting volcano, baby dinosaurs hatching, and dinosaurs fighting 13-J1126.

Carson-Dellosa Pub. PO Drawer 16327, Greensboro, NC 27416. "Bone Up on Reading," dinosaur bulletin board CD654; dinosaur goal motivators (stickers) CD-0453, CD-0709, and CD-0402; Fantasaurus (13 wildly colored dinosaurs for bulletin boards) CD-0746; Fantasaurus stickers; *Dinosaur Reproducible Activity Books, K–1* and *2–3*; Find-the-Dinosaur theme pencils (green and other colors) CDP-54; Dinosaurs II stickers CD-0758; X-ray dinosaurs stickers CD-0768; *X-ray Dinosaur Books* with three-dimensional dinosaur models CD-0967; Dinosaur award pad CDN-049; *Dinosaur* multipurpose chart (22' × 28") CD-0327; dinosaur border (36') CD-0155; "Poke-& Peek" bulletin board maps U.S.—CD-678, World—CD-679; pop-out fantasaurus borders (sections fold forward to give a three dimensional effect) CD-0128; multipurpose dinosaur chart that can be laminated for writing messages CD-

0327; "Dinosaurs" motivational stickers CD-0709; extra-wide pocket chart (57″ × 40″) CD-5603.

Casual Living U.S.A. 5401 Hangar Court PO Box 31273, Tampa, FL 33631-3273. Fossil kits: brontosaurus 010410, tryannosaurus 010411; Audubon guides: *Eastern Forests* 010747, *Western Forests* 010748.

Children's Book Council. 67 Irving Place, New York, NY 10023. Mobile: "Dinosaurs" by J. O. Dewey. All ages.

Coronet, MTI Film & Video. 108 Wilmot Rd., Deerfield, IL 60015. Video & guide: *Alphabet of Dinosaurs.* Grades 1–3.

Creative Educational Materials. PO Box 18344, West St. Paul, MN 55118-0344. Dinosaur bulletin board T-1821; dinosaur figures for boards T-803; "Dino Trek" scalloped borders for boards T-1257; *Dinosaurs* activity book LW 265; rollagraph with "Terrific dinosaurs" JRM-RG02B; dinosaur stamp wheel with "Terrific dinosaurs" JRM-SW02B; dinosaur theme pencils JRM-7772B; dinosaur note pads SE-103; self-adhesive name tags with dinosaur illustration SE-804; stegosaurus mini-note pads SE707; fill-in-the-blank awards: "Dino-mite" SE-404; dinosaur reading bulletin board CD-654; pencils: dinosaur pals ATL-5077; dinosaur erasers 1125-18; "remarkable tags": dinosaurs T-1384; "Dino-mite" banner T-2810; "Dino-stars" incentive charts T-2525; reward seals showing dinosaurs IF4002; science enrichment: Dinosaurs (grades 3–4) IF 1814.

Creative Teaching Press. PO Box 6017, Cypress, CA 90630-0017. 8 1/2″ × 4′ panels of dinosaurs in scenes CTP 1450; dinosaurs and pterosaurs chart pack CTP 5184; fun facts charts of ocean, dinosaurs, solar system CTP 0601; big book and cassette *Dinosaur Dancing* CTP 3357 and CTP 3382; punchout paper reward "watches" (30 in set) with message of "Dino-Mite" CTP 0800.

Denison & Company. 9601 Newton Avenue South, Minneapolis, MN 55431. Songs and cassette: "Dinosaurs" in *Songs for the Flannel Board* by C. Walters & D. Totten TSD 1946-4B; story-telling apron of felt TSD 1825-5B; dinosaurs bulletin board to make TSD 1891-3B.

Dinosaur Catalog. PO Box 546, Tallman, NY 10982. Dinosaurobilia.

The Dinosaur Store. 2000 Massachusetts Ave., Cambridge, MA 02140. Source of dinosaur items.

DOK Publishers. PO Box 605, East Aurora, NY 14052. *Classroom Museums* by G. McCarthy & M. Marso DOK8317; dinosaur checkers EI-3006; dinosaur counters EI-1733; dinosaur chalkboard with writing guidelines EI-103; *The World of Prehistoric Animals Kit* with full-color cards and reproducible materials EI-3476; *Colossal Fossils Kit* with specimens from the Paleozoic, Mesozoic, and Cenozoic Eras EI-2132; textured vinyl dinosaurs EI-1016; *Dinosaur Box* with fact cards, activities, miniature dinosaurs EI-9134; *Dinosaurs* (Science Picture Library) EI-2856; self-inking stamps of dinosaurs EI-1567; *Fossilized Dinosaur Bones Kit* (10 specimens) EI-2144; *Dinosaur Stamp Kit* (6 stamps) EI-1770.

Dover Publications. 31 East 2nd Street, Mineola, NY 11501. Christopher's *Dinosaurs Iron-on Transfer Patterns;* Halls's *Easy to Make Stuffed Dinosaurs;* Hunter's *Dinosaur ABC Coloring Book;* Kalmenoff's *Dinosaur Dioramas to Cut and Assemble;* Kalmemoff's *Dinosaur Postcards;* Kalmenoff's *Days of the Dinosaurs Coloring Books;* Kalmenoff's *Ready-to-Frame Dinosaur Paintings;* Kalmenoff's *Dinosaur Stickers and Seals;* Menten's *The Little Dinosaurs Stained Glass Coloring Book;* Montroll's *Prehistoric Origami;* Pomaska's *Little Dinosaur Activity Book;* Pomaska's *Little Dinosaur Stickers;* Rao's *The Dinosaur Coloring Book;* Rao & Kalmenoff's *Fun with Dinosaurs;* Sandbeck's *Dinosaur Cut and Use Stencils;* Silver & Wynne's *Dinosaur Life Activity Book;* Smith's *Easy to Make Dinosaur Panorama;* Smith's *Easy to Make Apatosaurus Skeleton;* Smith's *Dinosaur Punchout Stencils;* Smith's

Fun with Dinosaur Stencils; full-color posters (34″ × 22″) include *Days of the Dinosaurs* and *Dinosaurs*; *My Dinosaur Notebook* (blank pages) 25300-7; Fun with Dinosaur Sticker Paper Dolls 26224-3.

ECS Learning Systems. PO Box 791437, San Antonio, TX 78279. *Shape-a-Story* has dinosaur patterns for shape pages and book covers FE6392; "Dinosaurs & Prehistoric Animals" learning Center 3155AP; dinosaur paper characters with stick-on costumes by N. Barbaresl 26224-3.

The Education Center. 1607 Battleground Ave., PO Box 9753, Greensboro, NC 27408. "Dinosaur days" desk tags D306; scalloped dinosaur borders D264; *Pocket Pals* skill game: *The Brontosaurus Chorus* (soft/hard) D2413; library card pockets D11015; loose game spinners D11050; spinners on cards for games D1065; *Dinosaur Discoveries* (language arts activities) D808; *Theme-a-Saurus II* (unit) D930; dinosaur superstickers rewards D4107; dinosaur superspots (stickers) rewards; 3″ diameter magnifying viewers D3471. *Lamination kit* (without heat) D8062; laminating film D8057.

Engine-Utility. PO Box 9610, Phoenix, AZ 85068. Reading center: *Danny and the Dinosaur.*

Fearon Pitman Publishers. 6 Davis Drive, Belmont, CA 94002. *Instant Borders* (1979) by A. Flores; *We Learn All about Dinosaurs* (names, habitats, life spans) FE 4595; *The Big Fearon Book of Dinosaurs* by D. Burkle, C. Muller, L. Petuch & E. Petuch FE 0698.

First Byte. 3333 E. Spring St., Suite 302, Long Beach, CA 90806. Software: *The Dinosaur Discovery Kit.* Grades K–3.

Fortune's Almanac. 50 California Street, 14th Floor, San Francisco, CA 94111. Art center: 30″ chalkboard in the shape of tyrannosaurus AEG051.

Frank Schaffer Publications. 1028 Via Mirabel Dept, 343, Palos Verdes Estates, CA 90274. Chart: *Dinosaur Life* FS-2367.

Globe Trotter Network/Barr Films. 12801 Schabarum Ave., Box 7878, Irwindale, CA 91706. Video & guide: *Charles Darwin: Species Evolution.* Grades 4–8.

Good Apple. 1204 Buchanan St., PO Box 299, Carthage, IL 62321-0299. *The Dinosaur Color & Pattern Book* by J. C. Brown (dinosaurs with moving parts) FE2322; *Story-Start Dinosaurs* by F. & S. Pagnucci FE0998.

Hammacher Schlemmer. 11019 Kenwood Road, Cincinnati, OH 45242. Set of 24 small light sticks to place inside a hand-held ball that glows in the dark 37006.

Hearth Song. PO Box B, Sebastopol, CA 95473-0601. Shadow puppet theater 6063; color-a-puzzle material 6058; "Chunki" nonstain chalks 6008; beeswax modeling clay 6004; giant colored pencils 6039; watercolor paints 6029; mosaic woodchips 6065; modeling wax 6026; block and stick crayon set 6038.

Hush-a-Bye Ltd. PO Box 829, New York, NY 10028. Pencils topped with dinosaur; dinosaur pin.

Impact 2000. 60 Irons St., Toms River, NJ 08753. Dinosaur figures 1/30th to scale: brontosaurus is 19.6 inches.

Incentives Publications. 3835 Cleghorn Ave., Dept H90, Nashville, TN 37215-2532. Self-stick Dino-gram notes IP 901-9.

Johnson Smith Company. 4514 19th Street Ct. East, PO Box 25500, Bradenton, FL 34206-5500. Black lightbulb to make fluorescent articles glow in the dark 6316.

Judy/Instructo. 4325 Hiawatha Ave. So. Minneapolis, MN 55406. Dinosaur flannel board aids IN1420; see-inside dinosaur puzzles with skeletons beneath pictures J903010; dinosaur puzzles for beginners J903008 and J903009; jumbo dinosaur alphabet puzzle JI4040; dinosaur floor puzzle J035008; giant floor puzzles of dinosaurs: tryannosaurus JO36032, stegosaurus JO36033, brontosaurus JO36031, triceratops JO36030; magnetic wooden stand-up dinosaur figures J611106; *Dinosaurs and Prehistoric Reptiles* (reproducible resource craft book) JI 8668; *Dinosaur* record album ATA 3225; *Dinosaur* cassette tape ATA 3227; *Dinosaur* duplicating book ATA 2651; *Young Scientists Explore Dinosaurs* (reproducible pages) GA652.

Just for Kids. 324 Raritan Ave., Highland Park, NJ 08904-0901. Self-inking dinosaur stamps 5111162; dinosaur necktie for a narrator or announcer to wear 50967; dinosaur cookie cutters 501775; dinosaur mold for gelatin, cake, muffins 507194; stuffed toy dinosaur in velour egg, velcro closing 5114; vinyl dinosaurs to float in water 511154; felt dinosaur shapes with trees, plants, volcanoes, and eggs on felt board 505701; 18 magnet dinosaur set and playboard 511667; dinosaur skeleton puzzle 500859; dinosaur stamps with ink pads 511162; 4 movable dinosaurs 511170; 50 dinosaur calling cards 510487; dinosaur calendar 509026; dinosaur stationery 5090570; dinosaur puzzle with accurate skeletons 500850; set of movable dinosaurs (legs move, heads turn, jaws open, tails spin) 511170; jumbo 22-inch puzzle of alphabet with dinosaur 509605; remarkable rocks 521302; dinosaurs hands-on science project with fossil dinosaur bone, excavation tools, magnifying glass, plaster of Paris, miniature dinosaur models, posters 533695; active volcano kit with papier mach, plastic work tray, information sheet 527838; grow-a-frog kit with container, food, instructions, and coupon for live tadpole (cannot be shipped to NE, AZ, CA, HI, AK) 501742; stick & life prehistoric animals 532895; dinosaur miniature models 532853.

Kaylor's School & Office Supply. PO Box 340, Highway 431 South, Albertville, AL 35950. Incentive pencils with imprint of Dyno-mite 1485J; fuzzy stickers of purple dinosaurs 3124EX, personal name dinosaur 3134EX; silver mylar sticker assortment with dinosaurs 3412HM; adhesive merit badges with "Dynamite Job" wording EU3416; dinosaur pencils 3466K; dinosaur erasers 3467K; dinosaur figurine erasers 1888D; dinosaur pencil tops 1890D; and dinosaur mini erasers 1352J.

Kids' Stuff/Incentive Publication. 3835 Cleghorn Ave., Dept. 889 Nashville, TN 37215-2532. Card match-ups to learn numbers, colors, and shapes 05024; dinosaur miniatures 531; mini-note pads of stegosaurus; *Dinosaur Learning Fun* with reproducible pages and stand-up figure pages 1P 100-6; dinosaur adhesive notes for attention getters IP 905-1; S. Cook's *Story Journal* IP 190-4.

L. W. Enterprises. Box 7985, La Verne, CA 91750. Smock with plastic pocket on back to hold book with caption, *Have you read this* or *Haz leido este libro?*

Learning Links. 2300 Marcus Avenue, New Hyde Park, NY 11042. Guides and paperbacks: *Cam Jensen and the Mystery of the Dinosaur Bones* S130; and *In the Dinosaur's Paw* S256.

Lillian Vernon. 510 South Fulton Ave., Mount Vernon, NY 10550-5067. Over-the-chair-organizer: red 646659 or black 502259; for field trips, *The Kids Car Songbook* with cassette 382259; dinosaur stickers 606159.

Listening Library. 1 Park Avenue, Old Greenwich, CT 06870-9990. Read-alongs with cassette: *Digging Up Dinosaurs and Putting Them Back Together* by Aliki; *Dinosaurs* by G. Gibbons; *My Visit to the Dinosaurs* and *Dinosaurs Are Different* by Aliki; *Danny and the Dinosaur* by S. Hoff. Filmstrips: *Dinosaurs* by G. Gibbons; *Dinosaurs Beware!*, *Dinosaurs Divorce*, and *Dinosaurs Travel* by K. Brown.

Mary of Puddin' Hill. PO Box 241, Greenville, TX 75401. Gummy candies in dinosaur shapes.

Meadowbrook. 18318 Minnetonka Blvd., Deephaven, MN 55391. *Dino Dots* (name-the-dinosaur quiz with dots to connect) by D. Dixon 2250.

Midwich Entertainment/Twin Tower. 18720 Oxnard St., Tarzana, CA 91356. Video: *Son of Dinosaurs* shows Calgary Prehistoric Park, Dinosaur Provincial Park, and Museum of Natural History, Los Angeles.

Miles Kimball. 41 West Eighth Avenue, Oshkosh, WI 54901. Four Dinosaur world puzzles 3631; dinosaur flash cards 3613; dinosaur stencils 4239; wooden dinosaur kits for assembly: tyrannosaurus 3616-7, triceratops 3620-7, pteranodon 3611-7, plesiosaurus 3617-7, brontosaurus 3621-7, stegosaurus 3636-7.

Music for Little People. PO Box 1460 Redway, CA 95560. Videos: *The Land Before Time* 8261; *Maia: A Dinosaur Grows Up* 875; *Dinosaurs! Dinosaurs! Dinosaurs!* 877; *More Dinosaurs* 876.

National Wildlife Federation. 1412 Sixteenth St. N.W., Washington, DC 20036-2266. *Ranger Rick's Dinosaur Book* and *Dinosaur Cookbook*; bean bag shape of tyrannosaurus rex 35457; to-assemble kits of triceratops and others 20079; life-like prehistoric models of diplodocus and others 20775; *Prehistoric Pop Up of Dinosaurs* 63973; *Draw 50 Dinosaurs and Other Prehistoric Animals* 67207.

Novel Units. PO Box 1461-Dept R, Palatine, IL 60078. Unit: *Danny and the Dinosaur*. Grades 1–2.

The Official Sticker & Toy Company. 348 North 30th Rd., Box 802 LaSalle, IL 61301. *Land of the Dinosaurs* magnet playboard 7033; 55″ inflatable tryannosaurus 7007; 160 "Prehistoric Pals" stickers 2458.

Pacific Science Center. 200 Second Ave. North, Seattle, WA 98109. *Dinosaurs: A Journey in Time* (1988) by D. Schatz shows how to make fossil casts, create a geologic time scale, build creatures from aluminum foil, assemble skeletons of two dinosaurs, and play a "Dinosaur Trivia" game.

Price/Stern/Sloan. 360 North La Cienga Blvd., Los Angeles, CA 90048. Dinosaur game with dinosaurs to punch out and stand up. All ages.

RS Records. Box 651, Brattleboro, VT 05301. Cassette: "Crazy for Dinosaurs" in *Family Vacation* 8806.

Saddleback Educational. 711 West 17th St., Suite F-12, Costa Mesa, CA 92627. Dinosaur checkers EI 3006; 300 dinosaur counters EI 1733; dinosauria posters (set of 4, 12″ × 3‴) EI 4016; dinosaur box (activity cards, miniature dinosaurs) EI 9134; fossilized dinosaur bones EI 2144; authentic fossils EI 2132; *Dinosaurs* big book, Pre-K EI 3313; Realistic viny dinosaur models (16″ tall) EI 1018; *Dinosaurs & Fossils* (35 science project booklets, grade 4 and older) EI 7151; dinosaur stamp set EI 1770.

Science Museum of Minnesota. Community Relations Dept. 30, E. 10th St., St. Paul, MN 55101. Free science museum packet about dinosaurs.

Spizzirri Publishing. PO Box 9397, Rapid City, SD 57709. Life line wall chart (70″ long) with over 200 prehistoric life forms in 600-million-year period; *Dot-to-Dot Dinosaurs* 078-1; *Dinosaur Mazes* 057-9. Educational coloring books and story cassettes: *Dinosaurs* 082-X; *Prehistoric Sea Life* 083-8; *Prehistoric Birds* 084-6; *Prehistoric Fish* 086-2; *Prehistoric Mammals* 087-0; *Count/Color Dinosaurs* 097-8. Coloring book: *Paleozoic life* 034-2; paddle "puppets" with facts on backs for tyrannosaurus M-622, pschycephalosaurus M-623, stegosaurus M-624, ceratosaurus M-625, triceratops M-626, apatosaurus M-627, parasaurolophus M-628. All ages.

Tapestry. Unique Merchandising Mart, Building 46, Hanover, PA 17333. Dinosaur-patterned toss pillow for reading corner E711911.

Teachers' Helper. 5301 Prospect Road, San Jose, CA 95129. Dinosaur name plates EU84391; dragons and dinosaurs unit TCM271.

Teaching Resource Center. PO Box 1509, 14023 Catalina St., San Leandro, CA 94577. *The Prehistoric Animal Parade Songbook* CSB-09; "Dinobet" (alphabet) stamp set 935-T.

Troll. 100 Corporate Drive, Mahwah, NJ 07430. Books: *Illustrated Dinosaur*

Dictionary B1312; *Discovering Prehistoric Animals* QD010; *Dinosaur Learning Activity Books* QD097; *How to Draw Dinosaurs* BH101; *Dinosaur Pop-Up Book* QD208; *Harold and the Dinosaur Mystery, Great Dinosaurs Pop-Up Book* BG685; *Home for a Dinosaur, I Can Read About Dinosaurs, More about Dinosaurs, Dinosaur Reference Library* (20 titles) QD129; *Student Thesaurus* BT041; and *Story of Dinosaurs*. Collections of objects: dinosaur costumes QG065 and QM060; dinosaur cookie cutters QD090; dinosaur models QA056; creative dinosaur templates QC140; dino-pac with saur models QA056; creative dinosaur templates QC140; dino-pac with dinosaur replicas QD055; "Dinobones" board games QD150; let's pretend dinosaur masks QG088 and QR079; *Volcano Kit* QM140; *Dinosaurs and Fossils* (Science adventure kit) QD183; *Dinosaur Craft Kits* QD147; authentic dinosaur models QA056; *Colossal Fossils Collector Kit* QC210. Student may subscribe to 8 issues of *Prehistoric Times Newsletter*.

United Educational Services. PO Box 605, East Aurora, NY 14052. *The Dinosaur Box* with 50 activities and 12 rubber dinosaurs; dinosaur pack of dinosaurs for dioramas.

Walden Video/Disney Studios. Dept 676, PO Box 305188, Nashville, TN 37230-5188.

Watten/Poe Teaching Resource Center. PO Box 1509, 14023 Catalina Street, San Leandro, CA 94577. Record: *Dinosaur Ride* by J. Valley RP-04.

The Wright Group. 10949 Technology Place, San Diego, CA 92127. Big books: *The Long, Long Tail* 9112778; *Dinosaurs* DWP 0317; *Ten Big Dinosaurs* DPM8927; *The Brontosaurus*, DPM9354. Small books: *The Bone Museum* (Social studies set) DWP0473; *Eight Big Dinosaurs* (Buddy books, set B) DPM0074; *Wesley and the Dinosaurs* (6 titles in set) DWG1461; *The Changing Earth* (Focus on science set) DWG6643.

Computer Software

Software. 7506 N. Broadway Extension, Oklahoma City, OK 73116. Software: *Dataventure: Return of the Dinosaurs*. Grades 4–8.

Bede Tech. 8327 Clinton Road, Cleveland, OH 44144. Software: *Coloring Book & Clip Art,* Vols. I & II. Grade 4 and older.

Continental Press. 520 E. Bainbridge St., Elizabethtown, PA 10722. Software: *Dinosaur Division*. Grade 4 and older.

Curriculum Applications. Box 264, Arlington, MA 02174. Software: *Dieting Dinosaur* ("Hangman" format). Grade 3 and older.

Educorp. 531 Stevens Ave, #B, Solana Beach, CA 92075. Software: *Dinomight Stack* is MAC hypercard stack to find dinosaurs by name, order, and suborder 7614. Grade 4 and older.

Learning Lab Software. 2100 Nordhoff St., Chatsworth, CA 91311. Software: *Dinosaur Days*. Grade 4 and older.

Math Learning Center. Box 3226, Salem, OR 97302. Center: *Dinosaur Blend* is integrated learning with worksheets and answer keys. Grades 3–6.

Minnesota Educational Computing Corp. 3490 Lexington Ave. N., St. Paul, MN 55126. Software: *Science Inquiry Collection: Fossil Hunter* determines geologic period in which fossil existed and in which rock is found by analyzing fossils. Grades 4–6.

Teacher Support Software. 1035 N.W. 57th St., Gainesville, FL 32605. Software: *The Literary Mapper* creates original literary maps. Grades 2–4.

Dinosaur Exhibits

Since exhibits are subject to time changes when open to the public, call or write before planning a visit to these displays.

California

Berkeley: Lawrence Hall of Science, Centennial Drive. Features "Mammoth Months" in September with "Dinamations" moving dinosaurs. 10:00–4:30 daily and to 9:00 on Thursdays. 415-642-5133

Los Angeles: Natural History Museum of L.A. County, 900 Exposition Blvd. 10:00 to 5:00 Tuesdays through Fridays, 9:00 to 6:00 weekends. 213-744-3466

San Diego: National History Museum in Balboa Park. Features 37-foot allosaurus and dinosaur classes. 10:00 to 5:00 daily. 619-232-3821

San Francisco: California Academy of Science, Golden Gate Park. Replica of dinosaur dig. Open 10:00 to 5:00 daily. 415-750-7145

Colorado

Boulder: University of Colorado Henderson Museum, 15th St. and Broadway. Features triceratops and pterosaur displays. 9:00 to 5:00 weekdays, 9:00 to 4:00 on Saturdays, 10:00 to 4:00 on Sundays. 303-492-6165

Denver: Denver Museum of Natural History, Colorado and Montview Blvd. Features diplodocus, stegosaurus, and dinosaur track site. 9:00 to 5:00 daily. For students who are planning a trip to a museum, a VHS videocassette, *Digging Dinosaurs* (1986, Centre Productions, 1800 30th St., Boulder, CO 80301), is available. Grades 2–9. 303-337-6357

Idaho

Pocatello: Idaho Museum of Natural History on the campus of Idaho State University. Features life-like scale model dinosaurs and other prehistoric creatures that are computer driven to simulate actual movement; shows 32-foot long roaming brontosaurus and huge tyrannosaurus in habitats. Idaho State University Campus. 208-236-3366

Montana

Bozeman: Museum of the Rockies, Montana State Univ., S. Seventh Ave & Kagy Blvd. Features triceratops skull, edmontosaurus and hadosaur eggs. 9:00 to 8:30 daily. 406-994-2251

Washington

Seattle: Pacific Science Center. 10:00 to 6:00 daily. 206-443-2001

Wyoming

Laramie: University of Wyoming Geology Museum. 9:00 to 5:00 weekdays, noon to 5:00 weekends. 307-766-4218

Yellowstone National Park. Grants Village visitor center. 8:00 to 8:00 daily. No calls.

Other Dinosaur Exhibits

Additional places for students to write and request information include:

Academy of Natural Sciences, Philadelphia, PA	Dinosaur Provincial Park, near Brooks, Alberta, Canada
American Museum of Natural History, NY	Dinosaur State Park, Rocky Hill, CT
Carnegie Museum of Natural History, Pittsburgh, PA	Dinosaur Valley State Park, Glenrose, TX
Dinosaur National Monument (near Vernal), Jordan, UT	Field Museum of Natural History, Washington, DC

Milwaukee Public Museum, Milwaukee, WI

New Mexico National History Museum, Albuquerque, NM

North Carolina Museum, Durham, NC

Provincial Museum of Alberta, Edmonton, Alberta, Canada

Field Museum of Natural History, Chicago, IL

Houston Museum of Natural Science, Houston, TX

National Museum of Natural History (Smithsonian Institution), Washington, DC

National Museum of Natural Sciences (National Museums of Canada), Ottawa, Ontario, Canada

Peabody Museum of Natural History (Yale), New Haven, CT

Royal Ontario Museum, Toronto, Ontario, Canada

San Francisco Junior Museum, San Francisco, CA

Science Museum of Minnesota, St. Paul

Stovall Museum, Norman, OK

Tyrell Museum of Paleontology, Drumheller, Alberta, Canada

Utah Museum of Natural History, Salt Lake City

W. H. Reed Museum, Laramie, WY

Zoological Gardens, Calgary, Alberta, Canada

Educational Resources Information Clearinghouse (ERIC)

An additional resource is:

Clearinghouse on Reading and Communication Skills. Indiana University, Smith Research Center, Suite 152, 2805 E. 10th Street, Bloomington, IN 47408-2698. Audio journal/cassette/read-along stories: *Parents and Children Together*. Publications: TRIED (teaching resources in ERIC database) on teaching techniques. Learning packets, K–12: topics include Expanding Thematic Units Beyond the Textbook, Using Folk Literature, Guiding At-Risk Students in the Language Arts Classroom, and Integrating the Language Arts

Modeling Materials for Maps and Scenes

Students may read and discuss directions to make the following for their projects:

Cornstarch clay: (1) combine 1 cup salt, 1/2 cup cornstarch, and 2/3 cup water; (2) place in pan and cook over low flame; stir constantly until mixture thickens; (3) remove from heat and cool until it can be handled; (4) place on aluminum foil or wax paper and knead well. Use immediately or store several days in wide-mouthed jar with lid. After storage, clay should be kneaded before using.

Flour and oil dough: (1) heat 2 cups salad oil and 1 cup water; (2) if bright color is wanted, stir in 2 tablespoons of powdered paint; (3) add all at once 1 cup of flour; stir and knead well. Dough will keep for several days when placed in jar with lid.

Papiér-maché: (1) soak 3/4-inch strips of newspaper overnight in water; (2) drain off excess water and tear strips into small pieces; (3) add wheat paste until modeling consistency you want; (4) apply to outline map or scenes. Let dry several days.

Paste and paper strips: (1) cut newspaper into 1-inch strips; (2) build up terrain of scene or map with crumpled paper held in place with tape; (3) dip strips into wheat paste and place strips over crumpled paper forms until covered with one layer of strips; (4) add second layer; (5) let dry and then paint with tempera colors.

Paste and plaster of paris: (1) mix 1 cup of wheat paste with 4 cups of water to make thin mixture; (2) mix in 1 cup of plaster of paris, 2 cups of fine sawdust, and 1 gallon of torn tissue strips; (3) mix thoroughly and use immediately.

Paste and sawdust: (1) mix wheat paste to consistency of heavy cream; (2) stir in fine sawdust to consistency of biscuit dough; (3) mix well and knead. Use immediately and let dry five days.

Powdered soap and starch: (1) mix 1 part of liquid with 4 parts powdered soap; (2) beat the mixture until it is fluffy; (3) apply it to map outline or table scene immediately. This mixture dries hard but crumbles easily when dropped or bumped. The quick drying mixture enables students to finish projects in one or two days' time.

Topic C: Knowing Resources to Support Any Thematic Unit: Literature Selection Aids

For Authors and Artists

Commire, A. (Ed.). *Something about the Author.* Detroit: Gale Research. Annual. Gives information about authors, a list of works for each, anecdotes and quotations, and related bibliography for further information on life and work.

Commire, A. (Ed.). *Yesterday's Authors of Books for Children.* New York: Gale Research, 1977–78. Information about authors who died before 1961.

Holtze, S. H. (Ed.). *Fifth Book of Junior Authors and Illustrators.* New York: H. W. Wilson, 1983. Authors and artists who have gained prominence since 1977 are listed along with biographical sketches.

Illustrators of Children's Books. Boston: Horn Book. Each volume in this series has essays about function and development of illustration in children's literature. Brief biographies and bibliographies for each author and artist are given.

Kirkpatrick, D. (Ed.) *Twentieth Century Children's Writers* (2nd ed.) New York: St. Martin's Press, 1983. Biographies, bibliographies, and essays for over 800 writers arranged by author with title index.

For Audiovisuals and Software

Gothberg, H. M. *Television and Video in Libraries and Schools.* Hamden: Library Professional Publications, 1983. Ways in which TV/video can be integrated into library activities.

Munz, L. T., & Slauson, N. G. *Index to Illustrations of Living Things Outside North American: Where to Find Picture of Flora and Fauna.* Hamden: Library Professional Publications, 1981. Provides locations for more than 900 illustrated plants and animals. Index of over 200 books.

Neill, S. B., & Neill, G. W. *The Cumulative Guide to the Highest-Rated Educational Software.* New York: R. R. Bowker, 1989. Entries suitable for students preschool through grade 12.

Thompson, J. W., & Slauson, N. G. *Index to Illustrations of the Natural World: Where to Find Pictures of the Living Things of North America.* Hamden: Library Professional Publications, 1977. 6,000 entries, each arranged alphabetically by popular or common name. Index lists species by scientific name.

For Award-Winning Children's Books

Children's Books: Awards and Prizes. New York: Children's Book Council, 1981. Describes U. S., British, and international awards for children's literature. Author and title indexes.

Jones, D. B. *Children's Literature Awards and Winners: A Directory of Prizes, Authors, and Illustrators.* Detroit: Gale Research Co. Annual. Lists awards for literature in English-speaking countries. Author and illustrator indexes.

Peterson, L. K. *Newbery and Caldecott Medal and Honor Books: An Annotated Bibliography.* Boston: G. K. Hall & Co., 1982. Chronological list for each award with plot summary and critical commentary for each. Indexes by author, artist, title, and subject.

Roberts, P. L. *The Female Image in the Caldecott Award Winning Books.* Monograph #2 University of Pacific Research Laboratory. Stockton: University of Pacific Press, 1976. Reviews the female/male image in the picture books since the first Caldecott award.

Weiss, J. S. *Prizewinning Books for Children: Themes and Stereotypes in U. S. Prizewinning Prose Fiction for Children.* Lexington, MA: Lexington Books, 1983. Discusses themes of children's books that have won U. S. prizes. Arranged by theme with books for each theme.

For Bibliographies by Theme

Appraisal—Children's Science Books. Cambridge, MA: Harvard Graduate School of Education and New England Round Table of Children's Librarians. Published three times a year with ratings and parallel reviews.

The Arithmetic Teacher. National Council of Teachers of Mathematics. Published 8 times a year. See "New Books for Pupils" column.

Austin, M. C. *Promoting World Understanding through Literature, K–8.* Littleton, CO: Libraries Unlimited, 1983. Overview of the cultures and literatures of African Americans, Mexicans, and Native American Indians. Annotated bibliographies with grade levels for each culture with activities. Title and subject indexes.

Azarnoff, P. *Health, Illness and Disability: A Guide to Books for Children and Young Adults.* New York: R. R. Bowker, 1983. Annotated fiction and nonfiction are listed by author and indexed by title and subject.

Baskin, E. H. *More Notes from a Different Drummer: A Guide to Juvenile Fiction Portraying the Disabled.* New York: R. R. Bowker, 1984. Discussion and bibliography about the disabled in literature with entries by author. Indexes by title and subject, for preschool through grade 12.

Bernstein, J. E. *Books to Help Children Cope with Separation and Loss.* New York: R. R. Bowker, 1983. Part I discusses using books as therapy; Part II has annotated list by subjects; part III lists selected reading for adults. Indexes by author, title, subject, reading level and interest level, preschool through grade 12.

Bibliography of Books for Children. Washington, DC: Association for Childhood Education International, 977. Compiled by B. Baron, with books for preschool through the elementary grades grouped by subject.

Breen, K. (Ed.). *Index to Collective Biographies for Young Readers.* New York: Bowker, 1988. Over 1,000 collective biographies. Cross-referenced to look alphabetically for biographee, by occupation or area of renown, or by title of collective work.

Davis, E. *A Comprehensive Guide to Children's Literature with a Jewish Theme.* New York: Shocken, 1981. More than 400 books arranged by subject.

Dreyer, S. J. *The Bookfinder: A Guide to Children's Literature about the Needs and Problems of Youth Ages 2–15*. Circle Pines, MN: American Guidance Service, 1985. Discusses bibliotherapy with extensive bibliography. Has primary theme of the book, annotation, reading level and other forms (i.e. films, tapes, etc.). Indexed by author, title, and subject.

Fakih, K. O. *The Literature of Delight*. New York: R. R. Bowker, 1992. Some 1,000 titles of humorous fiction and nonfiction. Has subject, author, title, character, and grade level indexes.

Horner, C. T. *The Aging Adult in Children's Books and Nonprint Media: An Annotated Bibliography*. Metuchen, NJ: Scarecrow, 1982. Part I discusses how the aged are portrayed in children's books; Part II has annotated bibliography by grade level. Indexes by author, title, and subject. Multimedia list of filmstrips, motion pictures, recordings, and so on by subject.

Immroth, B. *Texas in Children's Books: An Annotated Bibliography*. Hamden, CT: Library Professional Publications, 1986. 654 books in 79 subject areas such as adventure stories, tall tale, biographies, picture books, teen novel from historical to contemporary. Alphabetical order by author with content descriptions and reading/interest level. Title and subject indexes.

Kennedy, D., Spangler, S. S., & Vanderwerf, M. A. *Science & Technology in Fact and Fiction*. New York: R. R. Bowker, 1990. Indexed by subject, author, artist, title, and Fry Readability Scale.

Lynn, R. N. *Fantasy Literature for Children and Young Adults: An Annotated Bibliography* (3rd ed). New York: R. R. Bowker, 1988. Over 3,000 fantasy novels and collections. Subject index.

Mathematics Teacher. Roanoke, VA: National Council of Teachers of Mathematics. Eight times yearly; see "New Publications" column.

Miller-Lachmann, L. *Our Family, Our Friends, Our World: An Annotated Guide to Significant Multicultural Books for Children and Teenagers*. New York: R. R. Bowker, 1991. Fiction and nonfiction about minority people in U. S. and Canada and people in native cultures in Africa, Asia, and Central America. Annotated with maps of regions.

Morrison, F. B., & Cusick, K. *Golden Poppies: California History and Contemporary Life in Books and Other Media for Young Readers*. Hamden, CT: Library Professional Publications, 1987. Fiction, nonfiction and nonprint materials about California for grades 1–12. Annotations and grade levels.

Newman, J. E. *Girls Are People, Too! A Bibliography of Nontraditional Female Roles in Children's Books*. Menuchen, NJ: Scarecrow, 1982. Has entries grouped into categories of minority groups.

Reading Ladders for Human Relations (6th ed.). Washington, DC: American Council on Education/National Council of Teachers of English, 1981. Annotated list arranged by age levels in areas such as interacting in groups, appreciating different cultures, and so on. Indexes by author and title.

Science Books: A Quarterly Review. Washington, DC: American Association for the Advancement of Science. Reviews are listed according to subject with recommended titles.

Siegal, M. *Her Way: A Guide to Biographies of Women for Young People*. Chicago: American Library Association, 1984. Alphabetical list of famous women with profiles and bibliography of books on each person. Indexes by author, title, biography, nationality, ethnic group, and vocation.

Ulom, J. C., compiler. *Folklore of the American Indian: An Annotated Bibliography*. Washington, DC: Library of Congress, 1969. Entries grouped by culture areas.

Williams, H. E., & Golden, K. M. (Eds.). *Independent Reading*. New York: Bodart, 1980. Cross-referenced subject headings.

For Books by Types and Genres

Cianciolo, P. J. *Picture Books for Children* (2nd ed.). Chicago: American Library Association, 1981. Lists of picture books in concept areas of Me and My Family, Other People, The World I Live In, and The Imaginative World. Annotations and age levels, preschool through grade 6.

Roberts, P. L. *Alphabet: A Handbook of ABC Books and Activities for the Elementary Classroom* (2nd ed.). Menuchen, NJ:Scarecrow, 1992. Contains more than 200 reviews of ABC books for K–6 with creative extensions for use in alphabet-in-a-topic collection and alphabet-in-a-milieu collection; groupings include animals and insects, ABC puzzles, letter transformations, ABC science and technology, and others. Author-title index.

Roberts, P. L. *Alphabet Books as a Key to Language Patterns: An Annotated Action Bibliography.* Hamden, CT: Library Professional Publications, 1987. Alphabet books are categorized related to patterns of accumulation, alliteration, letter-object-word arrangements, repetition, rhyme, and word associations.

Roberts, P. L. *Counting Books Are More than Numbers.* Hamden, CT: Library Professional Publications, 1989. Annotations of counting books arranged in categories of related objects and unrelated objects. Number stories have themes of animals and insects, carnival and circus, family and community, farm and country, monsters, mysteries and puzzles, and transportation.

For Literature-Based Projects

Bauer, C. F. *This Way to Books.* New York: H. W. Wilson, 1983. Ideas and techniques to involve children with books. Sections on story-telling, programs, book talks, poetry, games, crafts, and exhibits. Subject index for books, grades K–12.

Haglund, E. J., & Harris, M. L. *On This Day: A Collection of Everyday Learning Events and Activities for the Media Center, Library and Classroom.* Littleton, CO: Libraries Unlimited, 1983. Chronological list of personalities, occasions, and events with suggested activities. Subject index and reproducible activity sheets.

Kimmel, M. M., & Segel, E. *For Reading Out Loud: A Guide to Sharing Books with Children.* New York: Delacorte, 1983. Part I discusses value of reading aloud and suggests techniques. Part II lists read-aloud books with annotations that include plot, theme, listening level and ideas for use, grades K–8.

Laughlin, M. K., & Watt, L. S. *Developing Learning Skills Through Children's Literature.* Phoenix: Oryx Press, 1986. Professional reference for school and public libraries.

MacDonald, M. R. *The Storyteller's Sourcebook: A Subject, Title and Motif Index to Folklore Collections for Children.* Detroit: Neal-Schuman/Gale, 1982. Contains indexes by motif, title, subject, and ethnic/geographic origin.

Paulin, M. A. *Creative Uses of Children's Literature.* Hamden, CT: Library Professional Publications, 1982. Ideas for using books arranged by subjects such as art, booktalks, poetry, and puppets. Author/title/subject indexes.

Raines, S. C., & Candy, R. J. *Story Stretchers: Activities to Expand Children's Favorite Books.* New York: Gryphon House, 1989. 90 titles area arranged into such themes as growing, feelings, grandparents, colors, transportation, and so on for preschool through kindergarten.

Thomas, R. L. *Primary Plots: A Book Talk Guide for Use with Readers Ages 4–8.* New York: R. R. Bowker, 1989. Lists titles, annotations and thematic connections along with activities and suggestions for linking the book to a child's experience.

Extensions for Chapter 7

1. *Consider the component in the Core of Structure: Select Resources.* List some of the resources that you know about that would support the teaching of a thematic unit of your choice. Focus on several of the resources and plan some of the activities you could make in your thematic unit to incorporate these materials.

2. *Discuss what was learned.* As a group, discuss what you learned in this chapter about locating resources for literature-based instruction. Ask two class recorders to write the resources under headings on the writing board. Divide into smaller groups and discuss the rank-order in which your group would place specific material from the most to the least significant from your point of view. If necessary, material can be ranked equally in the list. Return together to the larger group and ask someone to tell your group's final rankings and some of the reasons to support the choices.

Readings

Kellough, R. D., & Roberts, P. L. (1990). *A resource guide for elementary school teaching* (2nd ed.). New York: Macmillan.

Chapter 8

How Can I Meet the Needs of Diverse Students?

Teacher Reflections for Chapter 8

Chapter 8 assists you in:

- Considering learners and their diversity
- Linking learners and literature
- Reviewing the component in the Core of Structure to implement a thematic unit in literature-based instruction: Meet Needs of Diverse Students

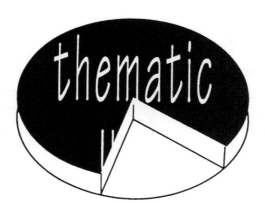

Component in Core of Structure to Implement a Thematic Unit for Literature-Based Instruction: Meet Needs of Diverse Students

Vignette for Newcomer Mei Mei: *I Hate English*

"'I hate English!' Mei Mei said in her head in Chinese," is the opening of Ellen Levine's book, *I Hate English*. Mei Mei is a recent immigrant to New York's Chinatown from Hong Kong. She is comfortable at home and in Chinatown because people look and talk the way people do in Hong Kong. She is uncomfortable at school because everything is in English. She understands most of what she hears in this strange new language but she refuses to speak it until an astute teacher helps break down this barrier in a surprising way. Reading to Mei Mei, the teacher told her a story about a boy who lived in New York more than 100 years ago whose family wanted to move to California. The teacher told about his family who crossed the country in a covered wagon. Mei Mei didn't know the words for *covered wagon* in Chinese and didn't want to listen any more because "she didn't want English to have words that she didn't know in Chinese. . . ." After the story, the teacher explained that in America almost everything happened in English—going to American movies; asking for ice cream, pizza, and other foods; reading signs at the zoo; and talking with others. The teacher took Mei Mei for a walk outside and talked to her about everything—books, foods, pets, teachers, schools, and more. The teacher read everything in print in the environment—store signs, street signs—forwards and backwards. Even Mei Mei's name was said backwards—Iem Iem! The teacher talked and talked until Mei Mei cried, "Stop! I want to talk," in English. Then it was Mei Mei's turn to talk about all that was going on in her head—Children's Day in Hong Kong, presents, dragon dances on Chinese New Year, her home in Hong Kong, and her friends. She talked for 22 minutes without stopping—and both Mei Mei and the teacher smiled and laughed together. They laughed so hard neither one could say a word in either language but "to this day, Mei Mei talks in Chinese and English whenever she wants."

Topic A: Learning and Diversity

The Nation's Report Card

Achievement of children, including those similar to Mei Mei, in fourth, eighth, and twelfth grades was compared in an analysis of *The Nation's Report Card*. This achievement was compared to student performance of 20 years ago and showed there was little gain in that time period. It seems that students' overall reading is about the same today and writing achievement has remained stable. However, minorities' performance has improved over the years—especially in reading (Bass, 1990). Other findings indicated:

- In reading, most students got the information of what they read but had "considerable difficulty" analyzing and synthesizing what they had read.
- In writing, some students had difficulty communicating effectively in writing; less than half of the students produced at least adequate informative and persuasive writing samples.
- In mathematics, only 21 percent of the 9-year-olds and 73 percent of the 13-year olds displayed a firm grasp of basic addition, subtraction, multiplication, division, and beginning problemsolving.

The Schools without Failure *Report Card*

"Much has been written on the difficulties of improving education in the central city," writes William Glasser (1969) in *Schools without Failure*. "From personal experience, I believe that most people who write about the schools have not raised the critical issue. They have been so obsessed with the social, environmental and cultural factors affecting students that they have not looked deeply enough into the role education itself has played in causing students to fail, not only in the central city but in all schools. . . . Very few children come to school failures, none come labeled failures; it is school and school alone which pins the label of failure on children." Looking into the role that education itself has played in causing students to fail, it seems it is time for schools to get rid of the label of failure by carefully selecting instructional strategies that promote flexible learning environments and that meet the needs of diverse students in the classroom. These instructional strategies include bilingual education techniques, cooperative learning, experiential learning, independent study, individualization, learning centers, mastery learning, multicultural education concepts, peer and cross-age tutoring, and self-instructional packets (Chapter 6).

A Classroom's Report Card

Indeed, elementary students are diverse. Tracy Kidder saw this and selected several students as "engines" to drive his book, *Among Schoolchildren,* an informative narrative that tells of a school year with a fifth-grade teacher, Mrs. Chris Zajac, and her classroom in Holyoke, Massachusetts. In Zajac's class, Kidder met Clarence, a 10-year-old bully and disciplinary problem who made frequent journeys to the pencil sharpener by the longest possible route. Clarence always entertained himself with a "cheerful little dance" that included a heel-to-toe walk and a pencil that did aerodynamic loop-the-loops before Clarence plunged the pencil "in the hole." Kidder also met Claude, the authority in the class on excuses for not doing his homework (his pen ran out of ink; he left his bookbag at home; he left his homework at home), but he surprised his teacher by building a model of a river for the school's year-end science fair. Kidder also met Judith, a top-notch student with leadership abilities who became shy when praised, and Pedro, who lived with his extended family that included four stepmothers ("My father never gets married with women"), his 69-year-old grandmother, and a transvestite uncle. Kidder's notes tell of daily occurrences, kids' conversations, interviews, and details about the classroom that present a meaningful narrative for all elementary teachers (Schumacher, 1990).

Topic B: Learners as Newcomers

Students Who Are Newcomers

In classrooms similar to the one Kidder wrote about, children who are newcomers have difficulties in feeling different, in being excluded, in being laughed at for having an "accent," in being called names, in negative labeling, and in other prejudicial acts. Newcomers also face difficulties in dealing with (1) stresses from being caught between two cultures and two worlds; (2) fear, tension, and hostilities between ethnic and racial groups; and (3) stresses in the family related to such things as drug addiction, unemployment, fear of deportation, family separation, gang activity, and unwanted pregnancies (Olsen, 1989).

Newcomers with English as a Second Language

As a factor in facing these difficulties, English Second Language (ESL) students should be encouraged to communicate in their language or dialect and by sharing ideas, engaging in verbal interaction, and gaining skill in oral communication with others in the classroom. Native languages of Limited English Proficient (LEP) students include Spanish, Vietnamese, Cantonese, Mandarin and other Chinese, Cambodian, Filipino/Tagalog, Hmong, Korean, Lao, and Japanese, and others.[1] Studying one of these languages can be a central role in the education of all students. For example, an English-speaking student who wishes to learn a language other than English may team up with another child who can serve as an other-language facilitator and a non-English-speaking child may team up with one who is an English-language facilitator. However, both students should continue using their own dialect at home and in a social context. Working together, the students can develop ownership of the classroom, take care of things that need to be done, and work together on various projects on the school campus and in the community. Through the projects, the teacher provides opportunities for a newcomer student to learn the English used in U.S. schools (and businesses) as a second language or dialect so the student can function and interact in situations that call for English.

Topic C: Learners and Limited English Proficiency

Learning a Second Language

James Cummins (1989) offers a sequential program of language proficiency for Limited English Proficient (K–6) students that includes primary language instruction, sheltered English instruction, and mainstream English instruction. In this sequence, Cummins points out that *primary language instruction* is reserved for activities and lessons about situations with few contextual clues—those that are the most cognitively demanding of students. *Sheltered English* is suggested for instruction of less difficult subjects with contextual clues for a nonnative speaker of English who has, in most cases, some English language proficiency. *Mainstream English* is reserved for students who have no trouble understanding instruction and are ready for native-like instruction in English for such subjects as art, music, and physical education.

Children's books are suitable for fluent English Speakers as well as LEP students. Some students may want to become proficient in a second language and select some of their books in the second language. To discuss these books, the English-dominant students should work closely with students who are proficient in the second language. Books from children's literature also enable Limited English Proficient children to maintain a flow of meaning by using existing knowledge and information observed from what they are reading (although they have not yet fully mastered the English graphophonemic system).

Sheltered English

To help LEP students acquire English, one instructional approach, commonly known as *Sheltered English,* consists of a variety of strategies employed by teachers to help students gain access to academic content and concepts.[2] The basic assumption of this approach is that students who are limited in English are not limited in their capacity for challenging academic content. By applying certain strategies that modify the dependency on high-level English proficiency, a teacher can provide access to content that is not "dummied down" for LEP students. Furthermore, the focus on content and concepts instead of language itself provides these students with improved opportunity for second language acquisition.

The theoretical basis of this approach is Stephen Krashen's Input Hypothesis on second language acquisition. Krashen claims that a learner acquires second language by concentrating on communication and meaning and that acquisition takes place if the learner receives language that is comprehensible. Furthermore, optimal condition for language acquisition requires a supportive, motivating, and low-anxiety environment.

Of foremost importance in using this approach is the nature and focus of the planned instructional activity. The activity should have its primary focus on a message, concept, or situation in which the learner can interact by using English in order to comprehend, express, and negotiate meaning. In order to accomplish this, the teacher needs to modify planning and delivery to address the language needs of these students. The strategy for sheltered instruction can be divided into three major categories: language simplification, contextualizing, and patterns of interaction.

Language Simplification

This includes making language more understandable to students by:

1. Reducing speed without distortion
2. Enunciating clearly with slight exaggeration
3. Emphasizing key words in sentences
4. Using simple sentences
5. Controlling the use of vocabulary and providing clarification
6. Avoiding idiomatic expressions
7. Repeating and rephrasing, using synonyms and antonyms
8. Clarifying the vocabulary for cultural context (see the following, Contextualizing)
9. Summarizing and paraphrasing

Contextualizing

This includes providing context that makes language and concepts more understandable to the students through:

1. Using gestures, facial expressions, or movements
2. Using real objects, props, or manipulatives
3. Using pictures, films, and other audio or visual cues
4. Using charts, maps, and other graphic organizers that minimize the need for complicated use of language to convey concepts and content
5. Using primary language to provide a context prior to introducing a new concept or content in English

Pattern of Interaction

This includes focusing on communication that is genuine, purposeful, and consistently monitored for comprehension through:

1. Questioning by the teacher to check comprehension (e.g., "Show me how you . . ." "Do you mean . . ." and "The words say that the dinosaur *awed its foe*. Is the dinosaur scared or the enemy scared?")
2. Asking who, what, when, where, and why questions
3. Encouraging the students to use clarification and make comprehension requests of other students and the teacher (e.g., "Do you mean _____ or _____ ?" "I can't understand, show me . . ." "Please repeat . . ." and "Please write it down for me.")
4. Planning interdependent communication activities between students (e.g., partners or buddies)
5. Planning small group and cooperative group work to maximize the opportunity and need to interact in English with others.
6. Reacting to the student's language that is not focused on the correction of errors in language structure, vocabulary, or pronunciation

7. Reacting to the student's error in communication that is focused on clarifying meaning and extending language use

The teacher also studies the students' diverse learning styles. To study the learning styles, the teacher observes the children in an ethnographic manner to learn enough about each of them, their languages, and their cultures to make teaching effective (Chapter 10). To make teaching effective, the teacher provides all children with language or dialect differences (either English speaking or non-English speaking) with many opportunities to participate in the experiences of putting stories on charts and then reading the words aloud with the assistance of the teacher. As part of this story experience, the children are encouraged to contribute their own histories and languages as part of the literature for the classroom, and when appropriate, they tell and read their stories to the class.

In a primary grade that is studying dinosaurs, a teacher encouraged students to tell stories to others and she gathered two students together for a discussion. The two were learning English while they were keeping their proficiency in their first language. Talking at home and in their neighborhood in their first language, the two had their major contact with English at school. To assist in this contact, the teacher talked with them in conversation and asked them to give a few sentences aloud similar to the ones she proposed with words generated from the class' trip to a museum (I saw a dinosaur. I saw a tyrannosaurus rex.) To help clear up meanings, the teacher showed some pictures of dinosaurs from children's books and samples of fossils as she and the two talked together. To connect literature to the use of computers, the two went to the computer in the corner of the room to write English sentences with a software program. Requesting help when it was needed, they thought of ways to use words in semantic maps with *The Semantic Mapper* (Kuchinskas & Radencich, 1986). Doing this, they organized their thoughts in English and expanded their vocabulary about what they knew about the topic. With the semantic maps, they could see changes in their knowledge as the semantic maps changed with each addition they inserted. Further, they composed a story with the *Language Experience Recorder Plus,* a speech synthesized word processor with primary print that *speaks* what the students write (Mason, 1987). With this software, they listened to English and heard the pronunciation and intonation patterns of the sentences they had written.

Topic D: Learners and Special Education

Students with Gifted Talents

Ward (1980) proposes differentiation education as a basis for programs for gifted and talented students. Supporting differentiation, Ward indicates that the students should be introduced to a theoretical and connected level of ideas as early as first grade. As part of this connection of ideas, events, and people, content for the students is explored and extended into all of the branches of knowledge and instruction is given about methods of inquiry (Clark, 1988). The students connect with the ideas that discoveries flow from personalities and that people take pleasure in their skills. They ask impertinent questions "on the way to the pertinent answer" (p. 153). To respond to the needs of the gifted and talented, the teacher requires many books related to the students' interests and reference materials: an atlas, thesaurus, almanacs, encyclopedias, and dictionaries. Trips may be scheduled often to a nearby library, along with many in-depth classroom discussions with resource people from the community that focus on higher level thinking to lead the students to interpret, apply, analyze, synthesize, and evaluate. With assignment choices, the students share their findings with others, lead discussions, give explanations, and demonstrate how to do something. They learn the techniques of interviewing, researching, and taking notes for lessons. They engage in making tapes, filmstrips, or slides; developing informational games; and participating in many special extracurricular activities that include making a contribution to the community, contributing to a district's science fair, or attending a reading association's workshop (Gallagher, 1985).

Students in Remedial Reading

In their report of a study in which sixth-grade remedial reading students made reading progress with a literature-based approach, Marjorie and Ronald Shumaker (1988) state, "In remedial reading programs, literature supplies multiple benefits . . . it suggests strategies for enduring and overcoming painful life situations and transitions." They maintain that literature written for children should be at the center of any remedial reading program, for literature enhances the child's self-concept and reduces the isolation of the struggling student. To respond to the needs of these students, the classroom teacher makes every effort to see that the experience of reading with literature is active, pleasurable, and motivational, for unlike the artificial language constructs of workbooks, literature uses the sounds and rhythms of real language and becomes a potent medium for writing.

Students with Hearing, Seeing, and Speaking Impairments

"Carefully selected literature can help to prepare the nonhandicapped children for the experience of knowing children with physical disabilities," write Monson and Shurtleff (1979). Literature can play a part in showing children different aspects of life and ways characters face personal crisis (Huck, Hepler, & Hickman, 1987). Understanding some of the problems disabled children face, the teacher makes individual arrangements for instruction. If a child has a hearing impairment, for example, a teacher asks the child to sit where the child can see the lip movements of the teacher as the teacher speaks clearly and slowly in complete sentences. The teacher puts all directions on the board and writes in large print. If needed, the teacher dictates test questions and assigns a partner to help interpret what is going on in the room. For a child with a seeing impairment, assistance by the classroom aide or another student is given. For instance, an aide helps darken lines on paper for younger students learning to print or provides raised letter models or word models for a child learning to write. Further, the teacher involves all the boys and girls, including those with impairments, in whole-group language that includes conversations, listening to stories and poems, choral reading, singing songs, chanting rhymes, and playing games (Hammill & Bartel, 1990).

Students with Learning Difficulties

Federal law requires a school district to test a student for learning disabilities when the parent requests the testing, but only if all other remediation approaches—such as remedial classes—have failed to help. Types of learning disabilities that can be diagnosed initially by a district's testing program include academic learning disability, attention deficit disorder, language learning disability, motor disability (perceptual motor disability), and social perceptual disability (Powers, 1990). A teacher's professional observations can assist in the diagnosis.

Academic learning disability can be exhibited by students who have trouble learning to read, write, and compute mathematics. Sometimes, a student will be accomplished in one of these areas but not in others. In spite of an academic learning disability, a student is often good in art, fixing things, making friends, and participating in sports. *Attention deficit disorder* is often shown by a student who has difficulty paying attention. A student have many thoughts and ideas in his or her mind and relate to what is being said by thinking of something else—a self-distraction behavior. Often, a student will be distracted by noises in the classroom. *Language learning disability* includes a student who is having trouble learning to listen and talk. A student hears others speak but has a difficult time understanding what the words mean. This lack of comprehension results in others (adults and peers) inferring that the student is not listening.

Motor disability (*perceptual motor disability*) is seen in students who have difficulty holding a pencil, crayon, or paintbrush in the hands. The handwriting of the student is difficult for others to read and sometimes this results in a low grade at school because the academic work looks messy. At times, the student is seen as clumsy; often she or he is not good at sports. *Social perceptual disability* is found in students who have trouble understanding the way others feel and who show inappropriate behavior. For example, a student with this disability often cannot understand the signals other adults and peers send with their words, voices, or bodies. This means that the student does not understand the meaning of an angry voice ("watch it!") or that a frown indicates that the sender is unhappy. A student with this disability has problems making friends and getting along academically with teachers and other students at school. If professional observations indicate behaviors related to a learning disability, the teacher should refer the student for an initial diagnosis by the district's testing program.

Students Exposed to Drugs

Drug-exposed or drug-affected students are those whose mothers have probably been exposed to different drugs—crack, marijuana, alcohol, and methamphetamines. The majority of these students can lead normal, healthy lives and can and do learn in the classroom. However, intervention must come early enough to help the mother and the child. Realizing that these children are more like their peers than unlike them, the teacher will be interested in knowing that drug-exposed children are born in every neighborhood, to every race, and across all socioeconomic lines. Indeed, according to one study by the National Association for Perinatal Addiction Research and Education in Chicago, there is no significant difference in the number of middle- and upper-income women who are using drugs during pregnancy versus low-income and minority women (Jackson, 1990). The National Institute on Drug Abuse reports that over 375,000 drug-exposed babies are born each year and that these children have unique characteristics (Jackson, 1990): decreased head circumference, anemia, growth retardation, neurobehavioral problems, and language development and attention problems.

Some drug-exposed students score in the normal range on standardized tests and are placed in regular education classrooms; others are placed in special education classes but mainstreamed into regular education classrooms for more and more of their education. A teacher of emotionally handicapped children sees the effect of drugs, "Drug abuse has taken its steady toll on the children. For some, it is a physical problem; they were drug babies or fetal alcohol syndrome babies. For others, it is a problem of severe stress." Realizing this, the teacher implemented an effective literature-based reading program with 8- and 9-year old students that sustained the students' interest and maintained their comprehension of the books the whole class was reading. The most profound effect of the program was the students' positive attitudes toward the books (D'Allessandro, 1990).

To provide educational services for young drug-exposed children, Slavin Elementary School in Los Angeles has a program for children ages 3 to 5 called the Children Prenatally Exposed to Drugs Program. In the program, there is a team that includes a developmental psychologist, pediatrician, and psychiatric social worker who all work with the students and the caregivers. In this school-home partnership, regular home visits and phone contacts are scheduled with the parent/guardian of the children. The drug-exposed children in the program have mood swings, tremors, and can withdraw into their own private worlds; they are slow learners and biologically vulnerable; some have poor social and play skills, show irritability and heightened response to stimuli; and many have dysfunctional homes or multiple caregivers. They are children who need a hand to hold, a story to listen to, or someone to talk to during the day. Some of them develop irregular attachments to adults—they show either too much or too little response. Teaching techniques used in the program include a structured curriculum with learning by doing, small teacher-child ratio, and a setting with predictable routines, rituals, and schedules to provide continuity and reliability. There are a minimum of toys and other materials that could be distracting to the children.

Topic E: Learners and Literature

Literature for Understanding Newcomers

Students need to read and listen to literature that presents accurate and respectful images of individuals in all cultures. Related to helping students develop an accurate and respectful image of others, the teacher may read or suggest stories to students that develop an understanding of what it is like to be new to an area and reflect the experiences of newcomers: The following stories are suitable for a literature-based unit about newcomers.

For Primary Students (K–3)

Clutching a picture of his new momma and poppa, a white house, a dog, and a teddy bear quilt, a small boy remembers how he left the orphanage in the Far East and went to his new life in Turner's story, *Through Moon and Stars and Night Skies*. Flip's parents adopt his little brother from Korea in *Mail-Order Kid* by Joyce MacDonald, and Felita is an unhappy newcomer when her family moves into a new neighborhood in Mohr's *Felita*. In Mohr's *Going Home,* Felita is made to feel like a newcomer again when she visits relatives in Puerto Rico and is called a *gringa*. New people move into a New York City apartment building and 7-year-old Nora feels the need to expand her circle of friends in *New Neighbors for Nora* by Johanna Hurwitz.

For Elementary Students (Grade 4 and Older)

A 14-year-old street child from Juarez, Mexico, wants to cross the Rio Grande into the United States in *The Crossing* by Gary Paulsen, and a 9-year-old Chippewa Indian girl adapts as a newcomer when she is left in the care of an Irish-Austrian family who lovingly care for her in Wosmek's *A Brown Bird Singing*. In Mark's *Trouble Half-Way,* Amy realizes that regional dialects make her a foreigner in her own country. An 11-year-old boy's memories turn to his beautiful Vietnam land before it was destroyed by war in Clark's *To Stand Against the Wind* (Viking, 1978), and a horse helps a family and an adopted Vietnamese boy realize their values in Dunn and Mayhar's *The Absolutely Perfect Horse* (Harper, 1983). A Vietnamese girl adjusts to her American home in Surat's *Angel Child, Dragon Child* (Raintree, 1983), and in Lord's story, *In the Year of the Boar and Jackie Robinson* (Harper, 1984), the love of baseball helps a Chinese girl make friends in America. In Yep's *Sea Glass* (Harper, 1969), Craig faces the problems of leaving the Chinese community and learning to live in a non-Chinese community, and Rinko, a 12-year-old Japanese-American girl in Uchida's *The Happiest Ending* (Atheneum, 1985), rescues Teru, a family friend from Japan, from the arrangement of marrying an older stranger. Russel, a contemporary Eskimo boy, leaves the people who hunt animals with snowmobiles and returns to the old Eskimo ways in *Dogsong* (Bradbury, 1988) by Gary Paulsen. An elderly Eskimo mentors Russel, a newcomer to the old ways, as the boy faces his ordeals with nature, visions, treks, and learning the old ways.

Literature for Fostering Self-Esteem

Children in the primary grades who are newcomers need a colorful classroom with posters or bulletin boards to reflect diversity and to boost cultural self-esteem. For example, when a teacher chooses diversity and cultural self-esteem as a theme for a literature-based unit, a poster can state the motto of the United States, *E Pluribus Unum* (Out of many, one) and others can read "Yo Soy Latino" or "I am Original Native American and Proud" (Olsen, 1989). Newcomers with English as a second language can begin to build self-esteem through lots of oral activity in which they combine and orally interpret English. For example, young children can see their names displayed in English and in another language (the dominant home language of the majority of the children in the room). They can listen to numbers in English and then in the dominant home language. To do this, different students can take turns being leaders and lead a number count in English and then count in their language so the children develop an awareness of the other languages spoken by others in the class.

A counting book, *Ten Little Rabbits* (Chronicle, 1990) by Virginia Grossman and Sylvia Long, reflects diversity with simple rhyming verses that introduce a number of rabbits in Indian clothing to represent the tribes of the Plains, Pueblo, Great Lakes, and others. The rabbits weave, fish, and show a different aspect of American Indian life on each page and the author's notes give information about Original Native American Indian customs and clothing. The "Count Your Way" series by Jim Haskins (Carolrhoda) includes *Count Your Way Through Israel* (1990) with counting from 1 to 10 in Hebrew and facts about the language, history, and peoples of Israel; *Count Your Way Through Africa* (1989) uses Swahili as an example of Africa's linguistic and cultural diversity; *Count Your Way Through Korea* (1989) includes numbers in Korean; and *Count Your Way Through Mexico* (1989) uses Spanish to represent Mexico's diversity.

In the classroom, a teacher of older students may display a pledge to promote self-esteem and show class guidelines that support respect for all. With visuals to build concepts, the teacher may suggest literature-based units with themes such as "Walk a Mile in My Shoes," "Tribes," or "My Country 'tis of Me: Discovering Citizenship through Cultural Heritage" (Kohn, Lutholtz, & Kelly, 1988) to interest students in studying something meaningful that is related to self-esteem. Through class meetings on self-esteem and discussions of any incidents of prejudice, all students should be encouraged to discuss the idea of "who loses what?" in the books they read and in prejudicial incidents at school. Understanding the feelings and emotions of those living with prejudice can be presented to older students (grades 5 and 6) through literature that shows characters from different cultures: Taylor's *Roll of Thunder, Hear My Cry* (African American [Dial, 1976]); Yep's *Dragonwings* (Asian American [Harper, 1975]); and O'Dell's *Sing Down the Moon* (Original Native American [Houghton, 1981]).

Literature for Developing Cultural Understandings

Awareness of cultural similarities and acceptance of cultural differences and the language a child brings to school should be a major focus in the classroom. Literature fosters this awareness and acceptance, and several books for young children point out similarities in themes across cultures. For a theme of family love, a teacher may read about Michael, who develops a caring relationship with his great-great aunt Dew in Mathis's *The Hundred Penny Box* (Viking, 1975) or about a Navajo girl and her loving relationship with her grandmother in Miles's *Annie and the Old One* (Little, Brown, 1971).

To show that girls and boys in different cultures look forward to their parents' return from work, *At the Crossroads* (Greenwillow, 1991) by Rachel Isadora tells of young South African children who wait excitedly for their fathers to return from the mines. To foster the understanding of ways one can learn from another culture, a little girl explains how her parents met and married and why on some days she eats with chopsticks, and other days with knives and forks in *How My Parents Learned to Eat* (Houghton, 1984) by Ina R. Friedman. To point out similarities of children in different cultures, different chores and responsibilities of an African boy and a Western boy are shown in *A Country Far Away* (Watts, 1989) by Nigel Gray. With the text "Today was an orindary day. I stayed home," a viewer sees parallel illustrations—the African boy's village home as he tends the goats and the Western boy who washes the car with his father. Children all over the world eat rice and in *Everybody Cooks Rice* (Carolrhoda, 1991) by Norah Dooley, Carrie looks for her brother at dinnertime in an multiethnic neighborhood and each family gives her a taste of the rice dishes they are cooking. The recipes are at the end of the book and provide an opportunity for reading, assembling ingredients, cooking, and tasting rice dishes prepared by multiethnic families.

To promote the understanding of similarities of people in different culture groups among older students (grade 6 and older), a teacher may suggest several books to emphasize the similarities of the characters through a theme such as "We're a Lot Alike: That's the Place to Begin." For example, the feelings of pride in one's heritage is found in Hamilton's *Zeely* (African American [Macmillan, 1967]); Yep's *Child of the Owl* (Asian American [Harper, 1977]); Garza's *Family Pictures/Cuadros de familia* (Hispanic American [Children's Book Press, 1990]); and Highwater's *Anpao: An American Indian Odyssey* (Original Native American [Lippincott, 1977]). For another example, a theme about ways imaginative thoughts influence people and their lives can begin with Fox's *How Many Miles to Babylon?* (African American [White, 1967]); Yep's *Dragonwings* (Asian American [Harper, 1975]); Krumgold's *And Now Miquel* (Hispanic American [Crowell, 1953]); and Sneve's *High Elk's Treasure* (Original Native American [Holiday House, 1972]).

Literature for Developing Awareness of Similarities of Cultures

The classroom's diverse population also may be reflected in folk literature from different cultures, another theme for literature-based instruction. For instance, when reading the version of Cinderella from China aloud to the children, the teacher can introduce the story from the point of view of other cultures, too. To introduce the story from the culture of China, the teacher may select *Yeh Shen: A Cinderella Story from China* (Philomel, 1982) by Ai-Lang Louie. The features in the other versions can be compared with the features in *Yeh shen*. Mistreated by her stepmother, Yeh Shen's wish to go to the festival is granted by an old man through the power of magic fish bones. Her slippers are woven of golden threads in a pattern like a fish's scales, her gown is azure, and her cloak is made of beautiful blue feathers. Other Cinderella stories are found in *In the Land of Small Dragon* (Vietnam [Viking, 1979]) by Ann Nolan Clark; *The Egyptian Cinderella* (Egypt [Crowell, 1989]) by Shirley Climo; *Moss Gown* (southern United States [Houghton, 1990]) by William Hooks; *The Talking Eggs* (Africa [Dial, 1989]) by

Robert D. San Souci; *Mufaro's Beautiful Daughters* (Africa [Lothrop, 1982]) by John Steptoe; and "The Poor Turkey Girl" (Original Native American Indian [Univ. of Arizona, 1986]) in *Zuni Folk Tales* by Frank Cushing—a version for adults that should be revised by the teacher before reading or telling it to students.

Literature for Fostering Collaboration and Cooperation

Related to cultural similarities and differences, a teacher may select the theme of collaboration and cooperation for a literature-based unit. Language minority children from Mexico and Central America value collaboration and cooperation as the best way to solve problems in real life (Olsen, 1989), so some children may have a difficult time making sense of storybooks in which the primary characters speak English and are in competition with other characters rather than working together as a team. For these children, their social orientation is toward the group and not the individual. Even when language-minority children are helped to comprehend the language of the story, they may be at a loss when it comes to understanding the idea that one character solves the problem without the help of others.

To use stories effectively with these children, a teacher needs to be aware of stories to read in which collaboration and cooperation motivate the main characters in the story. With these books, the students can draw on their first language cultural experiences to approach literacy in a second language. They need to hear or read stories where each character cooperates and contributes to the success of all of the characters and where the success of all is not possible without the contribution of the others. They need stories where the characters have a concern about social development, responsibility/service to the group, and mutual prosperity. The following "cooperation" stories support a literature-based unit with a theme of "Friends" or "Working Together."

For Very Young Children

Showing friendship in stories related to a dinosaur theme is found in Clark's *The Bouncing Dinosaur* (Farrar, 1990) where Boris, a bouncing dinosaur, is befriended by a rabbit and a monkey, and in Holt's *Baby Kermit and the Dinosaur* (Random House, 1987) where Baby Kermit's toy dinosaur comes to life in a dream and rescues Baby Piggy from a fire. In Blackwood's *Derek the Knitting Dinosaur* (Carolrhoda, 1989), Derek, a small dinosaur, knits every afternoon with his mouse friend instead of joining his rough siblings.

For Primary-Grade Children

Allen's *On Granddaddy's Farm* (Knopf, 1989) shows how children help Granny with chores while Grandfather is away working for the railroad. In Thiele's *Farmer Schulz's Ducks* (Harper, 1988), family members have a family meeting, cooperate, and offer solutions for Farmer Schulz's dilemma: his duck pond is across a street from his farm and the traffic has increased. In Wilhelm's *Let's Be Friends Again!* (Crown, 1986), a big brother becomes angry when his little sister frees his pet turtle, but becomes her friend again. Best friends Paul and Jim work together to solve a problem in Cohen's *Best Friends* (Collier, 1971), and three friends have a picnic at the beach and enjoy telling one another stories in Marshall's *Three by the Sea* (Dial, 1981). Animal characters are also best friends in Delton's *Two Good Friends* (Crown, 1974) where Duck and Bear are friends with different skills, and in Johnston's *The Adventures of Mole and Troll* (Putnam, 1972) where Mole and Troll work together to accomplish their goals. In Lobel's *Days with Frog and Toad* (Harper, 1979), Frog and Toad help each other, and in Marshall's *George and Martha* (Houghton, 1972), Martha and George share experiences as friends.

For Upper Elementary Students

A Pueblo tale from New Mexico,"The Little Girl Who Scatters the Stars," found in Monroe and Williamson's *They Dance in the Sky: Native American Star-Myths* (Houghton, 1987), implores all people to live as a related family. Mary Jane, a member of a large family, sets up a Runathon to raise money to support the library in Ryan's *Frankie's Run* (Little, Brown, 1987), and in Nelson's *Devil Storm* (Watts, 1987), young Walter and Alice Carrol become friends with Tom, an elderly black man, and enjoy his childhood stories. Energetic Mrs. Abercorn befriends two young brothers and helps them discover trust and friendship in Fosburgh's *Mrs. Abercorn and the Bunce Boys* (Four Winds, 1986), and Wendy finds a best friend who turns out to be Honor, a black child of a biracial marriage in Adler's *Always and Forever Friends* (Clarion, 1988).

Literature for Fostering Dignity and Worth of All Cultures

In selecting literature that shows the dignity and worth of all people in different cultures, the teacher will be concerned about evaluating the books for sensitivity and can turn to Bhalia's (1972) selection criteria: the books should (1) emphasize the dignity and worth of all, (2) have factual accuracy, (3) show interactions among multiethnic groups, (4) have objective treatment of social problems, and (5) show contributions of special groups. In addition to reading about people from different cultures, students will be engaged in independent reading and some will want to review many books about their heritage. For interested students, the following books foster pride in one's heritage.

African Americans

To develop an appreciation for the African American culture with traditional literature, the teacher may introduce older students (grades 4 through 6) to stories such as Hadithi's *Lazy Lion* (Little, Brown, 1990), Bryan's *Turtle Knows Your Name* (Atheneum, 1989), and *Beat the Story-Drum, Pum-Pum* (Atheneum, 1980), or present some of the characteristics of the tales of the American south with Hamilton's *The People Could Fly: American Black Folktales* (Knopf, 1985). After getting acquainted with folk literature, the students may be presented with historical and contemporary fiction such as Hamilton's *The House of Dies Drear* (Macmillan, 1968).

For younger students, there are intergenerational stories—Flournoy's *The Patchwork Quilt* (Dial, 1985), Howard's *Chita's Christmas Tree* (Bradbury, 1989), Walter's *Justin and the Best Biscuits in the World* (Lothrop, 1986) and Stolz's *Storm in the Night* (Harper, 1988). With biographies, older students can get acquainted with the people who have made a difference in African American history and some of these people are found in Miller's *Frederick Douglass and the Fight for Freedom* (Facts on File, 1988) and Meltzer's *The Black Americans: A History in Their Own Words, 1619-1983* (Crowell, 1984). Related to the biographies the students read are also historical fiction titles to support and enlarge their understanding of the times of historical heroes. For instance, biographies about times in the 1850s can be expanded with a book such as Hurmence's *A Girl Called Boy* (Houghton, 1982).

Asian Americans

Students may be engaged in developing an appreciation for the Asian American culture with traditional literature found in a collective anthology such as Sadler's *Treasure Mountain: Folktales from Southern China* (Atheneum, 1982) or a single version, Hong's *How the Ox Star Fell from Heaven* (Whitman, 1991). Other sources from other areas are (from Arabia) Lang's *Aladdin and the Wonderful Lamp* (Viking, 1981), (from China) Yeps's *The Rainbow People* (Harper, 1989), (from India) Jacobs's *Indian Fairy Tales* (David Nutt, 1984), (from Japan) Haviland's *Favorite Fairy Tales Told in Japan* (Little, Brown, 1967), (from Korea) Hyun's *Korea's Favorite Tales and Lyrics* (Tuttle/Seoul International, 1986), (from the Middle East) Van Woerkom's *Abu Ali: Three Tales of the Middle East* (Knopf, 1976), (from Vietnam) Graham's *The Beggar in the Blanket and Other Vietnamese Tales* (Dial, 1970), and (from Turkey) Kelsey's *Once the Hodja* (McKay, 1943).

Hispanic Americans

To foster an appreciation for the Hispanic American culture with traditional literature (Schon, 1990), the teacher may suggest to younger girls and boys a tale from Mexico about a crafty lamb who fools a hungry coyote, *Borreguita and the Coyote* (Knopf, 1991) retold by Verna Aardema, and for older students, there are titles such as Beals's *Stories Told by the Aztecs: Before the Spaniards Came* (Abelard, 1970), Joseph's *A Wave in Her Pocket: Stories from Trinidad* (Clarion, 1991), and Carlson and Ventura's *Where Angels Glide at Dawn: New Stories from Latin America* (Lippincott, 1990). To get acquainted with realistic fiction, older students may be introduced to Carlstrom's *Light: Stories of a Small Kindness* (Little, Brown, 1990) or Krumgold's *And Now Miguel* (Crowell, 1953). To introduce nonfiction, Marrin's *Aztecs and Spaniards: Cortes and the Conquest of Mexico* (Atheneum, 1986) and *The Mystery of the Ancient Maya* (Atheneum, 1985) by Meyer and Gallenkamp present information about the original inhabitants. Further, students should be invited to read and talk about historical fiction, biographies, and autobiographies to get acquainted with people who made an impact on Hispanic American history. Several historical fiction titles to consider, all published by Houghton Mifflin, are O'Dell's *The Captive* (1979), *The Feathered Serpent* (1980), *The King's Fifth* (1981), and *The Amethyst Ring* (1983).

Original Native Americans

To develop an appreciation for the Original Native American Indian culture with traditional literature, a teacher may present students with some of the myths and legends found in Haviland's *North American Legends* (Philomel, 1979), Hamilton's *In the Beginning: Creation Stories from Around the World* (Harcourt, 1988), or Monroe and Williamson's *They Dance in the Sky: Native American Star Myths* (Houghton, 1987). To present related nonfiction— biographies, autobiographies and informational books—and to get acquainted with the people and times of the history of Original Native Americans, the teacher may introduce Baylor's *When Clay Sings* (Scribner's, 1972), Marrin's *War Clouds in the West: Indian & Cavalrymen, 1860–1890* (Atheneum, 1984), or *Indian Chiefs* (A Child's Collection, 1990) by Russell Freedman and read about the moral dilemmas of the Indian leaders to fight or yield to the pioneers in the 1840s. Facts from these books and others can be expanded with selections such as Hudson's historical fiction, *Sweetgrass* (Tree Frog, 1984), and related contemporary stories—Keegan's *Pueblo Boy* (Dutton, 1991) and White Deer of Autumn's *Ceremony in the Circle of Life* (Raintree, 1983).

Literature for Fostering Dignity and Worth of Developmentally Disabled

"When Paul was born, something was wrong," writes Bernard Wolf in his story, *Don't Feel Sorry for Paul* (Lippincott, 1974). "On his right hand, where there should have been five fingers, there was only the stump of a flexible wrist. On his right foot, where there should have been five toes, there was only the stump of a flexible heel. . . . What went wrong? Not even the medical experts can say. Who was to blame? No one. Nevertheless, Paul is handicapped and has had to learn to live in a work made for people without physical handicaps." Students like Paul and other special needs children are mainstreamed into the regular classroom and ask for acceptance and accommodation from the teacher (PL 94-142, Education for All Handicapped Children Act). One method of accommodation is relating the teaching technique to the learner's response when the teacher presents material by gesturing or constructing something, by presenting pictures, by stating words, and by writing words. The learner responds by gesturing or constructing, by identifying pictures or objects within choices, by stating words, and by writing words. A student can respond in different ways and thus increase the options of interaction between the teacher and the student.

To promote the understanding of similarities between students, to foster sensitivity, and to break the stereotypes that relate to peer cruelty, the teacher can focus on ways that attitudes toward those with disabilities and introduce books that show this sensitivity and change: For grades 1 through 3, (deafness) Kneeland's *Cookie* (Turtle, Jason, & Nordic, 1989); (physically disabled, wheelchair use) Holcomb's *A Smile from Andy* and Holcomb's *Patrick and Emma Lou* (both Turtle, Jason, & Nordic, 1989). For grades 4 through 6, with settings in 1800s (epilepsy) Howard's *Edith Herself* (Atheneum, 1987); and (mental disability) Carrick's *Stay Away from Simon* (Clarion, 1985). Settings in 1900s (mute) Callen's *Sorrow's Song* (Little, Brown, 1979); (visual impairment) Little's *From Anna* (Harper, 1972); (cerebral palsy) *Mine for Keeps* (Little, Brown, 1962); (mental disability) Cleaver's *Me Too* (Lippincoot, 1973); and (mental disability) Byar's *Summer of the Swans* (Viking, 1970).

Literature for Understanding the Resilient Child

To face living with prejudice, developmental disabilities, and other difficulties, students need to be aware of what it takes to be resilient. To promote the understanding of traits of resilient children and adults in cultures other than one's own, several books focus on characters who show the traits that have been determined by research to be the characteristics of resilient children (Cecil & Roberts, 1991). Each trait of resiliency (or all of the traits) can be selected as a theme for a unit and supported with stories that feature a book character who exhibits one or more of the characteristics. Several selections for students (grades 4 through 6) focus on these traits and support the theme of resiliency for whole-group discussion, one-to-one conferences, or independent reading:

1. *Trait: Ability to gain people's attention in a positive way.* Williams's *Cherries and Cherry Pits* (African American [Greenwillow, 1986]); Wallace's *Chin Chiang and the Dragon's Dance* (Asian American [Atheneum, 1984]); Behrens's *Fiesta* (Hispanic American [Childrens, 1978]); Highwater's *Moonsong Lullaby* (Original Native American [Lothrop, 1981]); Fassler's *Howie Helps Himself* (physically disabled [Whitman, 1974]).

2. *Trait: Ability to plan ahead and solve problems.* Mitchell's *Shoes for Everyone: A Story about Jan Matzeliger* (African American [Carolrhoda, 1986]); Waters and Slovenz-Low's *Lion Dancer: Ernie Wan's Chinese New Year* (Asian American [Scholastic, 1990]); DeMessieres's *Reina the Galgo* (Hispanic American [Dutton, 1981]); Ashabranner's *To Live in Two Worlds: American Indian Youth Today* (Original Native American [Dodd, Mead, 1984]); Little's *Mine for Keeps* (ceberal palsy [Little, Brown, 1962]).

3. *Trait: Development of a talent or hobby.* Flournoy's *The Patchwork Quilt* (African American [Dial, 1985]); Paterson's *The Master Puppeteer* and Hitz's *Lu Pan The Carpenter's Apprentice* (Asian American [Harper, 1975 & Prentice-Hall, 1978, respectively]); Phillips's *The Picture Story of Nancy Lopez* (Hispanic

American [Messner, 1980]); Tobias's *Maria Tall Chief* (Original Native American [Crowell, 1967]); Slepian's *The Alfred Summer* (cerebral palsy [Macmillan, 1980]).

4. *Trait: Feeling of autonomy.* McKissack's *Jesse Jackson* (African American [Scholastic, 1989]); Yeps's *The Serpent's Children* (Asian American [Harper, 1984]); O'Dell's *Carlota* (Hispanic American [Houghton, 1981]); Baylor's *Hawk, I'm Your Brother* (Original Native American [Scribner's, 1976]); Southall's *Let the Balloon Go* (spastic condition [St. Martin, 1968]).

5. *Trait: Persistence in the face of failure.* Hamilton's *M. C. Higgins, the Great* (African American [Macmillan, 1974]); Yeps's *Sea Glass* (Asian American [Harper, 1969]); White's *Cesar Chavez, Man of Courage* (Hispanic American [Garrard, 1973]); Ashabranner's *Morning Star, Black Sun: The Northern Cheyenne Indians and America's Energy Crisis)* (Original Native American [Dodd, Mead, 1982]); Pollock's *Keeping It Secret* (hearing impairment [Putnam, 1982]).

6. *Trait: Positive vision of life.* Carew's *Children of the Sun* (African American [Little, Brown, 1980]); Newton's *The Five Sparrows: A Japanese Folktale* (Asian American [Watts, 1987]); Politi's *Song of the Swallows* (Hispanic American [Scribner's, 1949]); Baylor's *A God on Every Mountain Top: Stories of Southwest Indian Mountains* (Original Native American [Scribner's, 1981]); Garfield's *Follow My Leader* (blindness [Viking, 1957]).

7. *Trait: Relationship with a caring "other" person.* Clifton's *Everett Anderson's Goodbye* (African American [Holt, 1983]); Yagawa's *The Crane Wife* (Asian American [Morrow, 1981]); Clark's *Secret of the Andes* (Hispanic American [Viking, 1952]); Goble's *Beyond the Ridge* (Original Native American [Bradbury, 1989]); Bridgers's *All Together Now* (developmental disability [Knopf, 1979]).

8. *Trait: Sense of humor.* Aardema's *What's So Funny, Ketu?* (African American [Dial, 1982]); Li Shufen's *Stealing the Magic Fruit* (Foreign Languages Pr., 1985]); Snyder's *The Boy of the Three-Year Nap* (Asian American [Houghton, 1988]); Delacre's *Arroz con Leche: Popular Songs and Rhymes from Latin American* (Hispanic American [Scholastic, 1989]); Goble's *Iktomi and the Berries* (Original Native American [Watts, 1989]); Wrightson's *A Racecourse for Andy* (developmental disability [Harcourt, 1968]).

9. *Trait: Sense of control over her or his life.* Patterson's *Martin Luther King, Jr. and the Freedom Movement* (African American [Facts on File, 1989]); Dunn and Mayhar's *The Absolutely Perfect Horse* (Asian American [Harper, 1983]); Roberts's *Henry Cisneros: Mexican American Mayor* (Hispanic American [Childrens, 1986]); Morrison's *Chief Sarah: Sarah Winnemucca's Fight for Indian Rights* (Original Native American [Atheneum, 1980]); Roy's *Move Over, Wheelchairs Coming Through* (physically disabled [Houghton, 1985]).

10. *Trait: Positive experiences at school (including success in sports or music).* Knapp's *Sports Great Bo Jackson* (African American [Enslow, 1990]); Yashima's *Crow Boy* (Asian American [Viking, 1955]); Beckman's *Pudeo ser Maestra (I Can Be a Teacher* (Hispanic American [Childrens, 1989]); Pizer's *Glorious Triumphs: Athletes Who Conquered Adversity* (Original Native American and others [Dodd, Mead, 1980]); White's *Janet at School* (spinal bifida [Crowell, 1978]).

Extensions for Chapter 8

1. *Consider the component in the Core of Structure: Meet Needs of Diverse Students.* List opinions and research that could affect the way you teach or organize your classroom. Focus on several of the findings and plan some of the changes you could make in your teaching or in your classroom organization.

2. *Promote drug awareness.* In *Students Reaching Out* (California), teenagers visit grades 4 through 8 in elementary and middle schools to explain ways drugs and alcohol affect young bodies and minds. Financial support comes from grants, donations from the public, private and corporate sectors, and an annual benefit dinner. What similar program reaches students in your school?

3. *Consider a multicultural park.* Which students are interested in converting their playground (or part of it) into a multicultural park for the school and community? Plans for the park can include offering food festivals, crafts, celebrations, folklore and literature presentations, workshops on gardening, and onsite research affiliated with a nearby university for ethnic studies. If interested, what steps do the students suggest to support this?

Endnotes

1. Other languages include Original Native American, Arabic, Assyrian, Armenian, Burmese, Croatian, Dutch, Farsi, French, German, Greek, Guamanian, Gujarati, Hebrew, Hindi, Hungarian, Ilocano (and other Filipino), Indonesian, Italian, Mien (Yao) Pashto, Portuguese, Punjabi, Rumanian, Russian, Samoan, Serbian, Thai, Tongan, Turkish, Urdu, and Visayan.

2. Remarks about the use of Sheltered English for Limited English Proficient students asre contributed by Dr. V. Jew, Professor of Education, California State University, Sacramento.

Resources

Developmental Learning Materials (1987). Allen, TX: DLM. Software: *Create with Garfield.* Grades 1–3.

Harper, J. E. (1990). *Connect/Social Studies.* Sundance Pub. Program: literature and social studies. Grades 4–6.

Hermann, J. (1986). *Tiger's Tales: A Reading Adventure.* Pleasantville: Sunburst Communications. Software: graphics and stories. Grades K–3.

The Highgate Collection (1990). Austin: Steck-Vaughn. Literature: author's description of how piece was written. Grades 1–4.

The Learning Company (1989). *The Children's Writing and Publishing Center.* Fremont: Learning Company. Software: word processing and graphics. Grade 3 and older.

Scholastic, Inc. 2931 E. McCarthy St., Box 7502, Jefferson City, MO. Software: *Success with Writing.* Grade 2 and older.

Sunburst Communications. Pleasantville, NY 91985. Software: *Magic Slate.* All ages.

Readings

Bass, J. (1990). Students gain little in 20 years. *The Sacramento Union* (September 27): 1, 11.

Bhalia, S. (1972). *Trade book sources of social significance for culturally different children.* M. A. thesis, California State University, Sacramento.

Cecil, N. L., & Roberts, P. L. (1991). *Developing resiliency through children's literature.* Jefferson, NC: MacFarland.

Clark, B. (1988). *Growing up gifted* (3rd ed). Columbus, OH: Merrill.

Cummins, J. (1989). *Empowering minority students.* Sacramento: California Association for Bilingual Education.

D'Allessandro, M. (1990). Accommodating emotionally handicapped children through a literature-based reading program. *The Reading Teacher* 44 (4) (December): 288–293.

Glasser, W. (1969). *Schools without failure*. New York: Harper & Row.

Hammill, D. D., & Bartel, N. R. (1990). *Teaching students with learning and behavior Problems* (5th ed.). Boston: Allyn and Bacon.

Huck, C., Hepler, S., & Hickman, J. (1987). *Children's literature in the elementary school* (4th ed.). New York: Holt, Rinehart & Winston.

Jackson, S. (1990). Crack babies are here! can you help them learn? *CTA Action* (September): 11–13.

Kohn, R., Lutholtz, C. H., & Kelly, D. (1988). *My country 'tis of me: Helping children discover citizenship through cultural heritage*. Jefferson, NC: MacFarland.

Kuchinskas, G., & Radencich, M. C. (1986). *The semantic mapper*. Gainesville, FL: Teacher Support Software.

Mason, G. E. (1987). Technology development: It's not the hardware or the software; It's how you use it. *The Reading Instruction Journal* 29 (3): 2–7.

Monson, D., & Shurtleff, C. (1979). Altering attitudes toward the physically handicapped through print and non-print media. *Language Arts* (February): 167.

The Nation's Report Card (1988). Washington, DC: National Assessment Governing Board.

Olsen, L. (1989). *Embracing diversity*. California Tomorrow Immigrant Students Project Research Report. San Francisco: Fort Mason Center, Building B.

Powers, L. (1990). The learning barrier. *Reno Gazette Journal* (September 20): 1F, 4F.

Schon, I. (1990). Recent good and bad books about Hispanics. *Journal of Reading* 34 (1) (September): 76–77.

Schumacher, M. (1990). Among schoolchildren and other interesting people: How Tracy Kidder writes his books. *Writer's Digest* (November): 30–34.

Shumaker, M., & Schumaker, R. (1988). 3000 paper cranes: Children's literature for remedial readers. *The Reading Teacher* 41 (February): 544–549.

Ward, V. S. (1980). Differentiating the curriculum: Principle, design, and application. In *Curricula for the gifted*. Ventura, CA. Ventura County Superintendent of Schools Office.

Chapter 9

How May I Assess and Evaluate?

Teacher Reflections for Chapter 9

Chapter 9 responds to your needs about:

- Assessing and evaluating
- Reviewing the component in the Core of Structure to implement a thematic unit in literature-based instruction: Assess and Evaluate

Component in Core of Structure to Implement a Thematic Unit for Literature-Based Instruction: Assess and Evaluate

Vignette in Kindergarten: Reading without Pressure

Recently, a goal of one inner-city school in New York, where 92 percent of the children came from homes below the poverty level and 86 percent spoke no English upon entering school, was to offer the girls and boys in kindergarten an opportunity to learn to read successfully in an environment without pressure. After one year, all 255 children were able to read their own original stories as well as simple books. The program continued through first and second grades with success. However, when the children in second grade took a state-mandated phonics-based test, the children made a poor showing and the school returned to having all kindergarten and first-grade children spend an hour or more each day on phonics with a series workbook for each child. Despite evidence that effective learning took place through reading, the school officials dropped the program in favor of phonics study in preparation for the test (Braun, 1990).

Braun, former president of the International Reading Association, calls this a blind belief in the test. This is a belief that overrides the validity of the professional judgment of teachers engaged in literature-based instructional practices backed by theory and research studies. What a teacher observes in the students has validity. For instance, when a teacher observes that children are reading the stories they dictated and are also using those skills to read other stories, that observation has professional validity. This professional judgment leads to collecting evidence related to students' learning, to joining a teachers' support group, and to using theory and research to undergird what the teacher does in the classroom. Braun calls for teachers to take the lead if change in the classroom is to become a reality—a change that believes literacy has value beyond the statistical benefits of a school being able to cite what their limited English proficient students achieved on an English phonics test.

Topic A: Assessing Achievement in a Literature-Based Classroom

Skills can be highlighted in a literature-based context in a classroom through a variety of ways to help children learn about language. To do this, the teacher must consider the ways the students are managing the reading and writing they are trying to do. Then the teacher should determine what support or facts can be offered that will be helpful to the students. At times, the entire class will need teacher support; at other times, only a small group or an individual will need assistance. To interact with the students in different ways, Church (1990) offers these guidelines:

1. *Have authentic purposes.* Include authentic purposes and audiences for reading and writing (e.g., publish writing for others, prepare signs/posters and instructions, read to others, read and write letters, and read to younger children).

2. *Reflect with the children.* After reading a story to enjoy it, take time to reflect with children on the kinds of decisions the author made and explore ways the author used dialogue, indentation, punctuation, and use of descriptive words and language patterns with rhyme (phonics and word families).

3. *Schedule editing conferences.* Gentry (1981) identifies the sequence of stages that children go through regardless of when they begin to write—deviant, prephonetic, phonetic, transitional (beginning to learn patterns), and the correct stage (some mastery over conventional spelling). In your editing conference, emphasize what is needed for a particular child related to where the child is in spelling development. For example, for a child in the transitional stage, emphasize

spelling by focusing on one, two, or three words that presented problems to the young writer and talk about a useful spelling generalization that is related, a pattern that can be seen, or a memory aid.

4. *Encourage experimentation and cooperation.* Encourage children to experiment and use such marks as exclamation points and quotation marks while they help one another. Before a one-to-one conference or small-group instruction of new concepts and skills related to grammar, usage, and punctuation, observe the children's skills during free writing on topics of their choice related to the content area. Publishing original materials related to content should be emphasized since this provides an opportunity for the girls and boys to notice writing conventions and their importance in a meaningful way.

5. *Incorporate mini-lessons.* When some of the students are ready to use a particular strategy or need information about language, present a mini-lesson or a "For Your Information" (FYI) meeting. During this time, connect what you are talking about to a meaningful context for students by using examples from what they are reading and what they are writing.

6. *Encourage self-evaluation.* Provide an opportunity for students to keep track of the progress they are making with a checklist on which they record skills and strategies they have learned (see Chapter 9).

Usually, a teacher in an integrated classroom believes that a child's language and concepts of knowledge are related to the kinds of experiences he or she has within the range of concepts. Consequently, some of the typical and traditional ways of assessing or evaluating a child's learning are rarely used. Instead, a teacher focuses on the process of what a child is actually doing or is learning and uses general observation to collect information about how a child uses language and concepts across the curriculum.

A teacher evaluates a child's learning and language development informally while a child is active and engaged in meaningful activities in the classroom. Ways to do this include general observations as well as specific ones. Engaging in general observations, the teacher decides on a few students to observe each day. Using a record sheet, the teacher takes notes on what the children say and do. Several five-minute observations are recommended. In a column labeled "What Was Done?" the teacher writes down exactly what the child does with materials or items—not an interpretation of the behavior. Under another column labeled "Language," the teacher writes down what the child says and, if desired, what others say back to the child. Conclusions are noted in another space labeled "Instructional Plans." These plans are the teacher's conclusions based on the observations and are reminders for future intervention and suggestions that relate to the child. The record sheet is reviewed to detect patterns in the child's behavior. A pattern is the activity and language used that seem to indicate that the child is following a purpose—one that can permeate several of the child's activities. A teacher may record classroom observations as a basis for noting a pattern. These patterns may be written on an observation sheet (Reproducible 24) along with a record of the activities of the children as they interact in small groups. All of the members in the group can become the focus of a teacher's observations at times, and the teacher's interaction will support the work of the students—What book should be recommended? What questions should be asked?

Engaging in specific observations, a teacher focuses on a few students each day by reviewing their self-evaluation sheets. As an example of one type of a self-evaluation sheet, a student evaluates at the beginning of group work and responds to: What am I trying to learn? What do I already know? Will it help me while I am reading? and What is the best way for me to learn this? When the student finishes the work, another response is given to What parts gave me problems? What can I do to understand the hard parts? and When I finished, did I understand what I read?

Topic B: Using Language for Communication Purposes in Realistic Situations in the Classroom

How to Assess Listening

As examples of useful assessment techniques, a teacher can assess listening through student dictation and transcription, through story retellings, or through a structured analysis of what the students heard. Dictation and transcription, with partners, small groups, or whole group (Moffett & Wagner, 1983), engage students in taking dictations from other classmates, acting as recorders (scribes) for the group, or taping ideas on audio cassettes and then transcribing them. Older students may tape live conversations and discussions and transcribe them for hard copy for a group's review. Suitable for a taping-transcribing experience is Paul Fleischman's *Time Train* (HarperCollins, 1991), a reserved telling about a class trip from New York to the Dinosaur National Monument. Chronologically, the time clock turns backward and Civil War officers, bison herds, and woolly mammoths in an Ice Age scene pass by. The train finally reaches its last stop, a damp tropical scene filled with dinosaurs. Leaving the train, the children study the live dinosaurs and engage in play before the train returns them to New York.

Story Retelling

Story retelling is the way a student reproduces a story after hearing it read by the teacher. To start this, individuals retell the story to another person—a parent, the teacher, the classroom aide—who has developed a retelling guide that lists the major ideas in the story. The listening adult observes the extent to which the student has a sense of the text and story structure and mentions the main elements of the story—the setting, initiating events, actions, reactions, and outcomes.

Structured Analysis of What Is Heard

For a structured analysis, the teacher arranges for students to listen to a selection—recorded speeches, radio, television, recordings of debates, or live newscasts. After the students listen to the language used in the selection, they discuss questions based on the elements of who? what? to whom? why? what occasion? and how? (Wilkinson, Stratta, & Dudley, 1974). Observing, the teacher notes the extent to which each student has a sense of the elements when questioned about: *Who*: Who was the speaker and what do you know about the speaker? *What*: What is the speaker presenting (facts, opinion, instructions)? *To Whom*: Who is the audience? *What*: What is the purpose (and effect) of what is heard? *What Occasion*: What is the setting (series, celebration)? *How*: How do the speaker's voice, presence (self-assured), and expressions affect you?

How to Assess Speaking and Oral Language

With some children as catalysts who encourage others to read more, students who are in environments where they feel secure and valued are more inclined to participate and cooperate (Fisher & Terry, 1982). As examples of activities where their opinions are valued, students can engage in activities such as "Fishbowl Talk," "Directed Reading and Thinking Activity," and a "Directed Reading and Thinking Checklist Activity."

Fishbowl Talk

To engage in this activity, students sit in a small inner oval and discuss the assigned topic while the students sitting in an outer oval observe and evaluate the discussion using a checklist (Knowles, 1983). The checklist includes such items as (1) Who seems interested in the discussion? (2) What clever, powerful, colorful figures of speech are used? (3) Which suggestions are good ones according to your point of view? (4) Who is listening to the responses of others? and (5) Who is communicating their thoughts/feelings?

To focus on figures of speech, *Quick as a Cricket* (Child's Play, 1982) by Audrey Wood may be read to the students in a "fishbowl" situation. In the book, a child compares his behaviors to those of insects and animals. Contrasts are used in word pairs such as *small/large, sad/happy, nice/mean*. In a rereading, students can complete the lines (e.g., I'm as quick as a . . . ; I'm as slow as a . . .). Relating the lines to the topic of dinosaurs, students may be interested in creating other patterned lines (e.g., A dinosaur is as quick as a . . . ; A dinosaur is as slow as a . . .). The teacher can use this opportunity to observe the students and to make notations about aspects that cause difficulties. Notations may include information about the student's use of oral language in this communication situation, ways thoughts are communicated, and remarks about the quality of the students' participation.

Directed Reading and Thinking Activity
(Stauffer, 1975)

With a story, the fifth-grade students divided into small groups with assigned scribes (rotating reporters who write down questions) and all engaged in four activities: (1) they told their "hunches" about what might follow after reading the title, and the scribe recorded the hunches; (2) the entire text was read individually by students and then discussed to see which predictions were/were not confirmed; (3) activity 2 was repeated for the next section of the text and then the next until the total text was finished; and (4) the teacher entered the discussion and kept it going with "What do you think will happen next?" and "Why do you think so?"

Directed Reading and Thinking
Checklist Activity

To assess further, an activity checklist (Gillet & Temple, 1982) was developed by the fifth-grade teacher, expanded when necessary, and used selectively by observing only one or two items on the list when the students were in groups. When the students interacted in groups, the teacher rated each student with the ranks of *usually, occasionally,* or *rarely* on items related to participation in the group and to the use of the text. The teacher looked for examples of behavior that showed that the student(s) offered spontaneous predictions, participated willingly, made logical predictions, changed predictions, explained predictions, and showed tolerance to all points of view. The teacher observed the students' participation in the group and watched to see if the student(s) located information in text, used literal information, used context to clarify, analyzed words and meanings, and used charts, headings, pictures, and maps as aids.

How to Assess Writing Holistically

To evaluate students' writing holistically, the teacher read the students' writing, evaluated it, and assigned a numerical rating. Some guidelines for rating students' writing in this manner included: (1) highly inventive and mature presence of the characteristics expected and predetermined as criteria, (2) fairly successful communication of ideas through details and presence of characters, (3) some presence of the characteristics but communication of ideas are impeded, and (4) little or no presence of the characteristic (Hittleman, 1988).

Criteria Feedback

For general feedback to the students, a sixth-grade teacher gave an holistic impression (Cooper & Odell, 1977) of the writing with a marking scale. The scale (Manitoba Writing Assessment Program, 1979) included the terms *highly impressive*, *commendable*, *questionable*, *minimal*, and *insufficient material*. *Highly impressive* meant the writing was well above average in thought, sentence structure, and word choice, and was mostly free from errors. *Commendable* meant the writing showed command of thought, sentence structure, and word choice, and was relatively free from error. *Questionable* meant the writing was only functional in terms of thought, sentence structure, and word choice, and was in need of instruction. *Minimal* meant the writing was in need of remediation and appeared to be on a frustration level, and *insufficient material* meant below minimal.

Keep Track of Who's Writing What

The sixth-grade teacher charted where each student was in writing and noted if a student was on a first draft, second draft, or ready for an editing conference. Some students were in the process of rewriting, others were ready for a revision conference, and still others were doing self-editing (LaGreca, 1990). In the records, a teacher included written observations that documented the areas of learned values, attitudes, and use of expressive arts. The teacher placed a checkmark on the list of goals and objectives for the class/grade level in the front of each student's file when the classroom-based documents were collected for the file. The teacher considered each student's ability to self-evaluate and wrote notes to answer Did the student self-select, self-correct, and self-monitor? For those in need of further instruction, the teacher selected a children's informational book about writing as the focus for a mini-lesson. The purpose was to help students communicate, and the author gave them writing "secrets" they could use: (1) let writing "cool," (2) look it over and listen to the sound of it, (3) visualize it and analyze it, (4) punch it up, and (5) cut it down.

Specific Assessment

For specific feedback to the students, the teacher gave information about specific points in the writing and elaborated from a checklist (Manitoba Writing Assessment Program, 1979) with point values. The specific points for feedback in the students' writing were the topic and the middle and ending of the writing. The specific points and their values were: *For topic of writing:* When it included ideas that related to the topic (4 points); when writing fluctuated but had a focus on topic (3); when it deviated on topic (2); and when there was insufficient evidence (1); and *For middle and ending of writing*: When the writing had appropriate middle and ending (4 points).

How to Assess Conventions in Handwriting

On various occasions during the year, the third-grade teacher discussed handwriting samples with a transparency on the overhead, and the students kept a record of their handwriting progress and placed their self-evaluations in their student folders (portfolios). In teacher conferences, students reviewed their self-evaluations, discussed their progress, and set new and different goals for themselves. Here is one example of a student's record:

Student Guide for Self-Evaluation
of Conventions in Handwriting

How do I rate my writing?

5 = Excellent 4 = Good 3 = Average 2 = Fair 1 = Needs improvement

5 4 3 2 1

a. Is my slant the same?
b. Does my spacing look even?
c. Are the small letters/tall letters even?
d. Does my writing stay on the base line?
e. Can I identify one letter from another?
f. What handwriting goals do I want to plan for myself?
g. Other

How Students May Self-Evaluate Reading

A fourth-grade teacher encouraged the students to self-select much of what was read and written and to keep an individual reading and writing record. When the students did this, they were involved in evaluating what they wanted to read and write in the classroom. Before a conference with the teacher, each student would prepare for the reading conference about a book/selection read by writing some answers (Hunt, 1967) and recording his/her thoughts about:

1. Why did I choose this book/selection?
2. What made the writing easy/difficult to understand?
3. What made this a good/poor choice?
4. How would I compare this book/selection to others I have read?
5. Would I read more books by this author or on this same theme?
6. How would I tell about this book to someone else?
7. What happened in this book that I would like/not like to happen to me?
8. What did I learn from this book?
9. What were the high points?
10. How real/fanciful was the writing?

Assessing Oral Reading

To assess oral reading in a systematic way, the teacher made comments about what was observed (Moffett & Wagner, 1983) on a teacher-developed form:

Teacher Observation

Student_____ Date_____

Teacher Comments about:

a. Which kinds of mistakes are corrected? Are they important to meaning?
b. Which substitutions seem to constitute "reading into the text" such things as expectancies, preoccupations, or stereotypes?
c. Is the reader involved or is the reading mechanical?
d. Do phrasing and intonation fit the sense as well as the syntax and punctuation?
e. Which elements of the text are ignored (word endings, punctuation, headings, phrases, phonemes, etc.)?
f. Which combinations of sound-spellings trip up the reader (blends, vowel-consonant combinations, polysyllabic words)?

How to Assess Comprehension

A fifth-grade teacher assessed the comprehension of the students in various ways as the teacher observed the students working together with partners, small groups, whole groups, and one-to-one teacher-student conferences. Comprehension was revealed by the students' ability to accomplish tasks that involved categorizing, explaining, identifying the main idea, interpreting, and matching print with pictures. To demonstrate this, the students used cloze procedures, tape recorders, cartoons, and self-evaluation sheets to show they could do the following:

1. *Categorize when each received 3 (or 4) words on cards.* To do this, the student leader (or teacher) called out a category (e.g., word that rhymes, an action word, a food word, a dinosaur name, a descriptive words, and so on) and each looked at the cards to determine which word fit the category.
2. *Explain a cartoon related to the theme to another student.* This was one way for the teacher to assess and evaluate a student's comprehension of what was read. A "Herman" cartoon was one example the teacher used. In the cartoon, two older male observers are studying a dinosaur skeleton. The caption beneath reads, "They knew how to build skeletons in those days." The comic strip "Sally Forth" was another example. In a strip, the young daughter says to Mom, "I'm doing a crossword puzzle. How do you spell *pterodactyl?*" Mom, busy putting clother in a dresser drawer replies, "If you get the dictionary, I'll help you look it up." The girl replies, "You don't know how to spell it, do you?" Mom: "Yes, I do, I just want to teach you how to look things up." The next frame shows the young girl saying, "Mom doesn't know how to spell pterodactyl." The other child says, "Don't be too hard on her. Maybe she was absent the day the had spelling." Overhearing the children, Mom yells, "Cut it out, you two." *(The Sacramento Union, 1990).* Sitting by the student who explained the two cartoons to another, the teacher assessed and evaluated the student's comprehension of what was read.
3. *Identify a main idea.* The students told classroom peers one or two reasons why the title of the story was a good one.
4. *Interpret the ideas of others and answer selected riddles about the topic.*
5. *Match sentences with illustrations mounted on posters and discard the sentences that were unrelated to the topic.*
6. *Use cloze procedure.* The students completed incomplete cloze activities. They used a maze cloze (Guthrie et al., 1984), where the nouns and verbs of a reading selection were deleted. For each deleted word, three responses were given ty the teacher. One was the right answer, one was a word that was the same part of speech, and the third was a different part of speech. The students selected their choices. They also used an oral cloze procedure (Aulls, 1982), where the teacher placed text on an overhead transparency and covered key words with stick-on notes. As a group, the students read the text silently and then reread it together aloud. The covered key words were predicted and the stick-on notes were taken off for immediate self-check and feedback.
7. *Tape responses.* The teacher asked open-ended questions about a story and listened to the taped responses made by the students in their groups to discover the extent to which the students thoughtfully answered the questions.
8. *Evaluate.* To participate in self-evaluation during a unit study, the students responded to a "Self-Check on Reading about Dinosaurs" (Reproducible 25) and a "Self-Check on Reading Informational Books" (Reproducible 26).

How to Assess Participation in Group Work

In the classroom, participation in group work was encouraged and students met to consider some of their responsibilities with a guide sheet similar to this:

To Help Your Group:

a. In your group, identify a facilitator and a recorder.
b. Help the facilitator (and others) decide on the purpose of your group.
c. Help the facilitator (and others) decide on a group plan.
d. Write the plan and give a copy to the teacher.
e. Decide on what information is needed by the group.
f. Decide on who in the group will help collect and record the information.
g. Discuss the information when it is collected and recorded.
h. Discuss ways to organize all of the information collected by the group members.
i. Organize the information.
j. Discuss the conclusion the members of our group can make from the information.
k. Prepare the materials your group needs to present its findings.
l. Make a presentation to the class about the findings.
m. Meet again and discuss each member's positive contribution to the purpose of the group.

During the students' participation in group work, the teacher kept anecdotal notes of the children's involvement in the group's tasks. To do this, the teacher used observational forms and wrote notes on adhesive-backed note papers as the teacher walked around the room. As the teacher interacted with the children and observed the participation, the teacher had the option of observing generally, observing specific behaviors, or recording both general and specific observations. The notes about the extent to which the students participated were taken on an observation form like this:

Assessing Participation in Group Work
Student_____ **Date**_____

1. Participated in the group's task (identifying a facilitator and a recorder).
   _____always _____often _____sometimes _____seldom _____never
   Comments:
2. Participated in helping others (deciding on group's purpose and the group's plan).
   _____always _____often _____sometimes _____seldom _____never
   Comments:
3. Participated in writing/copying the plan and giving a copy to the teacher.
   _____always _____often _____sometimes _____seldom _____never
   Comments:
4. Participated in decision-making (what information is needed by the group).
   _____always _____often _____sometimes _____seldom _____never
   Comments:
5. Participated in decision making (who in the group will help collect and record the information).
   _____always _____often _____sometimes _____seldom _____never
   Comments:

6. Participated in discussion about information when it is collected and recorded.

   _____always   _____often   _____sometimes   _____seldom   _____never
   Comments:

7. Participated in organizing all of the information collected by the group members.

   _____always   _____often   _____sometimes   _____seldom   _____never
   Comments:

8. Participated in drawing a conclusion from the information with the members of the group.

   _____always   _____often   _____sometimes   _____seldom   _____never
   Comments:

9. Participated in preparing the materials the group needs to present its findings.

   _____always   _____often   _____sometimes   _____seldom   _____never
   Comments:

10. Participated in making a presentation to the class about the findings.

    _____always   _____often   _____sometimes   _____seldom   _____never
    Comments:

11. Participated in discussing each member's positive contribution to the purpose of the group.

    _____always   _____often   _____sometimes   _____seldom   _____never
    Comments:

12. Participated in making a positive contribution to the group's purpose

    _____always   _____often   _____sometimes   _____seldom   _____never
    Comments:

Topic C: Collecting Evidence of a Student's Progress

A Collection Folder: A Portfolio by Thirds

"Fortunately, informal methods of assessment can complement formal measures of evaluation by providing clear evidence of growth in reading and writing which is easily understood by parents, teachers, administrators, and students," states Kramer, (1990), a reading specialist. Evidence of a student's progress can be shown by a collection (portfolio) of reading and writing samples through the academic year (Kramer suggests collecting samples in September, January, and May). Before collecting a sample, the teacher may read a selection aloud, brainstorm writing ideas, provide an audience, and invite children to read what they have written to any student in the class. Writing samples (where children spell to the best of their ability) generated during a 10-minute period will be enough for a child's assessment portfolio. In May, the teacher should compare the writing sample to those collected in September and January to see the growth in writing and spelling ability. To collect reading samples, the teacher may schedule one minute with each student in the classroom three times a year. During this time, the teacher can invite the child to read for one minute from a grade-appropriate story. In January and May, the teacher may invite the child to read the same sections of the story. In each reading (if desired), a teacher may count the number of words read correctly to provide a set of numerical values that can be compared at the end of the academic year.

A teacher may prepare student portfolios and collect documentation of student progress from the beginning to the end of the school year. To do this, a file folder or notebook is selected to organize each student's work and to include the teacher's written observations. In the student's portfolio, the teacher should put a copy of the course of study goals and objects for the grade level in the front of the folder and use it as an inventory checklist. Through the year, the teacher should collect examples of the student's performance on the objectives by collecting documents that show the acquisition, mastery, and maintenance of skills in the classroom. The collection of materials collected during the year include homework, in-class assignments, unit tests, and creative projects. The teacher should date each work sample and put a note with it to link it to the related objective.

To engage students and parents, a teacher may develop a student portfolio in thirds. This means the student selects material to be inserted for one-third of the portfolio; the parent (adult in the home) selects from the work sent home for another third (and brings the work to school to insert in the portfolio at conference time); and the teacher selects the remaining one-third of the materials. In assessing, a teacher keeps each student's file (folder, portfolio) and shows the portfolio to the adults in the child's home to demonstrate the student's skills acquired, mastered, and maintained through the school year. In addition to the drafts and writing under revision, a teacher keeps copies of the finished products, too—letters that were mailed, memos that were sent, minutes of meetings, reports that were developed, and so on.

A Writing Folder Shows Student's Progress

Sometimes the collection folder can focus on one aspect of progress, such as the development of a student's writing. The teacher may ask students to construct a writing folder and to label the different pockets that will be needed. Each student will need a different headings on the pockets to show the different types of writing styles. For instance, in one pocket, the student may place all the first drafts; in another, the draft that the student is currently working on; and in still another, the finished drafts and/or the student's personal writings. Inside the front cover, each student can start a list of the books that the he or she has published or will publish in the classroom. On one of the pockets, the students should keep a list of ideas or topics that are "ticklers" for future writing. Inside the back cover, the teacher can place a sheet to list the writing skills that each student has shown through the year. To personalize the writing folders, the covers can be decorated and personalized by the students.

An Audiotape

To note a student's increased reading fluency and phrasing, a third-grade teacher kept oral records of each student's reading. The teacher taped and recorded a student reading aloud several times a year to have an oral record of his or her reading progress. The teacher used this oral reading as a basis for evaluation.

As a student reads, a teacher determines which reading strategies the student is using and then plans future instruction accordingly. For example, a sixth-grade teacher invited the students to read an alliterative tongue twister from alphabet books each week for several weeks. The teacher recorded each student and went back to listen to the tape to note the student's expression and fluency. Alliteration was one of the many language patterns the teacher found in alphabet books, and these language patterns provided a foundation for oral responses and engaged students in oral language (Roberts, 1987). The patterns built on the speech of the children as they repeated alliterative words, rhymed words, and played games with rhyme, repetition, and other elements of language. The books offered predictable elements that promoted success and enjoyment of reading (Bridge, 1978; Bridge, Winograd, & Haley, 1983; Holdaway, 1979, 1981; Rhodes, 1977) and enhanced the students' comprehension (Heald-Taylor, 1987; Rand, 1984; Tompkins & Webeler, 1983, Whaley, 1981). Some alliterative writing the teacher asked the students to consider included the following:

1. A pattern from *A Is for Angry: An Animal and Adjective Alphabet* (Workman, 1983) by Sandra Boynton. The teacher invited students to insert adjectives for A is for_____, B is for_____, and so on. When ready, the teacher asked students to substitute nouns or verbs in the pattern.
2. A pattern from *All about Arthur: An Absolutely Absurd Ape* (Watts, 1974) by Eric Carle. The teacher engaged students in responses about an acquaintance met (e.g., In the city of_____, Arthur met a_____ named_____).
3. A pattern from *Alphabet Zoop* (McCall, 1970) by Florence Parry Heide. The teacher asked the students to notice the pattern of animal-verb-food with the model, Alligator Adores Asparagus: __(animal name)__ __(verb)__ __(food)__ .
4. A pattern from *I Love My Anteater with an A* (Knopf, 1964) by Ipcar Dahlov. The teacher showed the students the sentence: I love my anteater with an A because he is_____ and do not love him because he is_____.
5. A pattern from *A-Z and Back Again: An ABC Book* (Tiger Books, 1986) by Carol Mills. The teacher read an example to the students, "Auntie Ada meets Albert the alligator who gives Auntie an apple," and asked students to work together and develop similar sentences for other letters in the alphabet.

A Conference and Conference Log

In a midyear conference in a sixth-grade class, the teacher and the student reviewed the student's daily journal, book response log, and writing folder. The individual conference was the teacher's approach to evaluate the reading and writing behaviors of each student. To discuss writing during a teacher-student conference, Graves (1983) has provided suggestions for supporting a student:

1. *Be predictable.* Always make the student feel comfortable in taking risks in his or her writing and give responses to help the student achieve success.
2. *Be focused.* Always select one or two features of the student's writing (e.g., purpose and the way the writing achieves that purpose). Save corrections related to conventions of mechanics until the writing is finished.
3. *Be ready to demonstrate solutions.* Always be ready to show (perhaps with chart and marker or overhead transparency) how changes might be made.
4. *Be ready to reverse the roles of teacher-student.* Always make the conference child centered and encourage the student to ask questions and make comments.
5. *Be ready to use the vocabulary related to writing.* Always use the vocabulary about the processes/technicalities of writing and encourage the child to use the vocabulary.
6. *Be humorous.* With your humor, a student will be encouraged to experiment, take risks, and thus grow and develop as a creative writer.

The student's writing was examined to see the progress in handwriting and the use of such things as number of drafts, revisions, and use of the editing process. Related to draft writing, the discussion was on the choice of topic, clarity of thought, use of complex sentences, the ability to synthesize information, and the use of descriptive details. Related to final revisions, the focus was on periods, capitals, paragraph indentations, and spelling. In the conference, the teacher encouraged the student to analyze the kinds of errors that were made and to talk about any problems the student was having. The strategies the student were using were discussed. Both could easily see the student's growth since the beginning of the year.

Student-to-Student Conference

For student-to-student conferences, a fifth-grade teacher engaged the students in a peer conference group (Crowhurst, 1979). The teacher divided the students into five or six groups. They passed around their drafts among the group members, read them, and each member wrote suggestions for improvement on response sheets. The authors passed along their ideas of what they needed in the way of help and feedback and ideas. Response sheets were given to the authors so that each author got a review of his or her writing from each member of the group. The response sheets suggested such phrases as (1) I like the way you . . . (2) This is interesting because it . . . (3) Can you tell me more about . . . and (4) Can you explain to me how. . . . The response sheets engaged students in becoming useful responders. To demonstrate this, the teacher showed the teacher's own writing to the class and asked for helpful ideas about ways to develop the writing.

Teacher-Student Conference Log

Relying on a conference log, a fourth-grade teacher scheduled meetings with students. After each conference, the teacher wrote notes about each student's conference. On a sheet with the student's name and the date, the teacher recorded the selection read and what the student recalled about the reading. The teacher recorded the extent of the student's comprehension and recommendations for the student. The teacher listed some of the skill needs and, if announced by the student, what the next reading would be. The teacher made notes on the related writing that was done by the student, signs of invented spelling, and made suggestions related to grammar and structure for a final revision.

A Learning Log, Journal, or Thinkbook

In a learning log, a student in a third-grade class wrote her sentences about what was being learned in school. Here, the student made comments about the learning and told what had been of interest, what went wrong, and what problems (difficulties) she had. She told of the new things she had learned and wrote about them in her own words, which helped her make the newly learned materials a part of her understanding.

A Life-Writing Journal Shows Student's Progress

In a second-grade class, a life-writing journal was a place for the students' personal writing about their interests and experiences. The students recorded incidents, holidays, hobbies, relationships, and wrote letters (Bentley & Butler, 1988). Participating in this, the girls and boys relied on their own thoughts, reflections, memories, and experiences, and recorded ideas that were important to them.

A Thinkbook Shows Student's Progress

In a third-grade class, a reading response thinkbook focused the students' personal reactions to a book read. The thinkbook was a spiral reading notebook for each student and the writing in it demonstrated the student's ability to synthesize and interpret information from silent reading and oral discussion. With the thinkbooks, the teacher kept the emphasis on enjoying and appreciating literature and stayed away from long written assignments. The teacher did not require book reports, believing that this might discourage the students from further reading. Instead of long assignments, the teacher asked the students to write a prereading prediction before reading a chapter and to write a brief summary after reading. Students also answered questions that were posed, gave an opinion of the book, and described the characters. They wrote a letter to the character, recorded some of the hard words they wanted to remember, wrote their personal reactions, and made comments about what was read. Collecting the thinkbooks weekly, the teacher read the students' reactions, wrote personal comments, and asked questions.

A Student-Teacher Cooperative Log Shows Student's Progress

With a student-teacher cooperative log, the teacher also communicated with each student. This log was a place where each student wrote about his or her daily progress in the afternoon each day. Students wrote about how they thought they were doing, what they wanted to read or study next, and what was interesting to them during the day. They wrote about what they wanted to learn next in reading or writing or in a study area. The teacher read the logs often and made written responses.

Journals, logs, thinkbooks, daybooks, and writing folders were used to demonstrate each student's movement from the stages of invented spelling to more conventional spelling. The materials were a record of the conventions of print and the skills of writing that the student was using and mastering. The teacher dated all of the samples of the writing to show the development of the student's language, interests, and perceptions. When the materials were collected, the teacher read them and commented on the student's ideas with no grading involved. However, the journals were counted as part of an overall grade, and students were recognized for the effort that went into thoughtful journal entries with award marks and bonus points. At the end of a unit, the students focused their attention on their journals before they started a new journal for a new unit of study and made an end-of-unit review of what they had learned, numbered the journal pages, added titles for the different pages of writing, made a contents page, decorated a title page, and wrote a self-evaluation summary for closure of their study.

A Record: Oral Responses, Anecdotes, and Readings

To gain insights into a student's understanding and appreciation of literature, the teacher can also generate a system for recording information about the students' oral responses as they participate in group discussions, whole-class activities, and shared book experiences. For instance, the teacher asks a student to retell a story orally, and, from the retelling, makes judgments about the extent to which the student can sequence, summarize, paraphrase, interpret, and recall the details. From the questions that a student asks, the teacher gains information about a student's language processing and thinking.

An Anecdotal Record Book Shows Student's Progress

The teacher should consider evaluation that is based on writing for real purposes, on the book projects, collaborative writing, and other activities that students engage in to respond to literature. To evaluate, the teacher may want an anecdotal record book in which to keep a profile of observations day to day. The teacher can look through each child's writing folder to look for patterns emerging over a period of time. Weekly, the teacher may ask the students to write about *Things I Have Learned* and give it to the teacher.

A Reading Record Shows Student's Progress

A teacher can look at the reading record kept by each student to see the number of books and the range of reading material (and the difficulty level) of books that have been read from week to week or month to month. A reading record will indicate the extent to which the students read and also show their reading preferences. With a reading record (folder, notebook), a student's reading progress can be documented from month to month.

A Comment Card and Report Card

A teacher can decide to keep a record of what a student does in the process of reading a 100- or 200- word sample. As the child is reading, the teacher notes the student's exact behavior. During a four-minute period, the teacher records the repetitions, insertions, word omissions, self-corrections, and substitutions, and sees where the students need help (and where help was given) in order to keep going in the reading. This record becomes a useful diagnostic tool for further instruction.

If a district requires that letter grades be placed on a student's report card (instead of a comment indicating progress), a teacher may use the writing and reading samples that have been collected to support the grades on the report cards. During conferences with parents, the samples will support the letter grade(s) the student has earned. To support the comment on cards, a teacher may want to use a checklist along with narrative paragraphs and place them in the report card.

A Group Inventory

A group inventory[1] can show a teacher the students' progress about locating components in books, about understanding the vocabulary in context, and about their use of graphic materials (i.e., charts, graphs, illustrations, and maps). Periodically, students are invited to respond to queries similar to the ones that follow in *How Well Written Was the Book?* to tell the teacher how well the author had written the text so the students could read it with understanding. The dictated or written results of a group inventory will help a teacher plan additional learning experiences for the students.

How Well Written Was the Book?

After looking at *The Dinosaurs' Alphabet* (Barron, 1991) by Richard Fortey, a paleontologist at the Natural History Museum, London, please answer:

1. After what dinosaur does the information about tyrannosaurus begin?
2. How did you find this information?
3. On what page did you find out more about duck-billed dinosaurs?
4. Where in the book does the author discuss when the dinosaurs lived?
5. Locate the page for A. Why do you think the author used bold text for the word *allosaurus*?
6. On the page for A, find the word *allosaurus* printed in syllables. Why did the author put those syllables there?

Words in Context

1. Turn to the second page (B page) and read the lines about the brachiosaurus. What is the meaning of the word *vast*? What clues helped you figure out the meaning of the word?
2. On the Z page, the lines begin with "I may be the last. . . ." Finish reading

the lines and then write/dictate in your own words what the words *dinosaur gazelle* mean. What clues in the pictures or print made the meaning clear to you?

3. The lines on the Y page begin with, "I polish my teeth. . . . " Read the lines and then, in your own words, write what the words *under the moon* mean. What clues in the illustrations or lines helped you with the meaning of the words?

4. On the X page, the lines begin with "A rare dinosaur I. . . . " In your own words, write the meaning of *rare* in the lines. Write an example of another meaning for *rare*.

Charts, Graphs, Illustrations, and Maps

1. Turn to page 65 of *Comparisons* (Diagram Group, 1980) and look at the chart about dinosaurs. How many meters long was the diplodocus, a huge plant-eater from the Cretaceous period?

2. Now look at the chart again. How many meters long was tyrannosaurus, the largest carnivorous dinosaur? How would you show the lengths of these dinosaurs with a line graph?

3. Look at the chart again. Which dinosaur had horns longer than the legs of an average person?

4. Turn to the chart again. Name three other dinosaurs.

5. Look at the illustrations of the dinosaurs and their physical appearance. In your opinion, what animals living today look like some of these dinosaurs?

6. Now that you have finished, sign this copy and give it to your teacher.

Homework

During a literature-based unit, students are encouraged to take the responsibility for completing any homework during a literature-based unit. Homework possibilities include partners contacting one another after school to assist each other in doing the tasks (when adults in the home give permission for a telephone contact or a personal contact in the neighborhood). For work at home, the students may write a story, complete rhymes, copy quotes from a favorite book, collect questions for an informational trivia game, or create original illustrations. Some mornings, a student-facilitator may call the roll and ask each to tell a story about how the homework was accomplished. Older students should be encouraged to name the story-telling activity about homework with a upbeat title such as "The Homework That Ate My Brain."

Topic D: Assessing Yourself

Before assessing introspectively, a teacher should consider some of the issues related to literature-based instruction. For instance, a review of the related literature shows that the proponents of literature-based instruction find an educational base in whole language and think of whole language as a philosophy rather than a method (Goodman, 1986, Stahl & Miller, 1989). Philosophically, a teacher of whole language can be one who believes in eliminating basal-type materials and any skills instruction, one who believes in literature-based instruction with specific time for phonics instruction, one who believes in integrating whole-language activities into these approaches, or one whose beliefs range somewhere among these views.

With a whole-language point of view, a teacher will be interested in evaluating the process of learning in the classrooms and the product(s) of the students. A teacher will have an interest in the students' attitudes, and the ongoing evaluation will take place daily—mostly through informal assessments. A teacher will evaluate the students in terms of where each one was at the beginning of the school year and where the student is currently. A teacher will consider alternative ways of evaluating instead of relying only on skills testing and standardized testing and will want to make careful teacher observations, keep ongoing records, make tape recordings of students reading, collect anecdotes of oral responses of students, listen to oral reading, use reading logs and writing journals or folders, and schedule conferences often with the students.

Extensions for Chapter 9

1. *Consider the component in the Core of Structure: Assess and Evaluate.* List some of the research findings that you know about that could affect the way you teach or organize your classroom. Focus on several of the findings and plan some of the changes you could make in your teaching or in your classroom organization.
2. *Read chapter headings.* Write a question for each chapter heading to guide your reading. On paper, write these questions under the chapter title. Would you suggest this approach for getting ready to read a chapter to the students in elementary school? Which grade levels?
3. *Discuss types of assessment.* Refer to *Watching Children Read and Write: Observational Records for Children with Special Needs* by Max Kemp (1989) or *The Primary Language Record: Handbook for Teachers* (Center for Language in Primary Education, 1989) or another resource about assessment. Choose from such types as interest inventory, word lists to be read aloud, cloze procedure, modified miscue analyses, repeating sentences as an indicator of short-term auditory memory, dictation of stories, use of handwriting and spelling samples, and a child's demonstration of knowing print concepts.

Endnote

1. Modified from the material discussed by C. Gunston-Parks (1990) Basic triage: Assessment tools in the content area classroom, *The California Reader*, 23 (3): 11–12, 13.

Readings

Aulls, M. (1982). *Developing readers in today's elementary school.* Boston: Allyn and Bacon.

Bentley, R., & Butler, S. (1988). *LifeWriting: Self-exploration through writing and life review.* Dubuque IA: Kendall/Hunt.

Braun, C. (1990). President's message: The International Reading Association: Agent of change. *Reading Today* 8 (1) (August/September): 3

Bridge, C. (1978). Predictable materials for beginning readers. *Language Arts,* 55, 593–597.

Bridge, C., Winograd, P., & Haley, D. (1983). Using predictable materials vs. preprimers to teach beginning sight words. *The Reading Teacher,* 36, 884–891.

Center for Language in Primary Education (1989). *The primary language record: Handbook for teachers.* Portsmouth, NH: Heinemann.

Church, S. M. (1990). Highlight skills in a whole language context. *Reading Today* 8 (1) (August/September): 22.

Cooper, R. D., & Odell L. (1977). *Evaluating writing.* Urbana, IL: National Council of Teachers of English.

Crowhurst, M. (1979). The writing workshop: An experiment in peer response to writing. *Language Arts,* 56 (7), 757–762.

Fisher, C. J., & Terry, C. A. (1982). *Children's language and the language arts* (2nd ed.). New York: McGraw-Hill.

Gentry, J. R. (1981) Learning to spell developmentally. *The Reading Teacher,* 34, 378–381.

Gillet, J. W., & Temple, C. (1982). *Understanding reading problems: Assessment and instruction.* Boston: Little, Brown.

Goodman, K. S. (1986). *What's whole in whole language?* Portsmouth, NH: Heinemann.

Graves, D. H. (1983). *Writing: Teachers and children at work.* Exeter, NH: Heinemann.

Guthrie, J., Seifert, M., Burnham, N. A., & Kaplan, R. I. (1974). The maze techniques to assess, monitor reading comprehension. *The Reading Teacher,* 28 (2), 161–168.

Heald-Taylor, G. (1987). Predictable literature selections and activities for language arts instruction. *The Reading Teacher,* 41, 6–12.

Hittelman, D. R. (1988). *Developing reading, K-8, Teaching from a whole-language perspective* (3rd ed.). Columbus, OH: Merrill.

Holdaway, D. (1979). *Foundations of literacy.* Exeter, NH: Heinemann.

Holdaway, D. (1981). *Stability and change in literacy learning.* Exeter, NH: Heinemann.

Hunt, L. C. (1967). Evaluation through teacher-pupil conferences. In T. C. Barrett (Ed.), *The evaluation of children's reading achievement* (pp. 111–125). Newark, DE: International Reading Association.

Kemp, M. (1989). *Watching children read and write: Observational records for children with special needs.* Portsmouth, NH: Heinemann.

Knowles, L. (1983). *Encouraging talk.* Toronto: Methuen.

Kramer, C. J. (1990). Documenting reading and writing growth in the primary grades using informal methods of evaluation. *The Reading teacher* 44 (4) (December): 356–357.

LaGreca, A. M. (1990). *Through the eyes of the child: Obtaining self reports from children & adolescents.* Boston: Allyn and Bacon.

Lichtenstein, R., & Ireton, H. (1984). *Preschool screening: Identifying young children with developmental and educational problems.* Boston: Allyn and Bacon.

Manitoba Department of Education (1979). *Manitoba writing assessment program.* A Report of the Measurement and Evaluation Branch. Manitoba Province: Department of Education.

McKowen, C. (1979). *Get your A out of college.* Los Altos, CA: William Kaufman.

Moffet, J., & B. J. Wagner. (1983). *Student-centered language arts and reading, K–13: A handbook for teachers.* Boston: Houghton Mifflin.

Rand, M. (1984). Story schema: Theory, research and practice. *The Reading Teacher,* 37, 377–383.

Rhodes, L. (1977). I can read! Predictable books as resources for reading and writing Instruction. *The Reading Teacher,* 34, 511–518.

Roberts, P. L. (1987). *Alphabet books as a key to language patterns: An annotated action bibliography.* Hamden, CT: Library Professional Publications.

The Sacramento Union (1990). "Hermann" and "Sally Forth" comics. June 13, p. F7.

Stahl, S. A., & Miller, P. D. (1989). Whole language and language experience approaches for beginning reading: A quantitative research synthesis. *Review of Educational Research* 57 (Spring): 87–116.

Stauffer, R. (1975). *Directing the reading-thinking process.* New York: Harper & Row.

Tompkins, G., & Webeler, M. B. (1983). What will happen next? Using predictable books with young children. *The Reading Teacher, 36,* 498–503.

Whaley, J. F. (1981). Readers' expectations for story structure. *Reading Research Quarterly, 17,* 90–114.

Wilkinson, A., Stratta, L., & Dudley, P. (1974). *The quality of listening.* London: Macmillan.

Chapter 10 _____

What Research Supports Literature-Based Instruction?

Teacher Reflections for Chapter 10

Chapter 10 deals with your perceptions about:

- A need for research in the classroom
- The importance of reading the research done by other researchers
- A way to infuse findings from research into the practices of the classroom
- A concern you might have to generate classroom research
- A need for support groups for teachers
- The component in the Core of Structure to implement a thematic unit in literature-based instruction: Use Research to Support Practice
- All of the components in the Core of Structure to develop a thematic unit

Component in Core of Structure to Implement a Thematic Unit for Literature-Based Instruction: Use Research to Support Practice

Vignette in Fifth Grade: Research in the Classroom

"As a classroom teacher, I find it necessary not only to study the research of others but also to generate research in my own classroom in order to develop my theory of learning and teaching practices," states Kittye Copeland (Patterson, 1990). Copeland, a teacher/director of a multigrade-level elementary school on Stephen's College campus, explored her issues of concern (such as the negative attitudes of students) through her ongoing classroom research. First, Copeland looked at her beliefs by writing down her thoughts about learning, decided what issue(s) should be considered, and took notes while talking to key students. Copeland read other research studies and asked someone to be her partner in research. In the issues related to finding reasons for fifth-grade student burnout in her classroom, Copeland designed surveys and wrote observational notes to gather information about the students' previous educational experiences and their attitudes toward learning. Then the answers of active, motivated learners were compared with the answers of students who were not motivated. In one survey, the findings revealed the learners' educational experiences *did* influence their attitudes about classroom instruction. Data from this classroom research provided Copeland with information that influenced her classroom practices, and she turned toward strategies that promoted more positive and caring attitudes in her classroom environment.

With ethnographic research methods, Copeland gives us a picture of what she did in the classroom. The picture is useful since it shows us the importance of the teacher's point of view of the instructional situation and shows us ways the teacher can collect information to support making changes in a classroom. However, a teacher is cautioned to remember that ethnographic studies such as this one do not support conclusions about the extent to which one approach is more effective or less effective than another approach. As a caution about Copeland's findings in this situation, a teacher will not find information that establishes that Copeland's classroom was more effective than any other classroom.

Topic A: Exploring the Cultures in Your Classroom

To explore the culture of your classroom, a teacher may employ the techniques of participation, observation, interviewing, and life history as useful tools to lead students toward developing understanding about the concept of culture. The anthropological field techniques help a teacher and students collect data in the classroom and assist in analyzing cultural systems of their own and others. The knowledge will make it possible for them to understand when and where the standards used by the school, teacher, parents and student meet, coincide, compete, or conflict.

Participating

To engage the students in participation in field work (a social process with interactions and face-to-face relationships), a teacher encourages the students to learn what the local people in the community do—to learn about the daily routines, the work, food, the language—and gain competencies necessary to participate appropriately in their culture. Students can get acquainted with people and visit them in their home to show an interest in learning about their culture and their ideas. As an example, the students may learn to use the local language and show sensitivity to local standards (manners, time, food, dress, hairstyle, speech). To participate, the students may learn how to introduce themselves and take leave from the groups in the local language, and, if possible, attend a community event in the company of a student who is an "insider." After the event, the student host can be invited to lead a discussion about the meaning and function of the event.

Observing

In the classroom, a teacher can observe the students in natural situations and learn from them as they go about their day-to-day activities. A teacher will gain knowledge about the children and their cultures as the teacher watches, listens, and reflects about what is seen and heard to establish cultural patterns of behavior as well as patterns of behavior specific to particular individual students. Additionally, the teacher encourages the students to notice the commonalities (and the diversity) in the peers that share a culture. As a commonality, for instance, the teacher may discuss the idea of everyone enjoying rice and read aloud *Everybody Cooks Rice* (Carolrhoda, 1991) by Norah Dooley, a story of Carrie, who looks for her brother in an ethnic neighborhood and finds every family cooking rice in a different way. The recipes at the back of the book offer students opportunities to gather ingredients, prepare food together, and sample dishes from different cultures.

During the professional observations of children, a teacher asks, What are the children doing; why and what does it mean to them? During a 15-minute period, a teacher can observe the verbal and nonverbal interaction of children at play in a nonschool setting in the community (Olsen, 1989) and write down the impressions of the children's behaviors. Later, a teacher can identify some of the underlying attitudes and values that could guide the observed behaviors. In observing the behaviors, the teacher should record basic details (e.g., the date, time, place, setting and the children/people involved). While recording, the teacher should be descriptive and use facts rather than opinions and judgments; be complete and write direct quotations; and be systematic and record sex, age, ethnic identity, social status, the context, and focus. Confidentiality should be maintained with those who give information to the teacher.

Interviewing: Informal and Formal

Both the teacher and the students can use formal and informal interviews to explore the cultures in the classroom. Informal interviewing consists of asking questions as part of the day-to-day participation process with others at school. Formal interviewing consists of seeking out specific children or parents to interview for information to specific questions. In both interview situations, the teacher and the students should ask the questions that relate to understanding what the collected observations mean from an "insider's" perspective.

Using Life-History Technique

A teacher should introduce the life-history technique to the students. A life history is information about a person's life that comes from the person or is told by others to show the diversity in roles, values, perspectives, and experiences of different individuals in one cultural group and the variation in a single culture. To initiate a life-history experience, the students can invite an elder from the community to school to tell his or her life story, record the visitor's information, and cross-check their notes for details and accuracy. As an option, they can tape record elders telling about their life and use slides or other pictures to illustrate the life history. Further, students can prepare a life history on themselves and focus on major events, crises, or significant people. When appropriate, a student's life history may be shared with the other students.

To give an example to older students (grades 4 through 6) of a life history found in fiction, the teacher may read Pam Conrad's *My Daniel* (Harper, 1989) and the poetic words of octogenarian Julia Creath Summerwaite who shares the memories of her brother's work, his life history, with her grandchildren when she flies to New York to visit her son's family. At the natural history museum, her grandchildren learn of the life of their great-uncle Daniel in Nebraska, his love for fossils, his search for a dinosaur, and the competition among paleontologists at that time as they looked for fossils. *My Daniel* has verbal flashbacks from the past to the present to link the story together, a device that makes this a suitable choice for a teacher read-aloud or a student read-a-part book.

Writing Essays

A teacher and the students can request personal essays from individuals or from groups of people on a single topic in an attempt to see cultural patterns. Topics could be ways students spend their weekends or ways their families celebrate a special holiday. When the students are engaged in writing essays about the topic, the teacher points out that they will not be graded, that they should just read for the ideas. The teacher reads and analyzes the essays for commonalities and differences, both in and between the groups represented (e.g., ethnic, age, and sex). Reacting to the data, the teacher gives sufficient time for the analysis and reads through the data to identify common themes and patterns. While reading, the teacher lists ideas that do not fit a pattern and the ideas that are unexpected. The findings are summarized to determine if additional data are needed. The teacher uses the findings to develop closer ties between the home and the school and to identify ways activities can be modified to build on the students' cultural patterns. In using the findings, the teacher makes the curriculum reflective of the varieties of cultures represented by the students.

Writing Personal Narratives

Personal narratives are natural starting places to foster writing growth of students. They may write together as partners to engage in firsthand experiences with narrative techniques as they explore memories of situations or early life stories and then follow events in their memories to a completed short story. Composing personal narratives will give the students time to think, talk, write, share, and publish together.

Topic B: Developing Individual Theory of Teaching and Learning

"Although there is no such thing as an archetypical whole-language classroom," says D. J. Watson (1989), "certain experiences consistently appear in whole-language learning communities: for example, reading of untampered texts, telling stories, student-generated writing, making personal and social connections to meaning, student choice and responsibility for learning, acceptance of errors, and always an emphasis on meaning."

Schema Theory

From the point of view of schema theory, a child's schema are mental representations of knowledge (Karmiloff-Smith, 1979; Piaget, 1975), and often a child meets cognitive conflicts that cause changes in her or his schema (Vygotsky, 1978; Bruner, 1986; Wells, 1986). When this occurs, a child's knowledge is restructured in specific domains (Smith, 1983). When cognitive conflicts occur in the classroom, the knowledge of a student is restructured in specific domains, too. Thus, the teacher can foster opportunities for cognitive conflicts in learning through integrative language and content learning experiences. The teacher will realize the need for more and more information about the students' cognitive conflicts and different cultural schemata to guide the teacher's instructional practices in the classroom (Lee, 1989). Indeed, different cultural schemata may affect the mental representations of knowledge for different students in a diverse classroom.

Whole Language

From schema theory also comes support for the concept of whole language as a set of beliefs about how language learning happens and as a set of principles to guide classroom practices (Moffett & Wagner, 1983; Goodman, 1986). From the view of whole-language learning, the child is an active, constructive learner who uses language for social purposes, and, in doing so, organizes and constructs language (Bates, 1976; Trevarthan, 1979). A child builds on prior knowledge (schema) and operates on ever-developing hypotheses about how oral and written language operate (Smith, 1983). In doing this, the child classifies experiences and learns through language (Halliday, 1982; Bruner, 1983). Learning that written text is a part of culture (Kagan, 1972), a child's schema are expressed through conventions of written language (Rosenblatt, 1978, 1983). In reading a language, a child reads to foster understandings (Smith, 1981), gains meanings (Smith, 1983), and learns that reading text is different from spoken text. Here, a child meets language differences since a situation, context, or the linguistics may be different (Wells, 1981, 1985).

From the point of view of whole-language learning, the expressive arts of language—speaking, listening, reading, and writing—are learned best in authentic speech and literacy events (Newman, 1985). These authentic events foster language development, which depends on cognitive development (schema) and vice versa (Wells, 1985). With this perspective, a teacher realizes that whole-language learning is a set of beliefs that supports guiding principles for classroom instruction—the daily teaching interaction with students. A teacher will find these interactions in the following:

Related to the Teacher
- *Assessing and evaluating.* The teacher evaluates a student's progress by documenting the work a student does in the class, by analyzing the student's reading, by noting the progress in spelling, and by keeping portfolios of anecdotes and student materials that include the student's writing to show the student's growth (Goodman, Goodman, & Hood, 1988).
- *Coaching by teacher.* The teacher coaches students through a student-generated writing process that includes prewriting, drafting, revising, editing, and conferencing.
- *Discussing in literature groups.* The teacher schedules literature circles as a way for students to talk in groups about books they have read (Atwell, 1987). Students make personal and social connections to meaning when the teacher supports story discussions and encourages students to talk about issues in literature and to connect what is read with their own lives.
- *Guiding by teacher.* The teacher stimulates interest and helps students relate present experience with previous experience with an emphasis on meaning.
- *Integrating of literacy curriculum with content.* The teacher infuses the expressive arts and skills of language arts with content by developing curriculum around themes.

- *Learning centered around students.* The teacher fosters student-centered learning and provides a literate environment. Student choice and responsibility for learning are encouraged.
- *Demonstrating by the teacher.* The teacher demonstrates reading and writing frequently as the students read and write.
- *Reading aloud.* The teacher reads aloud often and tells stories to students.
- *Reading is guided.* The teacher guides a child's reading of untampered texts (library books) and shows ways to predict, ask appropriate questions, and "map" what was read.

Related to the Students

- *Choosing by students.* Girls and boys choose their own reading material most of the time.
- *Creating original books.* Students write and illustrate original books that are read to others and kept in a class collection or given to other children in the school and in the community.
- *Learning by students at centers.* Skills are acquired in the context of literacy elements. Learning centers have labels, directions, and information on charts or activity cards to guide students' engagement with literacy elements in materials.
- *Reading books in class collections.* In literature-based instruction, reading materials relate to a thematic unit and are available for self-selection by the student.
- *Reading is silent and sustained.* Silent sustained reading occurs daily.
- *Reporting by students.* Students talk to partners and to members of small groups about what they have learned from books.
- *Responding to peers.* Students meet in response groups to read their writing and to hear peer responses.
- *Scripting stories.* Students turn stories into scripts, rehearse them, and present them either as a play, a tape, or a theater presentation. Stories can be told with a puppet show, a flannel or felt board retelling, or a show on an overhead projector using silhouette figures.
- *Selecting topics by students.* Students choose the topics they want to write about during a study.
- *Writing by students.* Students participate daily in the writing process.

From Schema Theory and Whole-Language Beliefs to an Integrated Curriculum

From schema theory and whole-language beliefs also come a view that learning language relies on the integration of curriculum—a classroom application that recognizes the importance of a child's schema. Integrating curriculum in a classroom indicates that a teacher accepts the place of a child's schema in learning and recognizes the value of a child's learning language in a developmentally appropriate way—with authentic use and integration across curricular areas (Moffett & Wagner, 1983). The integration of language and authentic use of language affects a child's restructuring of schema—an instructional goal for whole language teachers in today's classrooms (Edelsky, 1986; Lindfors, 1987). Researchers such as Marie Clay, John Downing, Emilia Ferreiro, Ken Goodman, Yetta Goodman, Jerome Harste, Frank Smith, and Gordon Wells demonstrate that children are much better at constructing their own knowledge than teachers are at teaching them. These individuals focus on the idea that teachers should nurture what the children know.

From an Integrated Curriculum to Literature-Based Instruction

To nurture what children know, the integration of language in the curriculum includes literature-based instruction since the instruction includes authentic use of language in untampered texts. To do this, a teacher integrates language with content in the different areas of the curriculum and infuses authentic literacy events such as the reading of children's books, writing as a process, student-selected inquiries, and related projects. A teacher's interaction with the students includes creating semantic maps, developing hypotheses, fostering an error-accepting environment, participating in collaborative learning, encouraging ownership of lines of inquiry, and implementing peer and teacher feedback.

Literature-based instruction presents specific content related to a specific domain of knowledge and, in doing so, affects the restructuring of a child's knowledge. To acknowledge a child's knowledge structure (and restructure), the teacher will be interested especially in the semantic maps of the students since the maps show a visual account of each child's concepts or schema at a given time (Lindfors, 1987; Wells, 1981) and her or his hypotheses (Smith, 1981, Wells, 1985). In an error-accepting classroom (Lindfors, 1987; Wells, 1985), the students use peer feedback as well as the teacher's feedback to restructure schema (Wells, 1985; Goodman, 1986). In a collaborative learning enterprise with the teacher and peers, the boys and girls use language to learn.

Furthermore, with thematic units, a teacher introduces content on a specific topic and integrates the arts and skills of language by developing the areas of the curriculum around a broad theme. The teacher and students together choose content and sometimes the theme. Often, an ethnographic record is kept as classroom research is conducted. Professional resources for elementary teachers, such as this book you are now reading, are valuable because they include records of classroom research and past experiences—ethnographic anecdotes—for those interested in literature-based instruction, thematic units, and authentic use of language.

Focusing on literature-based instruction, the teacher becomes further aware of Rosenblatt's theory (1978) about the importance of both the text and the reader in a literary transaction and realizes a recent study has identified the importance of a third factor in this response/transaction view—the role of the person sharing the book with the child. For example, one child shared a book with his parents. John Dickinson, a fourth-grade student in the Sacramento City Unified Schools District (California), who self-admittedly was not very interested in dinosaurs, contributed this information for a prereading word map to show the prior knowledge he had about the topic:

Dinosaurs are extinct. They were very big and lived millions of years ago.

After selecting and reading a book of his choice and discussing the content with a parent, John contributed this information for a postreading word map:

I learned that the reptiles and dinosaurs fought each other. The meat-eating dinosaurs ate the other dinosaurs for food. There also were plant-eating dinosaurs. I learned that the tglosaurus could swim. The gorgosaurus had gaping jaws with white jaggerlike teeth and was a meat-eater. The ornithomimus caught lizards and tore them apart with their hands to eat. They had long fingers and could reach up into trees to look for food.

In a adult-child book experience such as John's, the impact of the person sharing a book with a child, whether parent or teacher, is gaining importance as the third factor in the familiar two-factor view of literacy transactions.

Topic C: Reading the Research of Others

It seems that we need to hear from more writers about the effective components of reading programs as well as to ask researchers to respond to the question: What reading components are effective in fostering reading achievement? Regardless of the teacher's philosophy toward whole language, a teacher needs more answers about questions such as: Is silent reading effective? Is oral reading effective? Is word analysis effective? Indeed, information is needed about which components in reading programs are effective ones before the results of any one study can be interpreted clearly for instructional practices in the classroom. Some research organizations provide annotated bibliographies related to research on various topics, which will present some of the information a teacher needs that is related to instructional practices.

Classroom Update

- First-graders recalled a higher percentage of events from pupil-dictated stories over basal stories (Sampson, Briggs, & White, 1985).
- In a literature-based and traditional basal-reader comparison using over 400 elementary students, significant differences for the literature-based group were found with attitudes toward reading greater for grades 1 through 3. For grades 4 and up, students reported greater enjoyment of reading, greater use for information, and less anxiety about reading (Shapiro, 1990).
- Writing vocabulary generated by children in whole-language classes was compared with words in the basal reader series in the same district in Vancouver with the finding that children's writings generated 86 percent of the vocabulary in the basal series (Shapiro & Gunderson, 1988).

Topic D: Requesting Support from Parents

In order for parents to support what is going on in the classroom, they need to be brought into the process. A teacher may invite parents into the class to see activities from their child's perspective, send home newsletters, and plan parent evenings to talk about some of the current terms being used in education—developmental learning, invented spelling, process writing, process reading, ungraded papers, and the lack of worksheets. A teacher should discuss with parents the ways to see progress other than looking for report cards, scores on tests, and completions of workbooks. A teacher may discuss how such things as writing journals, writing folders, independence and fluency in reading, attitudes, and self-confidence are used as measures of a student's progress.

Incorporating the functions of the classroom with the interests and activities of parents can add value to the importance of the classroom and the teacher. The importance of social relations between the schools and the parents has been emphasized further in *Parental Involvement in Education* (U.S. Department of Education, 1991), a report that focuses on the role parents play in fostering their children's learning and in shaping their values. As another example of this relationship, a teacher can discuss some of the current practices (e.g., the practice of storybook reading to preschool children to foster a child's knowledge of constructing meaning from stories and the effect of group size in the classroom on interactive storybook reading). With interactions like this, parents will know what is happening in the classroom and feel a part of the learning process.

Topic E: Requesting Support after Preservice Education

Some preservice programs at universities and colleges offer not only theory, research, and practical applications of pedagogy but also provide continued support for new and beginning teachers during their first years in the classroom. Preservice support programs are developed by universities and colleges and often include support groups for teachers—especially first-year teachers. This support includes visits by consultants, workshops, summer and weekend classes, and educational teams who work with new teachers and other inservice teachers about student and classroom concerns. Contact your nearest university to find out what is offered.

Topic F: Requesting Support from Teachers in Your School

Support from Teacher Support Groups

"The majority of school districts in this country are very traditional; that is, most teachers follow lesson plans based on textbooks, teacher manuals, skills sheets, and periodic testing. There are small pockets of innovative change, but most of us continue to work in isolation using 'tried and true' methods and materials," states Regie Routman, a language arts resource teacher, in *Transitions*. As a teacher who wants to be in a "pocket of innovative change," you can gain support from the groups of teachers who attend professional meetings and inservice workshops (Patterson, 1990).

Also, coaching—one-to-one demonstrating and feedback—will be valuable to you. Coaching comes in several ways: videotapes of teachers in actual classrooms provide demonstrations of excellent process teaching. Volunteering to co-teach with another teacher gives you the opportunity to see demonstration lessons, to confer with each other, to try things out, to closely observe students, and to gain confidence in taking a risk when you are trying to change things in the classroom. In a coaching situation, you will find you develop a spirit of collegiality with others, are intellectually stimulated, and become more and more self-sufficient. For instance, you could invite another teacher and class at your same grade level into your room to see teaching demonstrations in whole-group reading or in process writing. Your teaching friend can observe the lesson, participate when needed, ask questions, help get a dialogue going, and later try out some of the teaching procedures in her or his classroom. Another time, an invitation from the other teacher is extended to you, and you and your class visit the colleague's classroom. You two will want to meet, give one another feedback, make suggestions, and, above all, provide encouragement to one another, realizing that teachers teaching teachers is a powerful way to establish a support group for making effective changes in your classrooms.

To initiate changes, you can invite several teachers in your building to meet monthly with you to discuss articles and books you have read, to talk about strategies and activities that have worked in classrooms, and to discuss any concerns and frustrations. Perhaps the group can meet for lunch once a month in one of the classrooms or in the school library or take the time for an evening meeting at a teacher's home. Keep the comradery and support going, so the meetings become invigorating ones for all involved. Articles of interests should be duplicated for all the members. Also from the group will come a sense of supporting one another as professionals through the teaching day and a sense of supporting others who are interested. Your support group should have an open door so any teacher (administrator, university member) interested can join the group. Such a support group can lead to social action for your professional needs in:

- Getting time and support for staff development
- Getting time during the work day for support groups to meet
- Requesting high-quality reading materials
- Getting information (workshops, consultancies, summer school courses) about alternative approaches to the basals such as shared reading, literature-based reading and writing, language experience, writing as a process, and guided questioning procedures
- Getting time for a teacher's three R's—reading, risking, and reflecting

The Total Core of Structure to Implement a Thematic Unit in Literature-Based Instruction

Using a whole-language approach to teaching reading and writing through literature will not excuse you from standardized test time in certain districts. Teaching children with a focus on whole language does not always transfer to standardized tests. Part-skills taught in traditional classrooms will more likely reflect items on standardized tests than those taught in the whole-language classrooms. So, there is a need to focus on what is similar between these two areas and synthesize a third approach that incorporates the best of both of these and minimize any weaknesses to help empower your students and yourself in coping with standardized tests. You and your support group can find the means to deal effectively with this in your classrooms.

With research findings as your professional underpinnings, you can develop your curriculum around topics or themes. Whether the topics are dinosaurs, dragons, or multicultural units, you can develop an across-the-curriculum approach that uses large blocks of time to explore the areas of work—themes through integrated units. Your teaching strategies will intentionally integrate knowledge from many disciplines and allow one area to assist in the learning of other areas in a thematic unit. The thematic unit will be the focus for students' inquiries, their language use, problem solving, higher-level thinking, and use of materials in the classroom. You will build upon the students' interests and give them some choice in deciding which aspects of the theme will be explored. To do this, you can arrange for the whole group to have shared language sessions together and for small groups and individuals to focus on activities in the classroom.

The thematic unit will be the students' focus for listening, speaking, reading, and writing in meaningful and purposeful ways. The unit will be open ended and give students an opportunity to explore aspects of the theme in several directions of study. If appropriate, you can diagram the possibilities in which the thematic unit can go and group related ideas under headings on a diagram and add to it as needed. With the diagram, you can determine your general/specific goals and the skills/concepts to be learned by students. From your goals, you can determine what resources and materials you will need. You will think of a way to introduce the unit and list the activities and experiences that will be included in the study.

To end the unit, you can suggest a culminating experience—a closing activity that involves the students and encourages their displays, group reports, whole-class activities, and perhaps a final presentation to another class or to parents.

Each area of information represented by the individual components in the total Core of Structure will affect the success of your thematic unit. For instance, after reflecting on the component about research and the other components, you will have a larger perspective about ways the students can become a community of learners. With this perspective, you will realize there are lines of inquiry for students to follow as well as inquiries and materials for you to follow and/or propose. With the Core of Structure, you will be knowledgeable about literature-based instruction related to a theme you select. To help you locate any additional books you want, research and database groups are available One such group is Children's Literature Educators Activating Research (CLEAR). The group provides annotated book lists on topics of your choice for supplementary reading, for class material, and for your reading clusters.

Total Core of Structure to Implement a Thematic Unit for Literature-Based Instruction

Reviewing the components in the Core of Structure and their related chapters in this book will enable you to infuse a literacy curriculum—listening, speaking, reading, writing—with content. To do this, you will arrange opportunities for the theme and related children's literature to be integrated with the arts, mathematics, science, and social studies. In these instructional situations, you will assess and evaluate, determine what it is about the subject matter that the students have learned, and perhaps generate research related to your educational concerns in the classroom.

Closing the Unit

For the closing of a study, the students sat in a circle around an imaginary classroom campfire. In a metal charcoal carrier, a red flickering "firebulb" flickered and simulated a small fire. Made with items from a garden supply outlet and a nearby lighting store, the classroom "campfire" was a charcoal carrier outfitted with cord and socket to hold a "firebulb." With the lights dimmed, reading around the campfire began. The teacher selected "The Mysterious Disappearance" from Goodman and Elting's book, *Dinosaur Mysteries* (Grosset & Dunlap, 1980) to read aloud. In an interesting way, the story told the theories of what may have happened to the dinosaurs: Were they drowned in a flood? Did they lack food? Did other animals destroy their eggs? Was there a disaster? The story closed with:

When it was all over, the earth must have been very quiet. There were no giant meat-eaters to roar at their prey and no pounding feet when plant-eaters ran to escape the terrible teeth. Some large crocodiles still swam and bellowed at times in swamps here and there. Some kinds of bird nested and called in the trees. But in the dry land below there were no creatures very much bigger or noisier than a cat. Will we ever know what really happened? Scientists are always learning new things about the world. Perhaps they will solve this greatest dinosaur mystery some day.

And the teacher ended the students' study of dinosaurs with, "Perhaps *you* will be the one to help solve this greatest dinosaur mystery—or another science mystery some day."

Extensions for Chapter 10

1. *Review the Core of Structure.* First, look at the graphic aid and read the text written on the components in the Core of Structure. Second, from your point of view, determine what the author meant by what was stated on the components. To do this, ask yourself questions you can answer with the use of the components in the Core of Structure. Third, answer the questions you developed and then generalize and make some conclusions about the information from the graphic aid.

2. *Begin a thematic unit for literature-based instruction.* Review the Core of Structure and its first component related to implementing a thematic unit in literature-based instruction. Review the related chapter and list all of the educational possibilities related to the component to extend the theme of your choice for the unit. For instance, once you have identified the theme, you can brainstorm ideas with a partner, list all of the books you think you might need, identify book extensions, and note your ideas for community interaction, class projects, and any lines of inquiry that connect your selected theme to the component. As you read the chapters and think about developing a unit, repeat this process with the other components in the Core of Structure and review the appropriate chapters in this book.

3. *Review this book's checklist.* In Appendix B is a checklist of information about this book. Review the material and indicate your level of knowledge about the topics covered.

Resources

C.L.E.A.R. (Children's Literature Educators Applying Research). PO Box 1128, Carmichael, CA 95609.

National Council of Teachers of English. 1111 Kenyon Road, Urbana, IL 61801. VHS videos for teachers: *PreWriting: Preparation for drafting in primary grades; Prewriting: Preparation for drafting in upper elementary classrooms; The writing conference: An effective way to help children revise their writing; Celebrating children's writing: How it happens; Managing literature-based classrooms.*

Readings

Atwell, N. (1987). *In the middle: Writing, reading and learning with adolescents.* Portsmouth, NH: Boynton/Cook.

Bates, E. (1976). *Language and context: The acquisition of pragmatics.* New York: Academic Press.

Bruner, J. S. (1983). *Child's talk: Learning to use language.* New York: Norton.

Bruner, J. S. (1986). *Actual minds, possible worlds.* Cambridge: Cambridge University Press.

Edelsky, C. (1986). *Writing in a bilingual program: Habla una vez.* Norwood, NJ: Ablex.

Goodman, K. S. (1986). *What's whole in whole language? A parent/teacher guide to children's learning.* Portsmouth, NH: Heinemann.

Goodman, K. S., Goodman, Y. M., & Hood, W. J. (Eds.). (1988). *The whole language evaluation book.* Portsmouth, NH: Heinemann.

Halliday, M. A. (1982). Three aspects of children's language development: Learning language, learning through language, and learning about language. In Y. Goodman, M. Haussler, & D. Strickland (Eds.), *Oral and written language development research: Impact on the schools.* Urbana, Il: National Council of Teachers of English.

Kagan, J. (1972). Do infants think? *Scientific American,* 2 (26), 74–82.

Karmiloff-Smith, A. (1979). *A functional approach to child language: A study of determiners and reference.* Cambridge: Cambridge University Press.

Lee, S. (1989). *Bilingual-bicultural pedagogy: Integrating Korean cultural schemata into American preschool-kindergartens.* Ph.D. dissertation, Southern Illinois University.

Lindfors, J. W. (1987). *Children's language and learning.* Englewood Cliffs, NJ: Prentice-Hall.

Moffett, J., & Wagner, B. J. (1983). *Student-centered language arts and reading, K–13* (3rd ed.). Boston: Houghton Mifflin.

Newman, J. M. (Ed.). (1985). *Whole language theory in use.* Portsmouth, NH: Heinemann.

Olsen, L. (1989). *Embracing diversity: Teachers' voices from California's classrooms.* San Francisco: California Tomorrow Immigrant Students Project.

Patterson, L. (1990). Teacher as researcher: Reach out and build your own support system. *Reading Today* (December/January): 22.

Piaget, J. (1975). *The development of thought: Equilibration of cognitive structures.* New York: Viking.

Rosenblatt, L. M. (1978). *The reader, the text, the poem: The transactional theory of the literary work.* Carbondale, IL: Southern University Press.

Rosenblatt, L. M. (1983). *Literature as exploration.* Urbana, IL: National Council of Teachers of English.

Sampson, M. R., Briggs, L. D., & White, J. H. (1985). Student authorship and reading: The joy of literacy. *Reading Improvement,* 25 (Spring): 82–84.

Shapiro, J. (1990). Research perspectives on whole-language. In V. Froese (Ed.), *Whole language: Practice and theory.* Boston: Allyn and Bacon.

Shapiro, J., & Gunderson, L. (1988). A comparison of vocabulary generated by grade 1 students in whole language classrooms and basal reading vocabulary. *Reading Research and Instruction,* 27 (2) (Winter): 40–46.

Smith, F. (1981). Demonstrations, engagements, and sensitivity: A revised approach to language learning. *Language Arts,* 58 (January): 103–112.

Smith, F. (1983). *Essays into literacy.* Portsmouth, NH: Heinemann.

Trevarthan, C. (1979). Descriptive analyses of infant communication behavior In H. R. Schaffer (Ed.), *Studies in mother-infant interaction* (pp. 227–270). London: Academic Press.

U.S. Department of Education (1991). *Parental involvement in education.* Washington, DC: Superintendent of Documents, U.S. Government Printing Office.

Vygotsky, L. S. (1978). *Mind in society: The development of higher psychological processes.* Cambridge, MA: Harvard University Press.

Watson, D. J. (1989). Whole language. *Elementary School Journal,* 90 (2) (November): 111–250.

Wells, G. (1981). *Learning through interaction: The study of language development*. Cambridge: Cambridge University Press.

Wells, G. (1985). Preschool literacy-related activities and success in school. In D. R. Olson, N. Torrence, & A. Hildyard (Eds.), *Literacy, language, and learning: The nature and consequences of reading and writing* Cambridge: Cambridge University Press.

Wells, G. (1986). *The meaning makers: Children learning language and using language to learn*. Portsmouth, NH: Heinemann.

Appendices and Reproducibles

Appendix A
What Are Some Guidelines for Substitute Teaching?

Appendix B
Checklist: How May I Review This Book?

Appendix C
What Dinosaur Books Are Available?

Reproducibles

After a page is removed from this book by tearing across the perforations, a page may be (1) placed with a spirit master to run through a copy machine to produce a master for reproducing duplicates on a spirit duplicator, (2) placed with a blank transparency and run through a copy machine to produce an overhead transparency for the overhead projector, or (3) inserted into an opaque projector for viewing by a small group or whole class.

Appendix A

What Are Some Guidelines for Substitute Teaching?

For some teachers, substituting is an interim job, undertaken only until a permanent position is secured. For others, it is a permanent career, undertaken for a variety of reasons. Janet D. M. Tucker taught as a full-time, third-grade teacher for 3 years, then chose to be a regular substitute teacher and has been doing this for more than 15 years. She considers herself to be a professional substitute and has ideas and experiences to pass along as a result of her successes and failures over the years. It is her firm belief that a substitute's main job is to teach self-esteem, courtesy, and a joy of learning. Often not in the classroom long enough to teach a great deal about an academic subject, Tucker suggests using the teacher's plans and an individual bag of tricks (shortcuts, math tricks, special stories, a joke or two) hopefully to make the day a little brighter for each child. Additionally, Tucker suggests showing courtesy and respect to each and every child so the day is a positive experience for everyone.

So You Want to Be A Substitute?

by Janet D. M. Tucker
Professional Substitute Teacher

Attitude

First of all, you must be comfortable with children. Do you feel confident around children? Can you guide without ordering? Do you expect to have directions followed without coercion or threats? Remember the adults you liked and who you respected as a child. Did they order you, threaten you, intimidate you? No. They treated you with respect and courtesy, and probably had an enormous sense of humor. A sense of humor is your best defense, especially in the upper grades and at the intermediate school level.

An experience several years ago in an eighth-grade class exemplifies the need for humor. I was setting up an educational movie none of the students wanted to see. Just as the movie started, the entire class got up and lined up to sharpen their pencils. I lost my cool and sent for the principal. Threats and warnings were issued. No one was comfortable or happy. If I had kept my sense of humor, the day could have been much better. I wish I would have turned off the movie and gotten in line, too. (The fact that there was no pencil sharpener in the room made the situation even humorous.)

Now, when I have to show a movie, I tell the class we are going to play "Trivial Pursuit." They are each, individually, to write two to five questions, with the answers, based on the movie. After the movie, I collect the questions and divide the class into teams. They work as a cooperative team, not individually, and attempt to answer their questions as I ask them. The team that can answer the most questions can leave early (or have some other privilege that is effective with that class). I try to structure it to have the teams tie so as not to have a loser. The result is that they learn something from the movie and have fun doing it. (Plan ahead and make the rules simple and clear.)

First Impressions

First impressions are vital. You do not have the luxury of building a relationship slowly. You must dress and act professionally. When I started substituting, I often wore slacks; they were comfortable, warm, and modest. Then I read *Dress for Success* and tried it. The behavior problems were cut in half. I could hardly believe it. Even in intermediate school, when I have a Physical Education class, I wear a dress and heels. I take tennis shoes to change into for the class, but I maintain my professional attire throughout the day. The results are worth any discomfort.

The next impression you will make is your voice and how you introduce yourself. You are not a top sergeant or general—you are a substitute teacher. Write your name on the board, high enough that the children cannot "fool around" with it. Explain why their teacher is not there and how long he or she will be gone. Show them the lesson plans left and explain that you are there to help them with the work their teacher wants them to accomplish. You are there to help them, not to take their teacher's place. Most children love their teacher and do not want the teacher replaced. Even those children who dislike their teacher are reticent to have someone in his or her place, so if you try to supplant the teacher, by your attitude, a change in rules or schedule, or anything else, you will have a battle over every direction during the entire day. It is a waste of energy—yours and theirs—and serves no purpose.

Assistance

If there is a student teacher in the room, allow him or her to take over—it will be a wonderful opportunity for both of you. If the student is not ready or is uncomfortable with the class, you can always step in. Rely on the student teacher as a backup. After all, the student teacher knows the routine, the children's names, and where everything is kept. Classroom aides also are worth their weight in gold. Rely on them. For further assistance:

- Try to learn the children's names as quickly as you can. A seating chart is a fantastic tool. Always call children by name whenever possible. Learn to recognize the ones you can ask for directions.
- Always know the school schedule—recesses, dismissal times, and so on. Also know the class schedule and stick to it. If reading is in the morning, leave it there. You do not have to stay fully with the lesson plans but you would be wise to stay with the schedule.
- If possible, meet the teachers next door or across the hall. They usually are glad to help if you are desperate.
- Have a backlog of "fill" activities from your personal bag of tricks. Activities include stories, puzzles, craft projects, and anything else that is fun. You should have activities for all the ages you might be teaching and for a variety of time slots. Short activities are good because you will find yourself with 5 to 10 minutes left at the end of a lesson or period more often than you would like. Other times, the regular teacher simply does not leave a lesson plan. Be prepared for all possibilities.

Classroom Management

If a child is motivated and busy, he or she does not get into trouble. However, this is not always easy for a substitute to accomplish at all times. If a class is starting to get unruly, it is usually easy to find one or two children who are working quietly. With sincerity, say, "I like the way Betty is working, and Joe is doing a super job." Often, the class will settle down immediately. Sometimes I will put the names on the board of the children who are following directions or working quietly. When they realize the names of on-task children are on the board, many will want to see their names up there, too. Sometimes, I let the children whose names are on the board go to recess early. I try to put every child's name on the board so I can go out and supervise until the playground supervisor gets there. Never put up names of children who are not working well. It defeats the purpose and becomes ineffective. Keep this practice positive.

In an intermediate school class that is really disruptive, it is more difficult. I will tell the students that for every minute that I have to wait for them to settle down, they can give me one minute at the end of the hour. Then, if they do settle down and work quietly, I will tell them they have earned the time back. Sometimes I have had to keep a plus and minus score on the board. If there are more minus minutes on the board, you can keep them in (for part of the recess but let them have a lavatory break) or have them come in at noon (after lunch and lavatory break) or after school (if they do not miss their only ride home on the school bus). Check with another teacher about the school's policy on this.

Tell students you will take roll to be sure they all show up. It will be a terrible day, but if you intend to go back to that school, you must follow through so they will trust you the next time. You will only have to do it once. Word travels fast. Do not ever say anything you cannot or will not follow through on. I also expect the classroom teacher to follow through on any assignments or discipline situations I have initiated. This also reinforces the trust the children have developed toward me. I have made it a practice not to return to substitute for a teacher who does not reinforce what I have done, as it is too difficult to maintain a relationship with the children.

The other side of the coin is giving time off for good behavior. If the class has worked very well for a long time, I will sometimes give them five minutes at the end of the period to chat. On occasion I will dismiss them early. It really depends on the school and the class. Sometimes you just cannot win. Chalk it up to experience. There are two or three classes in our school district I cannot handle. The teachers' techniques are just too different from mine and the children cannot adapt. I do not accept assignments for those classes. Remember, in all situations, you must never lose your cool.

Other Techniques and Hints

Your manner of teaching a group of children will reflect your personality and who you are. I am a small, active, outgoing woman. I tend more toward dramatics and upbeat classroom interaction, which works well for me and is consistent with my personality. As a substitute, I use much more energy than I did as a classroom teacher. I behave as though I am on stage, almost entertaining, especially if it is storytelling or music. However, I have seen very calm, methodical substitutes who are very successful. As a general rule, men in the elementary and intermediate school classrooms seem automatically to command a different presence than women. Differences in age, gender, and physical appearance all impact children's responses, so it is crucial for you to be aware of the effect you have on children and build on your own personal strengths.

It is not necessary for all the children to like you all of the time. There was an intermediate school girl who really had my number. She would yell, "Oh, no!" whenever she saw me arrive on campus and make a huge disturbance. I finally took her aside one morning and told her she did not have to like me—in fact, it was all right not to like me. However, she could not behave as she had been doing. That was not all right. She made a complete reversal and is now one of the best students I have had.

We do not have to know all the content all of the time. One time I had to substitute an advanced math class. I simply told the students, up front, that I could not help them and that they could get help from their neighbors. It worked great! Another time I did the same thing with a German class. It was a disaster. Another day to chalk up to experience.

The age of the children makes a great deal of difference in your techniques. Children of all ages can tell if you like them or are afraid of them. They all respond to positive reinforcement, courtesy, and humor. However, your bag of tricks varies according to the ages. Learn how to play "Hit the Bat." It is the best game I know for all skill levels. You can play with 2 to 20 children but it is best with 8 to 10. There is no pitcher. The batter holds the ball and hits it. (Primary grades can use a t-ball setup). If another student catches the ball, that student is up to bat. If it is caught on the ground, the batter puts the bat on the ground and the child who caught the ball rolls it, attempting to hit the bat. If the bat is hit and the batter does not catch the ball, the child is up. If the batter can catch the ball after it hits the bat, the batter stays up. When older children hit the ball a long way, they can set up relays to get the ball into the area of the bat. Or they can devise rules that will be fun for them. Adjustments in the procedures of the game are made according to the grade level and the individual children. I have used this game from first to eighth grades. It has saved the day for me many times. Unlike baseball and most other team sports, a child's lack of ability does not limit participation or cause a team to get upset. One most memorable experience with this game was when I had intermediate school boys' PE for a week. By the end of the week, everyone was playing either a serious game of baseball or a wild and crazy game of Hit the Bat. No one was benched or hiding behind the gym.

Recap

- Have a positive attitude about the children, school, and yourself.
- Maintain a professional appearance and attitude.
- Use all the assistance you can from student teachers, aides, and whomever else is routinely in the classroom.
- Be courteous, positive, and consistent.
- Use your own style and personality and develop a bag of tricks to reflect them.
- Have a huge sense of humor and always keep your "cool."

Read-Alouds

A teacher should not underestimate the value of asking a substitute to read a book aloud to the students. As an example of the value, Lloyd Alexander (1990), author of *Prydain Chronicles* series, tells of an impression he received from a book when a substitute teacher read aloud to his class: "In seventh grade one morning, we received the happy news that our English teacher had taken sick. Instead of tormenting us with spelling and vocabulary drills, her substitute read to us about such marvelous creatures as Mole, Road, Rat, and Badger. I hadn't caught the title and was afraid to ask, but the chapter haunted and enchanted me. Twenty years later, when at last I found out what it was and read the whole book, my enchantment only grew and has kept on doing so."

Read-Alouds for Younger Listeners, K—3

Planning for a substitute teacher during a dinosaur unit, there are several books for a teacher to leave in the classroom for read-alouds. For younger readers, *Dinosaurs, Dinosaurs* (HarperCollins, 1989) by Barton presents theories about the dinosaurs, their scientific names, pronunciation, sizes, and features of dinosaurs. Lines such as "There were dinosaurs with clubs on their tails" (ankylosaurus) and "There were hungry dinosaurs" (triceratops family eating plants) make it easy to read. After brightly colored drawings and a simple text, each dinosaur is drawn and named on the end papers, which turns the last pages of the book into a picture glossary with dinosaur names and a pronunciation guide. With this book, a teacher can display the creatures, discuss their comparative features, and give facts about the quality of their lives.

In *My Visit to the Dinosaurs* (Harper, 1987), Aliki explains the process of taking fossils from a digging site to a museum. The procedure includes uncovering the bones, brushing them with shellac, numbering them, drawing the position, taking a picture, and wrapping it carefully. When the bones are moved, they are covered with wet tissues and burlap and then wrapped in plaster. A teacher can move from facts to fancy for younger readers with *Dinosaurs Travel: A Guide for Families on the Go* by Marc and Laurie Brown (Little, Brown, 1983). The authors' light touch with dinosaurs humanizes the information and makes it palatable for young readers as they get hints from the silly dinosaurs about getting ready to travel. Seeing the dinosaurs ride an elephant and then all sleep in one bed at a relative's house does not denigrate the information.

Read-Alouds for Older Listeners, 4—6

For a read-aloud for older readers, *The Monsters Who Died: A Mystery about Dinosaurs* (Lippincott, 1989) by Vicki Cobb has an informative text about ways the scientist reads clues about the dinosaurs. In *Dinosaurs* by David Cohen (Watts, 1984), up-to-date information in the text is accompanied by the locations of dinosaur finds in North and South America on the endpapers.

Appendix B

Checklist: How May I Review This Book?

Review this book for the way it stimulated your thinking and for usefulness of the material. With a rating of excellent, good, fair, or poor, record your comments about each chapter on the following checklist.

Reflections	Ability of Chapter to Stimulate My Thinking	Chapter Material Useful

1. I can initiate a thematic unit. (Chapter 1)
2. I realize what planning I should do. (Chapter 1)
3. I reviewed the theory that supports literature-based instruction. (Chapter 10)
4. I reviewed the principles of whole language learning that support literature-based instruction. (Chapter 10)
5. I understand the ways a thematic unit can be infused with content. (Chapters 1–5)
6. I understand the ways a theme can be explored through a literature base. (Chapters 1, 2, 3)
7. I am aware of examples of themes for units. (Chapter 5)
8. I am aware of ways to integrate a literacy curriculum with content. (Chapter 2)
9. I understand that the theme of a Green Dinosaur Day is a day of integrated curriculum and enjoying language together. (Chapter 2)
10. I am aware of choices for projects that are available for the students. (Chapter 2)
11. I understand the purpose of enjoying active language about a content area such as dinosaurs. (Chapter 2)
12. I have identified my favorite titles related to a theme and know ways I would use them in the classroom. (Chapter 2)
13. I understand the benefits of silent sustained reading and silent sustained writing. (Chapter 2)
14. I am familiar with ways the teacher's demonstration of reading aloud affects a listener. (Chapter 2)
15. I can present a story to students in the classroom. (Chapter 2)
16. I realize some of the ways I can explore a theme for a unit. (Chapter 3)
17. I am familiar with a literature base for a thematic unit. (Chapter 3)
18. I have reviewed examples of choices for literature projects that are available. (Chapter 3)
19. I can initiate math projects. (Chapter 6)
20. I can initiate science projects. (Chapter 6)
21. I can select computer software. (Chapter 6)
22. I am aware of television, films, and filmstrips available to support a thematic unit. (Chapter 6)
23. To present an understanding and knowledge of the development of a period of prehistoric times, I have reviewed a sequence of events as a framework for knowledge. (Chapter 6)

24. I can provide information about the Triassic period (225–190 million years ago) and its inhabitants—crocodiles, sea beasts, and early dinosaurs. (Chapter 6)

25. I can provide information about the Jurassic period (190–136 million years ago) and its inhabitants. (Chapter 6)

26. I can provide information about the Cretaceous period (136–65 million years ago) and its inhabitants. (Chapter 6)

27. I can emphasize the contributions of people from different cultures to a theme. (Chapter 6)

28. I am familiar with children's books that have information about the theme. (Chapter 6)

29. I can initiate social studies projects. (Chapter 5)

30. I can initiate expressive arts projects. (Chapter 5)

31. I am familiar with literature to select to support the integration of social studies and the expressive arts. (Chapter 5)

32. I am aware of available resources for integrating social studies and the expressive arts into a literacy curriculum. (Chapter 5)

33. I understand the benefits of cooperative learning. (Chapter 4)

34. I am aware of activities where students work together with others. (Chapter 4)

35. I understand ways to develop language skills through content learning. (Chapter 4)

36. I can plan projects to facilitate the learning of content and speaking, reading, listening, and writing. (Chapter 4)

37. I can demonstrate ways to search for facts. (Chapter 4)

38. I am aware of various "everybody responds" techniques. (Chapter 4)

39. I can predict possible classroom problems when personalizing the study in the classroom. (Chapter 4)

40. I can organize the students' study in a group situation. (Chapter 4)

41. I understand ways informational books can enrich teaching and learning in a content area. (Chapter 4)

42. I can introduce students to books in different ways. (Chapter 4)

43. I am familiar with audiovisuals to support a theme. (Chapter 7)

44. I am aware of the value of artifacts related to a unit. (Chapter 7)

45. I know about computer software that will facilitate individual learning in the classroom. (Chapter 7)

46. I can introduce the students to the community through field trips and other resources. (Chapter 7)

47. I can assist students who are becoming bilingual speakers. (Chapter 8)

48. I can explain teaching strategies for working with diverse students. (Chapter 8)

49. I can help students who have impairments in hearing, seeing, and speaking (Chapter 8)

50. I can explain the way ongoing diagonsis of students works in a classrom. (Chapter 8)

51. I can discuss checklists related to literature-based instruction for assessing the needs of students. (Chapter 8)

52. I know of ways to assess myself as a teacher of literature-based instruction. (Chapter 9)

53. I am familiar with techniques to assess achievement of students. (Chapter 9)

54. I am familiar with self-appraisal approaches. (Chapter 9)

55. I will be able to assess group work. (Chapter 9)

56. I understand the need for research in the classroom. (Chapter 10)

57. I understand the importance of reading the research done by other researchers. (Chapter 10)

58. I recognize the value for support groups for teachers. (Chapter 10)

59. I can infuse findings from research into the practices of the classroom. (Chapter 10)

60. In the future, I might generate classroom research based on my educational concerns. (Chapter 10)

61. I recognize how each component related to literature-based instruction in the graphic organizer, Core of Structure, affects the development of a thematic unit. (Chapter 10)

Appendix C

What Dinosaur Books Are Available?

Aliki (1987). *My visit to the dinosaurs* (2nd ed.). Ill. by author. New York: Harper. In a museum, a boy sees herbivores and carnivores and learns ways a paleontologist studies things of the past. Pair with Aliki's *Dinosaurs are different* (Harper, 1988), and *Digging up dinosaurs* (Harper, 1988), and *Dinosaur bones* (Harper, 1990). Grades K–3.

Aliki (1990). *Fossils tell of long ago* (rev. ed.). Ill. by author. New York: Crowell. A reader makes discoveries about fossils along with ethnic children visiting a museum. Grades 1–3.

Andrews, R. C. (1956). *All about strange beasts of the past*. Ill. by M. Kalmenoff. New York: Random House. Paleontologist's story of the scientific expeditions and searches for early mammals. Pair Andrews's other early book, *All about dinosaurs* (Random House, 1954) illustrated by R. Voter. Grade 4 and older.

Arnold, C. (1990). *Dinosaurs down under: And other fossils from Australia*. Ill. by R. Hewett. New York: Clarion Books. With over 30 full-color photographs of fossils shown in "Kadimakara: Fossils of the Australian Dreamtime" (Los Angeles Museum of Natural History, 1988). Grade 4 and older.

Asimov, I. (1986). *Como descubrimos los dinosaurios? (How did we find out about dinosaurs?)* (E. Riambu, Trans.). Barcelona: Editorial Molina, 1986. Investigation of dinosaurs by scientists who are finding out more and more about the large creatures—a surprise to some students. Grades 4–6.

Asimov, I. (1988). *Did comets kill the dinosaurs?* Milwaukee, WI: Gareth Stevens. Data to use in classroom debates and other problem-confronting situations, including Sepkowski's nemesis theory about asteroids, comets, meteor showers, and a dark star causing the dinosaurs' disappearance. Grades 4–6.

Bakkers, R. (1985). *The dinosaur heresies*. New York: Morrow. Theories of dinosaurs as fast-moving, warm-blooded, noise-making creatures with a possibility of a pink pterodactyl. Grades 5–6.

Barlowe, D., & Barlowe, S. (1977). *Dinosaurs*. Ill. by S. Barlowe. New York: Random House. Pronunciation guides in illustrations. Grades Pre–2.

Barton, B. (1990). *Bones, bones, dinosaur bones*. Ill. by author. New York: HarperCollins. Scientists of different races, both male and female, dig, pack, load, and assemble what they find at a dig. Grades Pre–1.

Bates, R., & Seman, C. (1985). *The dinosaurs and the dark star*. Ill. by J. Dewey. New York: Macmillan. Compares methods used by scientists of the last two centuries to interpret the fossil evidence of dinosaurs, and states that a dark star, Earth's unseen companion, is one of the theories why the dinosaurs became extinct. Grade 4 and older.

Benton, M. (1984). *The dinosaur encyclopedia*. W. Barish (Ed.). Ill. by J. Channell and others. New York: Wanderer/Simon & Schuster. With information about paleontology, fossil hunting, and dinosaur record breakers, the reader learns how to collect fossils and what tools are needed. Pair with Benton's *Giant book of dinosaurs* (Smith, 1988). Grades 4–6.

Berger, M. (1986). *Prehistoric mammals: A new world*. Ill. by R. Cremins. New York: Putnam. Information about the animals who dominated after the Age of the Dinosaurs. Grade 4 and older.

Berger, M. (1990). *Stranger than fiction: Dinosaurs*. New York: Avon/Camelot. Facts about dinosaurs that can be cross-checked with other sources such as Berger's *Mighty dinosaurs*. Grades 3–4.

Berger, M. (1991). *How life began*. Ill. by J. LoFaro. New York: Dillon Press. Information about the formation of the earth, first forms of life, first animals, first vertebrates, first animals, first life on land, dinosaurs, mammals, and humans. Grades 2–5.

Berkowitz, H. (1986). *The dinosaurs: An educational coloring book*. Ill. by H. Berkowitz. New York: Hemart Books. Dinosaurs are shown in natural surroundings of millions of years ago. Pair with Llyn Hunter's *Dinosaur ABC coloring book* (Dover, 1988) with notes on dinosaur colors that point out ways scientists make guesses about dinosaur color by comparing fossils with present-day animals that have similar habits. For instance, a scientist knows that many hunting animals of today have spots to keep them concealed in foliage until they are ready to attack. This suggests that a hunting dinosaur, such as deinonychus, may have had camouflaging marks, too. Grades 4–6.

Boney, L. (1988). *Dinosaurs*. Ill. by author. Los Angeles: Price/Stern/Sloan. Introduction to the large creatures. Grades K–2.

Branley, F. M. (1982). *Dinosaurs, asteroids, and superstars: Why the dinosaurs disappeared*. Ill. by J. Zallinger. New York: Crowell. Discusses the latest about the extinction of dinosaurs. Grades 4–6.

Branley, F. M. (1989). *What happened to the dinosaurs?* Ill. by M. Simont. New York: Crowell. Explains possible causes for the dinosaurs' extinction. Grades Pre–2.

British Museum of Natural History (1985). *Dinosaurs and their living relatives*. Cambridge: British Museum of Natural History. Explains ways dinosaurs are related to other animals, living and extinct. A reader learns a method for working out the relationships among animals and is asked to use knowledge of present-day animals to work out the relationship among the dinosaurs. Bibliography, glossary, and index included for reference use. Grade 4 and older.

Butler, L. (1989). *Erni Cabat's magical world of dinosaurs*. Ill. by E. Cabat. Tucson: Great Impressions. Full-color full page paintings and 26 poems by Lollie Butler. Pair with Butler's *Erni Cabat's dazzling dinosaurs* (Great Impressions, 1989). All ages.

Carmine, M. (1991). *Daniel's dinosaurs*. Ill. by M. Baynton. New York: Scholastic. Fascinated with dinosaurs, Daniel imagines neighbors as plateosaurs and his teacher as a diplodocus until his mother broadens his interests with a visit to the aquarium. Glossary and pronunciation guide. Grades 1–2.

Carrick, C. (1986). *What happened to Patrick's dinosaurs?* Ill. by D. Carrick. New York: Clarion. Patrick tells his fanciful explanation of the life and times of the dinosaurs. Grades Pre–K.

Carroll, S. (1986). *How big is a brachiosaurus? Fascinating observations about dinosaurs*. Ill. by F. Marvin. New York: Grosset & Dunlap. Observations about dinosaurs, including the brachiosaurus, with its nostrils on top of its head and once thought to be the biggest dinosaur of them all. Grades K–3.

Clark M. L. (1981). *Dinosaurs*. Chicago: Children's Press. Describes different dinosaurs and how we learned about them. Grades K–4.

Cohen, D. (1977). *What really happened to the dinosaurs?* Ill. by H. Wells. New York: E. P. Dutton, 1977. Theories of scientists explain mystery of dinosaurs' extinction. Grades 1–3.

Cohen, D. (1984). *Dinosaurs and monsters*. New York: Watts. Information, illustrations, and key terms. Pair with Cohen's *Monster dinosaur* (Harper, 1983). Grades 1–3.

Cole, J. (1974). *Dinosaur story*. Ill. by M. Kuntsler. New York: Morrow. Beginning with allosaurus, retells the lives of several dinosaurs and gives facts about each. Grades K–3.

Conrad, P. (1989). *My Daniel*. Ill. by author. New York: Harper & Row. Eighty-year-old Julia Creath Summerwaite shares memories of her brother's work with her grandchildren when she flies to New York to visit her son's family. At the Natural History Museum, the children learn about great-uncle Daniel from Nebraska, his love for fossils, his search for a dinosaur, and the competition among paleontologists when he searched for fossils. Grades 5–8.

Cowley, S. (1989). *The mighty giants*. Ill. by M. Peterkin. New York: Warner. Paper-engineered pop-up illustrations about dinosaurs with name, enemy, and size of each dinosaur. Pair with Cowley's *The first dinosaurs* (Warner, 1990) and identify the creature(s) on the cover. Ask, "Is it a dimetrodon and should it be classified as a dinosaur?" Grades 3–4.

Craig, M. J. (1989). *Discovering prehistoric animals*. Mahwah, NJ: Troll. Illustrations complement the text. Pair with Craig's *Dinosaurs and more dinosaurs* (Scholastic, 1973). Grades 2–4.

Cremins, R. (1989). *Pop-up baby brontosaurus*. Contrib. by D. Dudley. New York: Dial Books for Young. Other titles in this series are *Pop-up baby coelophysis; Pop-up baby pteranodon; Pop-up baby stegosaurus; Pop-up baby triceratops; Pop-up baby tyrannosaurus rex*. Grades Pre–K.

Crenson, V. (1988). *Discovering dinosaurs: An up-to-date guide including the newest theories*. Ill. by B. Walters & J. Seward. Los Angeles: Price/Stern/Sloan. Discusses latest theories and scientists' hypotheses. Grades 4–6.

Crump, D. J. (Ed.). (1988). *Dinosaurs: Creatures of long ago*. Washington, DC: National Geographic. Introduction to prehistoric creatures. Grades Pre–3.

Cutts, D. (1976). *Los dinosaurios*. Mahwah, NJ: Troll. Spanish translation of picture book, *More about dinosaurs*, from *Now I Know* series. Available with read-along cassette or pair with another series title, *Story of the dinosaurs* (1975). Grades K–2.

Cutts, D. (1982). *More about dinosaurs*. Ill. by G. C. Wenzel. Mahwah, NJ: Troll Associates. First introduction to large creatures. Grades K–2.

Davidow-Goodman, A. (1978). *Let's draw dinosaurs*. Ill. by author. New York: Putnam. Steps to drawing the large prehistoric creatures. All ages.

Davidson, R. (1983). *Dinosaurs from A to Z*. Chicago: Childrens Press. Dinosaurs and information arranged in ABC order. Grades 4–6.

Dickenson, A. (1954). *The first book of prehistoric animals*. Ill. by H. Carter. New York: Franklin Watts. Drawings amplify the text and include a calendar of the earth from the present age of man back to age of ancient life. Discusses fossils found in other countries. A labeled "Prehistoric Who's Who" begins with allosaurus and ends with uintathere, a mammal named for Uinta County, Wyoming, where the fossil was found. Grade 4 and older.

Dinosaur habitats. (1989). New York: Putnam. Introduces environments of the large prehistoric creatures. Grades 3–5.

Dinosaur poster book (1990). New York: Courage Books. Has historical information on each dinosaur along with works of artists. Grades 2–3.

Dinosaurs (1990). Milwaukee: Raintree Publishers. Extends science concepts through "you" (reader-centered) science narratives. Pair with B. Armstrong's *Dinosaurs* (Learning Works, 1988) or G. Beaufay's *Dinosaurs & other extinct animals* (Barron, 1987). Grade 3 and older.

Dinosaurs and their living relatives. (1985). Cambridge: British Museum of Natural History. Inquiry method provides a way of working out the relationships among animals and using knowledge about present-day animals to work out relationships related to the dinosaurs. Grade 4 and older.

Dinsmore, M. (1988). *What really happened to the dinosaurs?* New York: Master Books. Discusses theory of extinction of the large prehistoric creatures. Grades Pre–2.

Dixon, D. (1987). *Hunting the dinosaurs.* Ill. by J. Burton. Milwaukee: Gareth Stevens. Explains ways paleontologist classify fossils, reconstruct, and restore them. Grades 2–4.

Dixon, D. (1987). *The Jurassic dinosaurs.* Ill. by J. Burton. Milwaukee: Gareth Sevens. Information and charts about 11 dinosaurs of the Jurassic period. Pair with Dixon's other titles: *Be a dinosaur detective* (Lerner, 1988); *The first dinosaurs* (Dell, 1990); *Hunting the dinosaurs* and *The last dinosaurs* (Gareth Stevens, both 1987); *The new dinosaur library* (Gareth Stevens, 1988); *The last of the dinosaurs, Learning about the dinosaurs, The very first dinosaurs, When dinosaurs ruled the earth,* and *My very first dinosaur library* (4 vols.) (Gareth Stevens, all 1989). Grades 3–6.

Dixon, D. (1988). *Be a dinosaur detective.* Ill. by S. Lings. New York: Lerner. A way to identify dinosaurs by their skeletons and match them to the food they ate. Grades 2–4.

Dixon, D., & Burton, J. (1990). *The new dinosaur library.* Milwaukee: Garth Stevens. Explores methods scientists use to study and reconstruct extinct species, Titles in this series include *The very first dinosaurs, When dinosaurs ruled the earth,* and *The last of the dinosaurs.* Each describes appearance, habitat, eating habits, and prehistoric cousins of the reptiles. Full-color photographs, pronunciation guide, key facts, and facts about famous digs and modern hunters. Bibliography, glossary and index. Grades 1–2.

Duffee, D. (1988). *A look around dinosaurs.* Ill. by A. Acosta. New York: Willowisp Press. Introduction to the large prehistoric animals. Grades 1–3.

Eldridge, D. (1979). *The giant dinosaurs: Ancient reptiles that ruled the land.* Ill. by N. Nodel. Mahwah, NJ: Troll. More about the large creatures. Grade 4 and older.

Eldridge, D. (1979). *Last of the dinosaurs, the end of an age.* Ill. by N. Nodel. Mahwah, NJ: Troll. Extinction of the large creatures. Grade 4 and older.

Elting, M. (1984). *The Macmillan book of dinosaurs and other prehistoric creatures.* Ill. by J. Hamberger. London: Macmillan. A reader goes through the stages from Precambrian period to Ice Age giants living in the Quaternary period. Glossary, index, and pronunciation key. Grades 4–6.

Elting, M. (1988). *The big golden book of dinosaurs.* Ill. by Christopher Santoro. Racine, WI: Golden Books. Brief chapters beginning with "Look Out, Little Dinosaur" and ending with "After the Dinosaurs." Grades 4–6.

Elting, M., & Goodman, A. (1980). *Dinosaur mysteries.* Ill. by S. Swan. New York: Grosset & Dunlap. Brief chapters address mysteries related to dinosaurs. Grade 3 and older.

Emberley, M. (1980). *Dinosaurs: A drawing book.* Ill. by author. New York: Little/Brown. Step-by-step directions about drawing dinosaurs. Pair with Emberley's *More dinosaurs and other prehistoric beasts* (Little, 1983). Grades K–3.

Fortey, R. (1990). *The dinosaur's alphabet.* Ill. by J. Rogan. New York: Barron's. In verse, each dinosaur (including maiasaura who hatches "reptile chicks" and nodosaurus who is a "dumpy, grumpy tank") tells about a distinguishing trait. Pronunciation guide. Grades Pre–3.

Freedman, R. (1983). *Dinosaurs and their young.* Ill. by L. Morrill. New York: Holiday House. Discusses the remains of duckbill dinosaurs, eggs, and the young. Offers conjectures about ways some dinosaurs cared for their young. Grades 2–4.

Fuchshuber, A. (1981). *From dinosaurs to fossils.* Ill. by author. Minneapolis: Carolrhoda. Traces fossil discoveries back to the huge creatures. Grades 1–3.

Gabriele, J. (1985). *The great age of the dinosaurs.* Ill. by M. Hurst. New York: Penny Lane. Pair with Gabriele's *The first days of the dinosaurs* or *The last days of the dinosaurs* (both Penny Lane, 1985). Grades 2–3.

Gallant, R. A. (1989). *Before the sun dies: The story of evolution.* New York: Macmillan. The story of how evolution occurred, how it continues today, and how evolutionary biologists keep finding new solutions to the puzzles. Grade 5 and older.

Geis, D. (1982). *Dinosaurs and other prehistoric animals.* Ill. by J. Hull, K. Shanon, & R. F. Peterson. New York: Putnam. Explains why these creatures flourished and then disappeared. Recipient of the Boys' Clubs of American award. See also *The how and why wonder book of dinosaurs.* Grade 5 and older.

Gerver, J., ed. (1986). *Day of the dinosaur.* Ill by K. McCarthy & others. New York: Random House. With clear text, introduces beginning readers to the time of the large creatures. Grades K–1.

Gibbons, G. (1988). *Dinosaurs, dragonflies, and diamonds: All about natural history museums.* Ill. by author. New York: Four Winds. With straightforward observations, tells how exhibits and collections in natural history museums are designed. Grades K–1.

Goodman, A., & Elting, M. (1980). *Dinosaur mysteries.* Ill. by S. Swan. New York: Platt & Munk. Mysteries include those that surround the sauropods (e.g., were their young born alive? Why have bellystones been found with fossil bones? and Of what use were the bellystones?). Grade 3 and older.

Gordon, S. (1977). *Un dinosaurio en peligro.* Jacksonville, IL: Permabound. Part of the Writing to Read program (Voy a Leer Escribiendo); beginning reader in Spanish. Grades K–2.

Granger, J. (1982). *Amazing world of dinosaurs.* Ill. by P. Baldwin-Ford. Mahwah, NJ: Troll Associates. Discusses prehistoric world of the large reptiles. Grades 2–3.

Greenberg, J. E., & Carey, H. *Dinosaurs.* Ill. by L. Birmingham. Chicago: Raintree. For emerging readers, introduces types of dinosaurs. Grades 2–3.

Greene, C. (1966). *How to know dinosaurs.* New York: Macmillan. Discusses ways to identify dinosaurs. Pair with *Dinosaurs* (Sterling, 1987) by L. B. Halstead and J. Halstead. Grades 3–4.

Greene, C. (1970). *Before the dinosaurs.* Illustrated by R. Cuffari. New York: Bobbs-Merrill. Gives a tour of the Paleozoic Era and the creatures who lived in it. Pair with Greene's *How to know dinosaurs* (Macmillan, 1966). Grade 4 and older.

Halstead, B. (1978). *A closer look at prehistoric reptiles.* New York: Glouster. Introduction to reptiles in this era. Grades 4–6.

Halstead, B. (1989). *Collins gem guide: Dinosaurs and prehistoric life.* Ill. by J. Halstead. Glascow: Collins. Observations of the fossil record up to the Age of Humans. Index. Grade 6 and older.

Halstead, L. B. (1978). *The evolution and ecology of the dinosaurs.* Ill. by G. Caselli. New York: Peter Lowe, Categorized into time periods, descriptions of species. Grade 6 and older.

Harvey, A. (1986). *The world of the dinosaurs: The question and answer book.* New York: Lerner. Question-and-answer format. Grades K–3.

Hoff, S. (1958). *Danny and the dinosaur.* New York: Harper & Row. At the end of a day of play, a museum dinosaur goes back to the museum. Spanish version is *Danielito y el dinosauro,* translated by Pura Belpre. Grades K–3.

Hopkins, L. B., sel. (1978). *To look at any thing.* New York: Harcourt Brace Jovanovich. Different poets offer perceptions and observations with a variety of verses. Pair with Hopkins's *Dinosaurs* (Harcourt, 1987). Grades K–3.

Horner, J., & Gorman, J. (1987). *Maia: A dinosaur grows up.* Ill. by D. Henderson.

New York: Running Press. Describes the life of a baby duckbill and stresses importance of recent discoveries in a fiction/nonfiction context. Grades 2–4.

Howard, J. (1972). *I can read about dinosaurs.* Mahwah, NJ: Troll. For emerging readers, facts about the huge reptiles. Grades 3–4.

Jacobs, F. (1982). *Supersaurus.* Ill. by D. D. Tyler. New York: Putnam. Facts about Jensen's discovery of the largest dinosaur. Grade 4 and older.

Johnson, R. E., & Piggins, C. A. (1992). *Dinosaur hunt.* Ill. by Gareth Stevens. Describes an actual dig in the Hell Creek Badlands in Montana which resulted in the discovery of the bones of a great bull lizard, the torosaurus. Grades 2–4.

Kauffman, J. (1976). *Flying reptiles in the age of dinosaurs.* New York: Morrow. One million years ago, variety of flying reptiles. Grades 4–6.

Kauffman, J. (1977). *Little dinosaurs and early birds.* Ill. by author. New York: Crowell. Explains the information fossils tell us about the way that small dinosaurs evolved and became birds. See also Kauffman's *Flying reptiles in the age of dinosaurs.* Grade 2 and older.

Kingdon, J. (1982). *The ABC dinosaur book.* Ill. by S. Fleishman. Chicago: Children's Press. Observations about dinosaurs are presented in alphabetical order from ankylosaurus to zanclodon. Pronunciation guide. Pair with S. Cowley's *The first dinosaurs* and *The mighty giants* (both Warner, 1990). Grade 3 and older.

Knight, D. C. (1977). *Dinosaur days.* Ill. by J. Schick. New York: McGraw-Hill. How we found out dinosaurs, their lives, movements, and travels. 18 species in a dinosaur family tree. Grades K–3.

Kroll, S. (1976). *The tyrannosaurus game.* Ill. by T. de Paola. New York: Holiday House. Jimmy, bored with a rain shower, begins a pass-it-along story with his friends at school. Grades K–3.

Lambert, D. (1987). *The age of dinosaurs.* Ill. by J. Francis & others. New York: Random House. Facts about dinosaurs. Grades K–3.

Lambert, D., & Diagram Group (1990). *The dinosaur date book.* New York: Avon/Diagram Group. Over 1,000 entries from *A* to *Z*. Grade 4 and older.

Lammers, G. E. (1990). *Dinosaurs.* Ill. by B. Thorsteinson. New York: Sterling. For independent readers, facts about different types of dinosaurs. Grades 4–6.

Langley, A. (1988). *Dinosaurs* (rev. ed.). New York: Watts. Presents a survey of different types of prehistoric reptiles. Grades 4–6.

Lasky, K. (1990). *Dinosaur dig.* Illustrated with photographs by C. G. Knight. New York: Morrow Junior Books. A photo-documentary about a family's dream to go West and dig for dinosaur bones and work with paleontologists and see their process of discovery. All ages.

Lauber, P. (1988). *The news about dinosaurs.* New York: Bradbury. 1988. Presents the latest scientific thinking about the colors of dinosaurs, relationship to birds, movements and agility, extent of feathers or lack thereof. Small world maps with animal habitats, facts and figures are in *Kenneth Lilly's animals: A portfolio of paintings* (Lothrop, Lee & Shepard, 1988). Grades 1–5.

Lipson, M. (1991). *Sew a dinosaur.* New York: Sterling/Lark. Instructions for sewing anatomically correct dinosaurs, creating puppets. All ages.

Liptak, K. (1992). *Dating dinosaurs and other old things.* New York: Millbrook. Describes various scientific techniques used to establish the age of objects from the past. Grade 6 (advanced) and older.

McCord, A. (1977). *Dinosaurs.* London: Osbourne. One of several titles in the prehistory series for older children. Grades 4–6.

McGowen, T. (1972). *Album of dinosaurs.* New York: Warwick. Pictures and print focus on 12 genus of dinosaurs. Grades 4–5.

McGowen, T. (1978). *Dinosaurs and other prehistoric animals*. Ill. by R. Ruth. New York: Rand. Combination volume of author's *Album of dinosaurs* and *Album of prehistoric animals*. Grades 4–6.

Mathews, R. (1989). *The great dinosaur pop-up book*. Ill. by K. Johnson. New York: Dial. Paper engineering of prehistoric creatures. Grades 2–4.

May, J. (1970). *Dodos and dinosaurs are extinct*. New York: Creative Education. With case studies of dodo birds and dinosaurs, idea of extinction is presented. Grades 5–7.

Milburn, C. (1987). *Let's look at dinosaurs*. Ill. by C. Newman. New York: Watts. Introduction for students reading independently. Grades 3–6.

Milton, J. (1985). *Dinosaur days*. Ill. by R. Roe. New York: Random House. Text, full-color illustrations, and pronunciation guides in text. Introduces different types with simple descriptions. Grades K–2.

Minelli, G. (1987). *Dinosauri e uccelli / Dinosaurs and birds*. Ill. by L. Orlandi. (M. Meringer, Trans.). New York: Observations on File Pub. Endpapers show colorful lines of evolution from Triassic to the end of the Cretaceous period with numbers beneath animal names and indicate chapters to turn to for further information. Discusses evolution theories relating to dinosaurs and birds with classification of birds and illustrated endpapers. Grade 3 and older.

Montroll, J. (1990). *Prehistoric origami*. Mineola NY: Dover Publications. Step-by-step folding directions for 23 prehistoric figures. Grade 4 and older.

Morris, C. (1988). *Fold your own dinosaurs: 12 challenging models to make*. New Zealand: Auckland Pub. Learn to make some basic folds— the reverse fold, rabbit fold, and bird base—before making your own pterodactyl, large brontosaurus, plated stegosaurus, fierce tyrannosaurus, and others. Grade 2 and older.

Moseley, K. (1984). *Dinosaurs: A lost world*. Ill. by R. Cremins. New York: Putnam Pub. Group. Pop-ups replicate the skeletal structures of selected dinosaurs. Pull-tabs allow a stegosaurus to move its tail, a triceratops to move its enormous armored head, and ankylosaurus to strike out with its rounded club-like tail. Grades 1–3.

Most, B. (1989). *The littlest dinosaurs*. Ill. by author. San Diego: Harcourt Brace Jovanovich. Small dinosaurs, 13 feet long or less, are described and compared to familiar similar-sized objects. Scientific names and pronunciation guides. Pair with Most's *Dinosaur cousins?* (Harcourt, 1987), *Four and twenty Dinosaurs* (Harper, 1990) and *The littlest dinosaurs* (Harcourt, 1989). Grades Pre–3.

Most, B. (1991). *A dinosaur named after me*. Ill. by author. San Diego: Harcourt Brace Jovanovich. Fanciful and humorous reflections about the large creatures with full-color illustrations. Scientific names, pronunciation guide. Pair with Most's *If the dinosaurs came back* and *Whatever happened to the dinosaurs?* (Harcourt, Brace Jovanovich, both 1984). Grades K–2.

Muller, C., & Jacques, E. M. (1987). *Dinosaur discovery*. Ill. by C. Muller. New York: Bonjour Books. For independent readers, discusses facts about fossil findings. Grades 4–6.

Murphy, J. (1989). *The last dinosaur*. New York: Scholastic. Story of what could have happened to the last three triceratop dinosaurs before their extinction. Pair with Murphy's *My pet tyrannosaurus* (Kimbo Educ., 1988). Grade 4 and older.

Neilson, C. (1989). *Dinosaurs*. Ill. by J. Kinnealy. Mahwah, NJ: Troll Associates. For beginning readers, illustrations introduce types of prehistoric reptiles in spiral bound format. Pair with C. Nemes's *A picture book of dinosaurs* (Troll, 1989). Grades 1–3.

Norman, D. (1988). *When dinosaurs ruled the earth*. Ill. by A. Milner. Toronto:

Stoddart Pub. Chapters arranged in ages of dinosaurs' rule with information about what each dinosaur looked like and how it lived and evolved. See also same edition illustrated by J. Sibbick published by Marshall Cavendish Publishers (London, 1988). Grades 4–6.

O'Neill, M. (1989). *Dinosaur mysteries*. Ill. by J. Bindon. Mawah, NJ: Troll Associates. Factual material and brief fictionalized accounts of different prehistoric beasts. Other titles in this series include *A family of dinosaurs, Life after the dinosaurs,* and *Where are all the dinosaurs?* (All 1989). Grades 4–6.

Packard, M. (1981). *Dinosaurs*. Ill. by C. Santoro. New York: Simon & Schuster. Time chart of the age of the dinosaurs and the age of humans with question and answer format and atlas. Grades 4–6.

Parish, P. (1974). *Dinosaur time*. Ill. by A. Lobel. New York: Harper & Row. Information about 11 types, including stegosaurus and tyrannosaurus. With simple sentences and pronunciation guides, pictures break frame and go into the text. For example, the neck of a dinosaur breaks a thick black line frame as it chews leaves while its tail leads back to a left-hand page to rest under a last line of text. Grades K–2.

Parker, S. (1988). *Dinosaurs and their world*. New York: Grosset & Dunlap. Information about meat gulpers and plant snatchers and some reasons why they became extinct as well as who their descendants might be. Pair with Parker's *The age of dinosaurs* (Gareth Stevens, 1986). Grades 3–4.

Pearce, Q. L. (1990). *Tyrannosaurus rex and other dinosaur wonders*. Ill. by M. A. Fraser. New York: Messner. Introduction to dinosaurs that mentions the a dinosaur speed demon, a fishing dinosaur, and the possibility that T. rex was a scavenger rather than a fierce predator. Pair with Pearce's *All about dinosaurs* (Simon & Schuster, 1989). Grades 3–6.

Penn, L. (1985). *Young scientist explore: Dinosaurs*. Ill. by K. Kasper. New York: Good Apple. For beginning readers, facts for exploring topic of prehistoric creatures. Grades 1–3.

Peters, D. (1986). *Giants of land and sea past and present*. Ill. by author. New York: Knopf. Compares big animals from all eras to the scale of humans. Grade 3 and older.

Peters, D. (1989). *A gallery of dinosaurs and other early reptiles*. Ill. by author. New York: Knopf. Includes 100 crested, finned, horned, spiked, and winged dinosaurs and other prehistoric reptiles shown to scale and in relation to one another as well as in relation to the 5-foot-tall youngster who is on the pages. Grades 3–6.

Petersen, D. (1989). *Apatosaurus*. Ill. with photographs. Chicago: Childrens. The giant apatosaurus (brontosaurus) was more like the elephant than the hippo (a visual and verbal metaphor for students to discuss and write about), and roamed the country as a leaf eater. Grades 4–5.

Peterson, R. T. (1988). *Peterson first guides: Dinosaurs*. Boston: Houghton Mifflin. Clear descriptions and facts about each species. Grades 4–6.

Peterson, R. T., & J. Kricher (1989). *A field guide to dinosaurs coloring book*. Ill. by G. Morrison. Boston: Houghton Mifflin. Present-day information about the colors of different dinosaurs. Black-and-white drawings. All ages.

Pringle, L. (1968). *Dinosaurs and their world*. San Diego: Harcourt Brace Jovanovich. Illustrations from museums, index, and table of contents from giant reptiles of long ago to where to see dinosaurs today. Presents a problem to solve—the puzzle of the duckbills' use of its hollow crest. Illustrations show artwork of Charles R. Knight and his restoration work, and *Notice of the iguanodon* by Gideon Mantell (1825).

Raintree Series.(1992). *World of dinosaurs*. Chicago: Raintree. Five easy-to-read books with facts given in story format. Topics include types of dinosaurs, how they lived, how we learned about them, and some of the theories that explain their disappearance. Grades 1–4.

Rogers, J. (1988). *Dinosaurs are 568.* Ill. by M. Hafner. New York: Greenwillow. First grader, Raymond Wayliss, discovers the dinosaur section in the school library and begins independent learning. Grades 1–3.

Roop, P., and Roop, C. (1987). *Dinosaurs.* New York: Greenhaven Press. Good overview of theories of the extinction of the dinosaurs. Grades 4–6.

Roop, P., and Roop, C. (1988). *Dinosaurs: Opposing viewpoints.* New York: Greenhaven. Discusses Alvarezes' theories, Muller's Nemesis theory, and other scientists' hypotheses and rebuttals. Grades 4–6.

Rosenbloom, J. (1981). *Dictionary of dinosaurs.* Ill. by H. Petre. New York: Julian Messner. Chart of dinosaur family tree. To show a lighter touch by the same author, discuss Rosenbloom's *Funniest dinosaur book ever* (Sterling, 1987). Grades 4–7.

Ross, W. (1972). *What did the dinosaurs eat?* New York: Coward. History of the plants during the Mesosozic Era of dinosaurs. Grades 1–3.

Rowe, E. (1975). *Giant dinosaurs.* Ill. by M. Smith. New York: Scholastic. Complete book of the great prehistoric creatures. Available in Spanish translation, *Dinosaurios gigantes.* Grades K–3.

Russo, M. (1992). *Weird and wonderful dinosaur facts.* New York: Sterling. Full-color illustrations and text give unusual facts about all types of dinosaurs. Grades 2–4.

Sattler, H. R. (1981). *Dinosaurs of North America.* Ill. by A. Rao. New York: Lothrop, Lee & Shepard. Extensive scientific details about 80 different dinosaurs of North America. Grades 4–6.

Sattler, H. R. (1984). *Baby dinosaurs.* Ill. by J. D. Zallinger. New York: Lothrop, Lee & Shepard. Fossils found to date of baby dinosaurs are discussed from the small mussaurus in Argentina to the maiasaura in Montana. Grades 1–3.

Sattler, H. R. (1989). *Tyrannosaurus rex and its kin: The mesozoic monsters.* Ill. by J. Powzyk. New York: Lothrop, Lee & Shepard. Information about structure, behavior, and habitats of this family of dinosaurs. Grades 3–6.

Sattler, H. R. (1990). *The new illustrated dinosaur dictionary.* Ill. by J. H. Ostrom. New York: Lothrop, Lee & Shepard. Alphabetical listing of over 300 dinosaurs and guides to meaning and pronunciation of the names. Bibliography and index. All ages.

Schlein, M. (1991). *Discovering dinosaur babies.* Ill. by M. Colbert. New York: Four Winds. Traces recent discoveries about ways dinosaurs protected and cared for their young. Grades 1–4.

Selsam, M. (1978). *Tyrannosaurus rex.* New York: Harper & Row. Tells how scientists build a dinosaur from fossils and make deductions about the dinosaur's way of life from the fossils. Grades 2–4.

Shuttlesworth, D. (1973). *To find a dinosaur.* New York: Doubleday. Text, photographs, and reproductions of paintings give information about early discoverers. Grades 4–6.

Silverman, M. (1990). *Dinosaur babies.* Ill. by C. Inouye. New York: Simon & Schuster. Information about dinosaurs and their young. Grades 1–3.

Simon, S. (1987). *The smallest dinosaurs.* Ill. by A. Rao. New York: Crown. One of the few books that concentrates on the small specimens of the species. Grades 3–4.

Simon, S. (1990). *New questions and answers about dinosaurs.* Ill. by J. Dewey. New York: Morrow Junior Books. Introduces the "terrible" lizards and answers questions about intelligence, families, and other topics. Grade K and older.

Steinger, B. (1986). *Oliver Dibbs and the dinosaur cause.* Ill. by E. Christelow.

New York: Four Winds. Dibbs and his fifth-grade classmates succeed in making the stegosaurus the state fossil of Colorado. Grades 3–5.

Stidworthy, J. (1986). *The day of the dinosaurs*. Ill. by C. Forsey. Morristown, NJ: Silver Burdett. Presents huge prehistoric creatures that dominated earth's life millions of years ago and discusses ways scientists recover fossils from washing down to acid bathing. Maps, diagrams, photographs, pronunciation guides, and numbered small inserts as keys show ways scientists put together evidence about lifestyles of dinosaurs. Grades 4–6.

Waldrop, V. H. (Ed.). (1984). *Ranger Rick's dinosaur book*. Washington, DC: National Wildlife Federation, 1984. Illustrations by such artists as Charles R. Knight, famous for his scenes of prehistoric life, and Rudolph Zallinger, Pulitzer Prize recipient for his mural, *Age of Reptiles*. Shows the making of a fossil, the first model of an iguanodon, fossil hunters Marsh and Cope, and discusses color patterns similar to that of crocodiles, leopards, and tigers. Lists of museums having dinosaur exhibits, diagrams, family tree, and pronunciation guides inserted in illustrations; with index. Grades 4–6.

West, R. (1989). *Dinosaur discoveries: How to create your own prehistoric world*. Photographs by B. and D. Wolfe. Drawings by M. Rabin. Minneapolis: Carolrhoda. Step-by-step instructions for drawing, cutting, and gluing paper shapes to form dinosaurs and prehistoric plants in three dimensions. Grade 4 and older.

Wilson, R. (1986). *100 dinosaurs from A to Z*. Ill. by C. Fitzsimons. New York: Grosset & Dunlap. Descriptions of dinosaurs are listed alphabetically with information about weight, length, where a fossil was found, and period in which the dinosaur lived. Grades 3–6.

Wilson, R. (1988). *The new dictionary of dinosaurs*. New York: Barnes and Noble. Alphabetically arranged articles tell about over 100 species, their size and weight, what they ate, and when, where, and how they lived. Grade 4 and older.

Wise, W. (1968). *Monsters of the ancient seas*. Ill. by J. Sibal. New York: G. P. Putnam's Sons. Black-and-white drawings with highlights of blue and yellow show the Mary Mantell story, the girl who found fossils as she collected shells. Key words and pronunciation guides. Grade 5 and older.

World Book staff (Eds.). (1987). *Dinosaurs!* New York: World Book. Survey of times and types of prehistoric creatures. Grades 3–6.

Yolen, J. (1990). *Dinosaur dances*. Ill. by B. Degen. New York: Putnam. Attending a prehistoric Cretaceous party, dinosaurs are dressed in their best and dance to the beat they like—all told in verse, (e.g., stegosaurus is in a ballet pose, tyrannosaurus is on his toes, and allosaurus does the "Twist and Shout"). All ages.

Zallinger, J. (1985). *Dinosaurs*. Ill. by author. New York: Doubleday. Information about prehistoric creatures with pronunciation guide, index, and time table. Grades 3–6.

Zallinger, P. (1986). *Dinosaurs and other archosaurs*. Ill. by author. New York: Random House. Information about birds and their relationships to the dinosaurs. Grades 2–3.

New Type of Small Dinosaur Discovered

Thursday, a scientist announced the discovery of a new species of horned dinosaur—a small, squat creature that foraged for plants along a warm inland sea that existed in Montana about 75 millions years ago.

Paleontologist Peter Dodson said the dinosaur was smaller than most, weighing only about 400 pounds. Dodson said it was not fully grown when it died, but probably would not have grown larger than 1,000 pounds and 12 feet in length.

"It challenges the notion that all dinosaurs were large," Dodson said at a news conference. "This plant-eater was only about 7 and 1/2 feet long and about 3 feet high at the hips. It was more or less the size of a large boar."

Dodson said Eddie Cole, a commerical fossil collector from Wall, S.D., discovered a rich fossil bed on the Careless Creek Ranch near Shawmut, Mont., 60 miles northwest of Billings.

Dodson, who led an excavation of the reptile's bones, named the new species of dinosaurs Avaceratops lammersi after Cole's wife, Ava, and the Lammers family, owners of the ranch. The scientist, who has spent most of his career debunking claims of new species of dinosaurs, said what convinced him the avaceratops was a new species was the shape of its squamosal, a bone of the skull.

Dodson said the dinosaur, which had two horns on its forehead and another on its nose, also was distinguishable from other horned dinosaurs by a solid, seashell-shaped bony ridge around the base of the skull and by pointy toes.

He said other horned dinosaurs have heart-shaped bony ridges, called frills, with holes in them. Their toes also have a different shape.

"Avaceratops represents one more brick in the wall of science, just one more insight into the diversity of life during the age of the dinosaur," said Dodson, who holds joint positions with the University of Pennsylvannia and the Academy of Natural Sciences, a Philadelphia museum. He said the reptile, which lived in a warm, wet environment similar to that of modern-day Florida, could be an ancestor of the triceratops dinosaur, which lived about 65 millions years ago.

Reprinted with permission of Associated Press; excerpt from *The Sacramento Bee*, Friday, December 19, 1986, p. B11.

Writing

Create a dinosaur character similar to this new species. Select a name and describe the dinosaur's age, dislikes, habits, and physical features.

Artwork

You are the director of a display on dinosaurs at the Academy of Natural Sciences. Use the clues in the article to create a picture for a replica of the new type of dinosaur that was discovered by the paleontologist, Peter Dodson.

What clues did you think about when you drew your picture?

First, I thought about:

Then I thought about:

Piecing Together Bones of "T Rex"

by John Noble Wilford

The most complete skeleton of a Tyrannosaurus rex ever found has been uncovered in eastern Montana. Paleontologists expect the fossilized bones to give them a much clearer picture of the anatomy of the fierce-looking carnivore that, in the popular imagination at least, epitomizes the great dinosaurs.

Researchers at the Museum of the Rockies at Bozeman, Mont., reported that the skeleton was virtually complete, from the 5-foot-long skull and teeth the size of bananas down to the tail. Some of the parts, especially the arms, had never been seen before.

In a telephone interview, Patrick Leiggi, a paleontologist of the museum, said: "T rex may be a household name among dinosaurs, but no one's ever found a complete one."

Among the first bones of the new skeleton to be identifieid were those of an arm. Since no lower arm bones had ever been examined, Leiggi said, one of the first important discoveries could be answers to questions about how the giant creatures used their stubby arms in combat, eating, or other activities.

Writing

Create a Tyrannosaurus rex dinosaur character with a dinosaur history. How old is the dinosaur? Who were the dinosaur's parents? Are there other dinosaur relatives in the group? Describe where the dinosaur lives and tell about an average day in the dinosaur's life.

Reprinted with permission of Associated Press; excerpt from *The Sacramento Bee*, November 7, 1989, p. D6.

This May Be the Biggest Dinosaur Ever

Bones from what appear to be the world's biggest dinosaur were found in an ancient streambed by a retired music teacher who said Friday he knew he had stumbled onto something unusual. Arthur Loy, of Albuquerque said he was hiking in the desert with a friend in the fall of 1980 about 60 miles northwest of Albuquerque when he came to the end of a cliff overlooking a valley.

"I happened to look at my feet and these bones . . . were sticking out, laying on their sides," he said.

The exposed bones remained mostly buried until researchers were able to begin excavation this year. Nine bones have been taken from the site by paleontologist David Gilette of the New Mexico Museum of Natural History. This one is absolutely breathtaking for its size," said Gilette, who christened the beast "seismosaurus"—the earth shaker. Gillette delayed announcement of the discovery until Friday because "we didn't want to say anything until we were sure what we had."

Gillette has so far recovered eight articulated—connected—bones from a 10-foot section of the middle of the dinosaur's tail and a thigh bone from the hind leg.

Extrapolating from those bones, Gillette estimated that the new dinosaur was probably 100–120 feet long, 18 feet high at the shoulder, and 15 feet high at the hip. It probably weighed at least 80 tons. "Ours appears to be the largest dinosaur ever discovered, and a good case could be built for it being the largest ever known," Gillette said in a telephone interview. For comparison, an African bull elephant weighs about 7 1/2 tons and a blue whale about 100 tons.

The bones were isolated from the 150-million-year-old Morrison formation, which lies in New Mexico, Colorado and Utah. The previously largest known dinosaurs, called supersaurus and ultrasaurus, also were found in the Morrison formation.

"That formation has been very productive of real big dinosaurs," said paleontologist Nicholas Hotten III of the Smithsonian Institution, "so there is nothing outrageous about Gillette's discovery."

Supersaurus was about 100 feet long and 25 feet high at the shoulder and weighed 60–70 tons. Seismosaurus, like supersaurus and the similarly sized diplodocus, is a member of the sauropod

Reprinted with permission of Associated Press; excerpt from *The Sacramento Bee,* Saturday, August 9, 1985, pp. A1, A24.

family of dinosaurs, chracterized by a long, graceful neck, a bulky body, and a long tail. Sinclair Oil Company has used a picture of a sauropod as its trademark.

Gillette believes that seismosaurus came later in the Jurassic than the other large dinosaurs because its bones were found higher in the Morrison foundation, indicating that they were buried more recently.

He and other paleontologists agree that the sauropods existed in large numbers for only a relatively brief time.

"It appears that there was a gradual diminishing of abundance and diversity of sauropods during the Jurassic," Gillette added. "That diminishment correlates with the diminishing cominance of the coniferous forest and its replacement by flowering plants . . . which supported mostly smaller dinosaurs."

"I don't think that it's any great mystery about the sauropods becoming extinct. They just lost out on living space and food; they were crowded out."

The super-giants probably lived in herds and, like elephants, the adults gathered around the young to protect their offspring, Gillette said.

The bones were recovered from what seems to be an ancient sand bar and the top was sealed by iron ore, which helped preserve the bones, Gillette said. Most of the bones could be locked in the same area and they were so large they probably could not have been washed very far downstream, Gillette said.

" We have much more than the tail still at the site," Gillette said. "We cross our fingers and hope for a whole skeleton." If the whole dinosaur were found, "it would probably take about 10-man-years to prepare . . . and $500,000 from excavation to mounting," Gillette said. "We're going to try not to dig more than we can handle," he said. "We'll have another dig this fall and have scheduled more for 1987."

Writing

Create a super-giant dinosaur character, select a name for it, and describe the huge dinosaur's physical features, its length and weight. Tell about its food and what its habitat was like.

Rank the Findings

Name _____ Date _____

1. Read a dinosaur article together with the teacher, discuss it with others in your group, and then complete the activity that follows the article.
2. Sign your work and place it in your dinosaur portfolios.
3. If you read and discuss more than one article:
   a. Discuss the material in each article.
   b. Evaluate the importance of each discovery mentioned in the article.
   c. Rank order the discoveries as: the most important finding, fairly important, and not too important at this time.

Name of Article

The most important finding:

Fairly important finding:

Finding not too important at this time:

4. In a discussion group, give the reasons for your rankings.

Dinosaur Capital USA: 113 Years Later, Morrison Formation Continues to Startle Scientists

by Peggy Loew

For more than a century, scientists have been digging into a vast dinosaur graveyard in the Rocky Mountains, unraveling the mysteries of the largest creatures ever to roam the planet. Here lie the fossilized bones of dinosaurs that lived 140 million years ago when the Front Range was a great semi-arid lowland with periods of rain and drought. Colorado was a flat landscape with large meandering streams, vegetation and open spaces. Man was still 138 million years away.

Called the Morrison Formation for a small town southwest of Denver where the first dinosaur skeleton was found here in 1877, the graveyard lies on either side of the Rocky Mountains from Idaho south to New Mexico. Paleontologists call it "the capital of dinosaur research."

In January [1990], a Colorado expedition found a jaw and vertebrae fragments west of Fort Collins that belonged to the rare, meat-gulping hunter epanterias. Robert Bakker, a University of Colorado paleontologist who led that team, says people weren't interested in dinosaurs before the 1877 discovery because they didn't know much about them. He said that before the Colorado find there were "miserable fragments" of fossils from Europe. "The Morrison finds really put American science on the map and continues to surprise us every field season," says Bakker, who has been working on the formation since 1974.

A group of preservation-minded people in Colorado has organized "Friends of Dinosaur Ridge" and is working on a project to protect a famous Morrison Formation outcropping southwest of Denver. The group has proposed a park a mile long and 200 feet wide. It would lie on the first ridge—a "hogback"—west of Lakewood, Colo., a Denver suburb. If the proposal is approved, Colorado Highway 26 would be closed from Rooney Road to Colorado 93.

Reprinted with permission of Associated Press; excerpt from *The Sacramento Bee*, Tuesday, April 10, 1990, p. D6.

Joe Tempel, environmental manager for the state highway department, described the proposed Dinosaur Ridge Park as an outdoor education laboratory, a "hands-on science, ecology, natural history park." The most extensive collection of Morrison dinosaur fossils are housed in the Carnegie Museum of Natural History in Pittsburgh. "The Morrison gives us the best picture of the really big dinosaurs that lived in the Age of dinosaurs," says David Burman, curator of vertebra fossils at the Carnegie. "Because of the nature of the environment it represented it has preserved more and better specimens of any formation in any period."

Scientists credit the Rocky Mountains with allowing them to study the dinosaur fossils. As the earth's crust rose and contorted, erosion exposed layers of sandstone, limestone, and shale. The layers display the fossilized bones, footprints, and environment of the Jurassic period. The Jurassic, a time from 205 million years to 130 million years ago, is the second geological period in the age of dinosaurs. The Morrison Formation appeared in the Upper Jurassic period, 140 million years ago, when the dinosaurs were at their largest.

The Morrison Formation is "part of one of the most complete records of the history of life you can find," says Dr. Richard Stuckey, paleontologist at the Denver Museum of Natural History. "There are episodes missing in the Rocky Moutains, but we do have a fairly complete record."

In 1877, the dinosaur graveyard was discovered by visiting scientists who found a apatosaurus and a stegosaurus near Morrison. That find was quickly followed by the discovery of an allosaurus and a camarasaurus north of Canon City, and dozens of dinosaurs north of Laramie, Wyo. Those discoveries kicked off a kind of "fossil gold rush" that continues today.

What Other Books Can you Find about the Morrison Fossil Finds?

Apatosaurus: Popularly known as the brontosaurus, one of the best-known dinosaurs. The 70-foot-long creature had a heavy body and legs and a long neck and tail.

Book found:

Diplodocus: Ninety feet long with most of the length from the long, thin neck and long, whiplike tail. Its name, which means "double beam," describes a special feature of the backbone, a piece of small bone that pointed forward as well as the normal piece that pointed back.

Book found:

Stegosaurus: Had a tiny, tubular skull with a brain the size of a walnut. It had small, flat plates on its neck and bigger diamond-shaped plates on its back and the first part of its tail. It grew to 30 feet long.

Book found:

Allosaurus: The largest carnivore in North America in the late Jurassic period. It was different from other meat-eating dinosaurs in the shape of its skull, which had a ridge along the top that ran from between the eyes to the tip of the snout. It was 35 feet long.

Book found:

Camarasaurus: A heavily built suaropod with a shorter tail and neck than the apatosaurus or diplodocus. Its head was short with a blunt snout, and its nosrils were on the top of its head. Those features had led scientists to believe it would have lived in water. It grew to 60 feet long (Loew, 1990).

Book found:

Choices, Choices, Choices #1

As you read a book of your choice, choose one or more to do:

- Make a title for each illustration you see in your reading.
- List the scenes.
- Find a figure of speech and explain it.
- Find single words that describe each dinosaur.
- List all words that tell action—what a dinosaur did.
- List all words whose meanings you do not know.
- Write a true-false statement for each page you read.
- Find a quote that makes you excited. Write it down and then illustrate it.
- Sign your work and give it to the teacher.

Choices, Choices, Choices #2

As you read, choose one or more things to do and check the ones you did. Sign your work and place this page in your portfolio when you have done one or more activities.

<u>What I Did</u>

- With words instead of colors in a picture, turn this sentence into a bigger sentence that tells us something we could see in our imagination: *The dinosaur stopped in front of the ____ .*
- With still more words, rewrite this sentence intolonger sentence: *By the ____ , the dinosaur halted abruptly in front of the gloomy cave.*
- As many times as you like, write endings for this sentence: *A dinosaur is ____ .*
- Using the sentences you made above, make a small study book for others to read.
- Sign your name: _____

Choices, Choices, Choices #3

Interested in This?

- The possible causes for the dinosaurs' extinction, such as disease, temperature change, animals devouring the eggs, and depletion of their food sources through comet showers.
- A way to classify dinosaurs

- A way to compare small dinosaurs to familiar and similar-sized objects
- Explain to others what you have read.

Read This:

What Happened to the Dinosaurs? by F. M. Branley (Crowell, 1989).

A Field Guide to Dinosaurs by the Diagram Group (St. Martin's, 1980).

The Littlest Dinosaurs by B. Most (Harcourt Brace Jovanovich, 1989).

If You Want to Find Out About . . .

If You Want to Find Out about This	Read This
• How asteroids, comets, meteor showers, and a dark star (nemesis) could have caused the dinosaurs' disappearance	*Did Comets Kill the Dinosaurs?* by I. Asimov (Gareth Stevens, 1988).
• Possible causes of the dinosaurs'extinction	*What Happened to the Dinosaurs?* by F. M. Branley (Crowell, 1989).
• How dinosaurs looked	*Dinosaurs and All That Rubbish* (Foreman).
• How scientists read clues about dinosaurs	*The Monsters Who Died: A Mystery about Dinosaurs* by Cobb.
• How to build a dinosaur from fossils	*Tyrannosaurus Rex* by M. Selsam (Harper & Row, 1978).
• How to make a model of rock strata	*The Big Beast Book: Dinosaurs and How They Got That Way* by Booth and Weston.
• How to collect fossils (What tools do you need?)	*The Dinosaur Encyclopedia* by M. Benton (Wanderer/ Simon & Schuster, 1984).
• How to create a geologic time scale	*Dinosaurs: A Journey in TIme* by Schatz and Pummel.
• How to draw dinosaurs, step by step	*Dinosaurs: A Drawing Book* by M. Emberley (Little/Brown, 1980).

Tell what you read about to others.

If You Want to Know About . . .

If You Want to Know about This

- How to draw 18 different types of dinosaurs
- How to find out what creature lived when

- How to group dinosaurs into categories
- How to identify dinosaurs by their skeletons, match them to the food they ate, and deduct the identity of dinnosaurs by the footprints they left

- How to match fossils with the creatures who have the same body forms today
- How to match old names of dinosaurs with current names
- How to pronounce 11 dinosaur names
- How to pronounce names of the smallest dinosaurs

Explain to others what you have read.

Read This

How to Draw Dinosaurs by La Placa

The Field Guide to Prehistoric Life by Diagram Group/Lambert

A First Look at Dinosaurs by Selsam and Hunt

Be a Dinosaur Detective by D. Dixon (Lerner, 1988)

They Lived with the Dinosaurs by Freedman

Dictionary of Dinosaurs by J. Rosenbloom (Julian Messner, 1981)

Dinosaur Time by P. Parish (Harper & Row, 1974)

The Littlest Dinosaurs by Most

Recognizing the Use of a Symbol

Show that you understand that an area may be shown with a variable (such as the locations of dinosaur diggings) that is represented by a symbol. Talk about what you see below.

Key: • = one dig

• • • •   •

• • •   • •

• •

• • • • • • •   •

            •   • • • • • •

• • • • • • •   • • • • •

• •   • • • • •

Now draw an area below and choose a symbol of your own to represent dinosaur diggings. Show the key to your symbol. Write about what you thought about, what you chose for a symbol, and what you learned.

My key:

My area:

What I learned:

Recognizing the Use of a Nonpictorial Symbol

Show that you understand that the use of an abstract symbol is arbitrary and can represent objects in the environment. Talk about what you see below.

Key: • = one dig
∧∧∧∧∧ = cliffs
=== = dry river bed

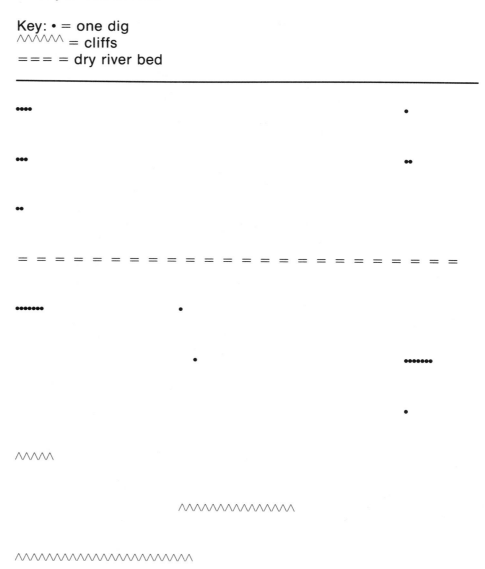

●●●●● ● ●● ● ●●●●●

●●● ●●●●●

_____

Create a story about what you find on the map above and then draw a map of your own below. Write what you learned about the use of a symbol.

My story:

My map:

What I learned:

Recognizing the Use of a Key

Show your ability to use a key to interpret a map containing symbols. Talk about what you see below.

Key: •   = one dig
      ∧∧∧∧   = cliffs
      = = =   = dry river bed
      *   = 1 fossil of tyrannosaurus rex
      Δ   = 1 fossil of supersaurus
      Ω   = 1 fossil of ultrasaurus
      #   = pottery shards

────────────────────────────────────

Second Dig

#######

First Dig

•••••***

= =

Third Dig   **Fourth Dig**

•••••••   ••ΔΔ•••∧∧∧∧∧

                                        Fifth Dig

                                        •

∧∧∧∧

                    ∧∧∧∧∧∧∧∧∧∧∧

∧∧∧∧∧∧∧∧∧∧∧∧∧∧∧∧∧

Sixth Dig   **Seventh Dig**

••••• • ••   • •••••

Eighth Dig   **Ninth Dig**

•Ω   •••••

────────────────────────────────────

1. How many dinosaur digs are there?

2. Which fossil find is nearest some cliffs?

3. Which fossil find is nearest the dry river bed?

4. Which dig has the fossil of tyrannosaurus rex?

5. Which dig has the fossil of supersaurus?

6. Which dig has the fossil of ultrasaurus?

7. How many fossil finds are on the map?

8. What fossil find was located in the sixth dig?

9. Write your thoughts about what you find on the map above.

10. Draw a map and a key of your own below. Tell what you have learned.

11. *Option:* Look for authentic maps in books such as *All about Strange Beasts of the Past* and *All about Dinosaurs* by Roy Chapman Andrews, where he suggests that you can roam in many different directions to get possible information from the fossil record. Show what you find to others.

Can You Categorize Words?

• Under the headings of features of dinosaurs, put a plus (+) if the feature is present and a minus (−) if it is not present.

	Protective Plates	*Spikes*	*Long Neck and Tail*
Ankylosaurus			
Brachiosaurus			
Compsognathus			
Diplodocus			
Edmontosaurus			
Fabrosaurus			
Gorgosaurus			
Iguanodon			
Kentosaurus			
Lambeosaurus			
Protoceratops			
Stegosaurus			
Tyrannosaurus Rex			

Discuss your markings with a partner. Sign your work and give it to your teacher.

Grouping Ideas Is as Easy as ABC

On a word map, find related ideas by marking words and phrases that are related in some way with A. Then mark other related words with B and still other related words with C. You make the decisions about the relationships. When you have all of the related words marked with A, write them in the A column. Do the same for the words and phrases you marked with B and C.

A Column   **B Column**   **C Column**

Write a main idea that tells about the information in the A column and then write main ideas for the B and C column.

Main Idea for A:

Main Idea for B:

Main Idea for C:

Read the main ideas and develop a summary statement that considers the information in the three main ideas.

Summary statement that has the information in the three main ideas:

Use Columns, Main Ideas, and Summary Statement to Make Your Outline

Use the summary statement you made as a topic sentence in this outline:

Topic sentence:

Write the main ideas for an A paragraph, B paragraph, and C paragraph in this outline:

A. Main idea (same as main idea for column A):

B. Main idea (same as main idea for column B):

C. Main idea (same as main idea for column C):

Write key words and phrases from the columns as supporting details.

A. Main idea (same as main idea for column A):

Detail _____

Detail _____

Detail _____

B. Main idea (same as main idea for column B):

Detail _____

Detail _____

Detail _____

C. Main idea (same as main idea for column C):

Detail _____

Detail _____

Detail _____

Now, you are ready to write your paragraphs from this outline.

Face-to-Face Survey

Do You Believe . . .   **Yes**   **No**

1. The first people and dinosaurs lived at the same time.

2. All dinosaurs were very big animals.

3. All dinosaurs had very small brains and were probably very stupid.

4. Dinosaurs were just like lizards and other reptiles living today, only bigger.

5. All dinosaurs were clumsy and slow-moving animals.

6. Dinosaurs were cold-blooded.

7. Dinosaurs died out because the earth's climate changed.

8. Insects were here before dinosaurs.

9. The largest dinosaur was the brachiosaurus.

10. The fiercest dinosaur was the tyrannosaurus.

11. Some dinosaurs lived in herds.

12. Other dinosaurs laid eggs.

13. Dinosaurs were terrible lizards.

14. The Age of Dinosaurs was about 150 million years.

15. Dinosaur skin has been found as a fossil.

16. Nearly all dinosaurs had small brains.

17. Pterosaurs had small bodies and huge wings.

18. The pteradon was the largest flying creature with a wing span of about 25 feet.

19. Mammals also lived during the Age of the Dinosaurs.

20. The Gingko tree grew in the Age of the Dinosaurs.

21. In the Age of the Dinosaurs, there were beetles, grasshoppers, termites, and flies.

Writing to a Paleontologist about Piecing Together Bones of "T Rex"

Read the news article "Piecing Together Bones of T Rex" to find out what new fossil discoveries have been made in Montana. What are your thoughts about:

1. **What dinosaur fossils were found that had never been seen before?**

2. **What question about this giant creature might be answered from this discovery?**

3. **Are you interested in writing to Patrick Leggi, a paleontologist at the Museum of the Rockies? Address: Museum of the Rockies, Montana State University, S. Seventh Ave. and Kagy Blvd., Bozeman, Montana 59771.**

Debate Cards

Debate Card: Dinosaurs were warm-blooded:

The bodies of dinosaurs work like swiftly moving animals with energy. Some stood on their back legs. They ran fast. They turned food into energy and warmth. Some lived as far North as Canada, where the sun shone briefly and days were cold and short in the winter. Since they lived in this country, they had to be warm-blooded because they would stay warm with little sun. If dinosaurs were cold-blooded they would have to find deep holes to hibernate for the winter. Scientists have found that dinosaur bones resembled the bone of warm-blooded animals.

Debate Card: Dinosaurs were cold-blooded:

The bodies of dinosaurs work the way that bodies of lizards work. The body gets heat from the sun, warm rocks, the ground, and the air. When the weather cools, so does the body of the lizard and the dinosaur. This is why they are cold-blooded. Dinosaurs had no way of controlling their own temperature.

Other dinosaur mysteries for debates are:

Mystery Subject #1: Tyrannosaurus had a use for the small front legs versus tyrannosaurus had *no* use for the small front legs.

Mystery Subject #2: Sauropods were swamp dwellers versus they were *not* swamp dwellers.

Mystery Subject #3: Duckbill dinosaurs were related to ducks versus duckbill dinosaurs were *not* related to ducks.

Mystery Subject #4: Dinosaurs and birds are relatives versus they are *not* relatives.

Mystery Subject #5: A cold climate disaster caused the extinction of the dinosarus versus a *hot* climate caused the extinction of the dinosaurs.

Descendants of Prehistoric Plants: Features of Leaves

Color	Length	Notches	Veins
Willow			
Ginko			
Maple			
Oak			
Chestnut			
Laurel			

With a magnifying glass or the use of the overhead projector, study these:

- *The ginko or maiden hair tree* has leaves about 5 inches long with parallel veins and notches at the center of the outer edge of the pale green leaves. It has been growing practicaly unchanged since the middle Paleozoic age where it appeared among the first fossil land plants.

- *The willow* has dark green upper surfaces and pale lower surfaces. When a breeze blows, the silver-white lower surface shows in contrast to the dark-green upper surface. The leaves are long, narrow, and slender, with no notches and small veins radiate from a central one.

- *The chestnut* has leaves about 8 inches long, sharp-pointed, and notched.

- *The oak* has large dull-green leaves from 4 to 6 inches long. Some leaves have grown to 12 to 16 inches long.

- *The laurel* leaves have different forms. They can be oval ones or in the shape of mittens with a thumb-like projection on one side.

- *The red maple* has a distinct three-part leaf that can turn red in autumn.

Write about what you learned.

Talking about What You Observe

1. ***Display the leaves and talk about them.*** Focus on the leaves by looking closely and telling something about them. Notice the edges. Are they uneven, rough, and pointed? Is the edge of one leaf like another? Describe how the leaves hang from their stems (flutter, dangle, tremble). Write the words on the board so you can use them as you write during the day.

   Write your thoughts:

2. ***Classify the leaves*** after after looking at them with a magnifying glass or on the overhead projector.

   Write your thoughts:

Reading Books about the Triassic Period

Imagine going back to the Triassic period. In the Triassic period (225–190 millions years ago), the continents were high with many deserts. Volcanoes and lava flows erupted near the Atlantic coast. There were trees that looked like pines that grew in forests in the West. There were some crocodiles, sea beasts, and early dinosaurs that were small.

Imagine going back to the age of the dinosaurs with Carrick's *The Crocodiles Still Wait,* where a 50-foot long mother crocodile defends her newly hatched eggs and her young from other dinsoaurs—including a tyrannosaurus rex.

Imagine seeing some of the animals of the Traiassic period. Look at *100 Prehistoric Animals from A to Z* or another book of your choice that tells about these animals:

- *Eryops,* an amphibian crocodile with short, strong, limbs was one of the beasts that lived in or near the sea during this period. It was a meat eater about 5 feet long.
- *Gerrothorax,* similar to a large tadpole about 3 feet long.
- *Lystrosaurus,* a mammal-like reptile about 3 feet long who lived in herds around the lakes and swamps.
- *Mandasuchus,* about 8 feet long, also closely resembled a modern crocodile or alligator and was a hunter of mammal-like reptiles.
- *Mastodonsaurus,* an amphibian about 10 feet long with teeth, also resembled the crocodile with its large heavy body and long tail. It lived on edges of swamps and lakes.
- *Mixosaurus* was a fish-like animal about 10 feet long that swam with its eel-like tail and ate fish and other sea animals.
- *Nothosaur* was a sea dweller about 20 feet long that had a long head with nostrils on the front of the snout, sharp teeth, a flattened tail, and webbed hind feet.
- *Placodus* was a sea-dwelling reptile about 7 feet long. It had a round body, short neck, long tail, and two kinds of teeth, and strong legs. It lived near lagoons and seas.
- *Protosuchus* was one of the first crocodiles with a long snout, strong jaws, and sharp teeth. Covered with bony scales, it was

about 4 feet long and lived both in the water and on the land banks near the water.

- *Tanystropheus* had a body 20 feet long and a neck 10 feet long (it resembled the long neck of a brontosaurus) and fished in rivers and waters.

Reading Books about the Jurassic Period

Imagine going back to the Jurassic period. During the Jurassic period (190–136 millions years ago), lands were probably low with large swamps. Shallow seas covered much of what is now Europe and filled narrow basins in the West. The weather became warmer than that in the earlier Ice Age and more moist. Repiles of many kinds swam in the water or even flew. The first birds appeared in part of the world now called Europe. Dinosaurs lived in western swamps. There were peterosaurs, plesiosaurs, ichthyosaurs, and the early dinosaurs.

Read about the creatures with these books:

- "Plesiosaurus" in *100 Prehistoric Animals from A to Z.* This active swimmer hunted fish. About 10 feet long, it had a strong tail, a long neck, strong jaws, and sharp teeth. Resembling a large turtle, its short front and back limbs were shaped like paddles.
- Dickenson's *The First Book of Perhistoric Animals* has a section called "Swimming and Soaring" about ichthyosaurus, plesiosaurus, and peterosaurs.
- Moseley's *Dinosaurs: A Lost World* has pop-up pages and facts to show what the dinosaurs looked like in three dimensions. Dinosaurs pop out from the pages and pull-tabs make a stegosaurus move its tail, a triceratops move its enormous armored head, and an ankylosaurus strike out with its rounded club-like tail. Models of skeletons of dinosaurs are seen for a coelophysis (swift runner on hind legs); plesiosauras (swimmer with broad, paddle-shaped legs); parasaurolophus (dinosaur with a crest on its head that curled back from the head like a horn); and allowsaurus (powerful runner with its front legs only half as long as its back legs).
- Dixon's *The Jurassic Dinosaurs* contains charts and information of dinosuars of the Jurassic period—the cryptocleedius, stegosaurus, and diplodicus. In the index, the use of capital letter in word means a *type* of dinosaur, such as Stegosaurus, and use of lowercase means a *group,* such as crocodiles.

- Arnold's *Dinosaur Mounain: Graveyard of the Past* shows life in the Jurassic age being uncovered in the National Dinosaur Monoument in Utah.

Creatures in the Early Jurassic Period

Countries Where
Fossils Were Found
England: Ichthyosaurus (ith ee o SORE us)

- *Dinosaurs: A Lost World* shows the illustration and pop-up skeleton of the ichthyosaur, a dolphin-like marine reptile that could swim as well as a fish and gave birth to live young in the water. About 40 feet long, ichthyosaurs had squat bodies, stubby tails, and broad paddle-shaped legs.
- *Creatures of Long Ago: Dinosaurs* has facts about icthyornis who flew through the air. Compare the shape of the legs to the flippers of some of today's animals.
- Oliver's *Dimorphodon* (whose fossils have been found in England) is a story of a female dimorphodon (a flying repile) who sleeps head-down like a bat and awakens to see struggling dinosuars. She flies away on an updraft, sees animal shapes in the deep water below, and finds a herd of plant eaters and a crocodile of long ago.
- *100 Prehistoric Animals from A to Z* describes ichthyosaurus as a fish-eating lizard with a tail like that of a shark. Resembling a dolphin and up to 25 feet long, it was a swimmer with limbs shaped like paddles.

Creatures in the Late Jurassic Period

Countries Where
Fossils Were Found
Africa: Allosaurus (al oh SORE russ)

- *Allosaurus: Troll Dinosaur Reference Library* has full-color illustrations and facts about the 42-foot-long allosaurus.
- Cole's *Dinosaur Story* retells the lives of five dinosaurs and gives facts about each. Beginning with the allosaurus, Cole relates one animal to the next one and ends with the tyrannosaurus rex.
- Sattler's *Baby Dinosaurs* discusses the size of the fossils of baby dinosaur fossil hartchings: the musaurus (size of robin), the psittacosaurus (pigeon size), stegosaurus (collie dog), centrosaurus (raccoon), and allosaurus (3 feet tall).

Africa: Brachiosaurus (brock ee oh SORE us)

- *Brachiosaurus: Troll Dinosaur Reference Library*. Found in Tanzania, fossils indicate the dinosaur was about 40 feet long.

- *The Largest Dinosaurs* (Simon) tells about six of the largest dinosaurs that ever lived.
- Colbert's *The Year of the Dinosaur* tells about one year in the life of a brontosaurus as it marches through the swamps, fights predators, and escapes a flood.
- Riehecky's *Dinosaurs* has diagrams and illustrations to show each dinosaur's unique physical traits along with background information.

Africa: Kentrosaurus (kent row SORE us)

- "Kentrosaurus" in Kingdon's *The ABC Dinosaur Book* tells about this dinosaur that was about 17 feet long with a double row of bony plates to protect the head and neck and several pairs of long, sharp spikes to protect the body and tail. Fossils found in Tanzania in Eastern Africa show this dinosaur to be a member of a herd and a plant eater.

Algeria: Brachiosaurus (brock ee oh SORE us)

- *Brachiosaurus* (Troll Dinosaur Reference Library) gives facts and illustrations about this 40-foot-long dinosaur.

Argentina: Mussaurus (moose SORE us)

- Sattler's *Baby Dinosaurs* discusses baby dinosaurs from the small mussaurus (size of a robin) in Argentina to the maiasaura (mah ee ah SORE uh) in Montana.

Australia: Allosaurus (al oh SORE russ)

- "Allosaurus" in *100 Dinosaurs A to Z* tells about the meat-eating dinosaur that was about 42 feet long and lived in Australia and other countries.

China: Mamenchisaurus (ma menk ee SORE us)

- *Mamenchisaurus: Troll Dinosaur Reference Library* gives facts and illustrations about this large dinosaur, 72 feet long, whose fossils were found in south central China.
- Rupert Oliver's *Mamenehisaurus* has a story about a long-necked plant eater as he becomes separated from his herd and finds other dinosaurs—gongubusaurus and yangchusnosaurs. At night, the dinosaur sleeps on its side, roams the darkness, gives a roaring distress call, and uses its tail to swing at a meat eater.
- *Let's Look at Dinosaurs* (Milburn) has facts about an obscure dinosaur, the Chinese yangchuanosaurus.

France: Compsognathus (comp SOG nah thus)

- "Compsognathus" in Kingdon's *The ABC Dinosaur Book* was as big as a goose with a mouth of sharp teeth. About 2 feet long, this was a small speedy dinosaur with some species having flippers instead of "hands." It was also found in Germany.
- *The Smallest Dinosaurs* by Simon describes seven of the smallest dinosaurs that ever lived.
- Most's *The Littlest Dinosaurs* compares the dinosaurs to familiar similar-sized objects. For instance, a 10-foot-long dravidosaurus would fit in a bush shelter and a 4-foot-high lesothosaurus could wear clothing of children.

Germany: Archaeopteryx (ark ee OP teri iks)

- Rupert Oliver's *Archaeopteryx* explains physical characteristics, habits, and environment of this winged creature. Written as a story, the brightly colored awkward flier encounters a lizard, teinuroosaurus, and alocodon. Notes at the end tell about ancestors, time period, and fossil find in Germany.
- *Dinosaurs: A Lost World* shows this first bird-like reptile with rows of teeth, a long bony tail, and three long fingers with claws. Found in southern Germany, it had clawed wings and a body covered with feathers.
- "Dinosaur Feathers" in Elting's *Dinosaur Mysteries* tells about the archaeopteryx who had a skeleton like a small running dinosaur, coelurosaurs. The similarity between the skeletons of an ostrich and a strutiomimus dinosaur is seen in the pictures.

United States: Allosaurus (al oh SORE russ)

- *Allosaurus: Troll Dinosaur Reference Library* gives facts and illustrations about this 42-foot-long dinosaur.

United States: Stegosaurus (steg oh SORE us)

- *Stegosaurus: Troll Dinosaur Reference Library* gives facts and illustrations.
- "A Lot of Puzzles in One Skeleton" in Elting's *Dinosaur Mysteries* questions the use of the two rows of plates along the back of the dinosaur. Were they hinged to the skin's surface? Did they grow out from under the skin? What was their use?
- Parish's *Dinosaur Time* has illustrations and text with information about the stegosaurus and other dinosaurs.

Colorado: Supersaurus (soup er SORE us)

- "Supersaurus and the Sauropod Mysteries" in *Dinosaur Mysteries* tells of the speculations about what they looked like. Found in western Colorado, Dry Mesa Quarry, the fossils included a shoulder bone 8 feet long and a neck bone 5 feet long. The size of these bones indicate the body was about 54 feet long.

Colorado: Ultrasaurus (ultra SORE us)

- Ultrasaurus takes up three pages to show its size in Peters's *Giants of Land and Sea Past and Present.* Found in western Colorado in Dry Mesa Quarry, the fossils included a shoulder bone 9 feet long, making it larger than the supersaurus.
- Simon's *The Largest Dinosaurs* concentrates on six of the lizard-hipped ones, the sauropods, from apatosaurus (ah pat uh SORE rus) to the Ultrasaurus (uhl tra SORE rus).
- Peterson's *Apatosaurus* states the giant apatosaurus (brontosaurus) was more like the elephant than the hippo, a dinosaur who roamed the country as a leaf-eater.

Colorado: Brachiosaurus (brock ee oh SORE us)

- *Brachiosaurus: Troll Dinosaur Reference Library* gives facts and illustrations about the 40-foot-long dinosaur.

Russia: Sordia pilosus (SORE dee ah pill o sus)

- "The Hairy Devil Takes Off" in *Dinosaur Mysteries* is a story of a flying creature with dense hair growth, the bill of a stork, the teeth of a crocodile, and the legs and backbone of a lizard.

Reading Books about the Cretaceous Period

Imagine going back to the Cretaceous period. In the Cretaceous period (136–65 million years ago), there were great seas over what is now North America and other continents. Lands became low. There were great swamps. The weather was mild and without great seasonal changes. Flying insects and birds increased, sea serpents declined, and dinosaurs with horns and armor increased. Rocks crumpled into mountains (Rocky Mountains) and appeared where lakes and swamps had been. Climate became cooler and more varied. The dinosaurs died out before this period ended.

Creatures in the Early Cretaceous Period

Countries Where
Fossils Were Found
Africa: Iguanodon (ig WAUN oh don)

- "The Case of the Poisoned Spike" in *Dinosaur Mysteries* tells a reader the spikes stuck out from each of the dinosaur's thumbs. Were they weapons? Did they hold venom? Fossils found in northern Africa indicate it was a plant eater and was about 29 feet long.

Belgium: Iguanodon (ig WAUN oh don)

- "Iguanodon" in Kingdon's *The ABC Dinosaur Book* states this dinosaur ate plants, lived in herds, walked on hind legs, was about 29 feet long (tall as a house) and had claws (or spikes) where his thumbs should have been.

Canada: Styracosaurus (sti rah co SORE us)

- "The Strange Case of the Great Horned Heads" in *Dinosaur Mysteries* says this dinosaur was found in Alverta, Canada. The fossils show the dinosaur was about 15 feet long with a long horn on the frill of its neck.

Canada: Triceratops (tri SERE ah tops)

- *Triceratops: Troll Dinosaur Reference Library* gives facts and illustrations.

Mongolia: Protoceratops (prot oh SERE ah tops)

- *Protoceratops: Troll Dinosaur Reference Library* gives facts and illustrations about this 6-foot long dinosaur who laid clusters of eggs.
- Sattler's *Baby Dinosaurs* discusses the eggs of protoceratops (potato size) and other dinosaurs.

Colorado: Triceratops (tri SERE ah tops)

- "Triceratops" in Moseley's *Dinosaurs: A Lost World* tells us large numbers roamed the plains of the American northwest. It had horns over each eye as long as meter sticks. Its skull measured 7 feet from its nose to its neck shield.

Montana: Styracosaurus (stie rah co SAWR us)

- "Styracosaurus" in Wilson's *100 Dinosaurs A to Z* states this plant-eating dinosaur was about 15 feet long. It was a spiked lizard with a horn on its nose, horns over each eye, strong jaws, and a spiked frill.

Montana: Dienonychus (die oh NIKE us)

- *Dienonychus: Troll Dinosaur Reference Library* gives facts and illustrations of this dinosaur, about 8 to 13 feet long, that had a sickle-shaped claw on each foot and ran on hind legs.

Montana: Proceratops (pro SERE rah tops)

- "The Great Egg Hunt" in *Dinosaur Mysteries* tells of the finding of the first meat-eating dinosaur eggs; the eggs were pointed, about 6 inches in length, touched each other, and stood upright in the nest.
- *Dinosaur* (Knopf, 1989) shows a dinosaur nest complete with eggs, a fossil skull that is 120 millions years old, and the texture of dinosaur skin.

Montana: maiasaura (may ee ah SAWR ah)

- Sattler's *Baby Dinosaurs* discusses the fossils of the maiasaura found in Montana.

Western U.S.: Iguanodon (ig WAUN oh don)

- *Iguanodon: Troll Dinosaur Reference Library* gives facts and illustrations about this 29-foot-long plant eater with spiked thumbs.

Wyoming: Dienonychus

- *Dienonychus: Troll Dinosaur Reference Library* gives facts about dinosaurs in series.

Creatures in the Late Cretaceous Period

Countries Where Fossils Were Found

Africa: Ouranosaurus (dure an oh SAWR us)

- "The Case of the Tall Sails" in *Dinosaur Mysteries* mentions the spiny bones covered with skin on the back of ouranosaurus, a plant eater.

Africa: Spinosaurus (spy no SORE us)

- "The Case of the Tall Sails" in *Dinosaur Mysteries* describes this meateater that was as long as 40 feet with a tail fin as tall as 6 feet high. Found in Niger and Egypt, the fossils indicate spiny bones were covered with skin on the backs of this dinosaur.

Canada: Triceratops (tri SERE ah tops)

- *Triceratops: Troll Dinosaur Reference Library* gives facts and illustrations about this 30-foot-long dinosaur whose fossils have been found from Canada to Colorado.

Canada: Parasaurolophyus (PAIR ah sawr oh lof us)

- "What Were the Last Dinosaurs" in *The World of Dinosaurs* states that the plant-eating parasaurs, about 33 feet long with curved hollow horns on their duckbills, were among the last dinosaurs in the last part of the period. Fossils have ben found in Alberta.

Canada: Edmontosaurus (ed MONT oh sore us)

- "What Did They Find in the Mummy's Stomach?" in Elting's *Dinosaur Mysteries* states that fossils found in Alberta in northern Canada show this duckbill dinosaur, about 43 feet long, ate pine needles, twigs, and seeds.

Mongolia: Tarbosaurus (tar bo SAWR us)

- "Tarbosaurus" in Wilson's *100 Dinosaurs A to Z* informs the reader that tarbosaurus, from 33 to 46 feet long, was a lot like a tyrannosaurus. It had two knife-shaped teeth in its upper jaw and was about 4 feet high on its hind legs.

Mongolia: Protoceratops (prot oh SER ah tops)

- *Protoceratops: Troll Dinosaur Reference Library* states the dinosaur fossils found in the Gobi Desert included dinosaur eggs in different sizes and shapes.

Montana: Edmontosaurus (ed MONT oh sore us)
New Jersey: Edmontosaurus (ed MONT oh sore us)

- "Edmontosaurus" in Kingdon's *The ABC Dinosaur Book* was the largest of the duck-billed dinosaurs. It was about 43 feet long with over 2,000 teeth that regrew when they wore out from grinding up plants. Other fossils found in Montana include a dinosaur skull with bone 9 inches thick on the top of its head and fossils of dinoaur eggs.

Utah: Parasaurolophyus (pair ah sore oh lo fus)

- "Lambeosaurus" in Fortey's *The Dinosaurs' Alphabet* says "crests are best" about this 33 feet long dinosaur with a curved hollow horn on its duckbill. It ate plants and was one of the last dinosaurs in the time period. It had a v-shaped crest on top of the head but scientists are not sure of the purpose of it: Was it for making warning sounds? For a better sense of smell? For recognition by other dinosaurs? To attract enemies away from its young?

New Mexico: Parasaurolophyus (pair ah sore oh LOP fee us)

- "Parasaurolophus" in Wilson's *100 Dinosaurs A to Z* states it was one of the last plant-eating dinosaurs of the time period, about 33 feet long, with a curved hollow horn on the duckbill. Inside this crest on its head, it had a long tube (or horn) that measured 39 inches in length. Was this a snorkel? Did it make noise? Was it used as a signal to others?

Texas: Pterosaur (TER o sore)

- "How Did the Pterosaurs Evolve?" in *The World of Dinosaurs* states they had small bodies, hollow bones, long heavy jaws, no teeth, and bony crests on their heads. Their huge wings were sheets of skin attached to bony "fingers" and reached out to a span of about 40 feet.
- Sattler's *Pterosaurs, the Flying Reptiles* has facts on the flying reptiles during the Dinosaur Age and includes the pteranodon, which may have been able to fly or glide along at 30 miles an hour, and the ctenochasma, which had jaws filled with hundreds of needle-like teeth

Kansas: Pteranodon (te RAN oh don)

- *Pteranodon: Troll Dinosaur Reference Library* gives facts about this flying reptile with a 27-foot wingspan.
- "Pteranodon" in Moseley's *Dinosaurs: A Lost World* says it was a giant among the pterosaurs with a huge wingspan. It had a body about 9 feet long, light hollow bones, and an unusual head with a crest. The wings were sheets of skin that grew and stretched between the fingers of its "hand" and the knee of its back leg.

Kansas: Tylosaurus (tie lo SORE us)

- "The Dinosaurs' Place in Prehistoric Life" in *The World of Dinosaurs* shows the tylosaurus, a 30-foot-long sea serpent, living in the time period with tyrannosaurus and triceratops.

Kansas: Elasmosaurus (e LAS mo sore us)

- "The Dinosaurs' Place in Prehistoric Life" in *The World of Dinosaurs* shows the elasmosaurus, a 40-foot-long marine reptile, living in the period with the huge dinosaurs—diplodocus and brachiosaurus.

Western United States: Ornithomimus (orn i tho MY muss)

- "Ornithomimus" in Hunter's *Dinosaur ABC Coloring Book* shows a slender bird-like dinosaur with strong leg muscles, large eyes, and a large brain, which probably coordinated it while it ran at speeds faster than 50 miles an hour.

Western United States: Tyrannosaurus (tie ran uh SORE us)

- *Tyrannosaurus: Troll Dinosaur Reference Library* gives facts and illustrations; "Tyrannosaurus" in Hunter's *Dinosaur ABC Coloring Book* states that it had a massive body, was ill-equipped for running, and perhaps was a scavenger.
- Sattler's *Tyrannosaurus Rex and Its Kin: The Mesozoic Monsters* has clear information about the structure, behavior, and habitats of this family of dinosaurs.
- Selsam's *Tyrannosaurus Rex* tells about the reconstruction of a rex from fossilized bones found in Montana in 1901.
- Sheehan's *Tyrannosaurus* is a prowling, charging, hungry animal who sleeps in a story that offers facts.

Tibet: Ornithomimus or Ornitholestes (orn i tho LESS tease)

- "Ornitholestes" in Kingdon's *The ABC Dinosaur Book* shows a related species, 11 feet long, ostrich-like, with long clawed "fingers" used to catch birds for food.

Observation Sheet for the Teacher

Record observations of students' activities and language that seem to indicate that the child is following a purpose.

Student's name_____   Date_____

Student's name_____   Date_____

Student's name_____   Date_____

Student's name_____   Date_____

Self-Check on Reading about Dinosaurs

Student's name_____   Date_____

Yes   Sometimes

I understand what I read.

I can find the main idea of a picture.

I can find the main idea of a paragraph.

I think about what I read.

I can tell what the author is saying.

I think about what I already know about dinosaurs as I read.

I figure out the words and read the rest of the sentence.

I figure out new words.

I use the dictionary to pronounce new words.

I use the dictionary to find the meaning of a word.

I find information in the library.

I find books about this study to read in the library.

I can read aloud with expression.

I know what I should learn from the book.

I know how to use an index in a book.

I know what I should study from a text.

I ask myself questions when I read.

Self-Check on Reading Informational Books

Yes No Sometimes

1. **I can use parts of an informational book.**
   I can use a Preface.
   I can use the Table of Contents.
   I can use maps, charts, and illustrations.
   I can use the Glossary.
   I can use the Index.
2. **I can use reference sources.**
   I can use the dictionary.
   I use the atlas.
   I know how to use an almanac.
   I know how to use an encyclopedia.
   I know how to use a card catalog.
   I know how to use a *Guide to Periodical Literature.*
3. **I can use graphic aids.**
   I know how to use maps.
   I study pictures.
   I know how to read graphs.
   I know how to read charts.
   I know how to make and read a time line.
   I study diagrams.
   I can understand main ideas.
   I can find supporting details for a main idea.
   I can tell fact from opinion.
   I can restate information.
   I can take notes.
   I can outline information.

Sign your name⎯⎯⎯⎯⎯⎯⎯⎯⎯⎯⎯   **Date**⎯⎯⎯⎯⎯